GCSE

LONGMAN
REVISE
GUIDES

PSYCHOLOGY

D0495725

Alison Wadeley

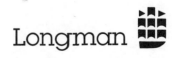

Longman

LONGMAN REVISE GUIDES

SERIES EDITORS:
Geoff Black and Stuart Wall

TITLES AVAILABLE:
Art and Design
Biology
Business Studies*
CDT: Design and Realisation
CDT: Technology
Chemistry
Computer Studies
Economics*
English*
English Literature*
French
Geography
German
Home Economics
Mathematics*
Mathematics: Higher Level and Extension*
Music
Physics
Psychology
Religious Studies*
Science*
Sociology
Spanish
World History

* new editions for Key Stage 4

Longman Group Limited,
Longman House, Burnt Mill, Harlow,
Essex CM20 2JE, England
and Associated Companies throughout the World.

© Longman Group Limited 1996

First Published 1996

ISBN 0582 28700–6

British Library Cataloguing-in-Publication Data
A catalogue record for this book is available from the British Library

Set by 27QQ
Produced by Longman Singapore Publishers Pte
Printed in Singapore

ACKNOWLEDGEMENTS

I would like to thank Wendy Young for agreeing to act as my title adviser, for her boundless energy and enthusiasm and invaluable help with marking students' answers. My thanks also go to my fellow psychology lecturers, Mike Cardwell, Anthony Curtis and Pam Prentice, for their interest and support during the preparation of this book and for their generosity in sharing their textbooks and academic expertise with me.

Most of all I am grateful to Ian who single-handedly facilitated the writing of this book through his willingness to be a double parent, cook and housekeeper and keep up a constant supply of cups of tea, words of reassurance and soothing background music. This book is dedicated to him and to Holly and Imogen, our two wonderful daughters, with love.

The author is grateful to the following examination boards for permission to reproduce their questions:

The Midland Examining Group (MEG)
The Southern Examining Group (SEG)
The Northern Examinations and Assessment Board (NEAB)

These boards accept no responsibility for the accuracy of the answers provided. They are the responsibility of the author alone.

CONTENTS

GETTING STARTED

Psychology is often defined as 'the scientific study of behaviour and experience'. A quick look at the chapter headings in this guide will give you an idea of what we mean by 'behaviour and experience' and how wide ranging psychology is. On your psychology course you could be studying anything from brain structure and function to the effects of crowding on people. One day you may be studying how people learn, another day you could be looking at the formation of relationships between people or the impact of divorce on children. You will certainly be dealing with research methods and a certain amount of data handling. Psychology is a very popular subject, probably because it has something to offer everyone from the hard-line scientist to the more intuitive artistic type!

GCSE Psychology is offered by three examination boards. They are:

- the Midland Examining Group (MEG)
- the Southern Examining Group (SEG)
- the Northern Examinations and Assessment Board (NEAB).

This chapter will tell you exactly what you must do to revise for the written papers for the GCSE syllabus you are following. Coursework is not dealt with by this guide. You will probably have completed it well before you sit the written examination.

CHAPTER 1
THE SYLLABUSES AND EXAMINATIONS

1. THE SYLLABUSES AND WRITTEN PAPERS

2. THE CHAPTERS IN THIS GUIDE

3. SOME ADVICE

4. THE NEAB SYLLABUS

5. THE MEG SYLLABUS

6. THE SEG SYLLABUS

ESSENTIAL PRINCIPLES

Here is what you should do before you start using this guide:

- Find out which of the three syllabuses you are following.
- If at all possible, get your own copy of the syllabus. If your teacher cannot let you have your own copy, write to the examining board enclosing a large (A4) self addressed envelope. They will send you a price list and an order form so that you can send off for your own. Addresses appear later in this chapter.
- All three syllabuses have a 'core' of essential ideas to be covered and a selection of other topics. They examine knowledge of these in different ways. If you are a NEAB student you will need to cover the whole syllabus. MEG and SEG have compulsory core sections but offer options too. You should be absolutely clear about the core and which options you and your teacher have chosen to follow so that you can pick out the relevant parts of this guide.
- Make sure you have seen sample papers for the written exam. At the time of writing, all the syllabuses are new for first examination in June 1996 so there are only sample questions available. Your teacher should have these. From 1996 onwards, you will be able to buy past papers and markschemes from the exam boards by writing to them for an order form as above. You should be clear about the layout of the written papers and what you will have to do *before* you sit the exam.

Once you are clear about the topics you need to cover, use the information on the following pages to help you locate the sections of the guide that you will need for your syllabus. *Always* read **Getting Started** at the beginning of each chapter for extra guidance.

The chapters are divided into numbered sections to help you quickly find what you need. When you have worked through the relevant sections, *always* complete the appropriate **Review Sheet** at the end of this book. The questions you need for your board may be identified. If they are not, it means you should do all the questions. This will give you vital practice in giving short, precise answers.

At the end of each chapter there are **Examination Questions and Answers**, at least one for each board. Sometimes, it has been necessary to extract a few questions from longer papers to illustrate what you might be asked. In all cases a rough guide to how long you should allow to answer the questions has been given.

Some of the questions are answered by the tutor and some by GCSE students. The latter have examiner's comments showing where there are strengths and weaknesses and how the marks would be awarded. You should try some of these questions so that you can compare your answers to those given and practise your timing. Do not be afraid to try questions from all the exam boards if they cover the topics you need. The more practice you have the better.

There is plenty of advice around about how to revise effectively and how to make sure that you are in the right frame of mind for the exam. Here are some key points:

BEFORE THE EXAMINATION

- **Start revising in good time**. Last-minute revision does work for some people but, on the whole, it is too risky.
- **Be clear about what you have to learn**. Use the *syllabus* to find this out.
- **Plan your revision carefully**. Make yourself a revision *timetable* to ensure you can fit in what you need to do. Be prepared to revise your timetable as you go along. Some topics will take more or less time than you imagined. Build in rest periods for relaxation and treats. These will help to keep you going. If you are working hard, you deserve them so take them without feeling guilty.
- **Revise *actively***. This means doing more than just reading over something. You may fool yourself into thinking you have learned a topic simply because you understand it and recognise the ideas when you read over them. This is not the

same as being able to reproduce those ideas in an exam. At the very least, you should rework your notes into as many different forms as you can, e.g. make 'brain maps' (see 13.5), or lists of key points on a postcard. Discuss the topics with your teacher and friends in class (or out).

- **Practise reproducing information** without the aid of notes, e.g. by completing the review sheets or trying the examination questions yourself. Try to ensure that you have a practice run of the exam before the real thing. Recite model answers to yourself while you are lying in the bath. Risk social ridicule by telling the dog all about Pavlov's conditioning experiments every time you take it for a walk. Shock the cat with tales of the kitten carousel. Worry your parents with accounts of child-rearing styles and their effects. Alienate your friends by telling them about the effects of alcohol on memory.
- **Expect to work hard.** Sadly, few of us are natural geniuses who soak up information with little effort. You will need to put in the hours, but remember it is the *quality* of your revision, not the *quantity* of time you spend on it, that matters most.

DURING THE EXAMINATION

- **Relax.** Well – relax as much as you can. A little bit of tension is a good thing because it energises you but too much anxiety can spoil things.
- **Ignore what others are doing** around you, especially the annoying person who uses up three pens in the first half hour and asks for extra paper before you've finished your first page. They're probably writing garbage anyway.
- **Plan your time carefully** and try to stick to your plan.
- **Read the instructions** at the start of the paper.
- **Follow the instructions.** You would be surprised how many students don't.
- **Read through all the questions** that are relevant to you at least once.
- **Take time to think** about each question, paying attention to the wording and the number of marks to be gained. If you are a NEAB student you will need to answer all the questions. If you are an SEG or MEG student the questions you choose should be those that will earn you the most marks. They may not be the ones on your favourite topics.
- **Answer the question that is set** and not the one you wish had been set. A good check of your longer answers is to ask yourself if someone else could work out what the question was from just reading your answer. If they could, you have probably done a good job.
- **Build in as much psychology into your answer as you can.** Use theories and research evidence whenever possible to back up your ideas.
- **Try to evaluate** the theories and evidence in answers to questions that invite evaluation. Not all of them will.

Now read the information on the following pages that applies to your syllabus and use the sections from the Revise Guide that you need. Whichever syllabus you are following, start with chapters 2, 3 and 4. These cover methodology, data presentation and interpretation and learning theories. They are absolutely central to all the syllabuses and the material in them comes up over and over again in other chapters. A good grounding in these will make it much easier for you to understand many of the other chapters. In addition, section 13.5 will give you some ideas about how best to use your memory. All NEAB and MEG students have to study this section in any case. Memory is not on the SEG syllabus but do not let that stop you from using the ideas in 13.5 to help you revise.

ADDRESS FOR ORDERING SYLLABUSES AND PAPERS

Northern Examinations and Assessment Board,
Publications Department,
12 Harter Street,
Manchester,
M1 6HL.

TIERS AND GRADES

Candidates following this syllabus can enter for one of two tiers named Option P and Option Q. You will need to decide in advance which Tier to aim for.

- Option P – Targeted grades C–G
- Option Q – Targeted grades A*–D.

Some overlap in these ranges of grades will be offered so that B is allowable on Option P and E is allowable on Option Q.

THE EXAMINATION

For both options, coursework accounts for 20% of your final grade. There is one written paper that will account for the remaining 80% of your mark. Spelling, punctuation and grammar are assessed in all parts of the examination accounting for about 5% of the mark in each part.

THE WRITTEN PAPER

This lasts for 2 hours for Option P candidates and $2\frac{1}{2}$ hours for Option Q candidates. All questions are compulsory. There will be a mixture of short answer and structured questions. The paper is divided into Section A and Section B. Section A covers methodology and handling data. Section B tests other areas of the syllabus using stimulus material as a starting point.

PLANNING YOUR REVISION

You should study all the Chapters and sections listed here. You are strongly advised to start with Chapters 2, 3 and 4 first.

Individual processes

- **Perception**. Chapter 12 section 12.1.
- **Learning**. Chapter 4.
- **Memory**. Chapter 13.
- **Emotion**. Chapter 16.

Interpersonal processes

- **Development of social behaviour**. Chapter 7.
- **Social perception**. Chapter 5 sections 5.1, 5.2, 5.5, 5.6, 5.7, 5.8.
- **Social influence**. Chapter 6 sections 6.1, 6.2, 6.3, 6.4, 6.5, 6.7. Chapter 10 sections 10.4, 10.5.

Methods of investigation

Chapters 2 and 3 cover what you need for this part of the syllabus.

5 ▷ THE MEG SYLLABUS

ADDRESS FOR ORDERING SYLLABUSES AND PAPERS

The Chief Executive,
University of Cambridge,
Local Examinations Syndicate,
Syndicate Buildings,
1 Hills Road,
Cambridge,
CB1 2EU.

TIERS AND GRADES

Candidates following this syllabus can enter for the Foundation or the Higher Tier:

- Foundation Tier – Targeted grades G–D
- Higher Tier – Targeted grades D–A*.

You will need to decide in advance which Tier to aim for.

THE EXAMINATION

For both Tiers, the coursework (a practical exercise) counts for 20% of your final mark. There are two written papers and these will account for the remaining 80% of your final mark. Spelling, punctuation and grammar are assessed in all parts of the examination accounting for about 5% of the mark in each part.

THE WRITTEN PAPERS

The first paper lasts for $1\frac{1}{2}$ hours and tests you on the syllabus 'core'. There are three sections A, B and C and you need to answer all the questions set. The second paper lasts for 2 hours and tests you on the four 'options' of which you will have studied two. You are required to answer all the questions set on your two chosen options. Common 'themes' of methodology, ethics, applications and cultural diversity will run through both papers.

PLANNING YOUR REVISION

You are strongly advised to start with Chapters 2, 3 and 4 first.

Themes and processes (compulsory)
- **Methodology**. Chapters 2 and 3.
- **Ethics**. Mainly Chapter 2 but ethics appear in many other contexts too.
- **Applications**. Various chapters. You will pick up this information as you go along.
- **Cultural Diversity**. Various chapters. You will pick up this information as you go along.

The core (compulsory)
- **The Behaviourist approach**. Chapter 4 sections 4.1, 4.2, 4.3, 4.5, 4.6, 4.7.
- **The Cognitive approach**. Chapter 13 sections 13.1, 13.2, 13.3, 13.4, 13.5, 13.6.
- **The Biological approach**. Chapter 16 sections 16.1, 16.2.
- **The Social Psychology approach**. Chapter 5 sections 5.5, 5.6, 5.7, 5.8.
- **The Developmental approach**. Chapter 10 sections 10.1, 10.2.
- **The Humanistic approach**. Chapter 15 section 15.1.

Options
You need to study two of these.

Option 1 Cognitive psychology
- **Perception**. Chapter 12.
- **Problem solving and creativity**. Chapter 14 sections 14.3, 14.4.
- **Development of language**. Chapter 11 section 11.2.

Option 2 Developmental psychology
- **Attachment**. Chapter 7 sections 7.1, 7.2, 7.3, 7.4, 7.5, 7.6, 7.7.
- **Cognitive development**. Chapter 11 section 11.1.
- **Sex and gender**. Chapter 9.

Option 3 Social and environmental psychology
- **Social influence**. Chapter 6 sections 6.3, 6.4, 6.5, 6.8.
- **Crowds and crowding**. Chapter 6 section 6.7.
- **Territorial behaviour and privacy**. Chapter 6 section 6.6.

Option 4
- **Biological bases of behaviour**. Chapter 16 section 16.1.
- **Ethological approach**. Chapter 18.
- **Aggression**. Chapter 17 sections 17.1, 17.2, 17.3.

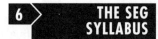

ADDRESS FOR ORDERING SYLLABUSES AND PAPERS

Publications Department,
The Southern Examining Group,
Stag Hill House,
Guildford,
Surrey,
GU2 5XJ.

TIERS AND GRADES

Candidates following this syllabus can enter for the Foundation Tier or the Higher Tier:

- Foundation Tier – Targeted grades G–D. Allowed range of grades G–C
- Higher Tier – Targeted grades D–A*. Allowed range of grades F–A*.

You will decide with your teacher which Tier to aim for.

THE EXAMINATION

For both Tiers, the coursework (a practical exercise) counts for 20% of your final mark. There is one written paper and this will account for the remaining 80% of your final mark. Spelling, punctuation and grammar are assessed in all parts of the examination accounting for about 5% of the mark in each part.

THE WRITTEN PAPER

This part of the examination lasts for 2 hours. There is one question paper divided into five sections:

- **Section A** is compulsory. The questions are drawn from the syllabus 'core' and there are 15 marks available in total.
- **Section B** is compulsory. Again, the questions are drawn from the syllabus 'core'. You will be given brief details of a flawed study and asked questions based on the given study and the methodology part of the syllabus. There are 25 marks to be earned here.
- **Sections C, D, E.** You must study at least two of these three sections. The question paper will offer a choice of two questions in each section. You are required to answer two questions but no more than one from each section. There are 30 marks for each question.

PLANNING YOUR REVISION

You are strongly advised to start with Chapters 2, 3 and 4 first.

Compulsory core. Section A. Ways of explaining human action

The compulsory core part of this syllabus is picked up partly through directly studying the topics specified in this part of the syllabus and partly through studying topics in the optional sections. A quick checklist of the main concepts in Section A is given below. You should come back to this checklist when you have finished your revision to ensure that you understand the terms and can give examples in each case.

1. The influences of inborn characteristics

See chapter 18 in particular. You will also meet these concepts in many other chapters:

Instincts.
Twin studies.
Maturation.
Heredity (as in nature–nurture debate).
Reflexes.
Sensitive period.

2. The role of learning in shaping behaviour

Chapter 4 covers these concepts. Again you will encounter them often in other chapters:

Classical conditioning.
Operant conditioning.
Social Learning.

3. Social and cultural influences

These appear in many chapters. You will encounter them as you work through the Optional Sections. Use the index to the guide to ensure you know some specific examples:

Affiliation.
Cross-cultural perspectives.
The role of the environment (in nature–nurture debates).
Social norms.
Social roles.

4. The influences of thinking and perception

These appear in many chapters. Use the index to guide you to specific examples.

Transduction.
Processing information – selection, organisation, inference.
Mental representation – schemas, mental images, concept formation.

Compulsory core. Section B. Psychological methodology

Chapters 2 and 3 cover what you need for this section.
1. **Ways of discovering and testing psychological knowledge.**
2. **Carrying out practical research.**
3. **Ethical concerns in research.**

Optional sections

Remember you need to study at least two of the sections C, D and E.

Section C. Social and antisocial relationships

1. **Making attachments to others.** Chapter 7.
2. **Widening social relationships.** Chapter 8. Chapter 6 sections 6.1, 6.2, 6.3.
3. **Prejudice.** Chapter 5 sections 5.2, 5.4, 5.5, 5.6, 5.7.
4. **Aggression.** Chapter 17 sections 17.3, 17.4, 17.5.

Section D. Individuality and identity

1. **The development of personality.** Chapter 15.
2. **Intelligence.** Chapter 14 sections 14.1, 14.2.
3. **The development of gender.** Chapter 9.
4. **Towards a concept of self.** Chapter 10 sections 10.4, 10.5

Section E. Cognitive and social competence

1. **Cognitive development.** Chapter 11 section 11.1. Chapter 12.
2. **The development of moral behaviour and moral judgements.** Chapter 10 sections 10.1, 10.2, 10.3.
3. **Pro-social behaviour.** Chapter 6 section 6.5.
4. **Construction of social reality.** Chapter 5 sections 5.1, 5.2, 5.3, 5.4.

CHAPTER 2

METHODOLOGY AND ETHICS

GETTING STARTED

All GCSE syllabuses require you to know something about the research methods used by psychologists when they are trying to find things out about human and animal behaviour. In the first of two methodology chapters we will look at some of these methods. In each case you need to know at least one example of the method being used in actual research. You also need to know some of the strengths and weaknesses of various methods. This will help you to evaluate the research findings arising from them and to answer any examination questions calling on your knowledge of research methods. The first chapter ends with a look at some of the ethical concerns which all research psychologists must be aware of. These apply just as much to a first project by a GCSE student as they do to research carried out by an eminent university professor.

It is important to understand that no one method is 'better' than another. A good method is one that is best in the circumstances and that is competently used. In making a choice, the psychologist must consider the type of participant, the aim of research, practical and ethical considerations and so on. To assume that psychologists have a completely free choice of method in their research is wrong. The method often determines itself.

Because of the amount you need to know about methodology, the two methodology chapters make up a rather long section. Sample questions and answers for both Chapters two and three appear at the end of Chapter three.

NB The term **participants** is used to refer to the individuals who provide psychologists with the data they need for their research. It is to be preferred to the term **subjects** which you will find in all but the most recent psychology textbooks .

1. PSYCHOLOGICAL RESEARCH METHODS

2. ETHICAL CONSIDERATIONS IN RESEARCH

ESSENTIAL PRINCIPLES

1 ＞ PSYCHOLOGICAL RESEARCH METHODS

When psychologists carry out research, they have to make a choice between methods which are **unobtrusive** and tap into more natural behaviour and methods which are more **intrusive** and tightly controlled. In other words there is a pay-off between realism and control.

A very usual way of grouping research methods is to think of them as **non-experimental** and **experimental**.

NON-EXPERIMENTAL METHODS

Observational methods – some general points

These involve watching and recording the behaviour of interest. The observer may make written records or use video- or audio-recording for more detailed analysis later. It is a good idea, wherever possible, to make more than one observation of the same thing. The two sets of observations can then be checked to see if they agree or are consistent. If they do, this is known as **reliability** and it helps us to have confidence in the results. Two ways of checking reliability are:

- **inter-observer reliability**. Two or more observers check their observations to see if they agree.
- **intra-observer reliability**. Repeated observations from the same observer are checked against each other to see if they agree.

It is important to establish these kinds of reliability to safeguard against erratic or biased observations.

The setting in which observations are made can be either:

- **controlled** – set up by the observer, e.g. in a laboratory, or
- **naturalistic** – in a setting familiar to the participants.

Naturalistic observation would usually be more true to life but researchers cannot be as sure about what is influencing behaviour as they would be in a controlled environment. Whatever method is chosen, objective, unbiased observation and description is the aim.

Non-participant observation

In this kind of observation the researcher watches from outside the group. This may be done with or without the participants' knowledge. Sometimes *everything* a participant does over a specified period of time is recorded, other times the observer may sample particular types of behaviour or only record behaviour occurring in specified periods of time. Observations are often recorded into checklists or tables.

Ethologists and **comparative psychologists**, interested in animal behaviour in its natural environment, produce detailed catalogues of animals' behaviour known as **ethograms**. They may also use controlled observation in laboratory settings if they want to study an aspect of behaviour, such as factors affecting imprinting strength, more closely. Human behaviour is so complex that an ethogram would quickly become too cumbersome. The closest psychologists come to it is **diary description**, a special version of which is the **baby biography**. The famous developmental psychologist, *Jean Piaget* (1896–1980), made diary descriptions of the day-to-day development of his own three children and *Charles Darwin* (1809–82) used the baby biography. *Virginia Axline* (1964) kept a diary-like account of her psychoanalytic sessions with a child known as '*Dibs*'. Both Piaget and Axline sometimes also controlled aspects of the children's environment in order to observe the effect. An example of controlled observation is *Ainsworth*'s (1978) **strange situation** technique in which the type and strength of attachment of infants to their mothers is tested in a laboratory setting by observing infants' reactions when the mother leaves and a stranger enters the room.

These methods are useful because:

- they produce rich and detailed descriptive accounts of behaviour;

build in safeguards against erratic or biased observations

the observer must decide what to record

some good ways of observing very young children

strange situation

- they often provide ideas for further research;
- they can be used when other methods might be unethical.

Problems with them are:

- the observer's presence may influence participants' behaviour in unwanted ways;
- there are many uncontrolled influences which may affect participants' behaviour making it hard to know which are the important ones.

Participant observation

This involves becoming a member of a particular social group so that it can be observed from the inside. **Anthropologists** studying different cultural groups and psychologists or sociologists studying different social groups may use this method. Ideally, the group members should be unaware that the observer is watching them, although that is not always possible to achieve. In some cases the researcher might infiltrate the group under an assumed identity. In other cases, the observer would 'come clean' about their identity and hope to be accepted to the point where their presence had a minimal effect on the behaviour of the group. In a short-term participant observation, *Festinger* (1956) and his associates joined a group called *The Seekers* who believed they were in touch with extra-terrestrials who had warned that the world was about to end. Festinger was able to observe what happened when the forecasted disaster did not occur and thus gained some insight into how the attitudes of group members changed.

participant observation can yield rich insights

This method is useful because:

- the observer may achieve a depth of understanding not possible by other methods;
- participants' behaviour will be more natural if they do not feel they are being observed;
- it allows access to groups that would probably not be granted if the group members knew the researcher's purpose.

Problems with it include:

- difficulties with recording observations unobtrusively;
- delays between making observations and recording them might mean that important details are forgotten or distorted;
- the more involved the observer becomes with the group the harder it can be to remain objective;
- it may be very time consuming and involve a great deal of commitment from the observer;
- the ethical difficulties involved in both observing others and in (sometimes) doing so without their knowledge and consent.

Case studies

a case is not always one person

A case study usually involves studying one instance of something in depth. Often, this will be an individual, but case studies can also be made of groups of people in a single unit such as a family, a married couple, long-stay patients on a psychiatric ward, a school class, inmates on a prison wing or workers in an office. The aim is usually to understand the case so that recommendations to improve things can be made and carried out, but it can also be for academic interest alone.

Case studies do not document every minute detail. They are usually quite specifically focused on one aspect of the case. This means that the method used to gather case material will need to be appropriate. It is a popular method with clinical and educational psychologists but there are other examples from many areas of psychology:

- *Sigmund Freud* (1856–1939) used clinical case studies to develop psychoanalytic theory;
- *Ebbinghaus* (1885) used himself as a case in order to study memory;
- *Gregory and Wallace* (1963) studied SB, a man who recovered his sight after over 50 years of blindness;
- *Sue Savage-Rumbaugh* (1990) continues to carry out case studies into the teaching of sign language to chimpanzees.

The method is useful because:

- it can give detailed information about unique instances of something;
- new ideas can grow from case studies, e.g. it is said that, although Freud carried out many case studies, he based his major theory of human behaviour on twelve key ones;
- a series of similar case studies could help to inform a researcher about how to deal with new ones;
- the information gathered is more likely to give a complete picture of the individual case rather than reducing it to a series of scores as might happen with other methods.

Problems with it include:

- the information gathered can be cumbersome and need interpretation. This opens it to bias on the part of the observer so it is often good to get a second opinion;
- the case material may not be useful outside the case itself;
- case material may include people's recollections from another time, e.g. adults recalling childhood, and these are not always reliable.

Surveys

This method is used for gathering information from large numbers of people to find out about their attitudes, habits or interests. The most common techniques of data collection are **interviews** and **questionnaires**. Interviews take many forms, some very informal, others more structured. A special type of interview is the **clinical interview**, e.g. as used by Freud and Piaget, where questions were asked and the answers pursued in order to reach a good understanding of the interviewee's thinking. Questionnaires can be thought of as a kind of written interview. They can be carried out face to face, by telephone or post. The questions asked can be open ended, allowing flexibility in the respondents' answers, or they can be more tightly structured requiring short answers or a choice of answers from given alternatives. The choice of questions is important because of the need to avoid bias or ambiguity in the questions, 'leading' the respondent or causing offence.

66 surveys can be good for large-scale research 99

An example of a survey is *The Hite Report* (1977) which involved 3,000 women aged between 14 and 78 living in the USA. They responded anonymously to postal questionnaires about their sexual attitudes and behaviour. A survey using interviews by *Sears, Maccoby* and *Levin* (1957) investigated child-rearing practices in the USA to see if they linked with children's behaviour.

The method is useful because:

- it can be good for collecting large amounts of data fairly quickly;
- if respondents are anonymous their answers may be more honest;
- it can provide ideas for further, more specialised research.

Problems with it are:

- the sample of people who agree to provide answers may not be representative of the population the researcher was hoping to test so generalisation is risky;
- people may respond in ways they think are socially acceptable rather than say what they really think;
- data collection and analysis can be very expensive and time consuming.

Correlation

66 correlation is not a method 99

Correlation is *not* a research method. It is a *technique of data analysis* applied to information gathered by means such as observation. To apply correlation we need to collect scores which are paired, e.g. aggression scores and TV viewing scores from a sample of children or attractiveness ratings of males and females from a sample of newly wed couples. Correlation tells us whether scores are related in some (specifically, linear) way and this can be expressed pictorially in the form of a scattergram, or numerically in the form of a correlation coefficient. This will be a value ranging from +1 through 0 to −1. The sign (+ or −) gives the direction of the relationship and the number (0 to 1) gives the strength of the relationship. (A correlation of +0.6 is weaker than a correlation of −0.7, for example.) Typical patterns of correlation are as follows (the scattergrams for these are shown in **Figs** 3.1 to 3.5):

- **perfect positive correlation** (+1), e.g. number of litres of petrol in your car and the maximum distance you can travel (perfect correlations are rare in psychology!);
- **imperfect positive correlation** (say, +0.6), e.g. number of hours spent studying outside class time during a course and end of course grades;
- **no correlation** (0), e.g. hat size and number of pets owned;
- **imperfect negative correlation** (say –0.7), e.g. number of hours spent in the pub during a course and end of term grades;
- **perfect negative correlation** (–1), e.g. number of miles travelled and the amount of petrol left in your car.

Correlation is useful because:

- it allows us to see how two variables *relate* to each other;
- it allows us to *predict* the likely value of one variable when we only have information about one of them, e.g. teachers can often predict students' final exam grades based on the students' average homework grades.

Problems with it include:

- it is purely a *description* of relationships between variables. It does not allow us to say one variable *causes* changes in another, e.g. there may be a positive relationship between how aggressive children are and how often they are smacked by their parents but we won't know the reason for this link from correlation alone.

EXPERIMENTAL METHODS

Non-experimental methods allow us to *describe* behaviour and see *patterns* in it. Experimentation goes a step further by allowing us to determine what *causes* things to happen.

An experiment is defined as a research method in which the experimenter changes some influence on the participants (an **independent variable** or **IV**) and observes and measures the effects of the changes on some aspect of their behaviour (the **dependent variable** or **DV**) while keeping all other sources of influence (**extraneous variables**) constant. Differences in behaviour under the various conditions can be put down to the IV only if extraneous variables have been properly controlled. Uncontrolled extraneous variables which interfere in a systematic way with the influence of the IV on the DV are called **confounding variables**. An example of this occurred in *Feshbach*'s study (1971). Boys in institutions were divided into two groups. Group A were restricted to viewing exciting TV programmes with aggressive content. Group B boys saw exciting, non-aggressive TV. Group B boys showed more aggression during this time which was thought to be because their TV diet did not allow them to express their aggressive urges. In fact, Group B boys knew about Group A's programmes and preferred them to their own. The frustration that this caused led to greater aggression. Frustration was thus a confounding variable.

There are four types of experiment but only **laboratory** and **field** experiments are *true* experiments in the sense that the experimenter has direct control over the IV. Experiments can be classified according to whether the experimenter controls the IV directly and whether the environment it happens in is naturally occurring or controlled by the experimenter (see Table 2.1).

correlation is not the same as causation

IV and DV

not all experiments are laboratory based

	The environment in which the experiment takes place is controlled by the experimenter	The environment in which the experiment takes place is not controlled by the experimenter
The IV is manipulated by the experimenter	**Laboratory experiment**, e.g. *Bandura*'s (1961) studies of imitation of aggression in pre-school children	**Field experiment**, e.g. *Feshbach*'s (1971) studies of the effects of TV 'diet' on the aggression levels of adolescent boys in institutions
The IV varies naturally (or fortuitously)	**Quasi-experiment**, e.g. where the effect of variables like male/female on some aspect of behaviour, such as aggression, are studied	**Natural experiment**, e.g. a study by *Williams* (1985) who studied aggressive behaviour of children in communities before, during and after the introduction of TV

Table 2.1 Types of experiment

The method is useful because:

- the amount of control possible in some experiments makes it possible for the experimenter to make causal statements about behaviour. This cannot be done with other methods;
- knowing what causes behaviour to change puts the experimenter in the position of being able to control it;
- in spite of rigorous control, there is always the chance that behaviour is not affected by the IV but by a confounding variable.

Problems with it include:

- lack of realism in certain kinds of experiment, especially the laboratory experiment, so that findings do not apply to real life;
- loss of control in the more 'true to life' experiments, such as the natural experiment, means it is more difficult to be confident about what causes what;
- ethical considerations (which are as important here as with any other method).

OTHER METHODS

Cross-sectional and longitudinal methods

If a psychologist is interested in the ways in which behaviour changes *over time* (with age) these are the two main research strategies available within which any of the data collection or treatment techniques described so far could be used.

The **longitudinal method** involves following up the *same group* of individuals on a number of *different occasions* over time. This could be daily, weekly, monthly, annually or whatever seems to be an appropriate time interval for as long as the research requires it. The television programme *35 Up* has revisited a group of boys and girls from widely differing social backgrounds at 7, 14, 21, 28 and 35 years of age. A good example from psychological research is *Eron et al.*'s (1972) study of children at 9 years old and then at 19 which showed a correlation between the amount of violent TV viewed at 9 and aggressiveness at 19.

The method is useful because:

- the psychologist can study *age-related changes* in behaviour (in other words, see how it develops);
- the impact of *early experience* on later behaviour can be seen;
- it is possible to see whether there is *consistency* between early characteristics, e.g. dependency, and later behaviour;
- using the same people over and over again cuts down on the number of individual differences which could affect the behaviour of interest (this is a kind of repeated measures design – see Ch. 3 p. 19);
- individuals can be studied in greater depth and detail.

Problems with it include:

- it can be very time consuming and expensive;
- there may be a high drop-out rate of participants, possibly meaning that the sample is no longer representative;
- research interests change over time so a study may literally be out of date before it is over;
- design faults or omissions in the original planning of the study cannot be undone.

The **cross-sectional** method involves taking samples of individuals to represent different age groups and studying them at the same time. Piaget is often quoted as a researcher who used this method when he studied aspects of children's cognitive development. Other stage theories such as those of Kohlberg and Freud can also be supported by cross-sectional research.

This method is useful because:

- it is usually quicker and cheaper than the longitudinal method;
- it helps us to see age-related changes in behaviour;
- it may be possible to study more children and this may mean that the samples are more representative;
- it is useful for helping to establish 'norms' of development.

Problems with it include:

- individual differences between age groups which could obscure the results;
- the information gathered may be more superficial than with the longitudinal method;
- as participants are seen just once, their behaviour at that time may not be typical;
- it may exaggerate differences between age groups and give a false impression of stops and starts in development rather than a smooth progression.

Both the longitudinal and cross-sectional method suffer from a further problem – that of ensuring that the method of testing at each age is *comparable*, e.g. is your test for 6-year-olds as difficult for 6-year-olds as your test for 8-year-olds is for 8-year-olds? If not it will be impossible to make comparisons between age groups.

Cross-cultural studies

cross-cultural studies can contribute to nature–nurture debates

These studies involve comparing two or more cultures to look for *similarities* and *differences* between them. If behaviour is similar across cultures we can think of it as more likely to be a universal human characteristic (**nature**) since it is the same regardless of differences in environment. Differences in behaviour are more likely to be due to environment (**nurture**). *Freud*'s (1856–1939) and *Piaget*'s (1896–1980) theories could be tested in this way to see if the stages of development they proposed were universal. In fact *Kagan* (1975) found that the stages of **cognitive development** proposed by Piaget were the same in Guatemalan, Kenyan and Japanese children except that Japanese children's rate of development tended to be faster and Guatemalan and Kenyan children, both living in rural village cultures, did not always reach the formal operational stage. In the 1930s *Margaret Mead* studied the expression of gender in New Guinea tribespeople. *Ainsworth et al.* (1978) studied the nature of attachment between Ganda babies and their mothers and compared it to that in USA mothers and babies. *Segall et al.* (1963) studied perception in Europeans and Zulus using the Muller-Lyer illusion.

This method is useful because:

- it is like a kind of natural experiment in which the IV (cultural differences) arranges itself. The researcher simply goes in and measures naturally occurring differences (DV);
- findings from cross-cultural research can challenge our assumptions about human behaviour, e.g. in Kagan's study, relatively impoverished Guatemalan and Kenyan children were not significantly disadvantaged in their rate of development compared to Japanese children who had access to all kinds of modern technology;
- it can help to clarify the nature–nurture issue over things like gender, perception, intellectual development and mental disorders.

Problems with it include:

- the time and expense involved;
- difficulties in translating test materials from one language to another in a way which retains the original meaning;
- difficulties in remaining **objective**, i.e. not allowing your own cultural biases to affect the way you view another culture;
- difficulties in deciding which of the large number of variables affecting people in different cultures are responsible for the observed differences between cultures.

Psychometric methods

These involve devising ways of measuring human characteristics such as personality, intelligence, abilities and achievements. Well-known measures of personality include

some psychologists believe we can test or measure psychological characteristics

the **Eysenck Personality Inventory** and **Cattell's 16 PF** questionnaire. Intelligence tests include the **Stanford Binet** test, the **British Ability Scales** and the **Wechsler Scales**. To use and interpret such tests, psychologists need special training. In the wrong hands, test results could be used in very damaging ways.

Good tests are **reliable**, **valid** and **standardised**. Reliable means that a test gives consistent results, e.g. over time. Valid means that the test is relevant and appropriate. Standardised means that it has been adjusted to fit the population it is intended for so that most people score in the middle part of the scale and fewer at the extremes.

These methods are useful because:

- it is relatively quick and easy to test large numbers of people;
- the results give us precise and objective measures;
- it is possible to compare people in an objective way;
- they can help in the overall assessment of someone and add to other information.

Problems with psychometric methods include:

- they tend to 'pigeon-hole' people because they do not allow flexibility in responses;
- the results may be misunderstood and given undue importance by the respondent (this is one reason why testers need to be well trained in how to deal with results);
- difficulties in devising tests that are free of culture, class or social bias;
- ethical concerns about who should know the scores and what happens as a result.

Archival data

data from the past can be revealing

Sometimes it is useful to psychologists to research into existing, historical records of events that have already happened. It is sometimes possible to discover patterns in behaviour that are linked to other events. The social scientist *Emile Durkheim* (1897) used such information in his research into suicide. More recently, *Heston* (1966) used archival data to test the role of inherited factors in schizophrenia. He looked into the backgrounds of children who had been born to schizophrenic mothers and adopted very soon afterwards. He used records from the child-care institutions that had arranged the adoptions as well as the children's school and court records. He found a higher incidence of schizophrenia in this group when he compared them to similar children of non-schizophrenic mothers.

ANIMAL RESEARCH

be clear about what psychological research with animals is for

Certain branches of psychology have depended heavily on the use of animals in research. This ranges from studying animals' behaviour in their natural environment through carrying out laboratory studies of behaviour to, at the other extreme, tissue research. It should not be confused with product testing or medical research and it is important to remember that vivisection is a minority and declining research interest in psychology. Examples of animal research include the work on learning by *Pavlov* (1849–1936), *Thorndike* (1874–1949) and *Skinner* (1904–90), work on training animals to use language by *Savage-Rumbaugh* (1990), and many studies into nature–nurture and perception, e.g. by *Held* and *Hein* (1963).

Some psychologists study animals because:

- they assume that we are both genetically and behaviourally related to other animals (an idea borrowed from *Charles Darwin* (1809–82). This means that we can look at simpler species to help us understand more complex human behaviour;
- for legal and ethical reasons it is easier to exert control over animals' experiences in research, e.g. selective breeding, deprivation or enrichment;
- we can compare generations of animals more quickly than we could humans, e.g. when examining the role of early experience on later behaviour or when carrying out selective breeding programmes;
- it is easier to be objective with animal subjects because it is more likely that a researcher will be able to remain emotionally detached from them.

Others object to the use of animals because:

- they feel that it is ethically indefensible;
- they think it is dangerous to transfer findings (**extrapolate**) from one species to another;
- they think that humans are unique and that the use of animals to understand humans is inappropriate.

2 ETHICAL CONSIDERATIONS IN RESEARCH

Ethics are *moral standards* and *rules of conduct* which psychologists must abide by in both research and practice. The *British Psychological Society* (BPS) and the *Association for the Teaching of Psychology* (ATP) have, between them, devised guidelines covering all areas of research and practice. You will find guidelines for GCSE students included in the psychology syllabuses. All of them stress that any research you do should be cleared first by your teacher to ensure that you are sufficiently competent and qualified, that the research is within the law and that it is appropriate and well designed. Here, we will concentrate on ethics in research with humans and look briefly at ethics in research with animals.

ethics matter at all levels of research

ETHICS IN RESEARCH WITH HUMANS

Here are some of the main considerations:

1. **Rights**. Respect the rights and dignity of the research participants at all times.
2. **Consent**. Obtain consent (preferably informed consent) from participants or someone qualified to speak for them.
3. **Deception**. Avoid using this if at all possible and only use it if absolutely necessary and if there is no other way of carrying out the study.
4. **Debriefing**. Whenever possible, offer full information to participants after they have completed your study. (Intention to debrief is not an excuse to deceive participants!)
5. **Withdrawal**. Participants need to know that they are free to withdraw from the investigation at any time or have their data destroyed if they so wish.
6. **Confidentiality**. All participants have a legal right to expect that the data they provide will be treated confidentially.
7. **Protection of participants**. Ensure that they are not put at risk, or harmed, either physically or psychologically.
8. **Observations**. As this may involve observing participants without their consent, you should not observe people unless they are in places where they would expect to be seen by others.
9. **Advice**. You should never give advice on the basis of research findings unless properly qualified to do so.
10. **Colleagues**. Psychologists should monitor ethical standards in each other's work.

ETHICS IN RESEARCH WITH NON-HUMAN ANIMALS

Animal research at GCSE level is quite rare and usually involves naturalistic observations. Nevertheless, you will come across animal studies in the theory part of your course so a quick look at ethical issues is necessary. Here are some of the main concerns:

1. **Legal issues**. It is illegal to carry out animal research involving pain, distress, surgery, drugs and euthanasia unless the research has been scrutinised and approved and the researcher has the relevant certificates from the Home Office.
2. **Know the species**. It is essential to know the needs, habits and behaviour patterns of the animal species being studied so that distressing them unnecessarily is avoided.
3. **Protect the species**. Studying the animal should not pose a threat to its survival, e.g. by disturbing its breeding patterns or care of its young or by using endangered species.

    The fewest possible number of animals should be used to gain meaningful results.

A Review Sheet for this chapter can be found on pp. 229–30.

CHAPTER 3

DESIGNING RESEARCH AND UNDERSTANDING FINDINGS

GETTING STARTED

All the GCSE psychology syllabuses have one thing in common – methodology is a *theme* underlying everything you study. This means you can expect to bring it in *anywhere*, not just in the questions which are obviously focused on methodology. Remember that psychological research can always be evaluated on methodological grounds so if you are stuck for something to say about a topic, try taking a look at the research methods behind it. Be prepared to think on your feet.

The MEG examination has two written papers and the first of these examines the syllabus core which all students prepare for. In this paper, you will need to apply knowledge of methodology and be able to interpret given 'stimulus' material including 'visuals'. The second paper examines the specialist options. Here too, you will have stimulus material and you will need to understand research designs and read 'visuals'.

The SEG examination has one written paper and includes a methodology question with stimulus material. You will need to interpret information and apply knowledge of methodology both here and in parts of other questions.

The NEAB written paper also includes methodology questions but, here, you will actually need to handle data, for example draw a scattergram or calculate averages. You will also need to interpret data and you may be able to bring methodology in elsewhere if you are flexible.

1. CONSIDERATIONS IN DESIGNING RESEARCH

2. PRESENTING AND INTERPRETING RESEARCH FINDINGS

ESSENTIAL PRINCIPLES

SELECTING PARTICIPANTS – POPULATIONS AND SAMPLES

A **population** in psychological research refers to the total number of individuals who qualify to take part in your research because they have the required characteristics. An example of a **target population** might be all full-time16–19-year-old students in the UK studying GCSE Psychology in a given year or it might be all the rhesus monkeys living on Cayo, Santiago or all the couples marrying at a particular register office in a given year. If it is possible to test all members of a population, the study constitutes a **census**. If not, **sampling** is carried out because:

- it is usually only practical to study a selection (sample) of the population;
- it is vital that the sample is carefully selected so that it is representative of the population;
- if the sample is representative then findings about it can be applied to (generalised to) the population from which it was drawn.

Sampling techniques include:

- **Random sampling**. The main feature of this technique is that each member of the population has an equal chance of being chosen. To achieve this, members of the population would be assigned a number. The numbers would be pooled and individuals' numbers selected using random number tables, computer-generated random numbers or by pulling the numbers out of a hat.
- **Opportunity sampling**. The researcher decides on the type of participants needed and approaches anyone who happens to fit that category. You may have been part of an opportunity sample if your teacher used you as participants for a class practical. You were the right kind of person in the right place at the right time.
- **Quota sampling**. This is used if there are important sub-groups in the population which might be missed using random sampling. The population is organised into groups and the samples selected from them in the same proportions that appear in the population. The researcher usually stops when enough representatives for each sub-group have been found so it is like a kind of elaborate opportunity sampling.

The only hard and fast rule about sample size is that the sample should be large enough adequately to represent the population so we can't say '100 is enough' or '10% is enough' or 'the larger the better'. In populations of very similar individuals, smaller samples may be representative. If individuals are very different, larger samples may be necessary.

HYPOTHESES

A hypothesis is a *precise* and *testable* statement that *predicts the outcome* of a research study. It is not a 'shot in the dark' because it is based on much careful theorising and/or research.

If we are doing an experiment, we predict a difference, e.g. 'There is a difference in the amount of aggressiveness shown by boys and girls.' For a correlation we say 'There is a relationship between the amount of aggression children show and the amount of violent TV they watch.' These are called **research hypotheses** or **alternate hypotheses**. With every research hypothesis there is a **null hypothesis**. For an experiment we might say 'There is *no difference* in the amount of aggressiveness shown by boys and girls. Any difference is due to chance.' For a correlation we would say 'There is *no relationship* between the amount of aggression children show and the amount of violent TV they watch. Any relationship is due to chance.'

Between them, the research and null hypothesis should cover all likely outcomes in the research. When the research is complete we *retain* one of them on the basis of the findings and *reject* the other.

Sometimes, psychologists feel confident enough to state the **direction** they think the alternate hypothesis will take, e.g. 'Boys are more aggressive than girls' or 'There is a positive relationship between the amount of aggression children show and the amount of violent TV they watch.'

OPERATIONALISING HYPOTHESES

Researchers need to be very careful to define precisely (**operationalise**) what they mean by the terms they use in hypotheses. This usually means that hypotheses have to be put into a measurable, or quantifiable, form. Aggression, for example, might be defined as 'a physical act that hurts or damages someone else or something'. Anxiety might be defined as 'a self report score of over 10 on an anxiety scale of 0–20 where 0 means not anxious and 20 means extremely anxious'. In observational studies it may be necessary to set up categories or checklists in advance so that it is possible to record, e.g. the number of aggressive acts per observation interval or the number of TV adverts fitting predetermined categories.

EXPERIMENTAL DESIGN

The simplest type of experiment involves collecting scores from participants under two different conditions to see if there are differences between them. In a laboratory or field experiment, it is usual to have a **control group** of participants and an **experimental group**. The control group lacks the influence of the IV and provides **baseline data**. The experimental group is under the influence of the IV so any differences between experimental group and control group scores must be down to the IV (providing the two groups were the same before the addition of the IV). An example might be to test the effect of alcohol on driving ability. The control group would have no alcohol and the experimental group would have alcohol. All extraneous variables such as previous driving experience, weather conditions, difficulty of the driving test, type of car, body-weight etc. (can you add to the list?) would need to be controlled (balanced across the two groups) so that the only systematic difference between them was the presence or absence of alcohol.

In a natural or quasi-experiment the IV arranges itself and you take what you get, e.g. male vs female, brown vs blue eyes, culture Y vs culture Z. There is no control group as such because the IV cannot be eradicated from one condition. Instead the researcher compares two levels of the IV.

There are three ways of collecting the two sets of data:

1. **The repeated measures design** is where participants take part in both conditions. This is good because:

   - it is economical in the number of participants used;
   - as the participants are the same in the two conditions there are fewer **individual differences** affecting the DV to worry about.

Problems with it include:

   - participants may become used to being tested and carry over the effects of practice or fatigue from one condition to the other. These are called **order effects**. To safeguard against them, we **counterbalance** order of presentation of conditions to participants so some do condition A first and some do B first. This is called the **ABBA** design. Alternatively, we can **randomise** presentation, deciding by tossing a coin which condition is done first;
   - participants may not return to be tested a second time;
   - it cannot be used in a quasi-experiment. Why?

2. **The matched pairs design** is where participants are organised into pairs on the basis of variables relevant to the investigation. (How would you pair drivers in the example above?) One member of the pair is then randomly assigned to condition A and the other to condition B. This is good because:

   - we don't have to worry about order effects;
   - it cuts down on the number of individual differences between conditions.

Problems with it include:

   - good matching is quite difficult to achieve (unless you have a large number of identical twins!);

know why we use control groups

- there will still be some individual differences remaining uncontrolled;
- it takes more participants than the repeated measures design;
- losing one person means you lose a pair of data.

3. **The independent subjects design** is where a sample of participants is randomly divided between conditions or the groups arrange themselves on the basis of a naturally occurring IV such as male/female. This is good because:

- it is relatively quick and easy to set up;
- it avoids order effects;
- random allocation should balance out individual differences in the participants.

Problems with it include:

- it takes more participants than the repeated measures design;
- the differences between the two groups are likely to be greater at the outset than in the other two designs.

OTHER DESIGN CONSIDERATIONS

1. **Demand characteristics**. These are features of the research situation which might alert the participants to the hypothesis being tested or the aim of the research. They may then change their behaviour depending on whether they feel cooperative, disruptive or anxious. To guard against this, the researcher may use the **single blind procedure** where steps are taken to ensure participants do not know the research aim or hypothesis. To ensure the researcher does not sway the results either, a better check is to use the **double blind procedure** where the researcher instructs someone else in how to collect the data but neither that person nor the participants know the hypothesis.
2. **Instructions to participants**. These need to be the same, or **standardised**, for all participants in a particular condition to avoid favouring some over others. They may be audio-taped and played to participants, written down for them to read or given by the same researcher to all participants.
3. **The situation**. The physical conditions in which the participants provide data should be the same for all.

<table>
<tr><td>2</td><td>PRESENTING AND INTERPRETING RESEARCH FINDINGS</td></tr>
</table>

66 know how to 'read' data 99

All the GCSE boards require you to submit coursework as part of the examination so you should have some experience of presenting research findings. Usually, this will entail putting numerical data into an understandable form and showing that data in a visual, or pictorial, way. One reason why this is valuable is that it helps you to understand the sort of data presentation you might encounter on an examination paper. This section, therefore, concentrates on common ways of presenting research findings in exam questions and how to interpret them.

CORRELATION AND SCATTERGRAMS

The 'visual' which illustrates different kinds of correlation is called a **scattergram**. Scattergrams typically show one of the patterns shown in **Figs** 3.1 to 3.5.

Imagine that we collected ten newspaper pictures of couples on their wedding day and separated the brides and grooms. Participants were then asked to rank order the grooms from least to most attractive and then do the same for the brides. Each picture would then have a rank score ranging from 1 (least attractive) to 10 (most attractive). The scores are shown in Table 3.1 and the scattergram in **Fig.** 3.6.

Fig. 3.6 allows us to say the following:

- it shows an imperfect relationship (the points are almost in a straight line);
- it shows a positive relationship (the line rises from bottom left to top right);
- the correlation coefficient is close to +1 (a good guess would be +0.8);
- newlyweds tend to match each other in their level of attractiveness;
- if we met a groom for the first time, we would be fairly safe in predicting his bride's level of attractiveness.

 remember this limitation 99

Fig. 3.6 does **not** allow us to say:

- matching in level of attractiveness causes people to get married!

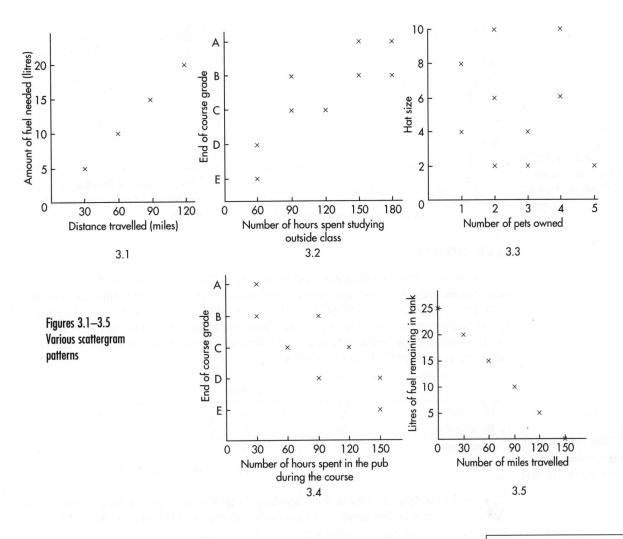

Figures 3.1–3.5
Various scattergram
patterns

Figure 3.6 Scattergram to show the
relationship between attractiveness
rankings for bride and groom pairs

Couple	Bride's rank	Groom's rank
A	5	4
B	10	9
C	2	3
D	3	1
E	1	2
F	6	6
G	4	5
H	7	8
I	9	10
J	8	7

Table 3.1 Attractiveness ranking for
brides and grooms

GRAPHS

> Caution! You may find the word 'graph' used quite loosely to mean any visual presentation of data

There are various kinds of graphs but one kind you are likely to encounter shows *change* in the amount of something over *time, trials* or *conditions*. Imagine that a teacher with a disruptive child in the class decides to ignore all acts of disruption to see whether it affects their frequency. The number of disruptive acts per five-minute interval are then counted for half an hour. See Table 3.2 and **Fig.** 3.7.

Fig. 3.7 allows us to say the following:

- exactly how many disruptive acts occurred in a given time interval;
- the number of disruptive acts drops sharply in the first four intervals (from 12 to 3) but after that it levels off;
- we may not be able to improve on the level reached at interval 6 as the 2 remaining acts may not be affected by being ignored.

Interval	Number of disruptive acts
1	12
2	8
3	5
4	3
5	2
6	2

Figure 3.7 Graph to show the number of disruptive acts shown by a child over 30 minutes of such acts being ignored

Table 3.2 Number of disruptive acts observed per 5-minute interval over 30 minutes

BAR CHARTS

In research projects which involve counting numbers of things into categories in order to *compare* them to other categories, bar charts are useful 'visuals'. Imagine that you are monitoring the content of TV advertisements to see if men and women are portrayed differently in them. One thing you might do is to count up the number of times adverts show female or male lead characters in particular roles. Here is a table showing results for 80 different adverts.

Table 3.3 Male and female lead characters in adverts classified according to role portrayed

	Male	Female	
Domestic role	6	26	
Workplace role	25	10	
Other role	6	7	
Total	37	43	**Grand total = 80**

The trouble with such data is that, because there are more males than females, it is difficult to compare the numbers in a meaningful way. For this reason they have been converted to *percentages* as shown in Table 3.4.

Table 3.4 Percentage of male and female lead characters in adverts according to role portrayed

	Male	Female
Domestic role	16	61
Workplace role	68	23
Other role	16	16
Total	100	100

We could now plot two bar charts to show these data in a clearer way but it would be clearer still to put them on to one composite bar chart so that immediate comparisons can be made. See **Fig**. 3.8.

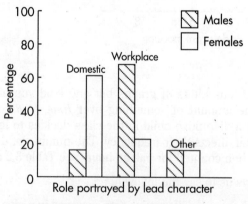

Figure 3.8 Bar chart to show the percentage of male and female lead characters in advertisements according to their role

Fig. 3.8 tells us that in our sample of 80 advertisements:

● males are most often seen in a workplace role (68%);
● males are seen equally in domestic and in other roles but neither occurs very often (16% each);

- females are most often seen in domestic roles (61%);
- females are more likely to be seen in workplace than in other roles but the difference is not very great (23% and 16% respectively);
- compared to males, females are shown in domestic roles nearly four times more often;
- compared to females, males are shown in workplace roles nearly three times more often;
- females and males are shown in equal proportions in other roles (16% each).

AVERAGES AND THE RANGE

Imagine you have carried out an experiment to compare the effectiveness of two reading schemes for young children. You decided on a level of reading ability which each child must attain and recorded the age in months at which they reached that level. See Table 3.5.

Child	Scheme A	Child	Scheme B
1	54	13	54
2	57	14	59
3	62	15	56
4	56	16	67
5	55	17	50
6	53	18	53
7	63	19	69
8	59	20	52
9	58	21	52
10	65	22	49
11	61	23	65
12	67	24	71
Mean A	59.2	Mean B	58.1
Median A	58.5	Median B	55
Mode A	none	Mode B	52
Range A	14	Range B	22

Table 3.5 Age of children in months achieving the required level of reading ability under Scheme A or B

How do we make sense of such data? Two ways are shown at the bottom of the table. The first is to compare the samples' *average* scores. We can work out the averages thus:

- the **mean** is the scores added together and divided by the number of scores in the sample. In Table 3.5 the means show that Scheme A children are, on average, a month later than Scheme B children in reaching the required level;
- the **median** is the central point in the scores when they are listed in order of size. In Table 3.5 the medians show that Scheme A children are, on average, 3.5 months later than Scheme B children in reaching the required standard;
- the **mode** is the value which occurs most often. There is no mode for Scheme A so this does not allow us to compare the two schemes.

The second way to compare the schemes is to examine how *varied* the scores are under A or B. The **range** allows us to do this. It is calculated by finding the difference between the largest and smallest scores in a set of data (in Scheme A this would be 67–53=14). The range for Scheme B (22) shows that there is a wider variation in the age at which children reached the required standard (although, on average, we know children do better on Scheme B).

HISTOGRAMS

bar charts and histograms have important similarities and differences

Bar charts and histograms are both ways of showing *how many times* a given thing occurs or *how much* of something we have. This is indicated on the vertical axis. On a bar chart, however, the categories chosen for the horizontal axis are not in any particular order of, say, size or importance. The horizontal axis on a histogram does show a scale where something has been measured so scores do have an order. The data in Table 3.5 can be organised in order of size. To plot them on a histogram, we can arrange the ordered scores into groups and draw **Figs** 3.9 and 3.10.

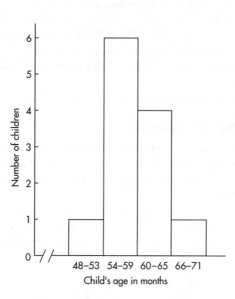

Figure 3.9 Histogram Scheme A   Figure 3.10 Histogram Scheme B

Comparison of these two histograms tells us:

● there is a bunching of scores in the middle of the scale for Scheme A;
● there is a bunching of scores at the lower end of the scale for Scheme B;
● there are more 'high-fliers' on Scheme B;
● the exact number of individuals appearing in each category.

Which scheme would you choose?

TYPICAL EXAM QUESTION

1. MEG specimen paper 3 (Higher) Section B. *Spend 15 minutes on this question*

Some psychologists decided to study prejudice in a natural setting by inviting 24 boys who were aged 12 to a 'summer camp'. The boys were all white and came from middle-class families. All the staff at the camp were actually psychologists. When the boys arrived, they were divided into two separate groups. The first week was spent trying to get each group to work together and develop a group spirit. Then the psychologists tried to create conflict between the two groups by having competitive games. The two groups became aggressive towards each other and fights broke out. In the last part of the study, the psychologists tried to reduce the prejudice between the two groups.

(a) The method used in this study was a field experiment. Why is this an appropriate method to use in studying prejudice?   [2]

(b) Describe how the psychologist might study prejudice using another type of method.   [2]

(c) Give one problem with the sample that was used in this study.   [2]

(d) Give one ethical problem with this study.   [2]

(e) Describe one way in which this study could be improved.   [2]

[*10 marks*]
(MEG)

TUTOR ANSWER

1. (a) The more realistic setting of a field experiment makes it less likely that participants would be affected by demand characteristics. These are features of a research situation that might give away the hypothesis being tested. If this study had taken place in a laboratory setting participants would have been more likely to question what the researcher was trying to do so the normal course of prejudice formation would not happen.

    (b) The psychologist could use psychometric methods, e.g. use the F-scale to measure the personality characteristic called Authoritarianism. High scores on Authoritarianism are thought to be linked to prejudiced attitudes so the psychologist could see if people's scores correlated with prejudiced attitudes or behaviour.

    (c) The sample only represents boys who are white and middle class so the study only tells us about prejudice formation in groups made up of this type of person. It tells us nothing about prejudice formation in girls or people from other races and social classes.

    (d) We could argue that the psychologists did not do enough to protect the boys from psychological harm caused by deliberately creating aggression and tension between groups which could have lasted beyond the study. Attempts to reduce prejudice afterwards do not excuse this. However, it could be argued that the research findings were important enough to justify treating the boys in this way.

    (e) The study might have told us more about prejudice formation if the sample had been improved. The psychologists could have taken a wider target population to include boys and girls from different racial groups and social classes. If the sampling were done carefully, findings could be generalised back to the target population.

STUDENTS' ANSWERS WITH EXAMINER'S COMMENTS

2. NEAB specimen paper (Tier Q) Section A

- *Answer **ALL** questions*
- *You are advised to spend approximately 40 minutes on this section.*
- *This section carries 50 marks.*

A1 A psychologist wanted to find out whether there would be a relationship between students' scores on an English test and their teacher's expectations of the scores they would obtain. From a class of 30 students, 12 were asked to volunteer to be participants. They were then given the English test and at the same time the teacher was asked to estimate the score of each participant.

The following table shows the two sets of scores.

Participants	Scores in tests (Maximum score = 100)	Teacher's estimate of scores (Maximum score = 100)
A	84	75
B	75	80
C	60	55
D	45	50
E	90	80
F	20	25
G	40	45
H	50	50
I	70	65
J	60	65
K	30	25
L	20	30

(a) On the graph paper, below, plot an appropriate graph of the data.   [4]

Title Scattergram to show the relationship between scores in test and
        teacher's estimate of scores

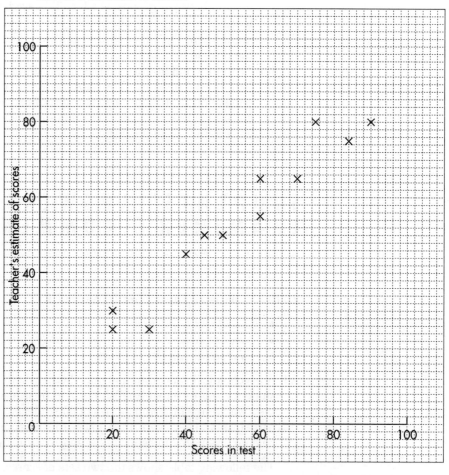

needs line of
fit 3/4

(b) Identify and explain the type of relationship shown in the graph.   [2]

explain what this
means 1/2

The graph shows a positive correlation between the students' scores and the
teacher's estimated scores.

(c) State an hypothesis for this study.   [2]

2/2

There is a relationship between students' scores on an English test and their
teacher's expectations of the scores they would obtain.

(d) Explain why this study is not an experiment.   [2]

mention IV and
DV 1/2

The test happened in natural circumstances with no interference or control
from the psychologist.

(e) What conclusion, if any, can be drawn from this study? [3]

The teacher was able to predict the outcome for each of the 12 students knowing the potential for each student.

[*Total 13*]

A2 A psychologist wanted to find out if there was any difference between the number skills of men and women. She decided to conduct her study in a College of Further Education and obtained a list of names of all students. She put the names of all the male students in one hat and the names of all the female students in another hat. The flow chart shows what she did next.

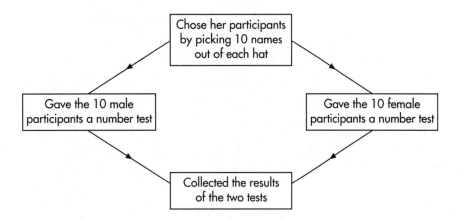

(a) Identify and assess the appropriateness of the sampling method used. [2]

Random sampling was used meaning everyone had a chance of being chosen.

(b) The table below shows the results of the study.

Scores on number tests	
Males	Females
20	10
25	35
30	35
25	10
15	10
10	25
25	20
35	15
15	30
10	10

Table 1 Scores on a number test for males and females

Complete the following summary of results using the data from Table 1. [4]

	Mean	Median	Mode	Range
Male Participants	21	22.5	25	25
Female Participants	22	22.5	10	25

(c) Apart from the control of environment variables, identify **two** variables which should have been controlled in this study and discuss the importance of their control. [4]

Age and IQ levels should have been controlled to make the test fairer.

(d) A GCSE student who saw the results drew the conclusion that the study showed women have better number skills than men.

How would you respond to this conclusion? [2]

❝❝ Yes, but appraise the
study 1/2 ❞❞

There is hardly any difference in the means, medians or the ranges but the modes show more women score low and more men score high.

[*Total 12*]

A3 A GCSE psychology student gave a volunteer sample of people two memory tasks.

Task A – To learn for 90 seconds an organised word list of 24 words. To recall the words in a period of 60 seconds.

Task B – To learn for 90 seconds a randomised word list of 24 words (not the same words as on the Task A list). To recall the words in a period of 60 seconds.

Task A and Task B were conducted in the same environmental conditions; the word lists were of equal difficulty.

Below are the results of the study.

Participant	Task A Score	Task B Score
A	*11	16
B	*13	16
C	11	*17
D	15	*18
E	*10	18
F	12	*15
G	*8	13
H	14	*7
I	10	*16
J	*8	15

* Denotes the task which was completed first by the participant.

(a) Write a suitable debriefing for the participants in this study. [3]

❝❝ explain much
more 1/3 ❞❞

Thank you for taking part in this study. I was testing to see if people remembered more words if they were organised into categories. Do you have any questions?

(b) Identify **two** appropriate experimental procedures which have been used in this study. [2]

❝❝ 2/2 ❞❞

Counterbalancing – the ABBA design. The word lists were of equal difficulty.

(c) Use the information given to you about how the study was conducted and the results obtained to write the Discussion section of a practical report. [10]

❝❝ good ❞❞

❝❝ discusses meaning of
findings
limitations
improvements
5/10 ❞❞

The mean for task A is 12.2 and for task B it is 15.1 so people scored more in task B. Nine out of ten did better on B. This isn't what we would expect. The organisation of words should have made them easier to recall. There must have been something about list B words that made them easier to remember even though the lists were of equal difficulty. We could say that randomised lists are easier to remember. Unfortunately, the sample of people is very small and they were volunteers so we cannot generalise. The study could have been done with a bigger, random sample to be really sure of the results.

[*Total 15*]
(NEAB)

❝❝ go on to examine data more thoroughly. Find another limitation. Explain what the findings mean in psychological terms. What are the implications of these results and how do they relate to other research findings? ❞❞

❝❝ 24/40 Some good answers here. On the whole more marks could have been gained by really reading the questions and doing as they ask. ❞❞

3. SEG paper 2, 1994. Section A

Spend 40 minutes on this question
Answer this question

In order to test the hypothesis that watching television helps children to learn, a psychologist selected a sample of 60 children aged between 5 and 15 years.

Half the children were shown a video aimed at teaching them how to solve a puzzle. Three weeks later, all 60 children were given a similar puzzle to solve.

As more of the children who had seen the video were able to solve the puzzle, the psychologist concluded that the children had learned this ability from the video.

(a) What hypothesis was being tested? [1]

 question paper says 'helps' 0/1

Children who watch television learn more than children who do not watch television.

(b) Rewrite this as a null hypothesis [2]

 2/2

Children who watch television do not learn more than children who do not watch television.

(c) What was the independent variable? [1]

 1/1

Whether the children watched television.

(d) How was the dependent variable measured? [1]

 1/1

This was the number of children who solved the second puzzle.

(e) What was the sample in the above study? [1]

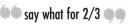 1/1

60 children aged between 5 and 15 years.

(f) What is a sample? [3]

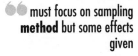 say what for 2/3

A sample is a group of people (adults, children etc.) taken to represent a larger population.

(g) Explain how the way in which the sample was chosen might have affected the result [5]

 must focus on sampling **method** but some effects given

2/5

We do not know how the psychologist chose the sample so it could have been biased. He might have selected children who looked bright so IQ wasn't controlled. Some of the children may have been very good at doing puzzles and all ended up in the video group. Young children could have found the puzzles much harder than the older children.

(h) How would you carry out a study of learning?

(i) State your hypothesis. [2]

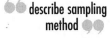 2/2

Children who attend a nursery every weekday learn more than children who do not attend nursery.

(ii) Describe how you would choose your sample and give reasons for your choice. [6]

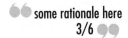 describe sampling method

 some rationale here 3/6

I would find 30 children who attended nursery every weekday and match them to 30 children who did not have any kind of daycare. They would all be between 3 and 4 years of age and from similar family backgrounds. I would then be able to compare these two groups. I would not include children with learning disabilities or hearing or sight problems as this could influence the results.

(iii) Outline the procedure you would follow and give reasons for your choice. [8]

good

I would test the nursery children weekly with puzzles aimed at their age group and see how long it took them to complete them. I would also get them to draw and paint, observe the quality of pictures and see how long they would concentrate on a particular picture.

I would test the nursery children and the non-nursery children in the same way. I could then compare the two sets of results to see how much the children improved over the course of the study. If the nursery children

66 generally more detail
needed 4/8 99

improved more I could say it was because they were at nursery. If not I would accept my null hypothesis which would say 'There is no difference in learning between children who do and do not attend nursery school.'

[*Total 30 marks*]
(SEG)

66 18/30 A good start but it is very important to really answer the question paying close attention to all its requirements. 99

A Review Sheet for this chapter can be found on pp. 231–2.

LEARNING

GETTING STARTED

Explanations of how animals and humans learn are central to all the GCSE syllabuses. They all require you to know about classical and operant conditioning and Social Learning Theory and how these apply to human learning. NEAB and Option 4 MEG students will need to pay special attention to the section on other approaches to learning. Ethical considerations are important whatever syllabus you are following. Option 4 MEG students will also need to look at the section on other approaches.

The learning theories emphasised here come from the influential and important Behaviourist school of psychology which sees our behaviour as mainly learned or determined by our experiences. The role of heredity in determining behaviour is important but less so than learning. This is a very optimistic view to take because it follows that we can unlearn unhelpful behaviour and learn useful behaviour at any time. Change for the better is always possible. Early Behaviourists insisted that psychologists should concern themselves only with that which could be observed and measured (i.e. overt behaviour which happened in response to stimuli, hence S-R psychology.) More recent approaches acknowledge the thought (cognitive) processes which go on during learning. We will see this in Social Learning Theory and in other theories.

- **Behaviourist** – a psychologist who believes that learning is the most important determinant of behaviour
- **Learning** – a relatively permanent change in behaviour that comes about as the result of experience
- **Stimulus** – any event or influence (internal or external) to which an animal or human reacts or responds
- **Response** – anything an animal or human does (internal or external) as a result of being affected by a stimulus.

ESSENTIAL PRINCIPLES

<table>
<tr><td>1 ></td><td>**CLASSICAL (PAVLOVIAN) CONDITIONING**</td></tr>
</table>

Classical conditioning is a type of learning which can explain how we develop fears, phobias (and other emotional reactions) and food aversions. *Ivan Pavlov* (1849–1936) was the first to study it formally.

Pavlov was studying dogs' digestive processes. Dogs automatically salivate when food arrives in their mouths but, after being in the experimental situation for a while, they would salivate in anticipation of food arriving as if they had learned to recognise the signs that it was on its way. Pavlov took control of these signs and showed that dogs could be trained to salivate to bells, lights and cardboard shapes instead of food. The classical conditioning process works like this:

❝❝ classical conditioning can build on innate reflexes ❞❞

- There must first of all be an *innate reflex* action (an automatic, involuntary response to a stimulus). Pavlov called these **unconditional reflexes**. (Unconditional means not dependent on learning. Examples include salivation to food, starting to loud noises, blinking to a puff of air in the eye.) Such reflexes consist of an unconditional stimulus (**UCS**) which brings about an unconditional response (**UCR**).

❝❝ CS and UCS are paired ❞❞

- The experimenter presents a neutral stimulus just before or along with the UCS. The new stimulus is called a conditional stimulus or **CS**. (Conditional means dependent on learning.) The UCR occurs as before.
- After several pairings of the CS and UCS, the CS alone will be enough to bring about the UCR. The animal now has a new **conditional reflex** – the response to the stimulus is dependent on learning and the name of the UCR changes to **CR** to show this.

Here is Pavlov's experiment expressed in these terms:

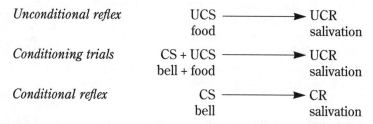

Unconditional reflex	UCS ————————→ UCR
	food salivation
Conditioning trials	CS + UCS ————————→ UCR
	bell + food salivation
Conditional reflex	CS ————————→ CR
	bell salivation

This model gives us an explanation for all kinds of learned behaviour. *Watson and Rayner* (1920) classically conditioned an 11-month-old boy called *Little Albert* to fear white rats. Albert was pre-tested with a white rat, a dog, a monkey, masks, cotton wool and burning newspapers. He was interested in these but not afraid of them. He was, however, startled by the loud noise of a steel bar being struck with a hammer. To condition Albert, Watson and Rayner used the white rat as the CS, the loud noise as the UCS and the startle response as the UCR. Over a period of 50 days, Little Albert received a total of seven conditioning trials, at the end of which he had learned to fear something which previously he had been interested in. The procedure looked like this:

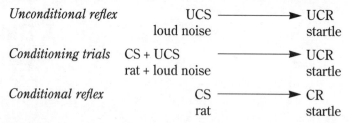

Unconditional reflex	UCS ————————→ UCR
	loud noise startle
Conditioning trials	CS + UCS ————————→ UCR
	rat + loud noise startle
Conditional reflex	CS ————————→ CR
	rat startle

Watson and Rayner thought that this process could explain the origin of many emotional reactions to stimuli. **Phobias** could thus arise through the accidental pairing of a previously neutral CS with a UCS. Other **emotional reactions** could arise this way too. Many people react positively or negatively to a piece of music, possibly because they heard it when they were in a heightened emotional state, e.g. leaving school, getting married, attending a funeral. Smells and sights can also evoke such reactions.

Seligman (1970) described the conditioning of a **taste aversion** in himself to Sauce

Can you think of examples that apply to you?

Béarnaise. He had contracted stomach flu, a UCS, which was naturally going to make him vomit (UCR), but before it had begun to make him feel ill he'd eaten out and had Sauce Béarnaise (CS). After his illness, Seligman found that the smell or taste of Sauce Béarnaise made him feel ill (a conditional reflex) even though it had nothing to do with causing his sickness.

OTHER FEATURES OF CLASSICAL CONDITIONING

One trial learning

Chapter 18 expands on this

Sometimes, we only need to experience one pairing of a CS and a UCS to develop a conditional reflex. Seligman's food aversion is an example of this. (It appears we are biologically prepared to learn some associations more readily than others. This poses a problem for Behaviourists who like to play down the role of biological factors.)

Generalisation

Once a conditional reflex has been established, the CR can be brought about by any CS which resembles the original one. Little Albert's fear transferred to a rabbit, a dog, a fur coat, Watson's hair and a Santa Claus mask. This is sometimes called **stimulus generalisation.**

Discrimination

Animals and people can learn to tell the difference (**discriminate**) between CSs if the UCS is paired only with a specific CS and not with others which resemble it, e.g. Pavlov's dog could be trained to salivate to a bell with a particular note because it signalled food and not to higher or lower notes which were never associated with food.

Extinction

Once a conditional reflex has been established, animals and people can learn not to respond to a CS if it is presented repeatedly without the UCS, e.g. the bell without the food or the rat without the loud noise. The CR apparently disappears or is **extinguished**.

Spontaneous recovery

This refers to the fact that, even after extinction, a CR may suddenly reappear to a CS for no apparent reason, e.g. a dog may suddenly salivate to a bell again even though the response had been extinguished. The CR will then extinguish again.

2 OPERANT CONDITIONING

be able to distinguish operant from classical conditioning

Operant conditioning is used to describe how we build up, sometimes very complicated, behaviour patterns over time. For example, it can explain how we learn skills like piano-playing, ice-skating or driving and how we learn a language. It can explain how animals learn tricks, how they learn their way round mazes and how we learn superstitions and habits like nail-biting. Behaviour patterns can be altered and refined through **trial and error** and built up from small beginnings by **shaping** (see p. 34).

Operant conditioning also differs from classical conditioning in that:

- there does not need to be an innate reflex to start with and
- the animal's behaviour is voluntary; it 'operates' on its environment to produce an effect (hence the name 'operant').

THORNDIKE AND INSTRUMENTAL CONDITIONING

Research into operant conditioning is usually said to have started with *Edward Thorndike* (1874–1949). He called his approach 'instrumental conditioning' and many textbooks regard this as the same as operant conditioning. (We don't need to worry about the distinction here.) Thorndike devised a **puzzle box** from which a cat would learn to escape by operating a catch and a lever. He timed how long it took a cat to escape from the box over several occasions (**trials**) and plotted the results on a graph.

The graph showed a steady rate of learning and no evidence of flashes of **insight** from the cat. It seems to learn how to operate the escape mechanism by trial and error, gradually dropping unsuccessful responses. The cat's behaviour was rewarded by escape and food. It learned to link the stimulus of being trapped in the box with operating the escape mechanism – a stimulus-response or S-R association. This led

Thorndike to state his **Law of Effect** which says that:

- if a response is followed by a satisfying state of affairs it tends to be repeated. Other responses fade away.

A learner driver is rather like a cat in a puzzle box. In the first lesson, many inappropriate responses are made (e.g. looking at feet, pressing the accelerator too hard) mixed in with some useful ones (e.g. looking in the mirrors, steering in the right direction). Appropriate responses have pleasant consequences (e.g. words of approval from the instructor) and inappropriate ones do not. They are ignored (or even punished, e.g. instructor grabs the steering wheel or jumps out of the car in terror). Inappropriate responses eventually decrease, appropriate ones increase in number and accuracy and driving becomes more skilled.

B F SKINNER AND OPERANT CONDITIONING

B F Skinner (1904–90) developed the theory of instrumental conditioning into a theory of operant conditioning using rats or pigeons in a kind of automated puzzle box called a **Skinner box**. A hungry rat would learn to press a lever (and the pigeon to peck a key) for food reward.

As Thorndike found, the animals learned gradually over time and became more efficient. Skinner concluded:

- behaviour was determined by its consequences and
- behaviour could be shaped and maintained by its consequences, and these are what we should concentrate on in order to change behaviour.

The order of events can be summed up as:

S ⟶ R ⟶ consequence
lever ⟶ press ⟶ food pellet is dispensed

Skinner described five consequences of responses. Four of these are shown in Table 4.1. The fifth consequence is to ignore the response.

	Given	*Taken away*
Pleasant	**Positive reinforcement**, e.g. a reward such as sweets, money, praise, attention, food pellets.	**Punishment by removal**, e.g. being 'grounded', refused use of car, pocket money stopped, freedom denied.
Unpleasant	**Punishment by application**, e.g. a smack, nagging, being given an unpleasant task to do, an electric shock.	**Negative reinforcement**, e.g. a lever press switches off an ongoing electric shock, a visit to the dentist stops toothache, a confession puts an end to torture.

Table 4.1 Four consequences of behaviour

It is important to remember that:

- both positive and negative reinforcement are rewarding, therefore they increase the level of responding, e.g. a rat would press a lever just as much for food pellets as for switching off a shock to its feet and
- punishment and ignoring of responses should lead to a decrease in the level of responding.

OTHER FEATURES OF OPERANT CONDITIONING

Shaping behaviour by successive approximations

it is important to understand how shaping works

The consequences of behaviour can be used to build up, or **shape behaviour**. An example might be training a dog to jump through a ring of fire. To start with, any response which could be the beginnings of the required behaviour is reinforced. The dog may be trained to walk through a yellow hoop for food reward. The hoop might then be wrapped in pieces of coloured paper which blow in the breeze like real flames. Eventually real fire would be used, then the height of the hoop off the ground would be increased so that the dog had to jump through it. Whole sequences of behaviour could be built up like this by increasingly closer steps in both animals and humans.

Generalisation, discrimination and extinction

These terms apply to operant conditioning as well as to classical conditioning. A learner who has learned to respond in a particular way to a stimulus will respond to similar stimuli in the same way. The learner can also learn to tell the difference between stimuli and only respond to certain kinds. Removal of reinforcement will lead to extinction of the learned response, i.e. it disappears.

Punishment

Skinner recommended that we should change behaviour through the use of reinforcement (preferably positive) and ignoring. Punishment should be *avoided* because:

the effects of punishment can be undesirable

- it teaches the learner what is inappropriate but not what to do instead;
- it may stop the unwanted response in the short term but the learner may do it when out of sight of the punisher;
- it can harm the relationship between teacher and learner;
- it can put the learner off learning.

Some psychologists believe that, in a warm and secure relationship, well-chosen punishment used as a last resort can be very effective but there is much debate about this!

Primary and secondary reinforcement

Primary reinforcement is something which *directly* satisfies a need, e.g. food for a hungry animal, warmth for a cold one, drink for a thirsty one, company for a lonely one. Secondary reinforcement can also reinforce behaviour because the learner comes to *associate it with the arrival* of primary reinforcement. Money is a good example. It has no value on its own but it can be exchanged for things like food and drinks so we do things for money. To a hungry rat, the lever in the Skinner box may be a secondary reinforcer because it is associated with food so the rat stays close to it.

Schedules of reinforcement

While the learner is in the process of learning something, it helps if the reinforcement happens after every correct response but we know from our own experience of learning that this does not always happen. Skinner investigated the effects of occasional (partial) reinforcement on the rate of responding and the rate of extinction when reinforcement was removed altogether. See Table 4.2

Name of schedule	Definition	Effect on response rate	Rate of extinction when removed	Example
Continuous reinforcement	Every correct response is reinforced	Low and steady	Fast	A child receives a star every time s/he reads to the teacher
Fixed ratio schedule	One reinforcement is given after every so many correct responses, e.g. after every 5th	A pause occurs after reinforcement, then response rate is high	Quite fast	A child receives a star for every 5 words correctly spelt
Variable ratio schedule	One reinforcement is given on average every so many correct responses	High and steady	Very slow	Any kind of gambling should pay off now and again
Fixed interval schedule	One reinforcement is given after a fixed time interval providing at least one correct response has been made	Fairly low, increasing as next reinforcement becomes due	Quite fast	Being paid by the hour
Variable interval schedule	Providing one correct response has been made, reinforcement is given after an unpredictable amount of time has passed, e.g. on average every 5 minutes	Steady, increasing as time passes	Very slow	A self-employed person receiving payment at unpredictable times

Table 4.2 Reinforcement schedules, rate of responding and speed of extinction.

> SLT expands on traditional learning theory in important ways

Social Learning theorists agree that we learn much of our behaviour through conditioning, but they add to the work of conditioning theorists in the following ways:

- They emphasise *social* reinforcers and punishers in conditioning, e.g. praise, attention, approval and disapproval, withholding love.
- They think we must also take account of the learner's *thought processes* which happen between the stimulus and response, even though we cannot observe and measure them directly.
- They can explain the sudden appearance of *novel* behaviour patterns, i.e. behaviour the learner has not shown before.
- They concentrate on *human learning*, particularly social and moral behaviour.

SLT's major contribution has been the study of **observational learning** or '**modelling**' (because the people we learn from model behaviour). Its main features are:

- learners can learn by watching others modelling particular kinds of behaviour;
- learning occurs apparently without any reinforcement; exposure to the model is enough;
- learning may occur without any obvious effort by the learner to learn or the teacher to teach;
- the observer may learn specific behaviour like someone else's mannerisms or very general behaviour such as an attitude to school.

Of course, we do not copy everything we see others doing so SL theorists have studied what kinds of models have the greatest influence. In 1965, *Albert Bandura* studied what effect seeing aggressive adult models had on pre-school children. Children were divided into three groups and, individually, watched a film of an adult beating up a large, inflatable clown doll called a **Bobo doll**. What happened next differed like this:

- for group A children (the controls) the film showed only the beating;
- group B children saw the adult praised and rewarded for the beating by another adult;
- group C children saw the adult punished and disapproved of for the beating by another adult.

When allowed the chance to play with the Bobo doll, children in groups A and B showed similar levels of imitated aggression towards it but group C children showed lower aggression. When 'bribed' to copy what they had seen, group C children could be just as aggressive as the other two groups. Bandura concluded:

> we do not always copy others

- seeing pleasant consequences for a model makes it more likely that imitation will occur, but seeing the model punished makes imitation no less likely than if no model had been seen at all;
- we all **acquire** (take in) behaviour from watching models but only **perform** (do) it if the consequences are likely to be acceptable.

In later studies, Bandura found that models were more likely to be imitated if they had the following qualities:

> characteristics of the model are very important

- they were seen as similar to the learner;
- their behaviour was appropriate, e.g. males doing traditionally male things;
- they were warm and friendly;
- they were effective or powerful;
- their behaviour was novel;
- their behaviour was consistent over time;
- their behaviour was consistent with their expressed views (it's no good a parent telling a child not to 'bloody swear'!).

Along with SL theorists other psychologists also think that there is more to learning than conditioning or the linking of stimuli and responses. They all emphasise the importance of **cognitive** (thought) **processes** in learning.

TOLMAN AND LATENT LEARNING

Tolman and Honzik (1930) ran maze-learning experiments with a difference. Over about 20 days three groups of rats learned to run a maze to a food box:

- group A rats were reinforced with food whenever they reached the goal box;
- group B rats were never rewarded on reaching the goal box;
- group C rats were not rewarded for the first ten days but received food upon reaching the goal box from day eleven onwards.

⟨⟨ rats seem to be capable of mental representations of a maze ⟩⟩

Group A rats learned the maze quickly. Group B rats did not improve their maze-running speed. Group C rats' speed improved dramatically after reinforcement was introduced. Tolman and Honzik concluded that the rats had learned a **mental map** (or **cognitive map**) of the maze which they could use as soon as it paid off. Also, rats trained to swim a maze do just as well when the water is drained and they have to walk. Both these findings suggest the rats are learning signs about the maze which they link together mentally, rather than a series of movements or responses which they do automatically or without thought.

KOHLER AND INSIGHT LEARNING

Kohler (1925) investigated insight learning in apes. This involved giving them problems to solve in order to get pieces of fruit which were out of reach, e.g. an ape might have to stack boxes to reach fruit suspended from the roof of the cage. Apes did not learn by trial and error. Instead, they tried a number of strategies and eventually solved the problem smoothly in an organised series of actions. Apparently the animals had 'thought it through' and experienced '**insight**' (the **Aha!/Eureka** effect) although we would have problems proving that this had happened!

HARLOW, LEARNING SET AND TRANSFER OF LEARNING

Transfer of learning is to do with *carrying over* learning from one situation to another to help solve problems. Learning set is one example of this. *Harlow* (1949) showed chimps rows of three shapes, e.g. two squares and a star. Under the star (the odd one out) there would be a raisin reward. By trial and error the chimp would eventually choose the right shape every time, regardless of its position in the row. Harlow went on to show they had a learning set because they were able to transfer it to new and different odd-one-out problems.

Humans also apply learning sets. When they do this successfully we call it **positive transfer**. When it is unsuccessful it is called **negative transfer**, e.g. some people may find it difficult to ride a moped after being used to a bicycle if the moped has a footbrake and a hand-operated accelerator. A bicycle has hand-operated brakes and foot-operated pedals for acceleration!

EDUCATIONAL APPLICATIONS

5 ⟩ **APPLICATIONS OF LEARNING THEORIES**

⟨⟨ know these applications ⟩⟩

1 Classical conditioning

Many stimuli related to school, subjects and teachers start off being neutral stimuli or CSs. These can become associated with unconditional reflexes and eventually bring about a conditional response. Here is one example that might come about through students having to study a subject in cold, cramped and uncomfortable surroundings:

Unconditional reflex	UCS —————▶ discomfort	UCR negative feelings
Conditioning trials	CS + UCS —————▶ subject matter + discomfort	UCR negative feelings
Conditional reflex	CS —————▶ subject matter	CR negative feelings

Of course, positive feelings could be built up by classical conditioning and positive or negative feelings would be open to generalisation, discrimination and extinction too. School phobia could also be learned by classical conditioning. How?

2 Operant conditioning

Reinforcement, punishment and extinction can all be applied to change behaviour in educational settings. Here are some examples:

- **Reinforcement**. In a **token system** children learn to earn tokens for obeying a few clearly defined rules of behaviour. The tokens are secondary reinforcers because they can be saved and exchanged for valued activities like painting, reading or running round the gym. Generally, teacher approval is also a powerful reinforcer, as is the approval of friends.
- **Punishment**. Physical punishment is not allowed in schools today. Teachers may apply punishment in the form of verbal warnings or reprimands. They may also use punishment by removal where the child is excluded from a valued activity or given **time out**, meaning that they have to spend time being quiet on their own before being allowed back.
- **Extinction**. Ignoring disruptive behaviour can be a very effective way of getting it to extinguish (as long as the behaviour is not damaging to the child or anyone else).
- **Programmed instruction** is a special case of operant conditioning being used in education:

  - material to be learned is *broken into parts* to be learned in a fixed sequence;
  - it might be in written form or presented by computer (CAL or computer assisted learning);
  - a **linear programme** presents one question after another, the learner answers one and moves to the next whether right or wrong;
  - a **branching programme** builds in remedial material. If the learner makes a mistake, the 'branch' teaches them why before going back to the main programme;
  - *immediate reinforcement* is given after each answer (the learner is told whether they are right).

  It is good because:

  - the learner determines the pace of learning;
  - individual learning packages can be devised;
  - it can teach factual things like foreign language vocabulary and mathematics.

  Weaknesses include:
  - the social side of learning is played down;
  - it is less useful for teaching evaluative and critical skills such as being able to argue or debate.

- **Stimulus control** can also be used to change behaviour. This means that the teacher organises the classroom in a way which encourages children to behave well in the first place, e.g. by positioning the desks in a particular way and making sure the children have something to do as soon as they get in. This reduces the likelihood that bad behaviour will occur and have to be dealt with and increases the amount of good behaviour which can be rewarded.

3 Social Learning

SLT includes conditioning and observational learning. Many of the above examples of conditioning in education apply here because the reinforcers and punishers are often social ones. SLT adds observational learning to the picture. For this to happen in an educational setting, the learner needs to observe someone who is already skilled. Good examples include the apprenticeship method of instruction, demonstrations and masterclasses. All the earlier comments about the type of model most likely to be imitated are relevant here.

> some psychologists find it useful to distinguish behaviour therapy and behaviour modification

CLINICAL APPLICATIONS

1 Classical conditioning

We can call treatments based on classical conditioning **behaviour therapies**. They concern either building up a wanted conditional reflex or extinguishing an unwanted one. Examples include:

- treatment of **nocturnal enuresis** (night-time bed-wetting). The enuretic child sleeps on a special blanket which sets off an alarm as soon as it detects moisture. The alarm is the UCS and waking up is the UCR. The sensation of having a full bladder and starting to urinate is the CS. After several conditioning trials, in which the child is woken every time s/he starts to urinate, this CS becomes linked to the CR of waking up and this should happen just before the child starts to wet the bed.

- **Aversion therapy**. This can be used to discourage someone from doing something which is harmful by conditioning them to associate the behaviour with something unpleasant. In theory it is possible to treat alcoholics in this way but the treatment is controversial and there is much argument about its effectiveness. An alcoholic would be given an **emetic** (which causes nausea and vomiting) just before taking a drink. They should then associate alcohol with sickness and avoid it in the future. Children involved in self-injurious behaviour like head banging could similarly be discouraged from such a response by being given an electric shock every time they show signs of starting to head bang.

- **Flooding and implosion**. One way to extinguish an unwanted conditional reflex such as a fear of spiders would be to face the person (flood them) with spiders immediately. The extreme fear the person feels cannot last forever and, eventually, it should subside to be replaced with an ability to cope in the face of spiders. With implosion, a person listens to a vivid description of the feared situation and, as with flooding, learns to cope with the panic.

- **Systematic desensitisation (SD) and graded exposure**. A less extreme way of extinguishing an unwanted unconditional reflex is to introduce a person gradually to a feared situation or object. In SD the person learns relaxation techniques then draws up a list of feared situations arranged in order from least to most threatening. They then relax and face each situation in turn starting with the least feared and working up the list at their own pace. One cannot relax and panic at the same time so the panic should eventually be pushed out. Graded exposure is similar except that relaxation training is not given. The individual finds their own way of coping at each stage.

2 Operant conditioning

Treatments based on operant conditioning are often called **behaviour modification.** Examples include:

- **Behaviour shaping**. *Isaacs, Thomas* and *Goldiamond* (1969) used shaping with a schizophrenic man who had been mute for 21 years. Using chewing gum as a reinforcer they began by requiring the man to make lip movements to earn the gum, then lip and eye movements, then a sound and so on. After five weeks of shaping, there was a breakthrough and the man spoke more from then on.

- **Token economies**. In an institutional setting, such as a long-stay psychiatric ward, patients can earn tokens (*secondary* reinforcers) for desirable behaviour such as self-care, care of the ward and creative activities. The tokens can be saved and exchanged for rewards such as sweets, cigarettes, cosmetics and leisure activities (*primary* reinforcers). Great improvements in behaviour have often been found but the token economy does not touch the underlying mental disorder.

- **Biofeedback**. Some psychologists claim that by taking a measure of a physical function such as heart-rate or blood-pressure, amplifying it and feeding it back to a person in the form of, say, a sound, the person can learn to control the function, e.g. lower heart-rate or blood-pressure. This would be extremely useful in controlling reactions to stressors or helping people to stay calm in situations they fear. The stimulus is the feedback, the response is to change the feedback and the reinforcement is knowledge of success and improvements in feelings of well-being.

3 Social learning

Via 'modelling' observational learning can be used to help people overcome unwanted behaviour patterns. A person who fears snakes, for example, might watch another person enjoying handling a real snake and then be encouraged to do the same. The nature of the model is, of course, important. The learner must see at least some similarities between themselves and the model and know that the model does not have some special power over snakes!

be able to cast a critical eye over applications

- The Behaviourist approach to explaining behaviour and learning is often regarded as the most scientific approach in psychology because it concentrates on behaviour that can be directly observed and measured and is very 'down to earth' in the way it explains things.
- The range of behaviours it can explain is very wide.
- Practical applications of the theory are, usually, very effective.
- Early Behaviourism has given rise to many useful theories such as SLT.
- Some critics say the basis of Behaviourism in animal research makes it inappropriate for explaining human behaviour.
- Others say it is *dehumanising* seeing people responding like puppets to stimuli, punishers and reinforcement (although later Behaviourists do take thought processes more into account). Humans, the critics say, are more complex than this.
- Some critics say that behavioural approaches to changing behaviour are just *cosmetic*. They do not treat the underlying problem. Behaviourists might reply that sometimes, maladaptive learning is all there is to a problem and there is no need to delve any deeper.

7 > **ETHICAL CONSIDERATIONS**

you can always use ethics as part of an evaluation

These focus mainly on applications and fall into three main areas:

- Objections to the use of *pain or other unpleasant stimuli*, e.g. in aversion therapy. Behaviourists reply that it is sometimes necessary to be cruel to be kind. A person may suffer in treatment but will be better off in the end.
- Objections to the idea of *control*. Who decides to control whom and for what reason? Behavioural techniques are very powerful and could do damage in the wrong hands. Behaviourists might reply that modern applications of learning theory involve the psychologist and client working as a team, deciding how to tackle a problem together.
- Objections to *depriving people of freedom* to choose how to behave. Many Behaviourist techniques may seem as if they take freedom away but Behaviourists reply that people are not free to behave anyway. They are influenced by reinforcers and punishers all the time in everyday life. All the Behaviourist does is to take control of these consequences of behaviour.

EXAMINATION QUESTIONS

1. MEG specimen paper 1 (Foundation) Section C, Source B. *Spend 27 minutes on this question.*

Source Priscilla the Pig

Operant conditioning techniques have been used to train animals to perform unusual responses. For example, Priscilla the pig was the star of a television advert for animal feed. She learned how to push a trolley and to place her favourite food in the trolley. Her trainers did this by breaking down the behaviour they wanted her to learn into small steps. They also gave Priscilla a reward when she made the right response.

(a) According to learning theory, what is meant by the term 'reinforcement'? [2]

(b) Give one example of a positive reinforcer which could be used in training Priscilla [1]

(c) According to learning theory, what would happen if the trainers stopped giving Priscilla a reward? [2]

(d) How could a parent use operant conditioning to teach a child to eat with a spoon? [3]

(e) (i) Outline some of the ways that operant or classical conditioning have been used to change human behaviour. [7]

(ii) What are some of the practical or ethical problems with using these applications? [3]

[*Total 18 marks*]
(MEG)

2. NEAB specimen paper (Tier Q) Question B2

Spend about 13 minutes answering this question.

Read the article below and answer the questions which follow.

Pupils learn it pays to be good

Lowfield is for children with emotional or behavioural difficulties who do not thrive in mainstream comprehensives even though many have high IQs. It has now been selected for special praise by Her Majesty's Inspectors in a national report.

Under the Lowfield scheme, children earn tokens for good behaviour, such as coming into lessons and sitting down quietly or for good work, but lose them for rudeness, laziness, disrupting lessons or violence. The tokens can be cashed in for extra swimming, football—or given tea and toast on Fridays.

Paul, ten, who has hundreds of tokens, says he tries to behave because of them. 'I was fined tokens for messing about the other week and I couldn't go to the adventure playground. They made me work instead, so I behaved the next week!'.

(a) The above article illustrates

one trial learning; ☐

a token economy system; ☐ (Tick the correct box)

programmed learning. ☐ [1]

(b) Using the terms 'conditioned response', 'primary reinforcement' and 'secondary reinforcement', explain Paul's change in behaviour. [6]

(c) Explain the disadvantage of trying to change Paul's behaviour in this way. [3]

[*Total 10 marks*]
(NEAB)

TUTOR ANSWERS

1. MEG specimen paper 1 (Foundation) Section C, Source B. Priscilla the Pig.

(a) Reinforcement is anything that strengthens a learned response and makes it more likely that the response will be made again.

(b) Priscilla could be rewarded with food every time she made the right response.

(c) If Priscilla stopped getting food rewards, eventually she would stop responding and her learned behaviour would disappear (extinguish).

(d) At first the parent should reward any attempt by the child to spoon-feed itself. Then the parent would be more selective, only giving rewards for better and better spoon-feeding. In this way the child's behaviour would be shaped by successive approximations until it was very skilled.

(e) (i) Classical conditioning has been used to change people's behaviour in educational and clinical settings. In education we could encourage a child to feel positive about school and everything to do with it. Teachers, subject matter and classrooms are neutral stimuli to start with but they can become associated with good or bad feelings, e.g.:

$$UCS \longrightarrow UCR$$
$$\text{laughter} \qquad \text{happy feelings}$$

$$CS \quad + \quad UCS \longrightarrow UCR$$
$$\text{teacher makes subject amusing} + \text{laughter} \qquad \text{happy feelings}$$

$$CS \longrightarrow UCR$$
$$\text{teacher and subject} \qquad \text{happy feelings}$$

In clinical settings alarm blankets can be used with children who bed-wet at night. The alarm blanket sounds a loud alarm (UCS) as soon as the child begins to urinate and moisture is detected. The child wakes up (UCR). Eventually the child will learn to associate the feeling of needing to urinate (CS) with waking up and will wake before wetting the bed. Classical conditioning has also been applied in aversion therapy using emetics to try to teach alcoholics to associate the taste of alcohol with nausea and vomiting.

Flooding and implosion are techniques for extinguishing unwanted behaviour such as a phobic reaction to spiders. The phobic person could be faced straight away with real spiders and kept close to them until the panic subsided (flooding). Implosion has a similar effect except that it involves the person imagining the feared situation in vivid detail. Systematic desensitisation is gentler. The phobic person learns some relaxation techniques and then draws up a list of feared situations from least to most feared. They then work up the list, facing each step in turn relaxing all the time. This technique could also be used in education to encourage a school phobic to go back to school.

(ii) These are techniques from the Behaviourist approach to learning. Some of the techniques, such as aversion therapy, have been criticised on ethical grounds because they involve deliberately causing pain or sickness. On the other hand, these are only short-term discomforts compared to the damage a person might do to themselves if they were left untreated. Another ethical issue is whether psychologists should take control of other people's behaviour and deliberately change it (although this would never be done without consent). Finally there is the issue of freedom to choose how to behave. People may feel pressurised to change their behaviour and the psychologist goes along with this in helping them to change. In their own defence, behaviour therapists argue that we are not free to choose how to behave anyway. Behaviour is controlled by natural reinforcers and punishers and all they are doing is using them in a more controlled way.

2. NEAB specimen paper (Tier Q) Question B2

(a) A token economy system.

(b) The teachers at Lowfields are trying to bring about a conditioned response of good behaviour in Paul. To do this, they need to find things that are directly reinforcing for him (i.e. primary reinforcers). Primary reinforcers that work in his case are swimming, football, time in the adventure playground and tea and toast on Fridays. To get these, he needs to earn tokens. These can be exchanged for primary reinforcers, hence they are known as secondary reinforcers. With time, Paul will learn to associate good behaviour with tokens and tokens with treats. It should follow that he will begin to behave well to earn tokens and this is what happens in the passage.

(c) The problem with token systems such as this is that Paul may only be behaving well for the tokens. There is no certainty that his good behaviour would continue if the tokens were stopped. He would need to be carefully weaned off the programme so that, eventually, he found that good behaviour was its own reward.

STUDENT'S ANSWER WITH EXAMINER'S COMMENTS

3. SEG paper 2 1994 Section B

Spend 40 minutes on this question

(a) What is learning? [3]

❝ good answer

3/3 ❞

Learning has been defined as 'a relatively permanent change in behaviour that comes about as the result of experience'. Psychologists see it as a gradual, continuous adaptation to our environment.

(b) What is classical conditioning? [8]

❝ use a diagram ❞

❝ be explicit about pairing stimuli

6/8 ❞

This is learning by making associations. While doing research on dogs' digestive systems, Pavlov noticed dogs would start to salivate when they saw the assistant bringing food. He decided to investigate, and within a few trials had taught the dogs to salivate to the sound of a bell by ringing the bell just before giving food.

He called the innate reflex of salivating to food 'unconditional'. The food was an unconditional stimulus (UCS) and the salivation an unconditional response (UCR). The bell was the conditional stimulus and the salivation that followed the bell alone the conditional response. Together the CS and CR make a new conditional reflex.

(c) Briefly describe how a child may learn by classical conditioning. [6]

❝ more detail needed but OK ❞

Little Albert is an example of how children may learn fears through classical conditioning. Watson and Rayner trained him to fear white rats by making a loud noise behind him every time he reached out to play with the rat. Soon the rat alone was enough to cause fear in Little Albert. His fear was reinforced by the loud noise. He also feared other furry things. This is known as generalisation. If he had learned to fear the rat and not other furry things, this would be discrimination. If the rat appeared without the loud noise, the fear would eventually extinguish.

❝ 5/6 ❞

❝ second example not needed ❞

Classical conditioning can also stop bed-wetting in children. They sleep on an alarm blanket which is moisture sensitive and sets off a bell as soon as it gets wet. Soon they learn to associate the need to go to the toilet with waking up and get out of bed before they wet it.

(d) What is programmed (learning? [5]

Programmed learning is used in education. Information is broken down and given in stages. The child has to answer questions at each stage and is offered

66 discuss more for 5 99

reinforcement for every correct answer so it is easily encouraged before moving on. Understanding is complete this way.

A linear programme presents information step by step, giving the correct answer after the child has had a go then moving on. A branching programme is more complex and flexible. If a mistake is made, there may be a branch to explain why it is wrong before going back to the question again. Skinner maintains that self-pacing and positive reinforcement will help the child to learn thoroughly.

66 4/5 99

(e) Explain how computer-assisted instruction is likely to help students learn.   [8]

66 explain how in more depth 99

CAI is based on claims by Skinner that any behaviour that is reinforced is likely to repeated. Behaviour that is ignored or punished will usually extinguish. In CAI the learner works at their own pace and should not make many mistakes. If they do, the computer can put them right. Teachers can monitor each child and the child is also getting one-to-one teaching from CAI. Many CAI programmes are so exciting that the child doesn't think they are working because it is so interesting. At the end, the teacher and child know exactly how much has been achieved.

66 good answer

CAI is probably best for teaching factual information like language vocabulary but it is less good at teaching a child to criticise and debate or at teaching appreciation of art or music. Some people argue too much CAI could be boring and put the child off but it is important that they get used to computers because they are so much a part of modern life.

7/8 99

66 25/30 Good answer simply needing more depth and detail in places 99

[Total 30 marks]
(SEG)

A Review Sheet for this chapter can be found on pp. 233–4.

CHAPTER 5

IMPRESSION FORMATION, STEREOTYPING AND PREJUDICE

GETTING STARTED

This chapter is to do with three important related topics concerning how we perceive other people and how we build an understanding of our social world.

NEAB and SEG syllabuses require a consideration of impression formation and stereotyping. These concern how we form initial impressions of other people and how these perceptions may be biased, inaccurate or based on snap judgements. SEG students then need to extend this to consider the role of filters in helping us to understand our social world. Much of our socially constructed knowledge comes to us from other people and this information may be filtered (selected and/or changed) by others before we receive it and then again when we receive it ourselves.

Prejudice is an important topic for NEAB, SEG and MEG students. For all syllabuses you need to know how psychologists explain the origins of prejudice and what these insights mean for the very serious problem of prejudice reduction.

1. IMPRESSION FORMATION

2. STEREOTYPING

3. SOCIAL FILTERS

4. PERSONAL FILTERS

5. PREJUDICE

6. SOME REAL-LIFE IMPLICATIONS OF PREJUDICE

7. SEXISM AND RACISM

8. PREJUDICE REDUCTION

ESSENTIAL PRINCIPLES

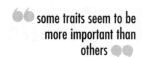

IMPRESSION FORMATION

When we meet people for the first time we make judgements about them and form impressions based on very little evidence. The field of **impression formation** concerns what information we base our impressions on, how enduring these impressions are and what biases and inaccuracies may arise.

Impression formation involves **selection**, **organisation** and **inference**. We choose to attend to certain items of information and arrange it so it makes sense. Inference means that we assume the existence of (infer people have) other characteristics even though we only have *actual* evidence of one or two.

CENTRAL AND PERIPHERAL TRAITS

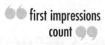 *some traits seem to be more important than others*

When we are forming impressions of others we tend to look for evidence of particular personality characteristics or **traits**. *Asch* (1946) discovered that some traits are more important than others. These are **central traits** and they can affect our whole perception of someone. Traits which do not have this general influence are called **peripheral traits**.

Asch gave people a list of traits said to belong to one person. They were then asked to use this description to help them choose more traits from a new list to describe this person. Some participants received a list like this:

   – intelligent, skilful, industrious, warm, determined, practical, cautious.

Others received a list like this:

   – intelligent, skilful, industrious, cold, determined, practical, cautious.

Asch found that *warm* and *cold* were central traits. Participants tended to infer traits such as happy, generous and good-natured to go with warm and others to go with cold. Other traits, such as polite–blunt, did not have this effect so could be called peripheral traits. Asch also asked participants to rank their final list of traits in order of importance and found that about half placed warm or cold first or second in the list.

Kelly (1950) gave students an introduction to a visiting lecturer which included either warm or cold in the description. More students stayed behind to talk to the lecturer described as warm and the ratings they made of him afterwards reflected whether he had been described as warm or cold earlier on. There seemed to be a kind of *halo effect* at work where the presence of positive traits gives the judged person an aura of goodness.

PRIMACY AND RECENCY EFFECTS

Asch went on to study whether the order in which we receive information about a person influences our impression. He gave some participants a description like this:

   – intelligent, industrious, impulsive, critical, stubborn, envious

and others a list like this:

   – envious, stubborn, critical, impulsive, industrious, intelligent.

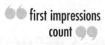 *first impressions count*

The first list presented positive traits first and negative ones second. For the second list the pattern was reversed. Asch found that, when participants chose more traits from a new list, there was evidence for a **primacy effect**. Participants who saw positive traits first inferred more positive traits than participants who saw the second list first – evidence that first impressions matter.

Luchins (1957) chose a slightly more realistic setting to study this. Participants read two paragraphs about a character called 'Jim'. In the first paragraph, he appeared to be an extravert and in the second paragraph he appeared to be an introvert. Another group of participants saw the introvert paragraph first followed by the extravert paragraph. Afterwards, judgements of Jim were far more positive from participants who had seen the extravert description first. They rated Jim as more likeable, good-looking and assertive. Again, first impressions matter most, possibly because:

- we ignore later information; or
- distort it to fit the first impression; or
- discount it in some way.

In an extension of the study, Luchins had participants read a comic for fifteen minutes between the first and second paragraphs. In these cases he found a **recency effect** in that participants' later judgements of Jim were more affected by what they had read about him most recently.

In an even more realistic setting *Jones et al.* (1968) asked participants to watch a student solve a series of problems. Some participants saw the student improve, others saw performance worsen (although overall the student solved the same number of problems correctly). Jones *et al.* thought there would be a recency effect in that an improving student would be judged to be more intelligent. However, the primacy effect still prevailed. The student who began well impressed people so much that they saw him as more intelligent and estimated he had solved more problems than the student who got worse.

What real-life implications do these studies have?

think what we can learn from this

- The research designs are rather artificial. Real-life impression formation is probably much more complicated.
- Primacy effects seem to be more important than recency effects but Luchins went on to find that, in longer-term, real-life relationships, recency effects seem to be more important.
- Negative first impressions seem to be much more resistant to change so we should work hard to make good first impressions on strangers, remembering that we never have a second chance to make a first impression.
- When people are judging others, e.g. when selecting someone for a job or deciding whether a person is innocent of a crime, they can be warned about the danger of primacy and recency effects. One way to do this is to insist they pay equal attention to all the information they are given. A person chairing an interview panel could do this as could judges in their summing up of a case for a jury. *Pennington* (1982) illustrated how important this is. He set up an imaginary rape trial in which some jurors heard the prosecution first followed by the defence. Others heard the defence first followed by the prosecution. Those who heard the prosecution first were far more likely to find the accused guilty even though they had the same information as the group who heard the defence first.

IMPLICIT PERSONALITY THEORY

Bruner and Tagiuri (1954) suggested that we each have our own idea about how personality traits go together, in other words, we have an **implicit personality theory** (IPT). IPTs help us to cope with large amounts of incoming information about people because they help to simplify the way we judge them. Asch had made a start on discovering people's IPTs. *Wishner* (1960) extended Asch's ideas to show that warm–cold only showed up as central traits when they were combined with certain kinds of other traits. He could reduce the influence of warm–cold by changing the traits they were listed with, e.g. warm–cold are central in lists including traits like generous or wise but peripheral in lists including traits like vain and reliable. *Rosenberg* (1968) went further to show that most traits could be arranged on the two dimensions *intellectual* and *social*. See **Fig.** 5.1.

IPTs help us to deal with large amounts of information

Warm comes into the cluster of traits seen as bad intellectual–good social along with a number of other traits. This helps to explain how 'warm' is central to traits like 'happy' and 'good-natured' but not to others that do not share a similar position on the two main dimensions. Cold is central to a different trait cluster.

2 ▷ STEREOTYPING

stereotypes also help us to avoid information overload

Stereotypes help us to simplify large amounts of incoming information about others. They are oversimplified, rigid and generalised ideas about people who share a particular characteristic, e.g. religious belief, nationality, sex or race. *Race* and *sex-role* stereotyping are very well-known examples but, sometimes, our stereotypes will be based on more *temporary* things such as hair colour or style of dress or something as *superficial* as a person's name. Stereotypes can be *positive* or *negative* and social

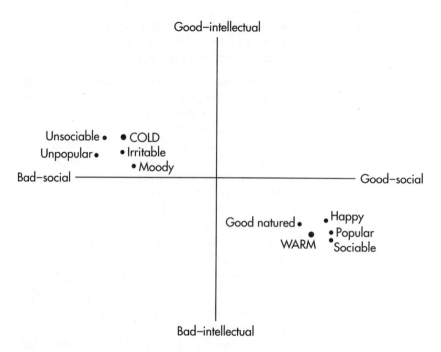

Figure 5.1 Rosenberg's two-dimensional model of trait clusters (simplified)

psychologists have found that negative ones in particular can lead to more serious problems, such as prejudice, because they encourage us to:

- overexaggerate differences between groups of people (e.g. men and women are like chalk and cheese);
- play down differences between individuals within a group (e.g. all students are the same);
- feel that hostility or discrimination against a stereotyped group is justified (e.g. all unemployed people are lazy, therefore, they deserve to have their benefit cut);
- ignore information which does not fit in with the stereotype.

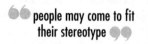

people may come to fit their stereotype

Some stereotypes persist because they have a *kernel of truth* in that we sometimes meet people who 'fit'. In addition, there is some evidence that members of a stereotyped group will start to believe in the stereotype themselves so that it can become a *self-fulfilling prophecy*. This might be one reason why girls take sciences less than do boys. Perhaps girls 'buy' the stereotype that they are no good at science.

RACIAL STEREOTYPING

Katz and Braly (1933) asked 100 American students to choose from a list of traits five characteristics which best described certain racial groups. Here are some of the findings:

- Americans – industrious, intelligent, materialistic, ambitious, progressive;
- Negroes – superstitious, lazy, happy-go-lucky, ignorant, musical;
- Jews – shrewd, mercenary, industrious, grasping, intelligent;
- Turks – cruel, religious, treacherous, sensual, ignorant.

In 1968, *Karlins* repeated this study and found that students still produced some stereotyped views but were much less willing to stereotype. This may have been because of greater contact with other racial groups but also because of greater awareness of the harm negative stereotyping can do.

SEX-ROLE STEREOTYPING

Deaux and Lewis (1983) showed the following stereotypes of men and women:

- women more than men were judged to be warm, emotional, graceful and small-boned, involved in child-care and cooking;
- men more than women were seen as independent, competitive, muscular and deep-voiced, involved in financially providing for others and capable of taking the initiative.

Not all these characteristics are negative. Other effects of sex-role stereotyping, both positive and negative, appear in sex and gender especially in connection with Social Learning explanations of sex-typing.

3 ▷ SOCIAL FILTERS

Almost everything we know about our social world reaches us from other people. They may give us information directly or we may find it out from the mass media such as newspapers, magazines, books, advertisements or TV. All these sources of information can be thought of as **filters** through which information passes. Each filter may select or change information in particular ways and, usually, each filter has received its information through other filters. The party game *Chinese whispers* shows how easily information can be lost or distorted when it passes from one person to another. Here are some important examples of social filters:

GATEKEEPERS AND THE MASS MEDIA

A **gatekeeper** is a person who supplies us with filtered information about the world that we would otherwise not have access to. Gatekeepers can be *family* and *friends*, *reporters*, *teachers* or *neighbours*. Some people argue that certain fields of interest, such as the sciences are male dominated because male scientists act as gatekeepers blocking out our awareness of the achievements of female scientists. The *mass media* are all examples of gatekeepers with TV and newspapers being amongst the most powerful and accessible. By careful selection of information, the media can make or break reputations overnight, they can stir people to action and create feelings in them about others that they may never meet. **Propagandists** knowingly exploit this power when they communicate false or inaccurate information for their own ends. **Censors** also use this power when they deliberately withhold or restrict information. Neither is necessarily up to no good. They can sometimes act for the good of people, e.g. propaganda about how smoking affects health could be used in health campaigns. News blackouts (censorship) following abductions can be helpful if they cut down the number of hoax calls received by the police.

RUMOURS AND GOSSIP

These are also examples of socially filtered information. They can reach us from other people or through the mass media. They seem to be most common when people are faced with uncertainty or social disruption, such as in wartime, or when there are disasters. *Knapp* (1944) identified three kinds of rumour:

- pipe-dreams which express hopes and wishes;
- bogies which express fears and anxieties;
- wedge-drivers which express messages of hate, hostility and aggression.

Bogies and wedge-drivers might be used by politicians on the campaign trail to do down their opponents and they might use pipe-dreams to help their own case. The little research that exists into rumours tells us that rumours are most powerful if there is high:

- interest on the part of the recipient;
- ambiguity in the information;
- anxiety in the recipient about the rumour.

Rumours, as they pass from one person (filter) to another, are also subject to:

- levelling – details which do not fit in well are dropped;
- sharpening – details which fit the story better are played up;
- assimilation – the rumour is elaborated to make a better story.

Rumours thus become distorted and more elaborate with every filter they pass through.

4 ▷ PERSONAL FILTERS

Once information reaches us, we can cut it down to manageable amounts if we filter it in our own way. Three factors are thought to be important in this:

1 Attention. We have a limited capacity to deal with incoming information. We have to select information to attend to and discard the rest. Our attention tends to be grabbed by things which are *intense, sudden, novel* or *repetitive* and by things which fit in with our *current physical state* or our *interests*. We seem to be able to develop a **set** to be more receptive to some things than others but too much of the same kind of information can lead to **habituation** where we stop attending.

2 Personal constructs. One thing people do to try to make sense of a vast amount of information is to organise it into a more manageable form. This makes the world a much more predictable and controllable place. One way of organising information about the social world is to use personal constructs. *Kelly* (1955) devised a way of testing an individual's personal construct system called the **repertory grid**. In this test, people are asked to provide a number of adjectives, or **constructs** (warm or cold, extravert or introvert etc.) to describe a number of other people (e.g. mother, boss, neighbour). The constructs chosen give an idea of the individual's unique ways of describing others to themselves, and consequently, how they understand others and fit them into their personal model of the world. If we meet someone who has characteristics which do not fit into our personal construct system, we may ignore the parts that do not fit, distort them until they do or, more rarely, change our personal construct system.

3 Scripts. People in social situations are often behaving according to a script. Having a script acts as a kind of filter governing how we will regard others and behave towards them. A waiter in a restaurant has a script as do the diners. They are all expected to behave in certain ways and do and say predictable things. Only when people step outside the script do we stop filtering and notice other things about them. Generally, however, much of our interaction is based on the shared assumption that people know their scripts and will stick to them.

5 PREJUDICE

Prejudice is often defined as an *extreme attitude*. It can be *positive* or *negative*. It can be about an *object*, an *issue* or a *group* of people. It is often *intense* and *difficult to change*. Well-known prejudices include **racism**, **sexism** and **ageism**. **Ethnocentrism** (*Sumner* 1906) refers to a general tendency to see everything, including other groups (out-groups), from the point of view of your own group (or in-group).
Like attitudes, prejudices are said to have three components:

prejudice is an extreme attitude

1. **A cognitive component**. This is what we *believe* to be true about the object of our prejudice, in other words a **stereotype**.
2. **An affective component**. This concerns the *emotions,* or *feelings,* we have about the object of the prejudice.
3. **A behavioural component**. This is to do with how we *act* towards the object of our prejudice. *Allport* (1954) suggested five ways in which this component might be expressed:

make sure you can define prejudice and discrimination

- anti-locution, e.g. hostile talk, sexist jokes
- avoidance, e.g. keeping a distance
- discrimination, e.g. excluding females from certain jobs
- physical attack
- extermination, e.g. massacre of members of a religious group.

Psychologists talk about prejudice as having at least three sources:

1. **individual** – from within the person, e.g. to do with their *personality* or *emotions* or their way of perceiving the social world;
these probably all work together
2. **interpersonal** – arising from influences within social groups, e.g. to do with *conformity* to *group norms, social learning* or *shared identities*;
3. **inter-group** – arising from *relationships between social groups* perhaps because they are competing with each other.

INDIVIDUAL EXPLANATIONS

The authoritarian personality
Adorno et al. (1950) took a psychodynamic approach to prejudice. They devised the **F-scale** (F for 'fascism') to measure what they called **authoritarianism**. A person who scores high on this scale tends to be:

- rigid in their beliefs
- conventional in their values
- intolerant of weakness
- punitive
- suspicious
- outwardly respectful of authority
- anti- all minority groups, especially those of lower status.

Psychodynamic approaches tend to look to *early experiences* to explain later behaviour. Accordingly, it was found that high scores on authoritarianism in adults tended to be linked to certain aspects of *child-rearing style* experienced by them in childhood, in particular:

 can we talk of a prejudiced personality?

- harsh discipline
- use of love withdrawal as punishment.

This seemed to lead to the child feeling insecure about the parents' love yet dependent on them for approval. The child would feel unconsciously hostile to the parent while outwardly being obedient. As an adult, the individual would continue to feel insecure and hostile towards others. Anger could be expressed by displacing it on to out-groups but the apparent deference to authority would remain.

Evaluation

1. Evidence has shown that authoritarianism and child-rearing style are *correlated* but not that child-rearing style *causes* authoritarianism. It could simply be that the child had learned prejudiced attitudes from observing the parent or that there is an underlying personality disorder which has nothing to do with child-rearing style.
2. The theory cannot explain why prejudice *comes and goes*, e.g. in line with political, or other, events. If the tendency to be prejudiced is a personality characteristic, it should not be so open to change.
3. The theory cannot explain how large numbers of people in a social group can all have *similar levels of prejudice* when their experiences of being parented are different.

this focuses on feelings

frustration does not always lead to aggression

The frustration–aggression hypothesis and scapegoating

In 1939, *Dollard et al.* proposed that, when individuals are thwarted on their way to achieving a goal of some kind, they will experience **frustration**. A common way of dealing with the frustration is to be aggressive (hence **frustration–aggression hypothesis**). The aggression is likely to be expressed as prejudice when:

- the thing which causes the frustration is *too big* or *vague* for direct retaliation (e.g. 'the economic situation' or 'life');
- the individual therefore has to find an object (*scapegoat*) on which to take out their frustration;
- there is a *less powerful out-group* available which can serve as a scapegoat;
- there is an *acceptable way* to express prejudice towards this out-group.

To illustrate this, a government minister might be frustrated because the unemployment figures are high. A suitable scapegoat might be *working women* because they do not (perhaps) have as much power as men. A way of expressing prejudice towards this scapegoat might be to block women's careers or attempts to find acceptable child-care. Another way would be to express the view that working mothers *should* give up their jobs to stay at home and rear their children.

Evaluation

1. *Hovland and Sears* (1940) found some support for this hypothesis when they discovered a negative correlation between cotton prices and lynchings of Negro people. When prices were high, lynchings were less common. When prices were low, lynchings were more common. Negroes could have been used as scapegoats for the frustration felt by farmers about the economic situation (but it is important to remember that this is a correlation so we cannot be sure about the cause of the connection).

2. Economic frustration does not always lead to prejudice. Even economically secure people, such as wealthy white South Africans, may still show prejudice towards Negro people.
3. Some types of prejudice are not easily explained this way, e.g. why should certain cultures show prejudice against birth control when there is no evidence to suggest frustration preceded their negative attitude?

Cognitive informational explanations

📖📖 this focuses on cognitions 📖📖

This explanation of prejudice focuses on the *cognitive* part of the prejudice, i.e. the **stereotype**. We tend to be more comfortable if our cognitions about something all fit neatly together and do not contradict each other. A prejudice serves to help us organise some of the vast amount of information we receive about other people in our social world into neat 'packages'. This takes away the guesswork and is altogether less effort, even if we are wrong! Information which *fits* in with our ready-made view of others tends to be more closely attended to and more easily processed. Information which does *not fit* with our prejudiced attitudes tends to be not as readily processed. We *reject* it, *discount* it, *distort* it or otherwise *dispose* of it. A prejudice is, therefore, more the result of our inability to deal with large amounts of information and our general laziness than from an emotional influence or personality type.

A stereotype is the cognitive part of a prejudice. Stereotypes help to perform this function of *pigeon-holing* people but they do make our judgements rather rigid. Once a stereotype has been 'activated' it is very resistant to change. This means it may become self-confirming because of our tendency to ignore information which does not fit in. We tend to see members of the **out-group** as more similar than they really are and do not bother to check out the accuracy of our ideas because we 'already know what those people are like'.

Baron and Byrne (1991) also talk about **illusory correlations**. This is the tendency to see relationships between things which do not actually exist. For example, a newspaper may report a violent crime committed by a black person. A white person reading about it may have little contact with either black people or violent crime. As a consequence, the event stands out to the reader and is remembered more easily. The two events, 'black' and 'violence' become linked in the reader's mind and help to contribute to a negative and inaccurate stereotype about black people.

INTERPERSONAL EXPLANATIONS

Conformity to group norms

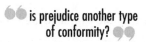 is prejudice another type of conformity? 📖📖

This explanation suggests that prejudice is just another aspect of responding to the *real* or *perceived* demands of others to conform to group norms. The reasons for such conformity include *compliance*, *internalisation* and *identification* (see Social Influence). *Minard* (1952) reported how white and black miners in a US town were friendly with each other below ground when they were at work. Above ground, only 20% of white miners continued to be friendly towards their black colleagues. It seemed the prevailing norms changed with the setting and prejudice appeared or disappeared accordingly. *Lieberman* (1956) found that workers' attitudes changed when they were promoted from the shop-floor to the post of shop steward (became more negative towards management) or foreman (became more positive towards management). Attitudes changed back again if they were demoted.

Social learning

📖📖 perhaps prejudices are learned 📖📖

SLT explains learning in terms of both conditioning and observational learning. Prejudices are seen as coming about in the same way as any other learned behaviour:

- In **classical conditioning**, a child may witness a parent being angry in the presence of, say, a member of an out-group. The negative feelings which this causes the child may eventually become associated with the previously neutral out-group person so that, in future, the out-group person, and other similar people, produce negative feelings.
- In **operant conditioning**, the child's expressions of prejudice in what they say and do would be shaped and maintained by others around them, e.g. parents, peers and teachers. These people would react positively, negatively, or not at all

to the child's behaviour so that they learn to repeat the responses which had pleasant consequences and inhibit those which were punished or ignored.

- In **observational learning**, children learn by watching and imitating the behaviour of certain 'models' around them who have certain characteristics. Initially parents may be the most important role-models, but later, children may also be influenced by peers, teachers and models in the mass media.

The learning approach to prejudice is a good complement to other approaches because it helps to explain how we decide which targets to direct prejudice towards. Frustration, for example, is a feature of life, but who we choose to direct the resulting aggression, or prejudice, towards may be learned by the processes described above.

Shared identities

This approach to prejudice has been put under the 'interpersonal explanations' heading but it really spans both this and the next section on 'inter-group explanations'. It was developed by *Tajfel* (1979) and is based on **Social Identity Theory** (SIT). The general idea is that, on an *interpersonal* level:

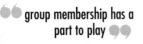
group membership has a part to play

- we get our social identities from the social groups to which we belong;
- we want to have a positive social identity;
- this means we need to belong to a group in which members share a positive identity.

On an *inter-group* level this means that we will compare our group to other groups in a way which enables our group to look better. We can do this by:

- emphasising how good, competent and worthy our own group is compared to an out-group;
- belittling the achievements of the out-group;
- comparing our group to an out-group on things which we are bound to score more highly on and dismissing things at which they do better as unimportant.

Tajfel found that a group identity could be a very *flimsy* and *temporary* thing. This led him to talk about **minimal groups**. He could create minimal groups in the laboratory using arbitrary labels or even by the toss of a coin. Once people had categorised themselves they would start to think of themselves as an in-group and others as an out-group and behave accordingly. Merely being told about the existence of an out-group could produce the minimal groups effect even though there was no contact with the out-group or proof that it existed!

INTER-GROUP EXPLANATIONS

Competition and cooperation

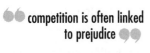
competition is often linked to prejudice

Tajfel has shown how competition between groups is not necessary for prejudices to develop but most inter-group explanations start with the assumption that such competition is a major cause of prejudice. The competition may be *economic* or *political* and is especially fierce if *resources are limited*. In these cases, a dominant group may exploit or derogate another group in order to get what it wants. Racial prejudice, for example, may be strongest when jobs are scarce or when there are disputes between countries over territory. *Aronson* (1992) describes how, during the 1930s, jobs in a small US industrial town became scarce. Prejudice against German immigrants appeared even though there had been no negative feeling before. Throughout the nineteenth century, prejudice against Chinese immigrants in the US came and went depending on the economic situation. When Chinese people were prospecting for gold, attitudes towards them were much more negative than when they undertook hard and, sometimes, dangerous work building the transcontinental railroad.

The problem with such reports is that they are *correlational*. We do not know if prejudice is caused by competition for resources or whether there is some other reason. To be sure we need deliberately to create groups, set them in opposition to each other and see if prejudice results. This is what *Sherif et al.* did (1961).

With the consent of the parents, Sherif used 12-year-old Boy Scouts on a camp. He divided them randomly into two groups which, at the start of the camp, did not know of each other's existence. Initially the boys spent time in their groups doing cooperative tasks and getting to know each other. Each group chose a name – in this case they called themselves *Rattlers* or *Eagles*.

Once the groups were settled, Sherif introduced them to each other and made them *compete* against each other for prizes, e.g. in football, baseball and tug-of-war. In addition, Sherif arranged *conflict* situations. An example of this was a party at which the Eagles arrived first. By the time the Rattlers arrived the food that was left by the Eagles was unappealing, unappetising and squashed. Name-calling degenerated into food-throwing until, eventually, a riot was in progress. Sherif stopped the competitions and conflict at this point but the hostility went on.

consider the ethics of this

6 ⟩ SOME REAL-LIFE IMPLICATIONS OF PREJUDICE

do you have any personal experience of these?

1. **Tokenism**. If a person sees themselves as a 'token woman' or 'token black person' who has been employed for reasons of sex or colour rather than ability, the effects can be negative. *Chacko* (1982) tested women managers. Some of them thought that they had been employed for reasons of ability. Others thought it was because of tokenism (i.e. their sex). The 'tokenism' group were less committed and satisfied in their work than those who believed they were appointed because of ability.

2. **Reverse discrimination**. *Fajardo* (1985) asked white teachers to grade essays which were especially chosen to cover a range of marks. Essays were identifiable as being written by either black or white students. Fajardo found that essays apparently written by black students were rated more highly by the teachers. This might seem to be a good thing if it resulted in black students seeing themselves as more competent and actually becoming more competent. The danger is that their expectations would be unrealistically raised and that they might make plans about life and career which would be dashed later on. White students, on the other hand, would be getting accurate feedback and would not run into such problems so often.

7 ⟩ SEXISM AND RACISM

We have looked at a number of explanations of prejudice, and some of their consequences, focusing on the individual or the group. Here we are going to take a wider view to see how prejudices such as sexism and racism may be expressed at an *institutional* level. (Examples of 'institutions' are the education system, the judicial system or the workplace.)

RACISM

in education

Racism may be kept going at an **educational level** in a number of ways, for example:

1. by providing inferior education for certain racial groups;
2. by keeping alive the idea that black people always score lower than white people on IQ tests;
3. through teachers communicating expectations to black pupils that they are less able than white pupils.

in law

In the **judicial system** there are many expressions of racism. Following the Brixton riots in 1981, the **Scarman report** gave examples of policing styles which may have contributed to a breakdown in relationships between certain racial groups and the police, for example:

- the use of Special Patrol Groups to control street crime was thought to be heavy-handed by local people;
- there was also evidence that the 'Stop and Search' law was applied more often to black people;
- inexperience in some police officers sometimes led to confrontations if the police officer was seen as being insensitive.

To help reduce such problems, Scarman recommended that more members of ethnic minorities should be encouraged to join the police, that new police officers should undergo special 'sensitivity training' and that there should be more contact between the police and the community. All these measures were aimed at reducing feelings of being discriminated against on both the part of the police and community members.

In the courts, studies in the US have shown that a black defendant is more likely to receive a prison sentence than is a white defendant (*Stewart* 1980). The race of a murder victim is also influential. If the victim is black, 4.5% of killers receive a death sentence compared to 11.1% if the victim is white (*Henderson and Taylor*, 1985).

 at work

In the **workplace**, *Jones* (1972) quoted survey results in the US to show that, compared to a white man of the same level of education, a black man would be earning much less. *Word et al.* (1974) provided evidence to show that white and black job applicants are treated in subtly different ways by white interviewers. For example, when interviewing black applicants, interviewers sat further away, made more speech errors and stopped the interview earlier than when interviewing white applicants. The effect of this was to make the black applicants appear more nervous and less competent.

SEXISM

in education

For some ideas about how sexism might affect boys' and girls' **educational achievement** see 'Gender and educational achievement' in Aspects of Self-Development (Chapter 10). Remember that girls (and others) often put their successes down to luck and boys (and others) often attribute their success to ability. The operation of sexism in education is a complicated mixture of *self-concept*, *expectations* of others, *gender-role stereotyping* and *discrimination*.

in law

In the **judicial system** females often seem to be at a disadvantage. In a mock trial *Cruse and Leigh* (1987) described a domestic crime in which the defendant had cut the victim with a kitchen knife. If the defendant were female, 69% of the jury found her to be guilty compared to 43% for the male defendant. Perhaps this is because physical violence fits more easily with the male stereotype than it does with the female one. Females are being punished both for the crime and for stepping outside the expected role. Similar biases may operate in rape cases where it is claimed that the woman somehow brought it on herself by the way she dressed or behaved. In such cases she is expected to take responsibility both for her own behaviour and for that of her male companion.

at work

In the **workplace**, women are generally under-represented in many professional or higher prestige occupations although opportunities may seem to be equal. Women seeking promotion talk of the *'glass ceiling'* – the point on the career ladder where they meet invisible blocks to moving upwards. *Baron and Byrne* (1991) suggest that the *male stereotype* (forceful, dominant, assertive) fits better with our stereotype of the successful career person than does the *female stereotype* (gentle, submissive, passive) and that women find it difficult to overcome this view. An added problem is that more *attractive women* seem to be seen as less appropriate for managerial roles than less attractive women (*Heilman and Martell* 1986). It's as if the female gender stereotype is more strongly encouraged for attractive women. Men's level of attractiveness does not seem to matter so much.

Many blatant examples of sexism in the workplace stage are now forbidden by law (e.g. sexual harassment, displaying suggestive calendars). Does this help to reduce sexism? The majority of working people would say 'No'. They argue that significant changes will not occur until employers recognise the problems that trying to combine work and family life present for both male and female employees. However, Baron and Byrne disagree. They say there is evidence of change for the better and quote research to show:

* increasing numbers of female managers;
* more acceptance of both men and women for leadership positions;
* no discrimination against women in evaluating their work performance;
* fairer job interviews;
* improvements in pay in female-dominated jobs.

8 > PREJUDICE REDUCTION

Explanations of prejudice which focus on individual, interpersonal or inter-group levels each have recommendations to make about reducing prejudice.

INDIVIDUAL SOLUTIONS

The authoritarian personality

Intervening at the level of personality is difficult. Authoritarianism would be passed down the generations as children reared by authoritarian parents rear their own children in an authoritarian way so some way must be found to break the cycle. One possibility would be to attempt to *change parenting style* so that it is:

- less harsh and hostile
- more loving and secure.

Another possibility would be to provide for authoritarian people to undergo *psychoanalysis* in an attempt to alter the balance of their personalities. Clearly, neither of these solutions is very practical.

The frustration–aggression hypothesis and scapegoating

It would be unrealistic to think of creating a world which never frustrates people. Frustration is a fact of life so, perhaps, what needs to be done is to teach people to see the reason for their frustration differently or to cope with their negative feelings in less destructive ways. These are solutions which will be discussed further in the next section and in the section on learning under 'interpersonal solutions'.

Cognitive informational explanations

Here, attempts to change prejudice focus on changing an individual's cognitions about an out-group. A good way to do this is to *challenge their stereotypes*. In the 1980s, *Fiske et al.* suggested that, when people meet someone else for the first time, they depend heavily on stereotypes to judge them because this is the least effort. She showed that, if people can be encouraged to pay attention to the other person's unique characteristics, stereotyping is reduced. It should be possible to encourage people consciously to confront and challenge their own stereotypes.

There is some evidence to suggest that the higher a person's level of education, the less prejudice they express. However, we do not know the reason for this correlation. It could be that higher education exposes people to more arguments against prejudice or it could simply be that they are clever at expressing socially acceptable views!

INTERPERSONAL SOLUTIONS

Conformity to group norms

Perhaps the only way to reduce prejudice in this situation would be to change the group's norms. Two studies which could be said to have achieved this are:

Aronson's jigsaw technique (1978)

In a class consisting of children of different races it was the norm to be competitive and to avoid working with children of a different race. The jigsaw technique was designed to overcome this:

- a story was divided into six paragraphs;
- the class was divided into groups of six;
- each member of a six-person group was given a different part of the story;
- each child had to learn their part of the story and teach it to the others in their group. At the end, all children aimed to know the whole story;
- children from different groups, but with the same part of the story, could work together in learning their part.

The aim of the technique was to get children working cooperatively together and to value each other's contribution equally. Aronson concluded that this experience helped children to:

- like each other more;
- like school more;
- achieve more;
- improve their self-esteem;
- see things from other children's point of view.

Jane Eliot's blue eyes–brown eyes technique

Eliot (1980) began her attempt to reduce prejudice with her class of 9-year-olds. On the first day she told her class that brown-eyed people were better than blue-eyed people. She said they were brighter and should have all kinds of privileges not open to blue-eyed people. Blue-eyed people were an 'underclass' and they would have to wear arm-bands so that they could be easily identified. In a short time, brown-eyed children started to oppress blue-eyed children. In turn, blue-eyed children became depressed and angry and their schoolwork suffered.

The next day, Eliot reversed the situation so that brown-eyed children were told they were the underclass and blue-eyed children were told they were superior. The children's behaviour changed accordingly. On the third day the children were allowed to discuss their experiences of being prejudiced against. They had experienced how unpleasant and unfair it could be and this understanding helped them to become less prejudiced.

At a class reunion years later, Eliot found the effect had *lasted into adulthood*. She continued to use this procedure in other settings, e.g. in training prison workers. (The effect seems not only to change group norms but also to raise people's consciousness which means that it works on both an individual and interpersonal level.)

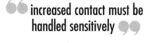

"Conformity to norms is only one reason why these two studies worked. Can you think of others?"

Social learning

If parents, peers and teachers are responsible for teaching children to be prejudiced, then it is with them that attempts to change prejudice should begin. However, they must first unlearn their own prejudices and this needs to be done at the individual level, e.g. through challenging their stereotypes or raising their consciousness. Only then will they be in a position to condition their own children or provide them with good models.

Shared identities

"multiple membership helps"

If prejudice results from people identifying themselves as members of a particular group, one way to reduce prejudice would be to get them to see themselves as members of several groups at once. Sharing characteristics with members of other groups should lead them to view them more positively. *Deschamps and Doise* (1978) created two minimal groups and then made a third group using a mixture of people from these two groups. Each group then had to create something which was judged by themselves and the other two groups. The mixed group both gave and received less negative feedback than the other two groups. (This solution could also explain how the jigsaw technique works. Children see themselves as members of the same class, as members of their own group of six and as members of the group with the same part of the story.)

INTER-GROUP SOLUTIONS

Attempts to reduce inter-group prejudice usually involve trying to increase contact between conflicting or competing groups. This has been tried in many settings, e.g. in *housing, schools*, the *workplace* and in *summer camps*.

In Sherif's study described earlier, Rattlers and Eagles were put into situations where they had to **work together** to achieve a solution, e.g. tow a broken-down truck or restore the camp water supply. In these cases, group hostilities had to cease. Sherif claims that boys eventually started to make friends across groups and to cooperate more.

In the 1950s *Deutsch and Collins* reported on an **inter-racial public housing** project where black families were either housed in separate buildings to white families or black and white families were mixed in the same block. They claim that the attitudes of white and black people became more positive towards each other in the mixed housing than in the segregated housing.

"increased contact must be handled sensitively"

It is important to remember that forcing contact on prejudiced groups is not always enough. It can make matters worse unless:

● the members of the two groups have equal status;
● the two groups have common goals;
● they are successful in achieving their goals (failure can make prejudice worse);
● everyone has a say in making decisions;
● contact is unavoidable and fairly rapid;
● neither group has practices offensive to the other;
● the social climate encourages reduction.

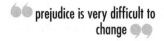

prejudice is very difficult to change

CONCLUSION

Clearly prejudice reduction is no simple matter. Why do so many attempts to reduce prejudice fail? Several suggestions can be made:

- Some attempts to reduce prejudice might tackle *only one component* of the attitude, e.g. the cognitive part and not touch on the affective or behavioural part. Sometimes a change in one part can bring about changes in another but this is not guaranteed.
- We do not always know what first caused the prejudice. It is *unlikely to be a simple cause*. All prejudices probably have an individual, interpersonal and inter-group part to them. If this is true, attempts to reduce prejudice which only tackle the individual level may have no effect on an interpersonal or inter-group level.
- It is very *difficult to measure* prejudice. When people answer questionnaires about their prejudices we do not know how honest they are being or whether what they say about an out-group and what they actually do towards it match up.
- People may be reluctant to let go of their prejudice if it pays off in some way.
- Prejudice may be so much *part of a society or culture* or so much part of their particular point in history that it is too much of a tall order to think of changing it much (although this is no excuse for doing nothing as change has to start somewhere!).
- Some prejudices may be *harder to alter than others*. As *Franklin and Franklin* (1986) observed 'white racists never become black and male chauvinists do not become women, but those who hold ageist views … grow old and … so fall victim of their own prejudices'.

EXAMINATION QUESTIONS

1. SEG sample paper (Higher Tier) Section C

Spend 35 minutes on this question

(a) Explain the difference between prejudice and discrimination [4]
(b) Compare and contrast **two** different psychological theories which attempt to explain prejudice. [14]
(c) From what you have learned in psychology, suggest **two** ways in which prejudice might be reduced. [12]

[*Total 30 marks*]
(SEG)

TUTOR ANSWER

1. SEG sample paper (Higher Tier) Section C

(a) Prejudice is often defined as an extreme attitude. Attitudes are made up of three components: the cognitive part includes our set of beliefs about something, the affective part includes our feelings about it and the behavioural part is what we do about it. Discrimination is the behavioural part of the prejudiced attitude, e.g. a person may think and feel negatively about the opposite sex and this may lead them actually to discriminate by blocking their promotion opportunities.

(b) One theory of prejudice is the psychodynamic approach of Adorno who devised the F-scale to measure authoritarianism. People with high F scores tend to be suspicious, conventional, rigid in their beliefs and outwardly respectful of authority but also anti- all minority groups. Adorno thought this was linked to the kind of parenting these people had experienced. Their parents were harsh and used love withdrawal as punishment. The children were consequently obedient but also felt angry, insecure and hostile to others. As adults they could continue to outwardly respect authority but displace their anger on to a scapegoat.

There is some evidence that child-rearing style and authoritarianism are correlated but this does not mean they are causally related. Also, people's prejudices should remain constant if they are part of the personality but prejudices seem to come and go as social conditions change. Finally, whole groups of people can have very similar levels of prejudice even though they experienced different parenting.

Adorno's theory is rather pessimistic because it suggests that change in prejudice would be very hard to bring about, also it plays down the importance of experience. Social Learning Theory can answer both these criticisms. SLT claims we learn most of our behaviour through conditioning and through observing and imitating certain others around us. As with the psychodynamic approach, parents are important but so are other people, and for different reasons. Through classical conditioning a child could learn to associate negative feelings with an out-group through being with their parents when they are reacting angrily to the out-group. In operant conditioning, parents and others would shape prejudiced attitudes in children by reinforcing anti- out-group attitudes and punishing or ignoring positive attitudes. Through observational learning, the child would observe others' behaviour and imitate prejudiced attitudes in role-models they admired. It is important that what the model says and does is consistent as children tend to copy what models do more than what they say. SLT is a good way of explaining how prejudices can change as we move from one role-model to another. It also helps to explain what we choose to direct our prejudice towards. Learned behaviour is always open to change so, if prejudice is learned there is no need to look on it, as psychodynamic theorists do, as something we can do little about.

(c) If we accept the idea of the authoritarian personality, one way to reduce prejudice would be to encourage parents to use less authoritarian parenting styles. This should help to stop authoritarianism being passed down the generations. Parenting would need to be less harsh and hostile and more democratic and loving. To enable the parent to do this they would need to undergo a long period of psychoanalysis in order to alter the balance of their personality. By the time this was achieved, it could be too late for the child! It is also a rather impractical way to deal with prejudice in large numbers of people.

SLT would focus on learning processes. People who children learn from would first need to unlearn their own prejudices so that they did not condition the child to behave in prejudiced ways. For classically conditioned prejudiced feelings, increased contact with out-groups could act as a kind of systematic desensitisation such that prejudiced people gradually become more positive and relaxed when with them. Operant conditioning principles could help to shape behaviour such that rewards for positive behaviour towards out-groups would be given and negative attitudes and behaviour ignored or punished. Observational learning leads to the suggestion that people should model positive behaviour towards all out-groups so that children observe and imitate positive behaviour too. The consistency of the models' expressed attitudes and behaviour is very important. They should practise what they preach since studies of observational learning suggest children tend to copy behaviour more than expressed beliefs.

STUDENTS' ANSWERS

1. MEG Module 5, Source A. Reducing racial prejudice

Spend 20 minutes on this question

Most of the research on how to reduce racial prejudice has been carried out on adults. However, more recently, psychologists have used children as participants (subjects). One study, which took place in a classroom setting, used children who were eight years old. The sample consisted of white, middle-class children. The children from the sample were randomly allocated into an experimental or control group. The experimental group used reading books which contained stories and pictures of different ethnic groups. The control group used reading books in which all of the characters were white. The psychologist used a questionnaire to measure the children's attitudes to other racial groups both before and after the study. The results are shown in the graph.

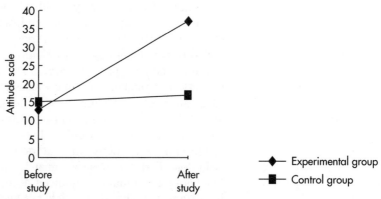

Measurement of racial attitudes in children (the higher the score, the more positive the attitude)

When attitudes were measured

(a) Using the graph shown above, what could the researcher conclude from this study?   [2]

66 2/2 99

Children in the experimental group who had read books containing stories and pictures of different ethnic groups had more positive racial attitudes than children who had read books in which all the characters were white.

(b) Give **one** criticism of the sample that was used.   [2]

66 2/2 99

The sample consisted only of white middle-class children so the findings could not be applied to other kinds of children.

(c) What is meant by the term *prejudice*?   [2]

66 very thorough

2/2 99

Prejudice is defined as an extreme (usually negative) attitude held about an object, an issue or a group of people. It is often intense and difficult to change and it can affect our thoughts, feelings and behaviour with respect to the object of our prejudice. Examples include sexism, racism and ageism.

(d) Why did the psychologist measure the children's racial attitudes before and after the study?   [2]

66 2/2 99

He needed to know what their attitudes were before they read the books so that he could see if attitudes had changed after reading the books. He could only know this by comparing before and after scores.

(e) The researcher used a questionnaire to measure the children's racial attitudes. What is **one** problem with using a questionnaire to measure prejudice?   [2]

66 2/2 99

Children might not be totally honest in their answers to the questionnaire especially if they were concerned about making a good impression on the researcher.

(f) Using your psychological knowledge, describe **one other way** in which psychologists have tried to reduce prejudice. [3]

> Another way to reduce prejudice would be to use Aronson's jigsaw technique. This could be used in school classes. Children would be split into groups of six and each group member would be given a different part of a six-part story, the object being for all members of the group to learn all six parts by teaching each other. Children with the same section of the story could work with children from other groups. Aronson found that this reduced prejudice in the classes where he tried it. There are many reasons why it might work. It ensures all children are equally important and that they must make contact with each other within their own group and across others. It teaches them to value each other's contribution and think of themselves as a group so that new norms of acceptance and cooperation develop. After being part of this technique, Aronson found improvements in children's self-esteem and greater liking for school and each other.

3/3

[*Total 13 marks*]
(MEG)

13/13 Top marks for a very clear set of answers

2. NEAB paper 2 1994

Spend 10–12 minutes answering this question

Chris has been invited to attend a job interview. She knows that you have studied a psychology course. She has asked you for advice on how to create a good impression. Give **two** suggestions supported by psychological evidence and/or theory.

(a) Suggestion 1. [1]

1/1

> First impressions count most so this is what she should work on.

Supporting evidence and/or theory. [4]

relate this to the interview

3/4

> In one study subjects were given two paragraphs to read about Jim. In the first paragraph he was described as extravert and in the second as introvert. Other subjects read the introvert paragraph first then the extravert one. It was found that the first paragraph was the most important in forming an impression of Jim.

(b) Suggestion 2. [1]

1/1

> She should come over as a warm person.

Supporting evidence and/or theory. [4]

again, relate this to the interview

> Asch found that warm and cold are central traits. If we think of someone as warm then we see them as having other good qualities. When Asch put warm in a description of someone and gave it to subjects, he found they judged the person as happy and generous. If he put cold in the list, the person was seen as miserable and mean.

3/4

[*Total 10 marks*]
(NEAB)

8/10 Clear content that needs to be directly applied to the problem described in the question

A Review Sheet for this chapter can be found on p. 235–6.

CHAPTER 6

SOCIAL INFLUENCE

GETTING STARTED

Social influence is a broad term used to refer to the effects of others on an individual's behaviour. The presence of others can be actual or implied. They may make no attempt to influence our behaviour or they may make deliberate attempts to do so. There may be only one other or many.

The topics in this chapter are just a selection of the many kinds of social influence and the three exam boards have chosen slightly different combinations. You will need to select those sections which apply to you so check in chapter one exactly which ones you need.

ESSENTIAL PRINCIPLES

The presence of others, either doing something alongside you or watching you do something, can have an effect on your behaviour. Here we will examine two processes known as:

- **social facilitation**, where the presence of others enhances performance – the two main influences here are **co-action effects** and **audience effects**; and
- **social inhibition**, where the presence of others may reduce the level of responding – this includes **social loafing** and **bystander apathy** (to be covered later in the chapter).

1 ⟩ SOCIAL FACILITATION

CO-ACTION EFFECTS

Co-action refers to situations when people are doing something alongside each other. Early studies by *Triplett* (1897) showed how racing cyclists did 23% better with a 'pacer' than when riding alone. He found a similar effect when schoolchildren were asked to reel in fishing lines together or alone.

These studies were extensively followed up by *Floyd Allport* (1924) over a wide variety of tasks, e.g. crossing out vowels in a piece of text, doing multiplication sums, making word associations or seeing how many times you could mentally reverse a visual illusion. In all these, the presence of others was helpful. Only when people were asked to produce good arguments for something were they better alone. In this case, the presence of others produces **social impairment**. Allport concluded that co-action increased the speed and quantity of output on certain tasks but not necessarily its quality.

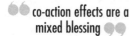
co-action effects are a mixed blessing

Zajonc (the name is pronounced to rhyme with 'science') wrote, in the 1960s, that co-action seems to be a biological effect because it is evident in other species. Examples of studies quoted by Zajonc included:

- *Harlow* (1932) who showed that albino rats eat more when feeding side by side than when alone;
- *Chen* (1937) who found that an Asiatic variety of ant works harder and faster on nest-building when co-acting than when alone;
- *Larsson* (1956) who showed that male rats, copulating in groups, achieved more ejaculations per hour than when copulating with no other males present.

AUDIENCE EFFECTS

Zajonc and Sales (1966) went on to study the effect on behaviour when it was performed in front of onlookers (an audience). Participants were asked to free-associate to a list of words. The time taken to respond to each word was measured. One group of participants began alone, another began with someone watching. Half-way through, the 'alone' participants gained an onlooker and the 'watched' participants lost theirs. The effect was that those who lost the onlooker slowed down and those who gained an onlooker speeded up.

Explanations of audience effects

1 The arousal hypothesis

Zajonc's arousal hypothesis states that the presence of others is innately arousing and this increases activity level.

The effects of arousal on behaviour, however, are not always facilitating. Zajonc said arousal increases the production of **dominant responses**. These responses are the most thoroughly learned or usual for you but they may not always be the best you can do. An audience *hinders* if your most usual level of performance is average or mediocre because that is what you are most likely to produce in front of onlookers. A very well-practised person's dominant responses are skilled ones so, in this case, the audience encourages these to be produced. Surprisingly, this effect is also apparent in other species. Table 6.1 shows the results of a maze-learning experiment.

Condition	Human's average errors made in learning the maze	Cockroach average time (secs) taken to complete the maze
Simple maze		
Alone	44.7	40.5
Others present	36.2	33.0
Complex maze		
Alone	184.9	110.5
Others present	220.3	129.5

Table 6.1 Human and cockroach maze-learning performance

 cockroaches are affected by an audience

Both humans and cockroaches seem to find the presence of others arousing and, when they are doing a demanding task, their dominant responses of rather unskilled behaviour seem to take over.

2 The distraction conflict hypothesis
Tedeschi et al. (1985) agree that the presence of others produces arousal but, when others are present and a task needs to be done, people experience a dilemma over how to share their attention out. Complex tasks take more attention so they suffer more easily than simple ones especially if they are not well practised. It is quite possible to do a simple task well and still have enough attention left to give to others around you.

3 The evaluation apprehension hypothesis
Another reason for the audience effect is that the performer may be concerned about how the onlookers are *evaluating* the performance. The strength of the effect increases down the following list:

- working alone
- in front of an audience of interested peers
- when performance is being taped for later evaluation
- the audience consists of experts.

Of course, if dominant responses are skilled ones, the effect will be enhancing, otherwise it could be disastrous! As well as this, we know that the larger the audience, the stronger the effect and that a *hostile* audience is usually impairing. Even so, a few individuals find hostility improves performance which suggests wide *individual differences* in responses to social influence.

Audience effects are small but reliable. It is difficult to say which of the above hypotheses is best because they probably all operate to some extent in every audience effect. The moral of the story is, if you are going to do something in front of an audience, expect it to arouse some feelings of excitement, nervousness or apprehension but, above all, make sure you are very well practised.

2 SOCIAL INHIBITION

This includes **social loafing** and **bystander apathy**. The latter is an important area to be covered later in this chapter.

SOCIAL LOAFING

Social loafing refers to the decrease in effort that an individual might make when working in a group. Some researchers have suggested that this is due to a reduction in, or *diffusion* of, a feeling of individual responsibility. *Ringelmann* (1935) demonstrated this by asking young male participants to tug as hard as they could on a rope. He charted kilograms of force exerted alone or with others. Participants in groups of eight appear to exert about half the effort each that they could exert alone. See Table 6.2:

Group size	Potential force (kg)	Actual force (kg)
Alone	63	63
Participant +1	126	118
Participant +2	189	160
Participant +7	504	248

Table 6.2 The social loafing effect and rope tugging

We also know the following about social loafing:

social loafing can be reduced

- If people believe their *individual effort* can be monitored, loafing disappears. *Williams et al.* (1981) showed this in a study where people were led to believe the volume of their shouting could be monitored when they were shouting with others.
- *Boring and repetitive* tasks seem to encourage more loafing. This can be overcome if the task can be broken into sub-tasks and individuals given responsibility for each one. In vote counting or envelope-stuffing for example, each person could be given a sub-section defined by alphabet to do.

3 > CONFORMITY

Aronson (1992) defines conformity as a change in a person's behaviour as a result of real or imagined pressure from a person or group of people. Laypeople think of conformity as giving in to group pressure. *Mann* (1969) offers a classification:

- **Normative conformity**. A person conforms to be accepted by a group and avoid rejection. There are two ways to do this: (a) **compliance**, where a person goes along with the group but, privately, holds different beliefs, and (b) **true conformity**, where the person agrees with the group and goes along with it.
- **Informational conformity**. People may go along with the group because they are not sure how to behave so they look to others for guidance and copy them.
- **Ingratiational conformity**. Here, people conform because they want to impress others in the group or gain their approval.

There are two types of non-conformity:

- **Independent behaviour**. A person sticks firmly by their beliefs even at the risk of falling out with the group.
- **Anti-conformity**. A person always goes against the group, usually out of perverseness. (Ironically, this person's behaviour is just as much determined by what the group does as is the conformist's!)

these are classics

STUDIES OF CONFORMITY

Sherif

Sherif (1935) showed conformity to judgements of the **autokinetic effect**. This is a visual illusion in which a stationary, bright point of light in a darkened room appears to move. Sherif collected participants' individual judgements of direction and amount of the light's movement. He then asked them to make judgements along with others. In these groups, participants' judgements started to agree, even though there was no discussion. Different groups reached different conclusions and individuals who seemed high in self-confidence tended to draw the others along. It seemed that each group had established a **group norm**, in other words an idea of what was appropriate behaviour in the group. Even when people were on their own again, they tended to stick to their original group's norm.

Asch

*Asch (*1956) tested participants in groups of six to nine and told them they were taking part in a perception study. Unbeknown to the participants, the other group members were all **stooges** of the experimenter's. Group members were seated in a semicircle to take part in a series of line-judging tasks.

In each task, participants had to decide which of three comparison lines was closest in length to a stimulus line and call out their answer in order, one by one. The real participant was always last but one to answer. On certain trials, all the stooges deliberately made a wrong judgement. Asch wanted to see how often the real participant would go along with it. For 50 real participants, Asch found a mean average of 32% of answers conformed to the group. (Participants tested individually could do the task with 100% accuracy!) When being debriefed, participants confessed that they did not agree with the stooges at times but felt unable to act independently. Reasons they gave were:

- they did not want to mess up the results;
- they thought they had misunderstood the instructions;
- they had failing eyesight;

- they were judging width, not length;
- it was an optical illusion.

Variations on the original study

Asch found the following factors affected the percentage of conforming responses:

1. **Task difficulty**. If differences between the lengths of the lines was reduced, conformity increased.
2. **Group size**. With one stooge there was no conformity, with two 14% of responses were conforming, with three it was 30%. After this, increasing the number of stooges had no further effect.
3. **Having an ally**. Only one stooge had to support the participant for conformity to vanish.
4. **Losing the ally**. If the stooge supported the participant in the first half of the experiment and then switched to the majority opinion, participants' conforming responses rose to 28.5%.
5. **Participant's status**. If the participant believed the other group members were of a higher status they conformed more.
6. **Conditions of responding**. If participants could write their answers down, or keep them private, conformity vanished.

Evaluation

1 Crutchfield's (1954) version of Asch's study

Crutchfield modified Asch's testing methods so that he could test large numbers of participants all at once. He tested 50 military men on a three-day assessment programme. He used the line-judging task and many others, testing for agreement on statements of opinion such as 'The average American eats six meals a day' and 'US males have a life expectancy of 25 years'. Crutchfield found wide variation in people's tendency to conform. He also found that some problems produced more conforming responses than others. Generally, out of 50 participants tested on 21 tasks, the mean number of conforming responses was 38%.

2 Does Asch's study tell us anything about real-life conformity?

There is an obvious bias in the sample of participants Asch used (white, American males). There are also some comments on how the research design may have affected the results. Conformity may have been exaggerated by:

- having to speak out – if we are unsure, we usually reserve judgement;
- lack of communication – it is unusual not to be able to discuss a problem with other group members;
- triviality of the task – participants may have felt line-judging didn't really matter;
- lack of support – it is quite unusual to be without allies in a group;
- the average used – Asch quoted the mean as a measure of average. This tends to be very sensitive to a few high scores and was artificially inflated. Most people conformed very little and, if we take a median, rather than a mean, the average drops to 25%.

Conformity may have been decreased by:

- task simplicity – the line-judging task was easy!
- lack of group identity – the group was not truly a group. Participants knew they would not meet the others again and had no need to make an impression of any kind.

3 Majorities and minorities

Moscovici (1976) questioned whether majority influence alone was enough to explain Asch's results. He thought that a minority could also be influential providing it held consistently to its view. In an Asch-like study, where the majority were real participants and the minority consisted of two stooges who held consistently to their wrong judgements, the minority could influence the rest.

4 Cross-cultural relevance

In Lebanon, Hong Kong and Brazil conformity rates were around 30% but in the Bantu of Zimbabwe they were 51% (e.g. *Whittaker, Meade* 1967). *Perrin and Spencer* (1981) warn that the Asch effect could be 'a child of its time' reflecting the historical and cultural state of these countries and 1950s' USA. In fact, *Nicholson et al.* found about 30% lower rates of conformity in 1985 and no differences between British and American students. This might reflect a move towards greater individual independence and tendency to question authority.

5 Why did people conform?

- **Behavioural contagion**. Psychologists use this term to describe how social behaviour patterns can be catching. (Remember how easy it is to yawn just after you saw someone else do it!) People may conform almost without thought because of this influence. One person starts it and it catches on, e.g. religious fervour spreading through a congregation, or a party atmosphere at a social gathering.

Kelman (1958) has suggested three more reasons why people conform. These also provide us with three ways in which **group norms** may form:

- **Compliance**. As Mann had suggested, people conform to the group because they want to be accepted even though, privately, they do not agree with the group.
- **Identification**. People change to agree with the group because they want to be more like someone in the group that they respect or admire.
- **Internalisation**. People come to accept that the majority view is the correct one.

Post-experimental interviews suggested Asch's participants had complied compared to Sherif's participants who seemed to have internalised the group view.

6 Ethical considerations

Asch's study used *deception*, so the participants could not give *informed consent* and may not have felt *free to withdraw*. He *debriefed* them afterwards but, given that many of them seemed to find the situation unpleasant, it is arguable that they were not fully *protected* from psychological discomfort. What do you think of the ethics of the study? Did the outcome justify the method?

DEINDIVIDUATION AND CONFORMITY

In 1973, *Philip Zimbardo* showed how taking away an individual's **personal identity** could encourage them to conform. He set up a **simulated prison** and randomly assigned a group of 25 adult male, student volunteers to role-play either guards or prisoners. The study was to last two weeks. After being 'arrested' at their homes, the prisoners were issued with a number and given a loose smock for a uniform. The guards worked shifts and had military-style uniforms, clubs, whistles, handcuffs, keys and reflective sunglasses. They were told to 'keep law and order' and that physical contact with the prisoners was forbidden. Before long, the guards and prisoners had slipped into their roles. The guards became bossy and authoritarian and the prisoners grew passive and apathetic. Some of the prisoners were released early because they developed serious signs of stress. Zimbardo stopped the study after six days because of the obvious distress prisoners were experiencing. In the careful debriefing Zimbardo carried out afterwards, guards said they had enjoyed themselves! It seemed that the loss of identity was responsible for the conforming behaviour of both prisoners and guards.

66 role-playing became a little too realistic 99

Obedience is when a person behaves in a particular way because they have been told to do so by someone else (perhaps an authority figure). Some psychologists define it as an extreme form of compliance.

66 a very well-known study 99

STANLEY MILGRAM'S 'OBEDIENCE TO AUTHORITY' STUDY

Milgram (1963) obtained 40 adult male volunteers through a newspaper advertisement asking for people to take part in a study on 'memory and learning'. They were paid $4 and their car-fare for attending. When a volunteer arrived at the lab. an elaborate deception began:

- The participant was introduced to 'Mr Wallace' who was said to be another volunteer. He was, in fact, a stooge.

- The participant and Mr Wallace drew lots to decide who would be the teacher and who would be the learner. This was rigged so that the participant was the teacher.
- Mr Wallace was seated in a chair and his arms strapped to electrodes.
- From an adjoining room, the participant had to teach Mr Wallace some simple word associations. The participant was to use a special shock generator to give Mr Wallace an electric shock of increasing intensity for every wrong answer. In fact no shocks were given but Mr Wallace groaned and shouted with increasing distress with every one.
- The shocks went up to 450v but Mr Wallace made no sound after 315v.
- Whenever the participant became concerned and asked what to do, the experimenter was ready with some verbal prods such as 'Please go on'. Many of the participants seemed to find the procedures very distressing.
- 62.5% of the participants were prepared to obey instructions to go right up to 450v.

Variations on the original research

1. The study was repeated in a rundown office because it was thought the awe-inspiring university setting of the original study might have increased obedience. Only 47.5% of participants continued to 450v suggesting the setting is important.
2. Bringing the learner closer *decreased* obedience but even when the participant had to force the learner's hand on to a shock plate, obedience rate was still 30%.
3. If the participant was paired with another (stooge) teacher who threw the switches on the generator, obedience *rose* to 92.5%.
4. If the participant was teamed with two other (stooge) teachers, who dropped out early on, only 10% of the participants went on to the end.
5. The greater the distance of the experimenter from the participant, the less obedience occurred, e.g. if the experimenter gave instructions by telephone, obedience was only 20.5%.
6. In a study with 40 women participants, the obedience rate was 65%, similar to the men.

Evaluation of Milgram's research

1. Were Milgram's participants *really* deceived? Milgram thinks they were. From observing their stress and the debriefing afterwards, he was convinced the deception had worked.
2. Did the study tell us anything about obedience in *real-life* settings? *Hofling* (1966) used 22 wards of private psychiatric hospitals to test this. Boxes of so-called 'Astrofen' capsules were placed in the wards. Nurses on duty received a telephone call from 'Dr Smith' instructing them to give 20mg of Astrofen to his patient, Mr Jones. Dr Smith said he would sign the authorisation when he arrived on the ward in about ten minutes time. Out of 22 nurses, 21 obeyed the instruction even though:

- Dr Smith was unknown to them;
- Astrofen boxes were labelled 'maximum daily dose 10mg';
- They should only give drugs on receipt of written authority.

Real-life settings also involve complex relationships between the authority and obedient person. *Staub* (1990) considers that bystanders who are passive and who tolerate authority contribute as much to the effect as the authority itself, e.g. in allowing wartime atrocities to take place.

3. Do the findings *apply cross-culturally*? It is very difficult to compare studies because they often use different kinds of participants or 'learners'. However in a study in Australia, *Kilham and Mann* (1974) found 40% of male and 16% of female students were obedient. In Spain, *Miranda et al.* (1981) found over 90% obedience in students. Other findings vary between these two extremes.
4. Was the study ethically acceptable? *Diana Baumrind* (1964) criticised Milgram's research for deceiving the participants and causing them unacceptable amounts of distress. The prods to keep going could be seen as not allowing participants the right to withdraw. Milgram replied that:

- He had **piloted** his research design beforehand by asking fourteen psychology students and 40 professors what 100 participants might do in such a study. They estimated that most would stop about half-way through.
- He claimed people could withdraw if they wished.
- He went to great lengths to debrief the participants. Indeed, a follow-up a year later showed no lasting damage had been done. Many participants said they were glad to have taken part and had learned something of value about themselves.

5 ▷ EMPATHY, ALTRUISM AND BYSTANDER BEHAVIOUR

THE DEVELOPMENT OF EMPATHY

Empathy is being able to understand how someone else might feel in a particular situation (as opposed to *sympathy* in which you feel concern for someone else as well as being able to empathise). *Hoffman* (1981) has suggested that empathy develops in four main stages:

1. **Global empathy**. In about the first year of life, an infant may match the emotions it sees others express, e.g. crying when someone else does so.
2. **Egocentric empathy**. From about 12 to 18 months, the child may still mirror others' feelings but will also try to help, e.g. by offering something that they find comforting themselves, e.g. a toy or sweet.
3. **Empathy for another's feelings**. At about 2–3 years, a child will still mirror feelings to some extent but will offer non-egocentric comfort, i.e. to suit the other rather than themselves. Children become aware of an increasingly wide range of emotions and realise that others do not always want help.
4. **Empathy for another's life condition**. In late childhood or adolescence, the child can begin to appreciate another's general plight. As well as empathising with the immediate feelings, they can see it in a wider sense and will feel more strongly. For example, if another's sadness follows a tragedy, the child realises it is likely to last longer and be distressing. At this stage, they also know a person may hide their feelings.

ALTRUISM AND BYSTANDER BEHAVIOUR

Eisenberg (1990) defines **altruism** as 'intentional, voluntary behaviour designed to benefit another'. (To behave altruistically it is obviously important to have developed at least some degree of empathy!) Some psychologists doubt that there is such a thing as pure altruism arguing that there is always a pay-off somewhere. Many studies have tried to identify the circumstances under which people will be altruistic. One fruitful area of research is into bystander behaviour, i.e. whether people do something when they see someone in need or just walk on by. The latter is known as 'bystander apathy'.

❝❝ 'bystander apathy' ❞❞

The case of Kitty Genovese (1964)

Research interest in bystander apathy is said to have begun after a newspaper report of the brutal murder of 28-year-old Kitty Genovese in New York who was walking back to her home in the early hours of one morning. Her killer stabbed her repeatedly, was frightened off and returned twice more to stab her again over a period of 35 minutes. The incident was witnessed by no fewer than 38 people before someone eventually called the police.

Research studies into bystander apathy

1 **'A Lady in Distress...'** *Latane and Rodin* (1969). Volunteer male college students were asked to sit in a waiting-room and fill in a questionnaire. Meanwhile, the female psychologist looking after them went into an adjoining room. Shortly, participants heard sounds indicating that she had climbed on to a chair and fallen off, hurting her foot in the process. 70% of participants who were alone went to her aid but if participants were with another person (a stooge) who did nothing, only 20% helped. The inactivity of the other 'bystander' appeared to be inhibiting. Participants looked to others to help them work out what to do and saw no reaction at all so they, too, decided not to act. Psychologists have called this **pluralistic ignorance**.

2 **'Good Samaritanism. An underground phenomenon?'** *Piliavin et al.* (1969). One reason why people fail to help others might be that they can walk away from the

situation. In this study, bystanders could not avoid an emergency because they were in a train carriage on the New York subway. An adult male staged a collapse and the number of helpers was noted. The person who collapsed:

- was either *black* or *white*;
- sometimes smelt of *alcohol*;
- sometimes *bled* from the mouth;
- sometimes had a cane and appeared to be *disabled*;
- sometimes had a disfiguring *birthmark*.

In general, about 60% of collapses received help with the number of bystanders having little effect. Other findings included:

- males helped more often than females;
- the invalid received more help than the 'drunk' (95% vs 50%);
- 'drunks' received more help from members of their own race;
- blood and the birthmark slowed helping down but did not stop it.

3 Laboratory vs a real-life setting. *Latané and Elman* (1970) arranged for participants to be in a psychologist's office where they witnessed a theft of money. 52% of participants who were alone at the time claimed to have seen nothing but only 25% waiting with a stooge, who did not speak up, said they'd seen nothing. In an off-licence, the theft of a crate of beer was staged. 65% of lone witnesses reported it to the shopkeeper and 56% of witnesses paired with a stooge reported it.

When do people intervene?

Tedeschi et al. (1985) suggest that the decision to intervene is a five stage process. You must:

1 Notice the event. People may fail to act because an event has not attracted their attention or they pretend not to see it. In a study by *Latané and Darley* (1968) experimenters pumped harmless 'smoke' into a room where participants were filling in a questionnaire. They could hardly have failed to notice it but it still took them longer to move when a second impassive stooge was in the room.

2 Interpret it as an emergency. Perhaps the participants in the above study did not move because they thought the smoke was harmless or they saw through the ruse. It helps if a person needing help can make their need clear to others. Studies show that a woman being attacked by a man is more likely to receive help if she shouts 'I don't know you!' at the attacker, otherwise people tend to see it as a domestic row and stay away.

3 Accept personal responsibility. Lab. studies suggest that the presence of others brings about **diffusion of responsibility** and makes help less likely. *Moriarty* (1975), however, found responsibility could be *given* to total strangers. An experimenter sunbathing on a beach asked a neighbouring sunbather either (a) for a match or (b) to 'watch my things' for a while. The experimenter then left. A stooge then stole a radio from the experimenter's blanket. 20% of group (a) people challenged the thief compared to 95% of group (b) people.

4 Know what to do. People tend not to involve themselves if they do not know how to help. *Huston et al.* (1981) found that **heroes** who intervened in muggings or robberies were more likely to have been victims themselves or witnessed crimes. They had taken the time to think about what they would do in such circumstances. Large charities often encourage donations by showing what a certain amount of money can achieve so people know what to contribute.

5 Decide to act. Even when you reach this stage, you may not help for fear of embarrassment or risk to yourself. Research has also shown:

- people in a hurry tend to be less likely to help;
- people feeling guilty or good are more likely to help;
- contact with the victim beforehand, no matter how brief, tends to increase helping.

Piliavin's Arousal: Cost–reward model of helping (1969)

66 this model draws all the important factors together 99

Piliavin says that to see another in need of help creates **physiological arousal** but whether we intervene depends on weighing up the **costs and rewards** of helping or not helping. A simplified version of this model appears in Table 6.3.

	Cost of helping is high	Cost of helping is low
Cost of not helping is high Cost of not helping is low	Likelihood of help is **fairly high** but indirect, e.g. call the police Likelihood of helping is **low**. People may escape the situation reason it away.	Likelihood of helping is **high** and helping is likely to be direct Likelihood of helping is **fairly high**. People may think the person needing help will be able to cope. It may depend on social norms (see below).

Table 6.3 Piliavin's Arousal: Cost–reward model of helping

SOCIAL NORMS AND HELPING

Much social behaviour seems to be guided by unspoken rules about how one should react to a given situation. *Tedeschi et al.* (1985) describe the following:

1 The norm of reciprocity. This is when we feel we should help those who help us. This seems to be *universal* across cultures. It is as if we do not like to be indebted to others and always need to return a favour. In laboratory studies people tend to help others *in proportion* to the help they received from them. In real life, we may not feel the need to reciprocate if a gift is freely given or if we feel the other was forced to give.

2 The norm of social responsibility. This means that people who are more fortunate and advantaged feel *morally obliged* to help those who are less fortunate or in greater need. *Barnes et al.* (1979) found that students were more likely to help fellow students with their work if the need were due to lack of ability. People needing help because of laziness, were less likely to receive it. The norm is most powerful when:

- the need is very obvious;
- the needy person is not responsible for their situation;
- the costs to the helper are low.

3 The norm of equality and equity. The amount of help given often depends on ideas of fairness. How should it be shared out? The equality norm requires that everyone receives *equal shares*, e.g. a tutor might resolve to give exactly the same amount of extra help to everyone in a class. The equity norm operates when people receive what they *deserve*. The tutor might decide to spend more time with diligent, hard-working students and less with lazy ones.

Linked to all these norms is the just world hypothesis which is the idea that people get what they deserve and should receive less help if they can be held responsible for their predicament.

PERSONAL SPACE

Bell et al. (1990) define personal space as 'an invisible boundary surrounding us into which others may not trespass'. They liken it to an **expandable bubble** which is flexible and moves with us. *Invasions* of the space lead to withdrawal or other ways of evading the intruder.

Personal space has three main functions:

66 we need personal space 99

1. **to protect our well-being**, e.g. by helping us to avoid over-stimulation, over-arousal or stress caused by others being too close;
2. **to help us control aggression** – this is an idea borrowed from the ethologists who think the need to space ourselves out has evolved because it helps us to avoid aggressive encounters;
3. **to smooth social interaction** – people recognise each other's personal space signals and know what behaviour is expected or permitted.

Zones of personal space

Hall (1963) identified four social distances at which people may operate:

1. **Intimate distance** (0–1½ ft), e.g. for intimate contact and contact sports.
2. **Personal distance** (1½–4 ft), e.g. for contact with friends and other everyday contacts.
3. **Social distance** (4–12 ft), e.g. for impersonal, business-like contacts.
4. **Public distance** (12 ft and over), e.g. for public speaking or performing.

Culture and personal space

Hall's zones are based on studying North Americans. They live in a **low-contact culture** as do North Europeans. **Contact cultures** permit smaller distances between people. They include Mediterranean, Muslim and Latin American cultures.

Other factors affecting personal space

● Females interact more closely with liked than with disliked people. Males do not show this pattern.
● Female–female pairs interact more closely than male-male pairs.
● Adult norms of personal space take time to develop. Children seem to have learned them by the time they reach puberty.
● Schizophrenics, highly anxious people and violent prisoners need more personal space.

Space invasions

Failure to obey the rules of personal space can lead to confusion and embarrassment, e.g. across cultures where people have different norms. An invasion usually causes a person to react by reducing eye-contact, turning away, building barriers or withdrawing altogether. Here are two studies of space invasion:

1. **Onset and persistence of urination** (*Middlemist et al.* 1976). An experimenter occupied a toilet cubicle next to a row of three urinals. Using a periscope, he timed how long it took males to begin to urinate and how long they urinated for. Men using the closer urinal were slower to start urinating and urinated less than those further away.
2. *Felipe and Sommer's* **library study** (1966). Female participants were studying at a library table with six chairs on each side. There were two empty chairs to each side of the participant and an empty one opposite. An experimenter approached then did one of three things:

● sat next to the participant and moved closer
● sat in the next chair but one
● left two chairs in between
● sat opposite.

Participants were more likely to erect barriers, move away or shift their own chair in the first condition than in the others.

TERRITORIES AND TERRITORIALITY

Territory is a term borrowed from **ethology**. For both animals and humans it is a **defensible space** but the meaning of this applied to animals and humans is different. For animals: 'a territory is an area of space which is held and defended by a solitary animal, or a family group, and in which food is found and young are reared' (*Gross* 1992). For humans it is: 'a relatively stationary, visibly bounded area which is home centred' (*Bell et al.* 1990). For humans, territoriality is:

'a set of behaviours an organism or group exhibits based on perceived ownership of physical space' (*Bell et al.* 1990).

There are many grades of human territory ranging from a chair in a pub or a bedroom to the 'home' end at a sports ground or a sales rep's 'patch'. Imagine life without territories! Bell *et al.* classify human territories as follows:

- primary territory, e.g. home or office. It is 'owned' and highly personal. Unwelcome intrusions are serious;
- secondary territory, e.g. classroom. It is not owned but can be personalised. Some control over unwelcome intruders is possible;
- public territory, e.g. park or beach. It is not owned but can be temporarily personalised. It is difficult to control intrusions.

There is some evidence that **dominant individuals** are more territorial. If some parts of the territory are more *desirable* than others, they take the best bits for themselves. In more *uniform* territories, they appear less territorial because they roam more. If territory boundaries are unclear, disputes over territory can be very bloody. Groups who establish clear boundaries early on are less likely to get into disputes because the chances of intrusion are less.

Marking territories

Sommer (1969) tested the effect of different **territory markers** on keeping intruders out of a territory when the owner left. He found very *personal* markers like coats or diaries were more effective than less personal ones like newspapers or library books. Wall *graffiti* can act as a special kind of gangland territorial marker. Spraying over someone else's graffiti is a good way of contesting territory!

PRIVACY

Defending a territory or personal space can provide a person with opportunities for privacy. *Deaux et al.* (1993) define privacy as 'the extent to which one perceives control over contact with, or information about, one's self or group'.

Privacy is important because:

- We can keep personal control. People with private information about us are in a powerful position. They could even blackmail us!
- It allows us to relax and be ourselves. There is no audience to react to or impression to manage.

Altman's theory of privacy regulation

Altman (1975) suggests:

- we like a certain amount of contact with others but too much is stressful;
- our need for privacy varies from total isolation to complete openness and changes all the time;
- we regulate it in similar ways to regulating personal space and territory, e.g. by our non-verbal messages, markers or how we use our environment (e.g. shutting doors).

Zimring (1982) classifies spaces as follows:

- **public spaces** – e.g. pavements, shopping areas, parks and thoroughfares;
- **semi-public spaces** – e.g. restaurants and foyers;
- **semi-private spaces** – e.g. social clubs, dormitories;
- **private spaces** – e.g. bedrooms, bathrooms.

Architecture can have a significant effect on people's need for privacy. **Open-plan offices**, for example, should aid communication and encourage co-action but some studies show up to two-thirds of people claim it *spoils concentration*, is *noisy* and that there is *nowhere for confidential conversations*. Social influence research on co-action shows that open-plan arrangements might enhance the performance of simple repetitive tasks but upset performance of complex tasks.

7 CROWDS AND CROWDING

❝ a crowd is not always crowding ❞

Deaux et al. (1993) define crowding as 'a form of stress resulting from excessive, unwanted social interaction that may accompany densely populated environments'.

Crowding is **subjective** and **psychological**. What is crowding to one person may not be so to another. It also has much to do with how we perceive the crowd. A few people may seem crowding, a large number may not. There is no simple link between *numbers* of people in a space (**population density**) and *feelings* of being crowded. *Freedman* (1975) suggests crowds intensify emotions so a happy crowd can make you feel extra happy and an angry one make you feel extra angry.

Calhoun's animal research

Calhoun (1969) linked **high population** in Norway rats to a number of problems. He created a four compartment rat **universe** and provided rats with plenty of food, water and nesting materials. The compartments had the same things in them except some were more easily accessible than others because of the number of ramps connecting them. Rats bred rapidly increasing the original population of 48 to 80. Conditions then *deteriorated* markedly:

- nest building, courting, mating and rearing of young decreased;
- social organisation began to break down, e.g. inhibitions against aggression decreased;
- up to 75% of the young failed to survive.

Crowding and humans

It is tempting to draw parallels with Calhoun's universe and densely populated residential areas for humans but human behaviour is much more complicated. We have already seen the negative effects of others in earlier sections mentioning deindividuation, social contagion and bystander apathy. *Evans* (1989) suggests another effect. He says that crowding disrupts people's **social support systems** (i.e. the comfort provided by friends and family) because people react to crowding by withdrawal and so cut themselves off from support.

To test his ideas, Evans interviewed 175 heads of household in India. He measured:

- the number of people per room in their houses;
- their socioeconomic status;
- their feelings of being crowded;
- the amount of social support they received;
- any psychological symptoms.

Evans found that, as density of the population in a house increased, social support decreased and the number of psychological symptoms increased.

In student residences, *Baum and Valins* (1977) compared 17×2 person room dormitories (**corridors**) with 3×2 person room dormitories (**suites**). Corridor dormitory students complained more of unwanted social contacts and a desire to avoid others. They spent less time there and had less social support at the end of the first term than suite dormitory students.

In prisons, open dormitories create far more negative feelings than cells, although overcrowding in a cell brings problems of its own. When rehousing people, *Freeman* (1974) found that moving to better quality accommodation was no help if the design of the housing area did not allow for the right level and kind of interaction with neighbours.

The effects of crowding on people

Remember, there are wide individual differences in responses to crowds.

1. **Affect (mood or feelings).** Feeling crowded can lead to negative feelings of over-arousal, information overload and stress. There do seem to be some sex differences though. *Freedman et al.* (1972) found males feel more negative in high density than low density conditions but for females it is the opposite. They suggested females like others' company more and that males have larger personal spaces.
2. **Physiological responses.** *Evans* (1975) showed people have higher heart-rates and blood-pressure in high density areas than in low density ones.
3. **Illness.** There is some association here but it is complicated. *Cochrane* (1995) reminds us that it is the subjective experience of feeling crowded that matters not actual density of a population. *Freeman* (1984) suggests excessive social interaction leads to information overload. If we have no way of cutting this down, we experience feelings of stress and may become ill.
4. **Attraction.** People tend to feel less attracted to others if they are feeling crowded but this effect is more pronounced for men. It may be that females find it easier to share their distress at being crowded with others and so have more support. In studies where crowded females were not allowed to communicate they found crowding much more unpleasant.

5. **Withdrawal**. Interactions between people become much less frequent and intimate in high density settings.
6. **Prosocial behaviour**. This tends to decrease as density increases.
7. **Aggression**. It has been suggested that aggression increases if density is high and that the effect is more marked if resources are scarce.

8 THE LAW OF SOCIAL IMPACT

To finish this chapter, *Latané* (1981) proposed the law of social impact to account for the effect of all the social forces on individuals that we have discussed here. It has three factors which all interact with each other:
1. **Strength**. The impact of others will be greater if they are experts or significant to the individual in some other way.
2. **Number**. In general, the impact of others increases the more of them there are. This is true up to a point and then the effect tails off.
3. **Immediacy**. The closer people are, the more effect their presence will have.

EXAMINATION QUESTIONS

1. MEG sample paper 4 (Higher), Option 3 Sources A and B

Spend 25 minutes on this question

Option 3: Social and Environmental Psychology

*Answer **all** the questions in Sources A and B in this Option*

Source A: Space Invasions

When another person invades our personal space, we may feel stress and discomfort and may even try to escape from the situation. One study on the effects of invading a person's personal space was carried out in a hospital. A 'stranger' (who was actually a confederate of the researcher) approached patients while they were alone in the television room. The 'stranger' sat down six inches away from the patient. A control group of patients did not have their space invaded by the 'stranger'. The researcher recorded how many patients in each group attempted to move away. The results are shown below.

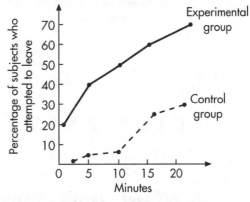

(a) What is the difference between personal space and territory? [2]

(b) Use the graph to answer the following questions.
   (i) What percentage of the experimental group attempted to leave after 15 minutes? [1]
   (ii) What percentage of the control group attempted to leave after 20 minutes? [1]

(c) Give two other factors which might affect the amount of personal space that we maintain between ourselves and others. [4]

(d) Give one ethical problem with this study. [2]

(e) Give one practical application of the research on personal space. [2]

Source B: Conformity

A psychologist decided to measure conformity in a laboratory setting. His experiment was based on a visual illusion called the 'autokinetic effect'. Participants were shown a spot of light in a completely dark room and asked to say how much the light moved (the light in fact was stationary, it only appeared to move). When the participants were tested on their own, the estimates varied a lot. However, when the participants made estimates in a small group, they changed their estimates so they were more similar to the estimates of the other people in the group. The psychologist concluded that a group norm had been established. The results are shown below.

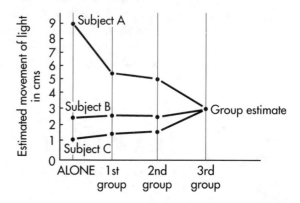

Experiment on conformity

    (f) Give an example in everyday life when conformity could be dangerous. [2]
    (g) According to the graph, what was the group norm estimate? [1]
    (h) Give **one** factor which might influence whether or not a person conforms. [2]
    (i) Describe how cultural background could affect levels of conformity. [4]
    (j) Evaluate the contribution of the research on conformity and obedience. How useful is this research in helping us to understand how other people may influence our behaviour? [9]

[Total 30 marks]
(MEG)

2. SEG sample papers (Foundation Tier)

    Spend 35 minutes on this question
    (a) Explain, using an example, the meaning of altruism. [6]
    (b) Describe **one** psychological study of altruistic behaviour. [8]
    (c) Explain **two** things which may affect whether or not one person helps another. [16]

[Total 30 marks]
(SEG)

TUTOR ANSWERS

1. MEG sample paper 4 (Higher), Option 3 Sources A and B

Space invasions

    (a) Personal space is an 'invisible bubble' into which others may not enter. The bubble is expandable and we carry it around with us. A territory is a fixed, defensible space. For some animals it could be an area of land. For humans territory is usually home-based.
    (b) (i) 60%
        (ii) 29%.
    (c) Personal space may be affected by the kind of relationship we have with someone. Hall thought we had different zones of personal space for different kinds

of relationship so that we allow intimate friends and medical doctors into the 0–18 inch zone but work colleagues are kept 4–12 feet away. Culture is another factor. North Americans and North Europeans live in low-contact cultures but Mediterraneans, Muslims and Latin Americans live in contact cultures and allow closer contact with each other.

(d) The invasion of personal space could have been distressing for patients so it could be argued that the researchers did not protect them enough especially as there is no mention of the researcher trying to debrief the patients afterwards.

(e) Workers complain that open-plan offices are noisy, spoil concentration and do not allow for private conversations. This could be taken into account when designing the layout of office space. People who have to work there will be happier if they have a space to defend.

Conformity

(f) Conformity could be dangerous if a person went along with the group just to be accepted by it and so ended up doing something risky such as taking drugs.

(g) The group norm was that the estimated distance that the light moved was 3 cm.

(h) The size of the group might affect how likely someone is to conform. In his line-judging study, Asch found that conformity peaked at about 30% of responses when the participant was with three or more others. There was less conformity with smaller groups.

(i) In Lebanon, Hong Kong and Brazil the rate of conforming responses was similar to Asch's (1956) figure of 30%. However, in the Bantu of Zimbabwe it was 51%. Nicholson found much lower rates of conformity than Asch in British and American participants in 1985. These findings suggest that conformity rate varies both with cultural background and with time.

(j) Asch's research suggests a number of factors that may affect how others may influence our tendency to conform. In his original line-judging study he found about 30% conforming responses but this figure was affected by group size, task difficulty, having and losing allies, who the other group members were and whether the participant could respond privately or had to call out the answer. Crutchfield used Asch's method to test larger numbers of participants on a wider range of tasks and he found conformity rates differed according to the type of question asked although the overall conformity rate was still 38%. Moscovici also found a minority could influence a larger group of participants if the minority were consistent.

Research studies like these have been criticised for telling us little about real-life conformity. People rarely have to speak out if they are in doubt. They can usually discuss things with others and find allies among them. Many of the tasks participants had to do were trivial and they were unlikely to meet other group members or the experimenter again so they may have behaved in uncharacteristic ways. We are also unlikely to find out their real reasons for conforming, e.g. were they showing compliance, true conformity, informational conformity, or ingratiational conformity? Finally, there are ethical issues to consider as participants were deceived and, sometimes, upset by the procedures.

Milgram showed how authority figures could influence a research participant to give electric shocks to another person while teaching that person a simple word task. (The study involved elaborate deception of the participants and no shocks were actually given.) Milgram found that 62.5% of participants were prepared to obey the researcher by giving shocks to the other person long past the point where he or she had stopped responding to questions. Participants obeyed less when they were in close contact with the other person and more if the electric shocks were given by someone else. Stooges who dropped out of the experiment seemed to encourage the participant to do the same. Milgram suggested that it was a natural human tendency to obey authority but that we could be encouraged to disobey by the example of others.

Some critics were concerned that Milgram's study was unethical in the use of deception and in causing distress to participants. Others wonder if it tells us anything about real-life obedience in other settings. Hofling, for example, found an even higher rate of conformity in nurses instructed to give a drug to a patient by a bogus doctor. Cross-culturally, wide variations in obedience rates have been found using Milgram's procedure suggesting that tendency to obey is not the same everywhere. Research with women participants shows similar results to those found with men. More recently, a useful development from early obedience research has been to consider the role of bystanders in tolerating powerful authority figures. Staub (1990) thinks passive bystanders are as important as the authority in bringing obedience about.

In conclusion, studies have told us much about the ways in which others can influence conformity and obedience rates in the laboratory but there is some doubt about whether such studies tell us much about these things in real-life settings or about different kinds of participants to the ones used.

2. SEG sample paper (Foundation Tier) Section E

(a) Altruism has been defined as 'intentional, voluntary behaviour designed to benefit another'. We usually think of it as selflessness or self-sacrifice for the good of another that has no pay-off for the altruistic person. In both animals and humans, parenting often seems to involve altruism on the part of the parents who might put themselves at risk for the good of their young. Some people argue that there is no such thing as truly altruistic behaviour and that there is always a pay-off somewhere. A person who donates bone marrow to a relative could be said to be behaving altruistically, however the bone-marrow donor could be acting for the rewarding attention it attracts, the thanks of other family members, time off work etc.

(b) Piliavin *et al.* used the real world setting of the New York subway to see if train passengers, who would not be able to walk away from an emergency, would help a fellow traveller who collapsed. The person who collapsed was an adult, male stooge. He was either black or white. Sometimes he smelt of alcohol or carried a cane, bled from the mouth or had a disfiguring birthmark. About 60% of collapses received help with the number of bystanders having little effect. Males tended to help more than females, the invalid received more help than the drunk, 'drunks' received more help from their own race and blood or a birthmark slowed helping down but did not stop it.

(c) Diffusion of responsibility when others are around works against the tendency to help. This means that, when others are around we tend to take less responsibility for dealing with an emergency. If we are to help someone in need it is important to accept personal responsibility. Moriarty found he could give total strangers sunbathing on a beach personal responsibility for another's belongings. Some sunbathers were asked by an experimenter for 'a match', others to 'watch my things'. The experimenter then left and a stooge stole a radio from his blanket. Of the 'match' group only 20% challenged the thief but 95% of the other group challenged him. The 'match' group had not had to accept personal responsibility so did not act. The other group had agreed to take responsibility and acted accordingly.

Knowing what to do is also important. People may not help others in need simply because they are unsure about what to do and so, while they are considering what to do, the moment is lost. Heroes who intervene in robbings and muggings have very often been victims themselves so they have had time to think what kind of help is useful and are not as unsure as other bystanders. The effect of this is that they can act more quickly, decisively and effectively and this may have the added benefit of encouraging others to join in.

Piliavin suggested the arousal: reward–cost model to take account of all the findings about helping behaviour. Seeing others in need of help creates physiological arousal in us but our decision about whether to intervene depends on how we weigh up the rewards and cost of helping or not helping, e.g. if the cost of helping is low and the cost of not helping is high, helping is highly likely. We may be happy to give a little time (low cost) to a friend in need because the costs of not helping (losing the friend) are high.

STUDENTS' ANSWER

NEAB specimen paper (Tier Q) Question B7

Spend about 18 minutes answering this question

Read the article below and answer the questions which follow.

Street crimes must be halted

In Sheffield, petty street robberies are causing new concern. This is all the more worrying because they are not the usual assaults carried out late at night in dark streets. They are made in broad daylight in busy shopping areas and often young people are both the thieves and the victims.

In recent weeks there have been several cases of teenagers stopped by gangs of youths – sometimes girls – and forced to hand over money or jewellery after threats of violence.

So far there have been no serious injuries but they are signs of a dangerous trend that needs stamping out as quickly as possible.

As so often happens, passers-by failed to help those in trouble.

One type of social influence is the **bystander effect**.

(a) Explain **two** reasons psychologists might give why passers-by fail to help in such situations. [4]

❝❝ Expand on this

They might not have noticed what was happening. They might not have realised it was an emergency. If people being robbed only scream passers by might think it's fun or a game. If the person shouted 'Help! I'm being robbed!' they might get some help.

3/4 ❞❞

(b) Apart from the bystander effect, discuss at least **two** other ways in which the presence of others has been shown to influence the behaviour of individuals. Use psychological theories and evidence in your answer. [10]

Social loafing. This is when people working in a group may not pull their weight. If people pull on a rope they can pull with a certain force but in a group they don't pull so hard. They seem to let others take over. If each person's effort can be identified, social loafing stops. It helps if they can be given responsibility for a part of the task so they can't hide.

❝❝ full marks so far ❞❞

Conformity. This is when someone goes along with the group even though they might not really want to. Asch did an experiment where a real subject was put into a group of stooges. They were shown a card with a line on it and had to pick the line that matched from another card with three lines on it. Sometimes the stooges deliberately gave the wrong answer. Asch found that 30% of subjects would go along with it. They seemed to give in so as not to lose face.

❝❝ 30% of answers not subjects

8/10 ❞❞

[*Total 14 marks*]
(NEAB)

❝❝ 11/14 Some good information that would benefit from expansion and more examples, possibly from real-life settings ❞❞

A Review Sheet for this chapter can be found on pp. 237-8.

ATTACHMENT

GETTING STARTED

We take it for granted in our culture that the development of attachment (a secure emotional bond between a child and its mother) is vital if the child is to grow up psychologically healthy. A little thought will make it immediately obvious that this is a situation which not all children experience. For one thing, not all children are brought up by their mothers. There may be several caregivers. For another, even if the child and mother do have plenty of time together there may be all kinds of reasons why attachment does not happen. How much does this matter to a child in the short and long term? This chapter sets out to show you the current thinking on these issues.

Attachment is an important topic on all the GCSE syllabuses but MEG and NEAB students could omit section 7.7 on divorce and MEG students can also omit section 7.8.

NB In the older research literature the word 'mother' is used on the assumption that it was usually the mother who cared for children. Nowadays, such an idea is out of date which is why the term 'caregiver' is used for more recent studies. Where you do see the term mother it will be when the original research actually did study mothers.

ESSENTIAL PRINCIPLES

Maccoby (1980) defines attachment as 'a relatively enduring emotional tie to a specific other person'.

When we attach or **bond** to another person, we can usually stay attached to them through periods of time apart but the attachment can be damaged or disappear altogether which is why it is said to be only 'relatively enduring'. The tie is made on an emotional level so we are affected emotionally if it is damaged or broken. Often the attachment will be two-way – the child and caregiver are attached to each other.

Babies seem to arrive in the world prepared to make attachments. Their appearance and behaviour help to keep caregivers close to them so attachment can happen. This makes good biological sense because human infants are relatively helpless and dependent on others for survival. Some things which make the infant attractive to caregivers are present immediately, others mature in the first weeks or months of life.

The infant's physical features

Infants of many species, including humans, have physical features which encourage caring behaviour from adults. The human baby's head is large in proportion to its body, its eyes and cheeks are relatively large, its nose and mouth small, its movements jerky and uncoordinated (spastic) and its cry is hard to ignore.

> ❝ babies can draw adults to them ❞

The infant's behaviour (sociability)

As well as looking and sounding right, there are many things the infant *can do* to encourage bond formation. *Schaffer* (1971) calls this ability to engage in social interactions with others '**sociability**'. What does it involve?

1. Face recognition. *Fantz* (1961) showed how infants seem to have an early (or even innate) ability to recognise faces. He used 49 infants aged between 4 days and 6 months old and found they would gaze at face-like patterns more than at patterns of equal complexity. *Barrera and Maurer* (1981) showed that, by 3 months, infants could distinguish a photo of their mother's face from strangers' faces. Infants also focus best at about the distance the mother's face would be from its eyes while it was breast feeding which should give plenty of opportunities for learning to recognise her.

2. Voice recognition. Research has shown that infants show more interest in human speech than in other sounds of similar pitch. *DeCasper and Fifer* (1980) showed infants could distinguish their mother's voice from a stranger's voice after only twelve hours of post-natal contact (but remember, babies can hear the mother's voice while in the womb).

3. Social smiles. Infants produce their first smiles within a few weeks of birth. At first they have no experience of the effect this will have but soon learn how positive the caregivers' reactions will be. Caregivers respond to the infant's early smiles as if the infant *meant* to communicate.

4. Social responsiveness. Infants quickly learn that their needs will be attended to if they cry so they tend to respond to being attended to by quietening. This is rewarding for the caregiver who is likely to react more swiftly and positively to a responsive infant giving plenty of opportunities for attachment to occur.

5. Taking turns. *Stern* (1977) showed that, as early as 3 months of age, infants can take turns in '**conversations**' with the mother. When she talks, the infant looks at her face and appears to listen attentively to her. The infant will then take a turn, moving and vocalising and then pausing so that she can take another turn. At first, the mother seems to do most of the work but they read each other's signals increasingly well until the baby makes just as much effort. Conversations move along like a complicated dance. The mother and infant have established a skill known as '**interactional synchrony**'.

Does early contact matter?

compare this to current hospital practices

Klaus and Kennel (1979) looked at the role of extended early contact using 28 mother and new-born baby pairs. Fourteen of the mothers had the (then standard) experience of holding the baby immediately after birth and then not seeing it for six to twelve hours. They would then see the baby for four-hourly feeds. The remaining 14 mothers saw their babies for about an hour after the birth and then had an extra five hours of contact with the infant each day.

Up to one year later, Klaus and Kennel claimed that the **extended contact** mothers behaved differently from the **standard contact** group, e.g. they soothed their babies more and had more physical contact with them. The extra early contact seemed to have made a difference to the *intensity* of the bond. However, 1980s research showed *little* or *no* effect and all studies show *small* or *non-existent* long-term effects. The question remains whether there is a **sensitive period** for attachment. (See Bowlby's work later in this chapter.)

Stages in the development of attachments

Bowlby (1969) described five stages in the development of attachments:
1. In the first few months of life the infant is generally socially responsive to others but does not show any particular preferences.
2. At about 5 to 7 months, the infant starts to show preference for certain individuals, e.g. smiling more at the regular caregiver. This is the first obvious sign that attachments are forming.
3. At about 7 to 9 months, the infant tries to stay close to the caregiver and will usually be upset if separated. Fear of strangers also appears.
4. At about 2 to 3 years of age, the child will be able to understand and tolerate separation a little better especially if it is explained and understood.
5. Attachment will gradually lessen as the child grows older. By school age quite long periods of separation will be possible without bad effects. In teenage years and adulthood new attachments will form until eventually the individual becomes an attachment figure for their own children.

---

3 > THEORIES OF ATTACHMENT

PSYCHOANALYTIC THEORY

feeding matters

Freudians think that activities essential to the infant's survival are at the root of attachment. Feeding is a very important part of the process. How the caregiver handles the infant's feeding needs, and the atmosphere of feeding, affect the quality of the attachment. If feeding is a happy and satisfying experience, the infant will become securely, emotionally attached to the satisfying breast and, eventually, to the mother herself.

LEARNING THEORY

another explanation of why feeding matters

Learning theorists agree with psychoanalysts that the feeding situation is important but for different reasons. Feeding is **reinforcing** because it reduces unpleasant hunger and is associated with other rewarding experiences like feeling warm and comfortable and receiving social stimulation. Things that satisfy needs directly, such as food, are known as **primary reinforcers**. With time, the mother becomes a **secondary reinforcer** because she is regularly associated with the arrival of primary reinforcers. The infant becomes attached to her because she meets its needs. She becomes attached to it because it responds positively to her caregiving.

ETHOLOGICAL THEORY

Influenced by **ethologists**, who study behaviour of animals in their natural environments, *Bowlby* (1958) thought that attachment resulted from instinctive responses which were necessary for survival. The infant's appearance and sociable behaviours are biologically designed to encourage closeness and caregiving in the parent. Attachment is a two-way process which is most likely to happen during a **sensitive period** in the infant's first months of life. This is rather like the **imprinting** process seen in some other mammals and birds. The feeding situation is just one of many opportunities for attachment to take place; it is not necessarily the most important one.

The attachment process and bonding are internal processes which we cannot see directly. The only way we can know if attachment has occurred is to watch the infant's *behaviour* for clues. A way of testing the strength and security of attachments was devised by *Ainsworth* (1978). She called it the **strange situation** assuming that, once an infant is attached, it will use the mother as a base to explore from but will also show fear of strangers. The procedure involves the mother, the infant and a stranger and takes place in a setting new to the infant where its reactions can be filmed. It involves a series of three-minute episodes in which the mother and stranger come and go from the room. Sometimes, the infant is with both of them, sometimes with one of them and sometimes alone. Ainsworth identified three types of attachment after testing a group of 1 to 2 year olds:

- **Type A. Anxious-avoidant**, 15% of the sample. These infants seemed to be indifferent to the mother. They were not obviously affected by their mothers' presence or absence. They generally disliked being left alone but could be comforted equally by either the stranger or the mother.
- **Type B. Securely attached**, 70% of the sample. These infants liked to stay close to the mother when playing. They were distressed when she left but were quickly comforted when she returned. The stranger could give some comfort but generally, infants treated the mother and stranger very differently.
- **Type C. Anxious-resistant**, 15% of the sample. These infants seem to have mixed feelings towards the mother (they were **ambivalent**). They sought contact with her and then resisted it. They also resisted contact with strangers. They often did not settle happily to play but kept glancing anxiously at the mother.

The percentages given above were taken from US studies, but what happens in other cultures? A study of German infants found 40–50% Type A and a Japanese study found 35% Type C attachments. However, we have to be very careful about interpreting these findings as child-care practices differ so widely and infants' experiences of being left alone will also be very different.

WHO DOES AN INFANT ATTACH TO?

Bowlby talked of **monotropy** by which he meant that the infant shows a marked preference for one attachment figure (usually the mother). *Hartup* (1989) said infants need to make **vertical** and **horizontal attachments**, that is to parents and to siblings or peers. Clearly, many different people may care for an infant. Can attachments be shared out?

Fathers

Fathers can parent as successfully as mothers. *Lewis* (1986) provided statistics to show that fathers were more involved in many aspects of child-care in the 1980s than they were in the 1960s but the change has not been dramatic. Much depends on whether their work takes them away from the child a great deal and on the cultural setting:

- *Hewlett* (1987) studied the Aka pygmies of Central Africa where the work roles of men and women are very similar. Fathers were near their children 88% of the time but mothers still spent more time on child-care.
- In Sweden, legislation since the 1960s has been passed to encourage greater involvement of fathers with children. This has had some effect but mothers still do more housework and child-care even when both partners are working (*Hwang* 1987).

Lamb (1977) thought infants formed equally strong attachments to both mother and father in the first year of life but that the kind of relationship was different. Fathers are more of a *playmate* and mothers more of a *caregiver* to go to in times of stress, which explains the differences in the examples above.

Siblings and peers

The findings here are varied. Older siblings may sometimes become attachment figures if they spend much of their time caring for their younger brothers and sisters. When children are closer in age there may be a problem with jealousy. *Dunn and*

Kendrick (1982) studied 40 first-borns before and after the arrival of a sibling and found a wide variation in reactions. Very early on the first-borns and siblings tended to develop *strong emotional relationships* mixing love and hostility with friendship and rivalry. Their attachment to each other could be deeper and more intense than attachments to parents but Dunn and Kendrick see this as important because they are learning how to relate to and influence others.

In an extreme example of peer attachment, *Freud and Dann* (1951) studied six German-Jewish war orphans who had lived together since their first year of life. At the age of 4, they were transferred to an English nursery called **Bulldogs Bank**. At first the children were wild and destructive and hostile to adults yet caring and gentle with each other, showing a sensitivity rarely seen between such young children. After a year they had developed other attachments to adult caregivers but these relationships were never as strong as their attachment to each other.

66 infants can attach to a number of people 99

> ## 5 > ALTERNATIVE CHILD-CARE PATTERNS

DAY-CARE AND CHILDMINDING

Working parents in the UK who cannot call on family or nannies to help, will probably use one of two common alternatives:

- **Nurseries**. These can be private or run by the state. Some of them take children from babyhood until they start school, others specify a starting age. Children can attend part time or full time and are cared for alongside other children by trained nursery nurses.
- **Childminders**. These are most often mothers who care for up to two or three other children, often fitting the care around their own family life. In the UK they should be **registered**, which means that the home where a child will be cared for is checked for agreed standards of health, safety and facilities.

Most of the research on the effects of day-care has been carried out in the USA. Much concern has been expressed about whether working parents are damaging their attachment relationship with their children by not being with them until they begin school. Reassuringly, researchers in the 1980s concluded day-care would not be damaging if:

- care was of high quality;
- there was a good carer to child ratio;
- there was low staff turnover;
- there were plenty of stimulating activities.

However, in 1988, *Belsky* compared children who went into day-care for 20 hours or more per week before they were one-year-old with children who had no day-care or less than 20 hours. Using the **strange situation**, he concluded that 43% of the first group were insecurely attached compared to 26% of the second group. Should we be alarmed? We still don't know because:

- reactions to the strange situation may not tell us much about the child's general emotional security;
- children of working mothers have more separation experience to start with so are not the same as children of non-working mothers;
- there might be other important differences between families with working and non-working mothers which can account for the findings.

On childminding there have been several UK studies. *Mayall and Patrie* (1977) studied minders in London and *Bryant et al.* (1980) studied minders in Oxfordshire. Both studies found that:

- children's physical needs were adequately met;
- minders tended to put their domestic and family duties first;
- children seemed less secure in the minder's home than in their own;
- minders did not feel it necessary to develop a close bond with the children;
- children scored lower than expected on tests of language and cognitive ability.

We cannot draw any firm conclusions from this because:

- There were no matched controls of non-minded children for comparison. The standard of care in the child's own home could have been the same, better or worse.

- We don't know whether any problems that had occurred for some children were because of being minded or whether they were there already.

It is not yet clear whether childminding does cause problems for children. There are 50,000 registered childminders in the UK and, probably, three times that number who are not registered. It is not possible to make general statements about them because there are wide variations. Many parents find childminding an excellent solution to the care problem, especially for very young children. Some of the advantages include:

> 66 the effects of day-care and childminding are not fully understood yet 99

- being cared for in a home environment similar to the child's own;
- a good adult to child ratio;
- a secure daily routine for the child;
- different toys to the child's own;
- the chance to spend time with playmates of a similar age.

> 66 childminding can have distinct advantages 99

Finally, *Melhuish* (1990) compared the effects on children of care by relatives, childminding and private nursery care. The children had started the care arrangements before 9 months of age. Results showed:

- no differences in the type of attachment to the mother;
- communication abilities at 18 months were best in children cared for by relatives, followed by minded children then nursery children. By three years of age the differences had all but disappeared;
- no differences in cognitive development although nursery children showed more understanding of pro-social behaviour such as sharing and cooperation.

In conclusion, it seems there are gains and losses to be had in different kinds of care and there is no strong evidence that the effects are long lasting.

ACROSS CULTURES

Ainsworth (1967) compared Ugandan mothers with US mothers. Ugandan mothers and children have a great deal of physical contact. Infants are carried everywhere by their mothers in slings, they sleep with the mother and are typically breast fed for two years. This greater contact seems to result in more anxiety on separation and earlier fear of strangers than in US babies. Ugandan babies seem to attach earlier than babies in the Western world.

Kibbutzim are Israeli agricultural communes which try to be self-sufficient. Mothers stay with their new-born babies for a few weeks and then gradually return to full-time work. By about 1 year of age a child will be mainly cared for by a children's nurse, called a **metapelet**, in the '**Children's House**'. Children usually return to their parents at the end of the working day. They have high quality day-care and good quality time with their parents. Such children seem to have *multiple attachments* to a number of caregivers but their strongest attachments are still to their parents.

6 ▷ WHAT IF IT ALL GOES WRONG?

Researchers generally agree that a secure attachment in early life encourages the child to explore the physical world and relate well to others. In the long term, it seems to follow that children can develop secure, trusting relationships with others when they are older. For some children, however, early experience is less than ideal. Psychologists differ in the extent to which they think this matters. First, here are some important terms and definitions:

- **Separation**. This is the physical parting of the infant and mother or caregiver. Separation does not always lead to deprivation if it is handled in the right way.
- **Maternal deprivation**. This is when there is disruption to an existing bond or obstacles which interfere with bond formation.
- **Maternal privation**. This is when the infant has never had a chance to form an attachment.

WHY MAY ATTACHMENT FAIL?

Here are some reasons why the infant, or caregiver or both might disrupt or prevent attachment.

- **Babies who are different**. This includes babies who are premature, have birth defects or inherited defects. They are not what the parent expected or pictured which can lead to problems.
- **Babies who lack attachment skills**. This includes babies who are blind so do not respond in ways parents can understand. Some babies are temperamentally difficult and drain the parents' coping resources.
- **Family problems**. This includes child abuse, neglect and divorce.
- **Lack of parenting skill**. This could be due to the parent's own lack of attachment experience when young, the parent's mental state (e.g. depression) or the parent's addiction to drugs or alcohol.

John Bowlby's 'maternal deprivation' hypothesis

Bowlby is a key figure in the field of attachment

Bowlby (1953) said: 'Mother love in infancy and childhood is as important for mental health as are vitamins and proteins for physical health.'

He went on to claim that it was essential to have: 'a warm, intimate, continuous relationship with the mother ... or permanent mother substitute'.

The second statement in particular caused a storm of protest mainly because of the pressure it put on women not to take work outside the home. What had Bowlby based his views on? He drew together ideas from *psychoanalytic theory, ethology* and *learning theory*. Here are some of his key pieces of evidence:

1. **Imprinting**. In many species of mammal and some birds, imprinting attaches the young animal to its parent. There seems to be a **sensitive period** soon after birth or hatching when this is most likely to occur. The end of the period is marked by **fear of strange objects** and unfamiliar others. Bowlby noted a similar process in human infants. They begin to attach at about 6 months and show fear of strangers soon after. Bowlby thought that, if attachment had not occurred by 2 to 3 years of age, it would probably be too late.
2. **Short-term problems**. Bowlby noted a sequence of **protest, despair** and **detachment** in children immediately following separation from an attachment figure. *Robertson and Robertson*'s (1967) films of the distress of young children in brief separation supported this idea.
3. **Later attachments**. If imprinting does not happen, the individual animal will find it difficult to relate to others in adulthood. Similarly failure to attach in human infants may mean that there will be problems forming relationships later in life. Bowlby thought that such people would be especially vulnerable if they did form a relationship but it broke down.
4. **Problems in development**. Studies of children in the 1930s and 1940s who had experienced long-term care in orphanages tended to show long-term problems in language, social and cognitive development. *Goldfarb* (1947) also showed how children who were adopted from such institutions early on made better progress than those left behind.
5. **Animal studies**. *Harlow and Harlow* (1958) carried out a series of studies in which infant rhesus monkeys were separated from their mothers soon after birth and reared in either **total isolation** or **social isolation** (where they could see but not get near other monkeys). Some of the monkeys had **surrogate** (model) mothers to feed from. When the isolated monkeys were allowed contact with normal monkeys they showed serious **behaviour problems**. They were either very distressed and withdrawn or extremely aggressive. When mature, they did not know how to relate to other monkeys. If they did mate successfully, they seemed unable to parent their own young and were often **abusive** to them. Later studies showed three months of isolation could be recovered from but six to twelve months of isolation did irreversible damage. The presence of the surrogate made little difference.
6. **Juvenile delinquency**. In 1946 Bowlby studied the family histories of **44 juvenile thieves**. He found that seventeen of them had been separated from their mothers for six months or more before their fifth birthday. He compared these to 44 adolescents who had emotional problems but were not thieves and found only two had experienced such separation. Of the seventeen 'thieves' Bowlby also noted that fourteen showed **affectionless psychopathy**. They seemed to have no feelings of affection, warmth or concern for anyone. Bowlby concluded that these adolescent problems linked directly to early experience of separation.

Evaluation of Bowlby's hypothesis

1. **Imprinting.** There are doubts about whether it is appropriate to talk of imprinting in humans. The sensitive period, if there is one in humans, seems to be very flexible. Children can start to attach as late as 2 or 3 years old and there are several studies of successful later attachment following adoption (e.g. *Tizard* 1977).

2. **Short-term problems.** The Robertsons found that children could overcome the problems of brief separation if they were cared for in a familiar environment by familiar people who made an effort to keep contact with the absent parent alive. This challenges Bowlby's idea of **monotropy** since the child can attach to more than one person and this protects them in the event of separation.

3. **Later attachments.** There is plenty of evidence to suggest that people can overcome early attachment problems and form trusting relationships later in life. *Koluchova*'s (1972) study of Czechoslovakian twin boys illustrates this. The boys' mother died when they were born in 1960. They spent the first months of life in an institution and progressed well. From the age of 18 months the twins then lived with their father and stepmother who severely neglected them. The boys were isolated from outside contact and lived in an unheated room or, as punishment, in a cellar. When they were discovered, aged 7 years, they were severely physically, emotionally, socially and intellectually retarded. At 8 years old they were put into the excellent foster care of two sisters. They began to attend a special school but by the age of 14 years had progressed to a normal school and had IQs within the normal range. Good quality care before and after the period of neglect appeared to undo the damage but it is also important that the boys had each other for company throughout.

4. **Problems in development.** Problems experienced by orphanage children probably resulted more from *lack of facilities* and *stimulation* than lack of an attachment figure. In addition, children who were selected for adoption may have been more advanced to start with than those left behind.

5. **Animal studies.** The extreme privation experienced by Harlow's monkeys is not often seen in humans. Later research has shown how **monkey therapists** (younger peers) can undo much of the early damage. They cling to the deprived monkeys and seem to make up for the early loss of contact comfort. The effects of early deprivation do not, therefore, seem to be irreversible.

6. **Juvenile delinquency.** *Rutter* (1981) questioned the link between maternal separation and delinquency suggested by Bowlby. In his study of 9- to 12-year-old boys on the **Isle of Wight**, he found that it was not necessarily separation that caused problems. Instead he found a positive correlation between anti-social behaviour in these boys and the extent to which there was a stressful family atmosphere in their early years. He found no correlation between separation experiences and delinquency.

IN CONCLUSION

The work of Bowlby and others has had important, beneficial consequences.

- Improvements in institutional care and an emphasis on fostering wherever possible.
- Improvements in how children are cared for in hospital, e.g. enabling parents to live in with their children and stay with them constantly.
- Improvements in therapy for children who have been affected by adverse early experiences.
- Improved training for carers of young children.
- Reassurance to working parents that Bowlby's initial ideas of monotropy and the need for mothers to stay at home with young children were overstated. Parents can now feel more confident about the type of care a child needs and know that, handled sensitively, it is not likely to cause problems for the child.
- We are now closer to understanding which children are more likely to be adversely affected by separation experiences, i.e. those aged between 6 months and 3 years, boys more than girls, those with an unstable relationship with the mother and those experiencing poor quality care in an unfamiliar environment.

| 7 > | **DIVORCE** |

Smith and Cowie (1993) estimate that, by the time a child is sixteen there is a one in four chance that they will have experienced their parents' divorce or separation. The process of divorce can be legally quite prolonged. *Wallerstein* (1985) says that there are also distinct phases which will affect the child:

- **the acute phase**, lasting about two years, when parents separate emotionally and physically;
- **the transitional phase**, emotional ups and downs while parents readjust;
- **the post-divorce stage**, where parents establish a new life.

Here are some of the main findings about the effect of divorce on children:

1. **Reactions to divorce** vary with age, temperament and sex of the child. **Pre-school children** may find it *hard to understand* and may *feel responsible* for it. They may show more obvious signs of distress such as sleep problems or *bed-wetting*. Older children's signs of distress may be *less obvious*. In **middle childhood** there is *greater understanding* of what is going on but children may still *fantasise about parents reuniting*. In **adolescence** there may be strong *mood swings* and problems over loyalty to one parent or the other.

    It is rare for children to welcome separation but some children are simply more temperamentally resilient than others and will weather the storm better.

    The loss of a parental role-model might affect the process of sex-typing and morality (see Sex and Gender (Ch. 9, p. 104–5) and Moral development (Ch. 10, pp. 113, 115–16), i.e. sections on Psychoanalytic theory and SLT).

2. **Long-term effects**. A study by *Hetherington et al.* (1982) compared children from divorced, mother-led families with children from non-divorced families. They found:

    - after one year, emotional distress in parents and children and behaviour problems in children;
    - improvements in these after two years;
    - after six years, evidence that children of divorced parents had grown up faster – they were more independent in a number of ways;
    - more tension between mothers and sons than between mothers and daughters;
    - a general trend that remarriage improved things although the adjustment to a stepparent could be slow and difficult.

    Another study in the US by *Wallerstein* (1987) found considerable **distress** in children of all ages following their parents' divorce. Long term, the children who experienced divorce during the early years of life were worst affected, many showing **mild depression** or sadness about what had happened. However, not all studies have such bleak findings.

3. **Joint custody**. It might be thought that joint custody would protect the child from the adverse effects of losing one parent but research shows no difference between joint and single custody arrangements in this respect. Generally, children are more likely to recover well if they can keep a good relationship going with both parents and they no longer have to witness their parents' conflicts. This seems to be more important than the custody arrangements themselves.

4. **Bee (1992)** summarises what we know about divorces which have the least and shortest term effects:

this is what would happen in an ideal world

- the families are financially secure after divorce;
- the child witnessed little parental conflict before the divorce and parents were able to get along afterwards;
- the child does not feel caught in the middle;
- the child sees both parents regularly and has good relationships with them;
- the child's life is not disrupted in other ways, e.g. by having to move house or schools;
- the parent they live with has a fairly stable life and emotional support from family and friends.

To conclude on a hopeful note, *Clarke and Clarke* (1976) said: 'it appears that there is virtually no psychosocial adversity to which some children have not been subject, yet later recovered, granted a radical change of circumstances.'

8 ▷ PARENTING SKILLS

❝ it is debatable whether good parenting can be learned ❞

Research into attachment has done much to improve our understanding of its importance and there are lessons to be learned from it about how to parent well. We must remember that there is no one recipe for successful parenting since every parent–child relationship is different. We can, however, make some general points about how to help the attachment process along:

1. Parental sensitivity

Ainsworth et al. (1978) talked about **sensitive mothering** as an important ingredient in the attachment process. A sensitive mother is one who can:

- see things from the baby's point of view;
- 'read' the baby's signals accurately;
- respond appropriately to the baby's needs;
- accept the baby in a positive, loving way;
- be available to the baby when she is needed.

Ainsworth thought such sensitivity led to **secure attachments**. Securely attached babies feel free to explore from the safe base of the mother and will tolerate brief separations without being overly distressed. Insecurely attached babies may be less ready to explore and anxious or ambivalent about separation from the mother.

2. Quality of contact

It is not how much time a parent spends with a baby that matters but *the way in which* the time is spent. Mothers may be with their children more but spend much of that time seeing to the child's practical needs. Fathers may be with an infant less but they may play with it intensively when they do have time. Parents in kibbutzim may only have a few hours a day with their children but they may be more inclined to give them undivided attention. The quality of interaction can thus affect the strength and type of bond.

3. Consistency of contact

Attachment is helped if a parent is a *predictable* and *reliable* part of the child's everyday life (providing, of course, that the contact is good quality and the parent is sensitive). Younger children in particular find it hard to understand time. If a parent does have to be away, it is important to maintain as much contact as possible by whatever means.

4. Appropriateness of contact

Children are different! *Thomas and Chess* (1977) talked of **easy** and **difficult** temperaments in babies and children and *Schaffer and Emerson* (1964) noted that some babies like a great deal of cuddling and contact but others resist it. Attachment will be helped if the parent can understand this and adapt their caregiving to suit the child. This calls for a high degree of sensitivity and, sometimes, a great deal of effort from the parent.

EXAMINATION QUESTIONS

1. NEAB paper 2 1993, Question 3

Spend about 12 minutes answering these questions

(a) What is meant by the term "socialisation"? [3]

(b) The following passage is a description of a baby and her parents.

> *The baby signals her needs by crying or smiling. She looks at the parents when they look at her. The parents, in their turn, enter into the two-sided 'dance' by coming near the baby when she cries or gurgles. They pick her up. They wait for and respond to her signals of hunger or other need. They smile at the baby when she smiles and they gaze into her eyes.*

What is meant by the term 'reciprocal behaviour'? Refer to the above passage in your answer. [3]

(c) A baby has to spend a week in hospital. What could be done to reduce the negative psychological effects? [4]

[*Total 10 marks*]
(NEAB)

TUTOR ANSWER

NEAB paper 2 1993, Question 3

(a) Socialisation is the process by which individuals learn to adapt their behaviour in line with the expectations of the society in which they live.

(b) Reciprocal behaviour happens when one person's behaviour encourages another to return the behaviour. In the example given, when the baby looks at its parents and smiles, they return its looks and smiles.

(c) Bowlby thought that any separation of a baby from its main attachment figure (e.g. mother) could result in maternal deprivation where the emotional bond between them is damaged. This is particularly likely to happen if the baby has entered the sensitive period for attachment. Others, such as the Robertsons, thought that damage could be kept to a minimum if things were kept as normal as possible for the baby. This could include visits to the hospital so that the baby gets used to the surroundings and the staff who will care for it. The baby should be able to take in familiar toys, blankets etc. The baby's daily routine should be kept to as much as possible and the main caregiver should stay with the child all the time including sleeping in. In this way, any distress the baby feels at being treated in hospital should not be complicated by distress through maternal separation.

STUDENTS' ANSWERS

1. MEG sample paper 4 (Higher), Option 2 Source B: Attachment

Spend 30 minutes on this question

In one study, psychologists followed the development of 65 children who were put in residential nurseries when they were very young. Although the children were well looked after in the nurseries, they did not have a chance to form an attachment bond with any of the nurses. Between the ages of 2 and 3, different things happened to the children. Some children were returned to their natural mothers, some were adopted and some remained in the institution. A control group of 30 children who had not been separated from their parents was also used. All the children were given intelligence tests at age 5. The results are shown below.

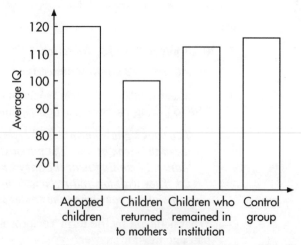

(a) Use the graph to answer the following questions.
   (i) What was the average IQ for children who remained in the institution? [1]

66 close enough 1/1 99

110

   (ii) What was the average IQ for the adopted children? [1]

66 1/1 99

120

(b) Why was it important in this study to use a control group? [2]

66 could be clearer

2/2 99

It is important to use a control group of 'normal' everyday children who hadn't experienced problems when they were younger as this gives a good idea of an average IQ for children of that age. This can then be compared.

(c) Why do the results of the study challenge Bowlby's theory? [2]

66 say what Bowlby predicted

1/2 99

The results challenge Bowlby's theory as the children suffered from maternal deprivation and had not made an attachment by the end of the critical period (three years), but they still managed a good IQ score which was higher than children returned to their mothers.

(d) Using psychological evidence, evaluate Bowlby's theory of maternal deprivation. [9]

66 good start 99

66 relevant evidence here 99

66 6/9 99

John Bowlby's theories of attachment and child-care were very influential although nowadays many of his conclusions wouldn't be acceptable, largely because mothers work and have a career as much as fathers do. Bowlby believed that humans have some biological need to have a close, loving bond with their mother or a permanent substitute mother. If this bond isn't formed, or is broken, emotional development, he claimed, would be disrupted. Bowlby used animal studies to see the effects of rearing animals without parents and concluded that being denied the chance to mix with other members of the species led to severe withdrawal.

Bowlby knew there was a critical period for imprinting in birds and applied this idea to humans. From his study of 44 juvenile thieves, Bowlby claimed that being separated from the attachment figure in the first five years led to affectionless psychopathy which could lead to delinquency. This study is biased and therefore inconclusive. It doesn't explain the thieves who weren't affectionless or study a group who had been deprived but not become delinquents. Also, the trouble with retrospective studies is that you are relying on people's memories of childhood and, in the case of the 44 thieves, could they be trusted?

[*Total 15 marks*]
(MEG)

66 11/15 Some good material here. Part (d) could have been expanded with some more clearly explained evidence 99

2. SEG paper 2 1994, Section B
Spend 40 minutes on this question

(a) What does maternal attachment mean? [3]

66 good 3/3 99

Maternal attachment is an emotional bond that forms between mother and child. Many theorists believe the process is two-way and instinctive.

(b) Explain, using examples, the difference between deprivation and privation [8]

66 go into more detail here

7/8 99

A child is said to experience deprivation if they have formed a bond with the mother but then experience separation from her so the bond is damaged. The twin boys studied by Koluchova had suffered deprivation. They had spent some time with their mother but were placed in a home when she died. When they returned to their father and new stepmother they were neglected and so could not repair the damage. Privation is when there is no chance at all to form a bond. The Bulldogs Bank war orphans studied by Freud and Dann had experienced this. They had been separated from their mothers when very young and moved around so much they never formed a bond with a mother figure.

(c) To what extent do you agree with Bowlby's views of attachment? In your answer, use psychological evidence to support your views.   [*10*]

" balance this with the other side of the argument

Bowlby's theory of attachment has been challenged and contradicted by many others. The Bulldogs Bank children did not bond with adults but they became very dependent on and devoted to each other. They were aggressive to adults and would not play with toys. However, over time they slowly improved and formed some relationships with adults. The twin boys in Koluchova's study were severely deprived, they were beaten and kept locked in a cellar. When they were eventually found they were scarred and malnourished and very afraid of other people. Their mental development was like that of a 3 year old. However, following adoption, by the age of 11 they were two normal boys physically and mentally but perhaps not emotionally. These two studies show that, with the right kind of care, it is possible for children to recover from and overcome deprivation and privation.

7/10 "

(d) From what you have learned in psychology, explain some of the ways in which fathers may affect their children's development.   [*9*]

From a psychoanalytic point of view, Freud believed fathers play a major role in the development of their children, especially their sons.

According to Freud the personality is made up of three parts: the id, ego and superego. The superego develops in the phallic stage when it is said that children unconsciously desire the opposite sex parent. This is the Oedipus conflict for boys and the Electra conflict for girls. Boys fear castration from their fathers if they are found out and girls fear further damage from their mothers who they believe have already castrated them.

" and daughters "

Fathers have an effect on their sons' moral development. The boy identifies with the father in order to make it impossible for the father to do the son harm. The son takes on his father's ideas of right and wrong, his sex-role and his mannerisms. However, this does not explain how single mothers manage to bring up their sons successfully.

" rather brief

Social Learning Theorists, such as Bandura, think boys learn from their fathers through observation and imitation. The father becomes a role-model for the child, as long as the father appears to be a loving, affectionate, powerful and influential figure for the child.

6/9 "

[*Total 30 marks*]
(SEG)

" 23/30 Plenty of psychological content. For full marks a good balance is needed in (c). In (d) more detail is needed. Some illustrative studies would help "

A Review Sheet for this chapter can be found on p. 239.

CHAPTER 8

AFFILIATION, FRIENDSHIPS AND ATTRACTION

GETTING STARTED

Affiliation, friendships and attraction appear on the SEG syllabus only. Affiliation is a core topic which connects with other optional syllabus areas such as attachment, divorce, friendships and attraction. Affiliation provides the background to these topics so all SEG students need to know about it. Only those students studying Option C need to complete the remainder of this chapter on friendships and attraction.

1. AFFILIATION

2. FRIENDSHIPS

3. ATTRACTION

❛❛ the company of others is important ❜❜

ESSENTIAL PRINCIPLES

THE NEED FOR AFFILIATION

People are said to have a need for affiliation, in other words, a desire to form relationships with others. There is good evidence to suggest that the company of others is important for our *psychological health* and even our *survival*. In infancy, prolonged periods of **social isolation** can have disastrous effects (see *Harlow*'s studies of maternal privation in rhesus monkeys in the Attachment chapter). The effects of social isolation on prisoners are also well known and solitary confinement has frequently been used to punish them. In normal attachment relationships, infants often turn to the parent when they need comfort or reassurance.

There are wide differences in people's need for affiliation. For example:

- some people, such as hermits or other recluses, actually *choose* isolation;
- some want to affiliate but lack the **social skills** needed to make friends so they are lonely even though others are around;
- some *crave* social contact and are very unhappy without it;
- for some, the effects of isolation may be unexpected. In 1938, *Admiral Byrd* looked forward to six months alone on an Antarctic weather station but the experience made him lonely and depressed. He was physically healthy and had radio contact with others but he became apathetic and even experienced hallucinations.

REASONS FOR AFFILIATION

Schachter (1959) suggested four reasons for affiliation:

1. The company of others *reduces anxiety* giving us a feeling of 'safety in numbers'.
2. Others can *distract* us from our worries thus indirectly reducing anxiety.
3. When we are unsure how to behave, watching how others behave can give us *ideas about what to do*.
4. We can make **social comparisons** with others. This means that, when we are evaluating our reactions to a situation, we use others to see how we measure up.

We also affiliate for positive reasons:

1. **Positive stimulation**. The company of others is fun and makes pleasurable activities and shared interests more enjoyable.
2. **Attention from others**. People seem to value positive attention from others.

STUDIES OF AFFILIATION

Reducing fear and anxiety

Schachter (1959) studied women undergraduates who had volunteered to take part in his research. Some were told they would receive *painful* electric shocks, others were told they would receive *mild* electric shocks. The women then had to wait ten minutes for the experiment to begin. They were offered the chance to wait *alone* or *with others*. 63% of the 'painful shock' group chose to wait with others but only 33% of the 'mild shock' group chose company. To find out more, Schachter tried a variation of the study (see next).

Affiliation in different situations

In a similar study to the one above, Schachter found that volunteers preferred to wait with others who were facing the *same thing* rather than with just anyone. He thought this difference was explained by the need to make social comparisons rather than by any of the other reasons he had suggested.

Kulik and Mahler (1989), however, found that 60% of patients awaiting heart bypass surgery preferred to share a room with someone who had already had the operation and was *recovering* rather than with someone who was awaiting the same operation.

Sarnoff and Zimbardo (1961) found that, if people were waiting to take part in a study which involved something *potentially embarrassing* (sucking on a nipple) they preferred not to wait with others in the same situation.

We seem to need to affiliate with different kinds of others for different kinds of support. If you were ill, for example, you might seek a doctor for information and practical support and a friend or fellow sufferer for emotional support.

STUDIES IN THE REAL WORLD

Argyle (1987) describes a number of studies of friendships and relationships in the real world. They seem to suggest that friends and other companions protect us from the stress caused by **emotional loneliness**. This can be felt even by people who have lots of company if the social contact they have is the wrong kind. This type of loneliness is associated with *depression, anxiety, boredom* and *loss of self-esteem* so what do we know that could help us understand why some people feel this way and others do not?

we can be lonely in a crowd

- Emotional loneliness may result from a **lack of social skills** which help us to make and keep friends. People differ in how socially skilled they are.
- People differ in their **need for affiliation** so what makes one person lonely may not affect another.
- Women seem to affiliate more than men. (Could this indicate a **sex-difference** in that women, more than men, seek out others to help them deal with stress?)
- Emotional loneliness tends to be avoided if there is someone to **confide** in.
- Women tend to have closer friendships than men and **disclose** more to each other.
- Women in general seem better than men at **relieving loneliness** in either sex possibly because of the kinds of things they are interested in talking about.

It appears that the general need for affiliation is only part of the story. If the company of others is to protect us from psychological harm and be positive for us, it needs to be the right kind of company at the right time.

2 > FRIENDSHIPS

If we accept that we need to affiliate with others, how do children learn to form friendships and relationships with others and how do these change as the child grows up? Psychologists have studied friendships in children both by *observing* them and listening to their *conversations* and by presenting them with stories about *friendship dilemmas* and asking them to comment.

THE DEVELOPMENT OF FRIENDSHIPS IN CHILDREN

From as early as 6 months of age, infants seem to be very interested in other infants and children. Even though they may be attached to the parent and spend most of their time near them, they still spend a great deal of time watching other children. Early on, there may even be some small interactions, such as passing a toy or smiling, but it can take up to three years for a child to learn how to interact really well with its peers. Toddler groups give the child contact with other toddlers but nursery schools and playgroups give plenty of chances to learn friendship skills when the child is more ready.

There are social stages in children's play which seem to reflect their social development. The stages are roughly age related:

- **Solitary play**. Play alone.
- **Parallel play**. Play alongside others but with no interaction.
- **Looking-on play**. Watching others play but not joining in.
- **Associative play**. This is sometimes called **joining-in play**. There is usually little or no sharing of activities or materials but lots of conversation.
- **Cooperative play**. Playing together, perhaps taking different roles to make the game 'work'.

Other trends are also noticeable. In the early years, children seem to seek out others to play with but, later on, their friends are important in helping them to move into adulthood. There are also changes in the sex of chosen friends:

gender differences in
choice of friends

- In the pre-school years boys and girls seem happy to play together;
- by about 6 or 7 years of age, children start to play mainly with friends of the same sex;
- by 10 or 11 years of age, boys and girls usually play separately with boys in larger groups than girls;
- by early adolescence, there may be small, mixed-sex groups which may join together into larger groups. Smaller **cliques** become larger **crowds** (*Dunphy* 1963);
- in late adolescence and early adulthood, there may be more **dating** pairs and, eventually, more lasting relationships between couples.

STAGES OF FRIENDSHIP DEVELOPMENT

notions of friendship
change with age

Selman (1980) presented children with **friendship dilemmas** (stories about trust or jealousy between friends) to encourage them to discuss what friendship meant to them. He found two things changed as the child moved through stages of friendship development:

1. How much a child could understand their friend's point of view.
2. How many friends a child had.

He identified five stages of friendship development but did not attach very specific ages to them:

Stage 0. Momentary physical playmate. 3–7 years. A friend is someone you play with and the friendship lasts as long as you are playing. Children are very **egocentric** at this stage and resolve conflict physically or by going to play with someone else.

Stage 1. One-way assistance. 4–9 years. A friend is someone who meets your needs and gives you help but you do not necessarily expect to return the favour! Children change friends quite often at this stage (although some friendships may last a lifetime!).

Stage 2. Fairweather cooperation. 6–12 years. The friendship forms and carries on if the going is good. There tends to be more give and take at this stage as children become better able to see their friend's point of view. A friendship tends to last longer although an argument could put an end to it.

Stage 3. Intimate mutual sharing. 9–15 years. These friendships might be quite intense and exclusive of others. Trust and intimacy become more important and the friendship can last through small conflicts.

Stage 4. Autonomous independence. 12 years upwards. In adolescence and adulthood friends recognise each other's need to have trustworthy friends as well as independence. Friendships can change and grow and stand quite serious disagreements. At this stage, friends can *let go* of each other so that there may be a number of very good friendships rather than exclusive loyalty to one best friend. These friendships can last over time and distance and are the most intimate of all.

SOME RESEARCH INTO POPULARITY

Some children seem to find it easier to make friends than others. If we agree that friendship is important to psychological health, how can we identify less popular children and what can be done to help them?

In 1983, *Cole and Dodge* carried out a four-year longitudinal study of 8–11 year olds' friendship choices. They classified children as:

- popular
- accepted
- average
- neglected
- rejected
- controversial.

Rejected children tended to stay rejected over the four years but neglected children became 'average'. Compared to average and popular children, rejected children:

- showed less cooperative play;

— lack of confidence?

- ● made less social conversation;
- ● argued and fought more;
- ● had fewer companions;
- ● tried to join in with others in rather forceful ways.

We do not know from research whether these differences caused the child to be rejected or were the result of being rejected. Whichever it is, it appears rejected children have problems with **social skills**. It may be that :

- ● they have difficulty 'reading' other children's signals and so respond inappropriately;
- ● they have difficulty giving out behaviour to which other children respond positively.

Psychologists have tried a number of ways of helping rejected children. They have had some success with allowing rejected children to see good social skills being 'modelled' on film. Direct training also helps to some extent but, surprisingly, improving a child's academic skills works even better. Clearly, having good social skills is not the only thing involved in popularity. Other factors have also been identified. More popular children tend to:

- ● be more physically attractive;
- ● mature earlier;
- ● 'match' well with other children in the group (some children may be neglected simply because they are different in some way from the others);
- ● fit in with the group's norms. For example, in higher school streams an academic child fits the group norm and is unlikely to be rejected whereas in a non-academic group, being clever could lead to rejection.

3 > ATTRACTION

We seem to need the company of others, but we do not choose just anyone for company. Also, we do not form relationships with everyone who seems attractive to us. Psychologists have identified a number of factors which influence whether we will go on from making someone's acquaintance to forming a relationship with them.

INFLUENCES ON ATTRACTION

1. Proximity

When circumstances bring people near to each other, relationships are likely to develop. *Pennington* (1986) warns that we must not confuse **actual distance** with **functional distance**. In other words, we might actually be very close to someone but find it difficult to interact with them. Being face to face makes interaction easier than being back to back!

A study into actual and functional distances was carried out by *Festinger et al.* in 1950. They studied the effect of the layout of married students' housing on friendship formation. The houses were arranged in U-shaped courts and all but the end ones faced inwards. People in the end houses had half as many friends as the others and friendships between people four or more houses apart were rare.

To test the effect of frequency of contact with others, *Saegert et al.* (1973) asked participants along to the lab. to 'test' various drinks and rate the flavours. During the testing it was arranged for each participant to be brought into contact with another person one, two, five, or ten times. Afterwards, participants rated the person for liking. It seemed that the more contact there had been, the more liking there was. Saegert called this the **mere exposure effect** and other research has shown it also works for *music, paintings* and *fashions*. It seems familiarity with something makes us more comfortable with it.

Frequency and *closeness* of contact with others is clearly important in attraction but not if it is of the wrong kind. We all know that too much contact can have negative effects (familiarity breeds contempt). We also know how uncomfortable too close proximity can be and how it can put us off someone else if they invade our personal space. *Hall* (1959) thought we carried **zones of personal space** round with us. These zones are like invisible bubbles which vary with the situation. (They are described in chapter six, p. 72.)

2. Physical attractiveness

Research suggests that we form relationships with people who have similar levels of attractiveness to ourselves. This is called **the matching hypothesis**. *Murstein* (1972)

❝❝ a kind of symmetry
– see 3 ❞❞

found evidence of matching in married couples and others have found matching in *dating* and *going steady couples*. However, it could be that we match with others to be on the safe side and *avoid rejection*. *Walster* (1966) randomly paired students into couples for a **computer dance**. The couples had been led to believe they had been matched in some way. Contrary to the matching hypothesis, couples who had been well matched by chance did not necessarily like each other more. Greater liking seemed to be for more attractive partners regardless of whether the match was good. In this case, students knew their partner would not reject them.

Physically attractive people also seem to evoke **stereotypes**. We expect a person who looks good to have a number of other desirable characteristics such as *sensitivity, kindness, competence* and *warmth*. *Dion* (1972) showed female college students pictures of boys who were said to have misbehaved. If the boy was attractive he was blamed less than an unattractive boy. *Gross and Crofton* (1977) found that essays written by more attractive women got higher grades and *Landy and Aronson* (1969) found that in mock court cases, attractive defendants got off more lightly than unattractive ones.

3. Similarity

We might think like attracts like when it comes to *personality* or *beliefs* and *values*. *Byrne and Nelson* (1965) measured students' attitudes to issues like religion, politics and music. Two weeks later they gave these people another questionnaire said to have been filled in by another student. If the attitudes expressed in it matched the student's own quite closely they rated the other student more positively than when the attitudes did not match well. Attitude similarity seems to matter more if the *issue is very important* to us but we can tolerate differences about less important issues.

Newcomb (1961) gave new male college students free accommodation in exchange for filling in questionnaires from time to time about their *attitudes* and *liking* for their housemates. Attitude similarity was the best predictor of how much the students liked each other at the end of the study.

On the subject of *personality, Cattell and Nesselroade* (1967) found that people in stable marriages had more similar personalities than people in unstable marriages. *Reader and English* (1947) found closer personality matching in friend pairs than in stranger pairs. We do not know why this is. It could be one reason why people got together in the first place or it could be that personalities grow more similar with time.

4. Complementarity

Too much similarity in a relationship could be comfortable but it could also be boring! People often claim that opposites attract. *Robert Winch* (1958) studied happy marriages and developed a theory of **complementary needs**. He suggested that opposite (complementary) needs can be important in a relationship but it depends on which needs are involved. An *extravert* personality who seeks constant activity and social stimulation may not mix very well with a more *introvert*, withdrawn type who needs peace and quiet. A person who squanders money may not pair well with someone who is very careful with money. On the other hand, a very caring and *nurturant* person may enjoy a relationship with someone who is child-like and *dependent* and a very *dominant* person may go well with someone who is *submissive*.

Campbell (1980) thought that similarity might be the main thing that draws people into a relationship but complementarity was the *cement* that made it last. Clearly, relationships are based on a *mixture* of similarity and complementarity. It is a question of getting the mixture right.

5. Reciprocal liking

We are attracted to people who like us, that is, we reciprocate their liking of us. (We also tend to dislike people who seem to dislike us.) *Backman and Secord* (1959) arranged for people who were strangers to each other to meet and talk in groups. Before they met, the participants were told that certain of the other group members would like them very much. The groups met on six occasions. After two meetings the participants were asked to say who they liked best. They tended to choose people who were said to like them. However, at the end of six sessions, participants chose other group members who *really did* like them. It seems we check another person's liking of us. The attraction lasts only if liking is seen as *genuine* and we genuinely like the other in return. *Deutsch and*

Solomon (1972) added that we like others who see us as we see ourselves and accept us as we are. *Linder* (1965) showed that we are more likely to reciprocate liking of someone who evaluates us negatively at first and then becomes *positive*. If they thought well of us all along, reciprocal liking is not as strong.

THEORIES OF ATTRACTION

The reinforcement—affect model

Byrne and Clore's reinforcement–affect model (1970) is based on **conditioning theory**. The basic idea is that other people behave towards us in ways which we find rewarding (**reinforcing**) or punishing. The **affect** part of the model refers to how this makes us feel. Reward makes us feel *good* and punishment makes us feel *bad*. As a result, we tend to like people who reward us more than punish us and dislike people who punish us more than reward us. Anyone or anything that is about at the same time as the rewarding or punishing person may also come to be liked or disliked.

Veitch and Griffith (1976) tested this model by arranging for people to hear either good news or bad news. They then had an encounter with a stranger and were asked to rate their liking of that person. People who had heard good news tended to rate the stranger more highly than people who had heard bad news. This model may explain something of the process of attraction but it seems to suggest we would become attached to anyone who was nice to us and this isn't always the case.

> a learning theory approach

Balance theory

Newcomb's (1971) theory focuses on *attitudes* and how they may make or break relationships. The model considers how two people A and B feel about something (X) that is important to them, e.g. an issue, another person or an activity. If A and B both like or dislike X there is no problem and the attraction remains steady. If there is disagreement about X, the unpleasant tension which results will encourage A and B to do something about it. They may argue about the issue until they come to an agreement or they may find that they cannot get over the disagreement and decide to part company.

In 1961, *Newcomb* showed how friendships among students tended to form between people who agreed about which other students they liked or disliked. This seems to offer some support for the model. However, we know that some relationships may persist in spite of serious disagreements and the model is not sensitive enough to explain why.

Social exchange theory

Thibaut and Kelley (1959) suggested that, when we are in a relationship, we have in mind what we deserve to get out of it. This is our **comparison level** (CL). If rewards from a relationship equal or exceed our expectations, we will tend to stay where we are. However, we also spend time looking around at the alternatives available (so we also have a **comparison level for alternatives** (CLalt)). If we could do better elsewhere, the prediction is that we move on. There certainly seems to be some anecdotal support for this if we consider the frequency with which Hollywood stars change partners!

The theory may explain some of the process of attraction but it is not sensitive enough to take into account other things that we know about relationships. For example, we may stay where we are for all sorts of reasons even when there are attractive alternatives. Some of us stay put because we reason 'Better the devil you know'. Others move on even though there is no alternative.

The repulsion hypothesis

Rosenbaum (1986) suggests that we are *initially* attracted to all kinds of people but *reject* some of them when we discover that their attitudes are different from our own. To support this idea, he asked students to rate some photographs of others for liking. Some students were given information that certain of the photographed persons had attitudes similar to their own. Others had no such information. This did not seem to influence the ratings at all.

Rosenbaum's hypothesis may make sense in some situations, but it does not fit with our general experience of being differently attracted to others whether we know them or not. Neither does it fit with other research about the importance of attitude similarity.

STUDENTS' ANSWERS

Spend 35 minutes on this question

(a) Describe one way in which psychologists have studied friendship formation in children. [6]

> Psychologists have studied friendship formation in children by observing children in their natural environment (e.g. playgroup), recording their behaviour and listening to their conversations. Some psychologists have presented children with stories of friendship dilemmas to discuss so that they can see what their understanding of friendship is like.

(b) Describe two ways in which friendship patterns change as children develop. [14]

❝ make it clear this is about gender differences ❞

> Children seem to be interested in each other from the start but it takes time for them to learn how to interact with other children and to make friends. In the pre-school years boys and girls play happily together but by 6 or 7 years they tend to play in same-sex groups. At 10 or 11 years, boys' groups will tend to be larger than girls' groups. In early adolescence, mixed-sex groups form and small cliques may merge together into larger crowds. Eventually there may be dating pairs and more lasting relationships.

❝ make it clear that this is about notions of friendship ❞

> Selman identified five stages of friendship development by studying children's responses to friendship dilemmas. At 3–7 years a friend is whoever you happen to be playing with. At 4–9 years a friend is someone who helps you. At 6–12 years a friend is kept as long as the going is good. At 9–15 years children may develop quite intense relationships with one special friend. After that people tend to have a few special friendships that can last over time and distance as well as a number of less intimate friends.

❝ 12/14 ❞

(c) Explain why one person may be attracted to another. [10]

> Some psychologists think we have a basic, biological need to affiliate with other people, yet we do not form friendships and relationships with just anyone. A number of factors are involved in attraction.
>
> Proximity is to do with how close people are to each other, but also how easy it is for them to interact and how often they see each other. Research evidence shows that people living in housing blocks tend to form relationships with those they live closest to. The 'mere exposure effect' describes how we come to like a person simply because we come into contact with them more often.
>
> Physical attractiveness is another factor. Murstein found evidence for matching of physical attractiveness in married couples and others have shown the same in going steady and engaged couples. We also seem to have stereotypes about physically attractive people that lead us to think they have other desirable characteristics apart from their appearance.
>
> Similarity in attitudes and personality may also draw people together. Newcomb found attitude similarity was the best predictor of how much students sharing accommodation grew to like each other. There is also evidence of personality similarity in married couples and friends although it is not certain whether this is a cause or effect of the relationship forming.
>
> Complementarity can also be important – the idea being that opposites could attract. On certain characteristics, such as nurturance and dependence, complementarity could work well but other characteristics, such as extraversion and introversion, may cause problems.
>
> Finally reciprocal liking is a very powerful factor in attraction and seems to keep a relationship together if it is felt to be genuine and we feel the other person knows us well and accepts us.

❝ 10/10 ❞

[*Total 30 marks*]

 25/30 An excellent answer with plenty of detail. There are just one or two areas where points could have been made more clearly ❞

A Review Sheet for this chapter can be found on p. 240.

INDIVIDUAL DEVELOPMENT PART ONE – SEX AND GENDER

1. SEX AND GENDER

2. THEORIES OF SEX-TYPING

GETTING STARTED

All three GCSE syllabuses require you to know the meaning of various terms related to sex and gender, as well as the relationship between biological sex and psychological gender.

Requirements for the SEG and MEG syllabuses are very similar so you are advised to look at all the material presented here. The NEAB requirements are less wide ranging. Biological, psychoanalytic and social learning approaches only are specified so you should concentrate on these, remembering that there is much to be gained from looking at other sections, mainly because they can help you to evaluate the three specified approaches. It would be a good idea for you to ensure that you have revised 'Learning' before tackling this chapter because many of the explanations described there are raised again here.

ESSENTIAL PRINCIPLES

> be able to explain
> these

DEFINITIONS

Sex – a person's biological type (that is, male or female) which is genetically determined.

Gender – a person's psychological type, that is, masculine or feminine, acquired through experience.

Sex or gender-role – the attitudes and behaviour expected by society of males and females.

Sex-role stereotype – a rather rigid idea about how males and females should think and behave.

Sex identity (or concept) – being able to label yourself accurately as male or female.

Gender identity (or concept) – being able to label yourself accurately as masculine or feminine.

Sex-typing – the process by which males and females acquire their sex-role and gender.

ANDROGYNY

Sandra Bem (1975) suggested that the masculinity/femininity distinction is too rigid. It is also possible for a person to be **androgynous,** that is to express *both* masculine and feminine characteristics. People may also be **undifferentiated** meaning that they are *low* on both. Bem's Sex-role Inventory (**BSRI**) is a questionnaire consisting of items measuring masculinity and femininity. Table 9.1 shows how a person may be classified after doing this questionnaire.

	High masculinity score	*Low masculinity score*
High femininity score	Androgynous	Feminine
Low femininity score	Masculine	Undifferentiated

Table 9.1 Bem's gender types

It has also been shown that:

- there is little sign of androgyny before 9–10 years of age;
- between 25–35% of teenagers are androgynous;
- there are more 'masculine' girls than 'feminine' boys;
- masculinity and androgyny tend to go hand in hand with higher self-esteem and feelings of psychological well-being (but this is probably due to the fact that both are high on masculinity).

WHAT DIFFERENCES ARE THERE BETWEEN MALES AND FEMALES?

In 1974 *Maccoby and Jacklin* published an extensive review of research studies into sex differences. They found that there is *no truth* in the following ideas:

- girls are more suggestible than boys;
- girls have lower self-esteem than boys;
- girls have lower motivation to achieve than boys;
- girls are less analytical than boys.

Regarding *differences* they found:

- boys are more aggressive than girls;
- girls have greater verbal ability than boys;
- boys have better spatial ability than girls;
- boys have better mathematical ability than girls.

The evidence was *mixed* for sex differences in the following:

- tactile sensitivity;
- fear, timidity and anxiety;
- activity level;
- competitiveness;
- compliance.

Maccoby and Jacklin concluded that there are far more similarities than differences between males and females.

The main problem for psychologists is to determine how biological and social influences interact in determining sex and gender. The following theories focus on different aspects of the same problem. They are not necessarily competing with each other.

BIOLOGICAL AND BIOSOCIAL EXPLANATIONS

Biological sex can be defined:

- **Genetically**. Sex is determined chromosomally. Females have two X chromosomes, males have one X and one Y chromosome.
- **Gonadally**. This refers to the reproductive organs. Males have testes, females have ovaries.
- **Genitally**. This refers to external appearance. Males have a penis and scrotum, females a clitoris and vagina.
- **Hormonally**. Both males and females produce the same hormones but males produce more androgens (e.g. testosterone) and females produce more oestrogen and progesterone.

For most of us, these are in accord with each other but a very few individuals, called **hermaphrodites**, have characteristics of both sexes.

The influence of hormones

Hormones are chemical messengers which are secreted by **endocrine glands**. The hormones travel round the body influencing all kinds of activities in organs or other glands. The hormones influencing sexual development are secreted by the **ovaries** in the female and the **testes** in the male. They determine development *prenatally* and *throughout life*. Their effect is most noticeable at **puberty** when they bring about **sexual maturity** – males and females develop **secondary sexual characteristics** and become fertile.

Here are some ways in which hormones can affect development:

- **The natural human form is female**. Foetuses would all develop into females unless the presence of a Y chromosome interfered with this by causing testosterone producing testes to form. Removal of testes from XY (rabbit) foetuses causes the foetus to develop into a female. Removal of ovaries from an XX foetus does not affect the femaleness of the foetus.
- **Androgenised females**. These females have experienced high levels of **androgen** while still in the womb. Sometimes, their external genitalia are ambiguous and they may be wrongly identified as males. *Money* (1972) found that such girls must be correctly assigned to the female sex as soon as possible, otherwise they may show inadequate sex-typing and be poorly adjusted. Nevertheless, they may be *tomboyish* as children and more masculine in their social behaviour and academic and work preferences as adults. However, they preferred male sexual partners and were successful mothers.
- **Late reassignment**. A study which questions the importance of early reassignment of a child wrongly sex-typed concerned girls in the **Batista family** of the Dominican Republic. These girls are XY males but the hormones which should make them male in the womb do not act until adolescence. At puberty, they literally change sex and develop male secondary sexual characteristics, but they do not seem to suffer psychologically.
- **Progesterone and IQ**. It has been suggested that children whose mothers receive progesterone to prevent miscarriage have significantly higher than average IQs. It may be that progesterone affects the development of the **cerebral cortex**.
- **Hormones and cerebral lateralisation**. We know that *verbal abilities* tend to be located more in the *left hemisphere* of the brain and *spatial abilities* more in the *right*. This is less pronounced (**lateralised**) in females than in males. It may be that the sex hormones affect the degree of lateralisation at a critical period in the foetus's development. Some people think this accounts for the more effective

spatial abilities of males and their superiority in the sciences. (But the latest research shows the ability gap is closing.)

Evaluation

Biological factors alone are not enough to explain gender differences. In most of the examples of hormonal action given above environmental and social influences creep in. For example, in many of the studies of hermaphrodites successful adoption of a gender role shows how both biological and social factors have a part to play.

66 hormones are not the whole story 99

PSYCHODYNAMIC EXPLANATIONS

Psychodynamic explanations of sex-typing have grown out of the **psychoanalytic approach** founded by *Sigmund Freud* (1856–1939). Here, we will look only at his ideas as one example of the psychodynamic approach.

According to Freud, we acquire our understanding of sex and gender as part of the general process of personality development. For a more detailed description of the structure of personality and how it develops see chapter fifteen.

Freud suggested all children go through four stages of personality development in the same order. Each stage is like a **sensitive period** when the child is most open to particular kinds of experience. They are the oral, anal, phallic and genital stages. The third (**phallic**) stage is most important in the development of gender.

The phallic stage lasts from 3 or 4 to 6 years of age. Freud thought that a child becomes very interested in *physical differences* between the sexes but most importantly, they are also going through an *unconscious* process called the **Oedipal conflict** (in boys) or the **Electra conflict** (in girls). Resolving this conflict is probably the most important step in personality development. Until it is done, boys and girls have a *sex identity* but not a *gender identity*. For boys, working through the Oedipal conflict happens like this:

66 remember this is all on an unconscious level 99

- the boy develops unconscious, *infantile, sexual desires* for the mother;
- he sees the father as a very powerful *rival*;
- he fears the father may discover the boy's desires and *punish* him for them;
- specifically, the boy fears the father will castrate him (*castration anxiety*);
- the id demands that the discomfort caused by this conflict is dealt with;
- the boy resolves the conflict by **identifying** with his father. This means he takes on many of his father's characteristics, *including his sex-role*. The boy becomes like a miniature version of his father. This defuses the threat from the father who is unlikely to hurt a child who is now a part of himself. It also allows the boy to express his affection for the mother without fear of punishment.

For girls the Electra conflict is similar to the Oedipal conflict except the girl desires her father and fears her mother's anger. The girl believes herself to have already been castrated by the mother and her fear is of *further damage* and *loss of her mother's love*. Identification with the mother resolves this problem and leads to the girl taking on her female sex role. Freud also suggested:

- the *stricter* the parent, the more *effort* the child will have to make to resolve the conflict – this means the *identification will be stronger*, making boys more masculine and girls more feminine.
- girls have *weaker gender identities* because the anxiety they experience is not as powerful as castration anxiety – this means less effort is needed to resolve the Electra conflict so identification with the female sex is weaker.

Evaluation

- It is difficult to explain how children in **single parent families** resolve their Oedipal or Electra conflicts. Freud would have predicted that they would be unable to develop a gender identity but there is no consistent evidence that children from single parent (or gay or lesbian) households are affected in this way. Any problems such children do have relating to the opposite sex can be explained in other ways.
- Freud used the case of **Little Hans** to back up his ideas about the Oedipal conflict. Four-year-old Hans had a fear that a horse might bite him. Freud interpreted this as an expression of Hans's unconscious fear that his father (represented by

❝❝ he had recently been very
startled when a horse fell down
near to him ❞❞
the powerful horse) might castrate him (represented by the biting). This interpretation has been much criticised. There are much simpler explanations of
Hans's fear of horses!

- Many of Freud's ideas about how the personality develops are *difficult to test*
  because they involve things like unconscious urges and instinctive forces. Such
  things cannot be directly observed or measured.
- Children's playmate and toy choices show that they *understand gender identity*
  earlier than Freud's theory predicts they would.

SOCIAL LEARNING EXPLANATIONS

SL theorists think much of our learning can be explained by **conditioning** and **observational learning**. Sex-role and gender are learned by the same processes as
any other behaviour. Parents and others will *selectively reinforce* gender-appropriate
behaviour in children. Also, models who are *similar* to the child and who show *gender-
appropriate behaviour*, are more likely to be imitated. This process starts very early.
One of the first things people want to know about a new baby is its sex.

The role of parents and others

Conditioning
Do we reinforce boys and girls for different kinds of behaviour? Here are some
research examples:

- **Baby X studies**. (e.g. *Seavey et al.* 1975.) If adults are asked to play with a baby,
  they treat it differently according to whether they think it is a boy or a girl, e.g.
  giving dolls to girls and trucks to boys, being gentler with girls and more boister-
  ous with boys.
- **Toddler and later childhood studies**. *Fagot* (1978) studied parents at home
  with toddlers aged 20–24 months and found girls were encouraged and praised
  for activities like dancing, helping and dressing up. Boys were praised for more
  physical activities and using construction toys like blocks. They were often
  actively discouraged from playing with 'girls'' toys such as dolls. Further
  research has shown it is fathers, rather than mothers, who are most likely to discourage boys from playing with feminine toys and that this tendency continues
  throughout childhood.

Peers
Lamb et al. (1980) studied 3–5 year olds at play. They found boys and girls tended to
play with sex-appropriate toys and that they were critical of each other for playing with
toys seen as more appropriate for the opposite sex. They were also critical if they saw
a girl using girls' toys in a *'boyish'* way or boys using boys' toys in a *'girlish'* way.

School studies
See the section on gender and educational achievement later in this chapter.

Observational learning
SLT predicts that children would pay more attention to *same-sex models* and learn
from them. There are many such models (teachers, peers and parents) for children
to learn from so there are plenty of chances to find out what males or females typically do. The mass media, such as books, newspapers and films and especially TV,
are an important source of models for children. Different cultures also provide different role-models.

Sex-role stereotypes and the media
When people stereotype others they identify one characteristic, such as male or
female, and then assume the person possesses all sorts of other characteristics which
go with the label. The typical *female stereotype* is of someone who is soft and pretty,
passive, nurturant, dependent, weak, emotional and domestic. The *stereotypical male*
is rugged, active, strong, independent, assertive, unemotional and dominant. A whole
range of typically male and female behaviours go with the stereotype. Do the media
give us stereotyped male and female role models?

Books

Collins *et al.* (1984) found:

- There are *twice as many male characters* as female characters in children's books.
- Male and female characters in leading roles were as *active and adventurous* as each other but there were far fewer female leads overall.
- Where males and female characters had *supporting roles*, these tended to be much more sex-stereotypical, e.g. boys active and independent, girls passive and dependent.

DeLoache et al. (1987) found that, when parents read to their pre-school children, 90% of characters whose sex is unknown are labelled as male. Children may not be exposed to the obvious stereotyping contained in books of the 1950s to 1970s but the subtle messages are still there. It is a male world in which males do *exciting, active* things while females *look on*.

are current books non-sexist enough?

Television

Research throughout the 1950s to 1970s showed that, as in books, there were twice as many male characters on TV as female characters. Also there are very few female cartoon characters. Females tended to be shown as dependent, over-emotional and less intelligent or able than men. *Davis* (1990) found that this picture had not changed in the 1990s. In addition:

- females' marital status is made more obvious than men's;
- women are four times more likely than men to be shown provocatively dressed;
- 20% of female characters are shown engaging in domestic activities compared to 3% of men;
- females are more likely to be shown as victims of violent crime than as violent criminals; males are just as likely to be victims as criminals.

In **TV adverts** *Harris and Stobart* (1986) showed that females are typically shown in domestic roles, producing arguments based on opinion rather than fact and advertising products to do with beautifying self or home. Men tended to be shown in roles outside the home, producing scientific arguments for products and advertising products such as cars and financial services. Voice-overs on other adverts were nearly always male. Even when males are shown doing domestic things in 1990s adverts it tends to be because the woman cannot do it or the male is making a mess of it. Does such stereotyping affect the viewer's behaviour?

the messages in adverts can be very subtle

The effect of media on gender stereotyping

Research in the 1970s suggested that the more TV children watched the more sex-typed their attitudes. Research in the 1980s shows this effect is weakening but it is still there. For example:

- *Williams* (1986) compared sex-role attitudes in three Canadian towns. **Notel** had no TV, **Unitel** had one channel and **Multitel** had four channels. After two years, Notel had one channel, Unitel had two and Multitel had four. Williams looked again at sex-role attitudes and found that children's ideas were much more stereotyped than before.
- *Morgan* (1982) studied adolescents over a two-year period and found the more TV girls watched, the more stereotyped their attitudes were. Boys were not affected like this but their attitudes were highly sex-typed to start with so there was little room for change.

Evaluation

- Children seem to express more stereotyped attitudes than do adults but this may not be reflected in their behaviour and they may grow out of it.
- Viewers will not absorb the image of males and females without question, especially if it is very different from their own experience. For example, most women on TV are shown in domestic roles, but ever-increasing numbers of women are employed outside the home.

Culture and gender

Not all cultures express gender in the same way. *Margaret Mead*'s (1935) comparison of three tribal cultures in Samoa and New Guinea illustrates this:

remember this research is 60 years, or more, old

- **Arapesh Indians**. These people showed no strong division into what is stereotypically male and female in our Western culture. Both males and females were gentle and cooperative. Both sexes were 'maternal' towards babies and children and shared in child-care. They were caring and peaceable.
- **The Mundugumor tribe**. These people did not show great differences in male and female behaviour. Instead they were all aggressive, argumentative and suspicious. Little attention was paid to children.
- **The Tchambuli tribe**. These people showed reversal of the Western stereotype. The women took charge of the economic affairs of the tribe. They were competitive and efficient. They reared their sons to be artistic, emotional, decorative and sentimental. (But it was still the males who went to war!)

Mead's research has been much criticised but it does call into question the power of social forces in shaping gender roles.

this is a more recent idea

Schlegel and Barry (1986) suggested the male and female roles children were exposed to depended on how much women contributed to **food-getting**. Some societies *gather* their food, wandering from place to place and living from day to day. Others can hunt and farm and *accumulate* food stores. They tend to be less mobile.

If food is mostly gathered, both men and women contribute a great deal to food-getting. If it is fished, hunted or extensively farmed, men tend to do more food-getting. If *both men and women* are very involved in food-getting, the culture tends to show the following pattern:

- Females are *more highly valued*. They are seen less as sex and reproductive objects. Men may take more than one wife and there is often a bride-price. Rape is extremely rare.
- Females have *greater freedom*.
- Girls are reared as *workers* and expected to be more *independent*.
- *Birth control is practised*. Pregnancies are more spaced leaving the women freer to contribute to work activities.

Compare this to sex-roles in our society now and, say, at the start of the 1900s.

Evaluation

- SLT is a neat and *economical* way of explaining differences in behaviour between boys and girls.
- Research does seem to show that males and females are *treated* differently but this may be because they *behave* differently in the first place possibly because of *biological influences*.
- *Golombok and Fivush* (1994) say that even in families who firmly believe in equality of the sexes, children are no different than those from more traditional families in their play activities, behaviour and choice of friends. Either parents can do little to alter their child's nature or there are so many influences outside the family that the parents' influence is swamped.
- More recent research emphasises the importance of the *setting* in determining whether boys or girls show **sex-stereotyped behaviour**. It seems that boys and girls acquire behaviours appropriate to both sexes and show them when the time is right, e.g. Boy Scouts might be happy to cook, clean and sew if they are on camp or earning badges and girls may be perfectly capable of carrying out car maintenance or leadership activities if they are working towards a Duke of Edinburgh Award. Cross-cultural studies also support the view that the setting is important.

COGNITIVE–DEVELOPMENTAL EXPLANATIONS

Kohlberg (1966) suggested that children need to develop an understanding of gender before they can take on a gender role. He suggested three stages:

1. **Gender identity**. 2–5 years. This is when a child can correctly identify them-selves as a boy or a girl.
2. **Gender stability**. 4–6 years. This is when a child knows they always have been and always will be one sex only.
3. **Gender constancy**. 6–7 years. This is when a child understands that changes in dress or other kinds of appearance do not change a person's sex. Before this stage, a child might claim that a man with long hair and make-up is a woman.

Evaluation

- It does seem to be the case that children with gender constancy watch same-sex models more **but**:
- Children seem to show sex-typed behaviour long before this.
- Kohlberg cannot explain the finding that children have serious problems adjust-ing to being assigned to the opposite sex if this is done after 3 years of age.

GENDER SCHEMA EXPLANATIONS

Bem (1964) has developed her ideas about androgyny into another approach. A schema is a **mental structure** which we use to take in knowledge about the world. A **gender schema** begins to develop as soon as the infant realises there are males and females. From then on, the child will sort all new knowledge about people, their objects and activities into the schema under the general headings of *male* or *female*. The schema helps them to organise and understand the world around them and acts like a magnet for new information. *Martin and Halverson* (1983) suggest the develop-ment of the gender schema goes like this:

- children realise there is a male–female distinction;
- they label themselves accurately as male or female;
- at about 4–6 years of age they focus on their own gender, learning how their gen-der play and talk and who they make friends with;
- at about 8–10 years old they will begin to pay more attention to the opposite gender so the schema expands to include more detailed information about both genders;
- after this, the gender concept becomes more flexible, e.g. girls know most boys don't play with dolls but they could if they wanted to.

Evaluation

- Gender schema theory can explain how children start to show sex-typed behav-iour and attitudes even *before* they have gender constancy. It is all part of the growth of their schema.

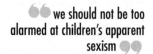 we should not be too alarmed at children's apparent sexism

- The theory sees the strong sex-role stereotypes that children hold as a *natural stage* in the child's understanding of gender. There is nothing to be alarmed about. Children's attitudes are not fixed for ever and will change depending on the experiences they have and the models they see.
- The theory neatly combines SLT and cognitive–developmental approaches into one.

EXAMINATION QUESTION

1. NEAB specimen paper (Tier Q)

Spend about 13 minutes answering this question

(a) What is meant by the term **sex-role stereotyping**?   [3]

(b) Explain **one** way in which **sex-role stereotyping** in young children could be avoided. Support your answer with theory and evidence   [5]

(c) Explain the difference between **sex identity** and **gender identity**   [3]

[*Total 11 marks*]
(NEAB)

TUTOR ANSWER

1. NEAB specimen paper (Tier Q)

(a) Sex-role stereotyping is a rather rigid idea, based on an individual's sex, about how they should behave. This idea is generalised to all males and females.

(b) Social Learning Theory suggests that children observe and imitate the behaviour of certain others (models) around them. One source of such models is television. Research suggests that the more TV children watch, the more sex-typed their attitudes. Williams found that the introduction of TV into a Canadian town that previously had none was related to a rise in sex-role stereotyping in children's attitudes. The solution would appear to be to ensure that TV content does not model sex-role stereotyped behaviour.

(c) Sex identity is when we understand that we are biologically male or female. Gender identity is when we label ourselves as psychologically masculine or feminine. These two types of identity do not always match up, and this may or may not cause problems for the individual concerned.

STUDENTS' ANSWERS

1. MEG specimen paper 4 (Higher), Option 2 Developmental Psychology
Source A Gender difference in spatial ability

Spend 30 minutes on this question

The early research on gender differences suggested that males are better at tasks which require spatial ability. Spatial abilities include being able to read maps, solve mazes or find your way around a town. In one study, twenty-six participants were given a spatial task in which they had to rotate figures mentally. The psychologist recorded the number of errors on the test and these results are shown below.

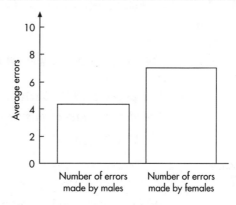

(a) Using the graph above, what was the average number of errors made by the female participants? [1]

good enough 1/1

Seven out of ten.

(b) As a measure of control, the psychologist made sure that all the participants were tested in the same environment. Describe one other measure of control that she could use. [2]

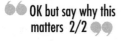
OK but say why this matters 2/2

She could standardise the instructions given to participants before they did the test. This would make sure they were all treated equally.

(c) (i) Briefly describe the biological approach to gender-role development. [4]

> Biological theories of gender-roles argue that boys and girls are genetically programmed to behave in typically male or female ways. These theories say that differences in behaviour can be explained by sex chromosomes (XX in girls and XY in boys) and hormones (testosterone in boys and oestrogens in girls). The strongest evidence for biological theory is that males tend to be more aggressive than females.

66 go for more detail, e.g. raise role of environment issue
3/4 99

(ii) Describe **one** study which supports the biological approach to gender-role development. [4]

> One study that supports the biological approach was done on monkeys. W. C. Young injected a pregnant monkey, whose foetus was genetically female, with a course of testosterone (male hormone). Every day from the 42nd to 122nd day of her pregnancy she received this injection. When the infant monkey was born it was genetically female but had developed normal male sex organs. It behaved like other male monkeys, challenging other males to fight for higher status in the group. When it was sexually mature it even tried to mount female monkeys. This investigation, which also tested other lower order mammals, showed that hormones can change the sex-role behaviour of those animals. These findings would not necessarily apply to humans, who are better able to control their behaviour.

66 good, but comment further
3/4 99

(d) Describe **one** study which shows there are cultural differences in gender-roles or gender-role development. [4]

> There are cultural differences in gender-role development according to the anthropologist Margaret Mead who conducted studies of tribes in Samoa and New Guinea. One study of the Tchambuli tribe (about 500 people) showed the opposite of what used to be the Western pattern. The women were industrious makers of mats, baskets, rain capes and mosquito baskets. The men spent most of their time carving, painting and preparing elaborate theatrical displays. They socialised their boys to be artistic and sentimental and their girls to be competitive. Both sexes were reared by the women and boys were not allowed to join male company until they were teenagers. The Arapesh tribe all behaved in ways that Westerners think are feminine and the Mundugumor all behaved in masculine ways. Mead's work suggests that gender roles are the result of how people are brought up in their culture, not the result of genetics.

66 well-structured answer 99

66 4/4 99

[Total 15 marks]
(MEG)

66 14/15 Concise, clear answers with one or two where the marks were only just earned 99

2. SEG paper 2 1993, Section B

Spend 40 minutes on this question

(a) What is 'gender'? [2]

> Gender is the psychological state of feeling masculine or feminine as opposed to the biological state of being male or female.

66 mention role of experience
1/2 99

(b) From what you have learned in psychology, explain **one** way in which children learn gender. [5]

> Social Learning Theorists would say that children are influenced by the important people around them. They might copy their behaviour. This is known as observational learning. Parents are role-models for their children and children will copy their behaviour and also that of other people they like or admire. This behaviour can then be reinforced by the parents by a reward such as praise. A father seeing his young son acting in a boyish way will praise him and this will condition him to repeat the desired behaviour. A mother might praise her daughter for helping with the housework so her behaviour is conditioned also. This behaviour can vary though as different cultures have different gender-roles and it must be remembered that sex hormones can influence behaviour too.

66 take care to make the answer sufficiently psychological 99

66 4/5 99

(c) Describe **one** example of gender difference shown by psychological studies. [5]

◖◖ add detailed description

3/5 ◗◗

Maccoby and Jacklin carried out a large study of differences between males and females. They found that one area where they differ is intellectually although the differences are small. Boys are a bit better than girls at maths and at dealing with visual problems. Girls are better verbally.

(d) Psychologists believe that much of our thinking and behaviour is based on social stereotypes. How can schools and colleges deal with such stereotypes in order to encourage gender and racial equality? [8]

Stereotyping is when we judge someone based on their sex and think of males or females as all the same. In schools and colleges this could lead teachers to treat boys as if they are always good at maths and sciences and girls as if they are only good at arts subjects, English and domestic work. Research shows that boys get more attention in school because they are noisier and more demanding. Girls tend to get left out. There are two things teachers could do to help. One would be to make sure they pay the same attention to girls and boys no matter what subject they are doing. Another would be to make sure children do not use books or watch videos that have sex-role stereotyping in them.

◖◖ mention overt and covert influences ◗◗

The same applies to racial stereotyping. Children from some races might be seen as less intelligent or only good at certain subjects. Teachers must make sure all the children have equal chances to do the subjects they want and take part in class. Social Learning Theory says that children learn from people they admire. If they admire a teacher who has racist attitudes they could start to be racist themselves. Teachers must model non-racist, non-sexist behaviour to children. Another way they could help is by having discussions with the children about racism and sexism to help them understand each other more.

◖◖ 7/8 ◗◗

[*Total 20 marks*]
(SEG)

◖◖ 15/20 Very good answer, with just a little more detail needed in places ◗◗

NB. SEG questions, such as this, set in 1993 and before, were marked out of 20. From 1994 onwards they were marked out of 30. Under the new scheme, full marks for the question above would be (a) 4, (b) 8, (c) 6 and (d) 12 making a total of 30. The student would have scored (a) 2, (b) 6, (c) 4 and (d) 9 making a total of 21 out of 30.

A Review Sheet for this chapter can be found on pp. 241–2.

INDIVIDUAL DEVELOPMENT PART TWO – MORAL DEVELOPMENT AND SELF

GETTING STARTED

Theories of moral development appear on the SEG and MEG syllabuses. A look at 'Cognitive Development' (section 11.1, pp. 127–32) to refresh your memory on Piaget's theory will help you to understand his explanation of moral development more thoroughly.

MEG students can settle for studying just the theories of moral development. The SEG syllabus requires you to consider in more detail the role of parents and peers in moral development, the relationship between moral development and behaviour and the development of pro-social reasoning.

Self appears only on the NEAB and SEG syllabuses. In this section we will look at origins of self and the effect of the expectancies of others on self.

1. THEORIES OF MORAL DEVELOPMENT

2. MORAL DEVELOPMENT AND BEHAVIOUR

3. PRO-SOCIAL REASONING

4. ASPECTS OF SELF-DEVELOPMENT

5. LABELLING, EXPECTATIONS AND SELF-FULFILLING PROPHECIES

ESSENTIAL PRINCIPLES

Gross (1992) says that moral development includes:

- *understanding* society's rules of behaviour;
- learning *how to behave* according to those rules;
- learning the *feelings* that go with good and bad behaviour, i.e. pride and worthiness vs guilt and shame.

<table>
<tr><td>1 ▷</td><td>**THEORIES OF MORAL DEVELOPMENT**</td></tr>
</table>

❝❝ these theories explain different aspects of morality ❞❞

THE PSYCHODYNAMIC APPROACH

Here we will take *Freud's psychoanalytic theory* as an example. He explains how we acquire moral *feelings*.

Look at all of the section on psychodynamic explanations of sex and gender in chapter eight. In particular you need to be able to describe how boys and girls resolve the **Oedipal** or **Electra conflict**. When they **identify** with the same sex parent, they take in many of that parent's characteristics. These include the parent's standards of *right and wrong* and internalising these gives us the third part of the personality known as the **superego**. The superego has two parts:

- the **conscience**, which gives us guilty feelings if we do wrong;
- the **ego-ideal**, which makes us feel good if we do right.

From this theory we can predict:

- Children with strict parents will suffer greater unconscious anxiety and have to work harder to resolve the Oedipal (or Electra) conflict. The identification will be *stronger* and so will the superego.
- Girls do not experience as much unconscious anxiety as boys so their identification will be *weaker* and so will their superegos.
- Children in **single parent families** should be less moral because they do not have the chance to resolve fully their Oedipal or Electra conflict.

Evaluation

- There is no direct evidence for the Oedipal and Electra conflicts because they cannot be *observed* and *measured*. Even the case of Little Hans, who was said to be suffering from castration anxiety, can be explained in simpler ways than Freud suggested.
- There is no evidence that females are morally weaker than males. If anything, they seem to be better able to *resist* temptation.
- If children from single parent families are found to be less moral there are *simpler explanations* for it than failing to resolve fully their Oedipal or Electra conflict. The parent may be single after a period of family conflict and/or divorce and may be under extra pressure from having to cope alone. Both of these things could mean that *consistent discipline* is not applied to the children and their behaviour is worse as a result.

COGNITIVE–DEVELOPMENTAL APPROACHES

These theories explain how we come to *understand* the rules of society, in other words, how moral *reasoning* develops.

Piaget's theory

Piaget (1932) collected evidence about the development of moral reasoning through observing children's play and *interviewing* them about moral problems. He identified two main stages of development in their reasoning:

Heteronomous morality (children up to 9 or 10 years old). Heteronomous means that their morality is controlled by *others* such as parents, teachers or other authority figures. At this stage:

- **Rules.** Children see rules as decided by *authority* figures. They are fixed and must not be broken.

- **Right and wrong**. Children's judgements of right and wrong tend to be based on the *amount of visible damage* caused rather than the intention behind it. For example, a child who breaks ten plates while helping to dry the dishes is seen as naughtier than a child who breaks one plate while stealing jam.
- **Punishment**. Children tend to suggest **retributive** (very harsh) or **reciprocal** (an eye for an eye) punishments for wrongful acts.

Autonomous morality (children over 9 to 10 years old). Autonomous means controlled from *within*. The child no longer needs others to say what is morally correct. At this stage:

- **Rules**. Children see rules as decided by *themselves*. They can be changed by agreement.
- **Right and wrong**. Children can take both the amount of damage and *intention* into account when judging how much someone is to blame for a wrongful act.
- **Punishment**. Children tend to suggest **rational** punishments adjusted to fit the crime.

Evaluation

- There is *cross-cultural* support for the idea of stages in moral development.
- Piaget's findings have been borne out many times in *replications* of his studies.
- Piaget may have *underestimated children's ability* to understand other people's intentions. If problems are presented on videotape, 6 year olds reason as well as 10 year olds.
- Real-life moral problems are *rarely as simple* as damage + intention so we need to test how children would deal with more complicated ones.

Kohlberg's theory

Kohlberg (1969) presented moral dilemmas to children and adults and asked them a series of questions to investigate their moral reasoning. One such dilemma concerned **'Heinz'** whose wife was dying of cancer. A druggist living in the same town had invented a drug which might save her but Heinz could not afford to pay what the man was asking. He tried and failed to borrow the money and, in the end, broke into the drug store and stole the drug. Kohlberg asked people questions such as 'Should Heinz have done that?' 'Was it wrong or right?' After people had responded to a number of moral dilemmas, Kohlberg was able to sort their judgements into three levels and six stages. People tend to *move up* the stages as they get older but *some never leave the first stage* and *most do not reach the last stage*. It is important to remember that it is the complexity of people's reasoning that determines the stage, not the judgement itself.

❝❝ the development of moral reasoning can be lifelong ❞❞

Level I Pre-conventional morality
- **Stage 1 Punishment and obedience stage**. The child's judgements concern avoiding physical discomfort or physical punishment.
- **Stage 2 Hedonistic stage**. The child's judgements concern gaining physical pleasures and rewards like sweets and cuddles.

Level II Conventional morality
- **Stage 3 Good boy/girl stage**. The child's judgements concern psychological rewards such as praise and approval from others.
- **Stage 4 Law and order stage**. The child becomes aware of the wider rules of society so judgements concern obeying those rules in order to avoid psychological punishment such as guilt.

Level III. Post-conventional morality
- **Stage 5 Contracts and legalistic stage**. Laws and rules are seen as guidelines which can be applied flexibly. Judgements concern achieving fairness or the greatest good for the greatest number.
- **Stage 6 Universal ethical principles stage**. People at this stage have developed their own set of moral guidelines which may or may not fit with the law. The principles apply to everyone, e.g. human rights, justice and equality. The person's judgements concern being true to their own standards, even if this is disapproved of by others.

Evaluation

- Other research has confirmed the *general sequence* of development suggested by Kohlberg (e.g. Kohlberg's own 20-year longitudinal study of 58 10-year-old boys).
- *Cross-cultural studies* (e.g. *Snarey* 1985) support Kohlberg's claim that his theory is *universal*. People everywhere follow the same sequence of development but in less developed rural cultures stage 4 is usually the highest stage reached compared to modern Western cultures where stage 5 is usually the highest.
- Some critics think Kohlberg's dilemmas only tap into people's reasoning about justice and fairness and *do not test wider moral issues* such as obligations to others or pro-social behaviour.
- People may *reason* at higher levels than they *behave* so Kohlberg's theory tells us what they *think* but not what they *do*.
- Kohlberg suggested that children's moral reasoning could be encouraged by *debating* moral issues with others at higher stages of development. There is some evidence that this does help children's reasoning to advance. The same effect can be achieved by parents who discuss moral issues with their children before punishing them.

Gilligan's ethic of caring

Gilligan (1982) suggested that because Kohlberg's theory is based mainly on research with males it is biased in their favour. On Kohlberg's classification women tend to be scored as morally inferior. Gilligan challenged this idea. She interviewed women facing **real-life dilemmas** such as deciding whether to continue an unwanted pregnancy. She concluded that men and women are *no different* in their ability to reason about moral issues. Instead, women's moral reasoning centres more on **care** and men's centres more on **justice**. On Kohlberg's dilemmas, judgements based on care score lower than judgements based on justice.

> is there a sex difference in the focus of moral reasoning?

Gilligan suggested women go through three stages of moral reasoning:

1 **caring for self**;
2 **caring for others**, perhaps sacrificing own needs to achieve this;
3 **caring for self and others** in a way which balances your own needs with those of others.

Evaluation

- *Bee* (1992) says that, in general, studies of sex differences in moral reasoning in children show no differences in the tendency to base judgements on care. In adults, however, women do seem to centre their judgements on care more than do men.
- *Walker* (1984) found no evidence that girls score lower on Kohlberg's scoring system.
- Gilligan has alerted us to a possible *bias* in the way we think of moral issues, in other words, it is determined by *males*.

SOCIAL LEARNING EXPLANATIONS

These approaches assume we *learn* moral behaviour through exactly the same processes as we learn any other behaviour. Look back at chapter four to refresh your memory. Social Learning theorists accept that we learn through both the processes of **conditioning** and **observational learning**. Other people, such as parents, peers and teachers are vital in these processes. Eventually, the *external* controls a child experiences should become *internal* ones so others are no longer needed to control the individual's behaviour.

Classical conditioning

Some of our moral behaviour is the result of learning **conditional reflexes** through **classical conditioning**. Here is an example of what might happen to a child who has just taken money from a parent's wallet. The parent's reaction to this should condition an **aversion** to stealing money which will generalise to similar situations. By the same process, parents should be able to condition positive feelings in a child for good behaviour.

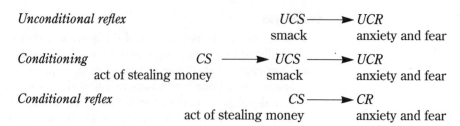

Unconditional reflex				UCS ———▶ UCR	
				smack	anxiety and fear
Conditioning		CS ———▶	UCS ———▶	UCR	
		act of stealing money	smack	anxiety and fear	
Conditional reflex				CS ———▶ CR	
				act of stealing money	anxiety and fear

Operant conditioning

Parents, and others, should also be able to *change* and *shape* moral behaviour by **selectively reinforcing** and **punishing** a child's good and bad behaviour.

Reinforcement and punishment

It is important to take into account the relationship between the child and the parent. Reinforcement and punishment work better in a *warm and secure relationship*. *Sears et al.* (1957) found that mothers who used *psychological* rewards and punishments such as love and disapproval had children with stronger consciences than mothers who used *physical* rewards and punishments such as sweets and smacks. Children may be more influenced by peers who they *admire* or whose approval they *value*.

All the comments made in the chapter on Learning about reinforcement and punishment apply to moral behaviour but here are some specific points:

- It is better to use positive reinforcement to *increase* good behaviour and punishment to *decrease* bad behaviour. This makes learning a happier experience.
- Punishment on its own does not show the child how to behave. It only shows it how *not* to behave.
- Punishment **models** to the child an unacceptable way of getting others to do want you want.
- Punishment can *damage the relationship* between punisher and learner.
- Punishment may encourage children to behave badly if it is the only way they can get *attention*.
- Reward and punishment can work well together if they are used *on mutually incompatible behaviours*, e.g. rewarding a child for sitting and working quietly but punishing them for shouting across the room.

⁶⁶remember punishment may have undesirable effects⁹⁹

Observational learning

Remember, we may learn a great deal from observing others but we do not always imitate what they do. Look back to the chapter on Learning to see how children learn from models and what sorts of models they imitate most. An important point here is that parents and other models should practise what they preach if they want children to copy them.

⁶⁶note well⁹⁹

2 ▷ MORAL DEVELOPMENT AND BEHAVIOUR

Do people behave in ways which match their level of moral development?

- *Hartshorne and May* (1928) gave 12,000 11–14 year olds opportunities to cheat, lie and steal knowing they would get away with it. They found great *inconsistency* in children's behaviour. They would cheat in some situations and not others and sometimes they would cheat or not cheat at different times in the same situation. Hartshorne and May concluded moral behaviour was not a consistent trait. It depended on the situation **but:**
- *Kohlberg* (1975) discovered that tendency to cheat decreased the higher a child's stage of moral reasoning **so,**
- *Bee* (1992) concluded moral behaviour is determined by a whole set of influences. The situation and level of reasoning are important but so are social pressures like **group norms, social norms** and the **costs and benefits** to someone of behaving morally or immorally. Until we understand how these things affect each other we will find it very difficult to predict people's moral behaviour.

3 ▷ PRO-SOCIAL REASONING

Much of the work on moral development described in this chapter concentrates on doing wrong, but what of helpful and altruistic behaviour?

Eisenberg's model of pro-social reasoning

Eisenberg (1986) presented children with moral dilemmas in which they had to decide between self-interest and helping someone else. She found five levels of pro-social reasoning which cover the age range from pre-school to teenage and beyond.

- **Level 1 Hedonistic, self-focused orientation**. 'If I help her she'll help me.'
- **Level 2 Needs orientated orientation**. 'She'll feel better if I help her.'
- **Level 3 Approval or stereotyped orientation**. 'I'll help because it's expected.'
- **Level 4a Empathic orientation**. 'I'll help because I can see how she feels.'
- **Level 4b Transitional empathic level**. 'I'll help because I feel I have a duty to.'
- **Level 5 Strongly internalised orientation**. 'I'll help because I feel a personal responsibility to do so.' (This stage differs from the previous one only in how personally committed the person feels.)

> some difficult terms to remember here

Implications

- At first this looks rather like Kohlberg's stages of moral reasoning, but researchers have found that scores on Eisenberg's and Kohlberg's scales are not strongly related. If anything, pro-social reasoning is *ahead* of moral reasoning.
- *Hay and Murray* (1982) showed that *parents* could help pro-social reasoning to develop up the levels by playing exchange games with their children. Children who are encouraged and shown how to give and take from an early age were more inclined to share later on. *Bee* (1992) recommends that parents will develop the highest level of pro-social behaviour in their children if they preach it, model it and reinforce the child for doing it.
- *TV* can also encourage pro-social development. *Freidrich and Stein* (1975) showed either a neutral programme or a pro-social programme called 'Mr Rogers' Neighbourhood' to 5- and 6-year-olds over four days. The 'Mr Rogers'' group showed better understanding of pro-social behaviour and were more pro-social too, especially if they were also encouraged to role-play what they had seen on TV first.
- *Rheingold* (1982) also found cross-cultural differences in pro-social development depending on how much children were allowed or encouraged to help parents. Children who are encouraged to do domestic chores and care for other children develop pro-social reasoning faster than in cultures where this is all done for them.

4 ASPECTS OF SELF-DEVELOPMENT

DEFINITIONS

There are many terms relating to self and textbooks often use them in slightly different ways. Here are some definitions:

- **self** – the part of us of which we are consciously aware, our inner world or sense of existence;
- **self-concept** – the set of attitudes or ideas we have about our self;
- **self-esteem** – how we evaluate, or feel, about our self. Our evaluation may be positive, negative or neutral;
- **ideal self** – how we would like to be.

> these four things may be grouped together under the main title of self-concept

DEVELOPMENT OF THE SELF-CONCEPT

Some psychologists think that the new-born and infant human does not have a sense of self as separate from the world. This is a very extreme form of **egocentrism** which disappears in a few months. By 18–24 months, the child will be aware of itself as an *object* in a world of separate objects. In later childhood and adolescence, the child will increasingly be able to *reflect* on the self, *evaluate* it and consider *how others regard* it. The self-concept will eventually be quite complex, incorporating, among other things, the many **roles** an individual plays.

Social psychologists think the self-concept is *social* in origin and can be shaped by three main influences:

1 Feedback from others

As children we receive much feedback from others whether we like it or not! *Cooley* (1902) referred to this aspect of self-concept as the **looking-glass self** because others

❝❝ consider the ethics of this ❞❞

provide us with a reflection of ourselves. To illustrate this effect, *Guthrie* (1938) described a student prank in which the class-mates of a rather dull and unattractive female student decided to treat her as if she were very desirable. They drew lots to decide who would take her out. After a string of dates, the female student's self-concept appeared to change. She allegedly became more confident and outgoing, smiled more and changed the way she dressed. In a way, she reflected the image others had given her.

Obviously, we do not soak up others' opinions like sponges. Much depends on whether we value their opinion. Also, as adults, we become very careful about letting each other know what we think. It is then necessary to be sensitive to more subtle feedback and we may not read each others' messages accurately.

2 Comparison with others

Festinger (1954) developed **social comparison theory** to explain this source of information about the self. Sometimes we can compare our self against an external standard, e.g. when we achieve an examination grade, we know how it compares to others' grades. When external standards are not available, we look to others in reality or in books, magazines or on TV to see how we compare. The other person must be similar to us in *relevant* ways. It is no good choosing an impossibly high standard to aspire to. If we compare ourselves to others and come off badly we can either change some aspect of ourselves or get them to change until we feel more comfortable.

3 Social roles occupied by the individual

A large part of our self-concept consists of the social roles we play in our lives. A social role is rather like an actor's role. It has a **script** and an expected pattern of behaviour, or **norm**, that we learn largely to *conform* to (although, just like an actor, we can sometimes interpret a role for ourselves and express it in our own way). It is mainly through parents and other important people that we learn how to play our roles. Some roles, such as the sex-role, may then last a lifetime, others, such as 'student' may be quite brief. It has been suggested that we conform to role expectations for the same reasons we conform in other ways, i.e. through **compliance**, **internalisation** or **identification** (see chapter six).

To find out which roles people consider important to themselves, a simple technique is the 'Twenty Statement Test'. A person is asked to list 20 answers to the question 'Who am I?' (Try it now before you read on.) *Mulford and Salisbury* (1964) tested over 1,000 adults in this way and found people most often mentioned four types of role:

- **family roles**, e.g. mother, brother – 70% of responses
- **occupational**, **roles**, e.g. student, shop assistant – 68% of responses
- **marital roles**, e.g. divorced, married, single – 34% of responses
- **religious roles**, e.g. Catholic, Muslim – 30% of responses.

Role theorists also talk of:

- **Inter-role conflict**, where the demands of two roles compete, e.g. being a teacher and having your own child, to whom you are also a parent, in your class.
- **Intra-role conflict**, where demands within a role compete, e.g. wanting to be a mother at home with the children as well as wanting to set a good example to the children by having a career.

If such conflicts become too difficult to resolve, problems can develop, especially if the role is a large part of a person's self-concept. The role may be played badly, abandoned altogether or, if possible, changed to fit the individual.

5 ▶ LABELLING, EXPECTATIONS AND SELF-FULFILLING PROPHECIES

There are many examples of the power of others' expectations over one's self-concept and behaviour in the psychological literature, e.g. see Guthrie, above. In another well-known study by *Rosenhan* (1973), eight psychologically healthy people individually turned up at psychiatric hospitals complaining of hearing voices. Once admitted, they behaved perfectly normally, but they found that the label of mental disorder was very difficult to shake off. In addition, some of the staff treated them differently, e.g. ignoring their greetings and explaining their behaviour in line with the label. In another area of research, *Rosenthal* (1966) showed how the expectations experimenters had about how their results would go often meant that they found what they expected to find. Such studies show that once a person has labelled themselves, or been labelled, their own and others' expectations of their behaviour can come true, hence the term **self-fulfilling prophecy**.

STUDIES OF THE EFFECTS OF LABELLING, EXPECTATIONS AND THE SELF-FULFILLING PROPHECY

In this section, we will look separately at *gender* and *educational achievement* and then take the two together.

Gender

Gender-roles are a very powerful part of the self-concept and they influence our behaviour in important ways. For information on how we acquire gender-roles and how they affect our behaviour, see chapter nine. **Sex-role stereotyping** is a very important influence here.

Educational achievement

Rosenthal and Jacobson (1968) published the findings of a study called **Pygmalion in the Classroom** about teacher expectations and pupils' achievement. Teachers at 'Oak School' were told that researchers needed to check out a new test on the children. It was also said that some children, especially *slow achievers*, could be expected to show *spurts* in academic development and that the test could *predict* which children would do this. (In fact the test was simply a well-established test of academic ability.)

Children were initially tested in the spring. The following September results were given to the teachers and the names of the **spurters** (about 20% of the children) were casually mentioned. Unbeknown to the teachers, this was false information and the 'spurters' names had been *randomly selected*. When the researchers returned to retest the children, they claimed that the 'spurters' had indeed shown a gain in academic achievement, especially in the *first grade* where there is the greatest room for improvement. The gains were greater than those made by control group children who had not been labelled as 'spurters'.

Evaluation

Such studies seem to tell us what we want to hear but we should not accept the findings too readily. There have been many criticisms:

- Many *ethical* questions can be raised about the **deception** involved in this study.
- Rosenthal and Jacobson's *methods* have been seriously questioned, e.g. for misrecording and misrepresentation of data. Also, many teachers said they had no recollection of which children were meant to 'spurt'. Perhaps the researchers were victims of their own **experimenter expectancy effect**!
- Numerous attempts to replicate the study have failed. *Brophy and Good* (1974) reviewed 60 attempted replications and found no strong evidence that expectancy effects worked as suggested. They did, however, find consistencies in some teachers' behaviour, e.g. they had higher expectations of children who were:

  - more compliant and obedient
  - more attractive
  - seated closer to the teacher
  - clearly spoken.

  Teacher expectations showed themselves through such things as giving these children more time to answer questions and more praise than other children.

- *Rolison and Medway* (1985) found both a label and information about a child's recent performance was important. More was expected of children labelled 'learning disabled' than of children labelled 'mentally retarded' and expectations were higher for those whose performance had recently improved.

Implications of expectancy studies:

- To be sure that the expectancy effect does work it would be necessary to label people as low achievers to see if it depressed children's performance. This would, of course, be *unethical*. Evidence for such an effect is therefore only *anecdotal*.

❝❝ the evidence is not particularly conclusive ❞❞

The best teachers can do is to be aware that negative labels could be damaging and try to guard against them.

- We do not know how an expectancy effect is meant to begin. Is it with the teacher or the child?
- Teachers do not have absolute control over children's attitudes to study and, sometimes, no amount of high expectancy will budge a child with no interest or motivation. Parents and peers may be far more influential than the teacher.
- To accept an expectancy effect is to undermine teachers' professionalism and commitment to help all children achieve the best they can.
- In case a positive expectancy does work, it would be safest to have high expectations of all children.

GENDER AND EDUCATIONAL ACHIEVEMENT

Golombok and Fivush (1994) quote evidence to show that boys receive *more attention*, both positive and negative, from teachers and that this difference starts as early as nursery school. At first, teachers focus on behaviour in school but once children know how to behave, teachers focus on academic work. Attention given to boys and girls then evens out but it is given for different things:

- boys are praised more for knowledge and criticised more for bad behaviour;
- girls are praised more for obedience and criticised more for wrong answers.

In spite of this, girls say they enjoy school more and they achieve more until adolescence when boys seem to go ahead. There are no differences in intelligence, so how does this happen?

Hyde and Linn (1988) reviewed 165 studies of gender differences in ability and found:

- girls were only very slightly better than boys in *verbal* ability;
- boys are only very slightly better than girls in *mathematical* ability.

 note this

They concluded that the differences were so small as to be unimportant. However, there does seem to be a marked difference in the *sciences* where boys out-perform girls. Why? Most researchers agree that academic ability of boys and girls is similar so differences must be due to social influences. Golombok and Fivush make some suggestions:

- **Teachers' expectations**. Some research shows that teachers pay more attention (both positive and negative) to boys in maths, physics and chemistry classes and this seems to make boys more sure than girls of their ability (but the evidence is mixed).
- **Children's expectations**. Some studies show boys seem to expect to do better in maths exams than girls. Girls do not seem as open as boys to positive feedback from teachers about their maths ability but, again, the evidence is mixed.
- **Parents' expectations**. Even if teachers and children do not have expectations, parents may do! Some studies show mothers and fathers put their daughters' maths ability down to hard work and their sons' ability down to talent. (The studies also show such ideas are shared by children and seem to affect their self-concept and motivation.)
- **Gender-role expectations**. It may be that the stereotype of the modest female who is not academically talented in sciences is holding girls back. Golombok and Fivush suggest that girls' self-esteem is more affected by *social acceptance* and *approval* and boys' self-esteem is more affected by their *academic achievements*. This may cause girls to reject things such as being good at science, which are thought of as unfeminine, and so they underachieve. Boys have no such problem.

HOW TO MODIFY NEGATIVE EXPECTATIONS

We have seen how important parents, peers and teachers can be as a source of self-concept for an individual and how others' expectations can affect self-concept and behaviour. The process is cyclical, see **Fig**. 10.1.

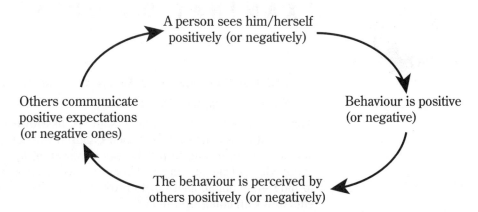

Fig 10.1 Self-concept and feedback
from others

This should give us some clues about how to improve a negative self-concept. Constant negative influences on this cycle will eventually affect the individual's self-esteem so that they begin to feel worthless and give up trying. We need to break into the cycle of negativity and improve self-esteem, but first, we need to know what affects self-esteem. There is little research on the effect of peers on self-esteem but we do know something about the role of parents and teachers.

The role of parents

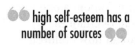

high self-esteem has a number of sources

In 1967, *Coopersmith* carried out a study of the origins of self-esteem in 1,700 10–12-year-old boys. He tested self-esteem by interviewing the boys, their parents and teachers and by testing the boys in other ways. He concluded there was no one factor which was responsible for high self-esteem but found that the following things could help parents improve their children's feelings of worth:

- **warm acceptance** by parents of their children;
- the setting of **clear standards** and boundaries of behaviour by parents;
- **consistent enforcement** of the standards and boundaries by parents;
- use of **reinforcement** rather than punishment;
- insistence on **respect** for parents;
- **reasonable expectations** of success by parents from their children;
- expecting and trusting children to take **initiative** from time to time.

The role of teachers

We have already seen that the evidence about the influence of teachers' expectations on their pupils' achievement is mixed. However, studies have shown a *low but positive* relationship between a child's self-esteem and academic achievement. (Incidentally, the effect is more marked for boys.) It would seem to make sense to try to improve pupils' self-esteem when they are underachieving. *Burns* (1979) makes recommendations to teachers which are similar to Coopersmith's recommendations to parents:

- **acceptance** of the child as s/he is and as a person worthy of respect and attention;
- set **clearly defined limits** and expectations about behaviour;
- **consistent enforcement** of limits and expectations;
- complete **honesty** (children can spot false praise straight away!);
- setting **interesting tasks** which are *challenging* but *manageable* (remembering that nothing succeeds like success);
- recognise the child's need to feel they have **succeeded by themselves**.

With individual children, it may also be possible to use **counselling** to help them close the gap between their self-concept and an ideal self which may be out of reach. Burns also raises other questions about education which you might like to consider:

- **Streaming** a child for academic ability can mean that they are labelled as a low achiever from the start. Burns thinks streaming can be disastrous for lower ability children. On the other hand, not to stream would mean less able children constantly comparing themselves to impossible standards.
- **The teacher's self-esteem**. Teachers with high self-esteem and trust in their ability to help pupils change are more likely to have a positive effect on their pupils' self-concept. How would a teacher develop and maintain high self-esteem?

EXAMINATION QUESTIONS

1. MEG June 1993 Module 2, Source C: Telling the truth about Lying

Spend 20 minutes on this question

Almost all children will tell a lie at some point. However, parents find lying very hard to deal with. Parents worry that their children will not have developed a sense of right and wrong. According to psychological research, by age 3 children have some idea about what is true and untrue. Children may lie for a variety of reasons. They may lie to hide some unhappiness or to protect themselves or their friends. How should parents deal with children who lie?

Psychologists provide three guidelines:

A   Parents should provide a good example to their children by not lying.
B   Parents should explain to their children **why** lying is wrong. Punishment alone rarely works.
C   Parents should consider whether there is an underlying cause for lying.

(Adapted from *The Independent*, 10/5/92)

(a) According to the text, name **one** way that parents could deal with the problem of lying. [1]
(b) Using your psychological knowledge, explain why punishment alone may not be effective in encouraging the moral development of children. [3]
(c) In this module, you have studied different theories about how children develop their moral standards. Choose **one** of the following theories and explain what that theory tells us about moral development.

– Psychoanalytic Theory (Freud)
– Social Learning Theory (Bandura)
– Cognitive Developmental Theory (Piaget and Kohlberg)

(HINT: You may like to describe your chosen theory and say what the theory's implications are for childrearing.) [9]

[*Total 13 marks*]
(MEG)

2. SEG sample paper (Higher Tier) Section D

Spend 35 minutes on this question

(a) What is self-concept? [8]
(b) Describe **one** example of how a social role contributes to a person's self-concept. [10]
(c) Explain how **either** self-fulfilling prophecy **or** labelling might affect an individual's self-concept and behaviour. [12]

[*Total 30 marks*]
(SEG)

TUTOR ANSWERS

1. MEG June 1993 Module 2

(a) Parents could set a good example to their children by not lying.
(b) Punishment should discourage a child from behaving in certain ways but it is thought to be ineffective on its own for a number of reasons: it does not teach

the child what it should have done instead, it models aggressive behaviour as a way of getting your own way with others, it may lead to feelings of resentment in the child or it may encourage the child to lie only when the punisher is not around. Punishment can be effective if it is used infrequently in a warm and secure parent–child relationship and it is accompanied by reasoning and explanation.

(c) Cognitive-developmental theorists such as Piaget and Kohlberg concentrate on the development of moral reasoning. Piaget observed children at play and posed moral problems to them. He found that younger children had hetero-nomous morality. This means their morality is controlled by others such as parents or other authority figures. They thought rules were fixed and could not be changed. Judgements of right and wrong were based on the extent of damage rather than the intention behind it. Chosen punishments tended to be harsh (retributive) or eye-for-an-eye (reciprocal). From about 9 years of age onwards children entered the stage of autonomous morality meaning that they were now self-regulating. They understood the need for rules, judged wrongful acts by looking at the intention behind them and chose rational punishments.

Kohlberg also presents a stage theory based on people's responses to stories of moral dilemmas. The stages suggested can take much longer to unfold and many people do not get past the early ones. There are three levels of morality (pre-conventional, conventional and post-conventional) each with two stages. In the first level the child is concerned with the physical con-sequences of behaving immorally. In the second level there is a wider aware-ness of society and the child is concerned with doing its duty and upholding the law. In the last level the individual is concerned with applying the law flexibly for the greatest good but in the very top stage, they have a personal conscience which they will not betray.

Both Piaget's and Kohlberg's findings have been replicated many times and there is some cross-cultural support for the theories. They have been criticised for using research methods that are open to interpretation, underestimating children's ability to reason and for not taking into account how complicated real-life moral problems can be. There is also the problem that people's moral reasoning does not always match their behaviour. Gilligan suggested that these two theories are biased towards males' preoccupation with justice. She tested women's responses to real-life dilemmas and suggested their moral rea-soning had more to do with caring than justice.

For people involved in child-rearing, these theories suggest that it is impor-tant to understand the child's level of understanding and to work within it when trying to teach them to behave morally. Both Piaget and Kohlberg thought it was important for children to be exposed to moral reasoning slightly in advance of their own because it would help them to progress.

2. SEG sample paper (Higher Tier) Section D, Question 6

(a) Psychologists often talk of self-concept as having four parts. The self is the inner world or sense of existence. The self-concept is the set of ideas we have about the self and is how we might describe ourselves. Self-esteem consists of the feelings we have (positive or negative) about the self and ideal self is the self we would like to be. Self-esteem is arrived at by comparing the self-concept and ideal self. The gap between them is important. It is important to be realistic about ourselves and not expect too much or too little.

(b) A social role is rather like an actor's role. It has a script and an expected pat-tern of social behaviour that the person can interpret in their own way. Generally there are limits to the interpretation of a role and there is usually a norm, or usual way of expressing it. Some psychologists think we conform to role expectations for the same reasons we conform in other ways, i.e. through compliance, identification or internalisation.

The Twenty Statement Test is used to find out the roles that make up a per-son's self-concept. Participants are asked to respond 20 times to the question 'Who am I?' Family roles account for 70% of people's responses to this test. 'Mother' is one example. Society expects certain things of a mother such as being domestic, caring for children and putting her family's needs before her own. This may be a comfortable role for some women but others experience role conflict. Inter-role conflict (conflict between roles) might occur if being a traditional type of mother clashes with being a career woman. Intra-role conflict (conflict within a role) could result from the woman wanting to be a friend to her teenage children but having to discipline them as well. Too much of these kinds of role conflict can lead to a person dropping the role although some, such as mother, would be harder to drop than others. How the woman plays the role of mother and how she deals with the conflicts it brings will affect how she views her self-concept. How this compares to her ideal self will affect her self-esteem. The outcome could be either positive or negative.

(c) A well-known study of the effects of labelling on educational achievement is 'Pygmalion in the Classroom' by Rosenthal and Jacobson. They gave a test of academic ability to a number of schoolchildren, picked some of the children at random and told their teachers that they could be expected to 'bloom' academically in the coming year. When they returned to test the children they claimed that the 'bloomers' had gained more academically than a matched control group. They argued that the label given to the children led the teachers to expect more of them. In turn, the children had picked up signals from the teacher and grown into the expectations the teacher seemed to have of them. The teacher had labelled the children who had then labelled themselves. This would have changed their self-concepts and led them to behave in different ways, perhaps being more enthusiastic about school work. This was especially true of first grade children with the greatest potential for change.

Critics of this study object to it on both ethical and methodological grounds. Ethically, it is questionable whether children and teachers should have been treated like this. There were also thought to be problems with the methods of recording data and doubts about whether teachers could even remember who was meant to bloom. Attempts to repeat the study have not given consistent results although there is some evidence that teachers do have higher expectations of some children, especially ones who are more obedient, attractive, clearly spoken and who sit close to the teacher. However, there is little good evidence that labelling and expectations do increase academic performance so it is probably best to have high expectations of all children just in case.

STUDENT'S ANSWER

NEAB paper 1 1992 Question B1. *Spend about 8 minutes answering these questions*

Read the passage below and answer the questions which follow

> **PISCES** *(Feb. 20–Mar. 20)* **You are by nature trusting and always take others' welfare into account. Such selfless qualities will stand you in good stead over the remainder of the week, attracting admiration from unexpected sources.**

Some psychologists would argue that the information above could become a self-fulfilling prophecy.

(a) What is a self-fulfilling prophecy? [2]

Self-fulfilling prophecy is thought to happen when someone is labelled in a particular way and they start to behave in a way that fits the labels and others' expectations.

2/2

(b) Use your knowledge of psychology to explain how a self-fulfilling
prophecy might occur.   [3]

expand on the effect of this
2/3

If a teacher labels a pupil as bright she may treat him in special ways, paying more attention to him and praising him more.

(c) Give an example of a self-fulfilling prophecy that could be harmful.   [2]

[Total 7 marks]
(NEAB)

use research to illustrate
2/2

A teacher might label a pupil as being slow and unintelligent. After a while, the pupil might start to believe it and behave in a slow and unintelligent way.

6/7 Very brief answers. A little more illustration by means of examples (preferably more detailed research) would make the marks more secure

A Review Sheet for this chapter can be found on p. 243–4.

GETTING STARTED

Cognitive development refers to how we come to know and understand the world and others around us. *Piaget* (1896–1980) was particularly interested in the development of logical thinking in children which is just one aspect of cognition that we tend to call intellectual development.

Option 2 of the MEG syllabus requires you to know about Piaget's and Bruner's theories of cognitive development. You need to be able to evaluate these theories and know how they apply to education. Language development fits under option 1 of this syllabus. You need to be able to describe the features of children's speech and know about some different explanations of language development. This section also brings in attempts to teach language to animals.

For the SEG syllabus you need to know about Piaget's theory only including how it has influenced practical aspects of child-care, for example, in the choice of toys for children and how playgroup activities are organised. Language development is not required by this syllabus.

The theories can seem complicated at first, mainly because there are *many* new words to get to grips with, but the ideas behind them are very straightforward.

1. COGNITIVE DEVELOPMENT

2. LANGUAGE DEVELOPMENT

ESSENTIAL PRINCIPLES

1 > **COGNITIVE DEVELOPMENT**

PIAGET'S THEORY OF COGNITIVE DEVELOPMENT

Many textbooks have it that Piaget's interest in children's intellectual development began when he was working on developing intelligence tests with Binet and Simon in Paris. Test items were being tried out on children and Piaget became just as interested in children's wrong answers as in their right ones. When asked 'Why do clouds move?' for example, children often had interesting ideas of their own rather than saying 'I don't know'. Piaget branched out on his own with a new set of assumptions about children's intelligence:

> Piaget challenged established ways of regarding child development

- Children's intelligence differs from an adult's in *quality* rather than in *quantity*. This means that they reason differently from adults and see the world in different ways.
- Children *actively* build up their knowledge about the world. They are not passive creatures waiting for someone to fill their heads with knowledge.
- The best way to understand a children's reasoning was to see things *from their point of view.*

PIAGET'S METHODS

Piaget studied children from infancy to adolescence. He used:

- **naturalistic observation** of his own three babies and sometimes **controlled observation** too. From these he wrote **diary descriptions** charting their development;
- **clinical interviews** with **cross-sections** of older children who were able to understand questions and hold conversations.

PIAGET'S VIEW OF THE INTELLECT AND ITS DEVELOPMENT

Piaget viewed the intellect as a **mental system**, which:

- is **structured** and **organised** to take in and deal with knowledge and information about the world. (We have other organised systems too, such as the digestive system which is structured and organised to take in and deal with food and drink.) The mental system both *changes* incoming information and *is changed* by it (just as the digestive system changes food and is changed by it).
- grows and changes through **maturation** – the genetic process of 'growing up' which is inevitable. Experience may speed up or slow down the process, and affect the quality of the system, but we all get there in the end.
- grows in a series of **stages** which are roughly defined by age and follow the same, *invariant* order in everyone. We cannot miss stages out.

> these ideas are not as difficult to understand as they look

The intellect is made up of **schemas** and **operations**. These are mental structures for taking in and using information. A baby has a number of **innate (inborn) schemas** which take the form of **reflex actions**. Through these, the baby 'knows' how to grasp or how to suck. These schemas grow and change as the child matures and new ones develop. In middle childhood, **operations** appear. These are more complex mental structures which allow us to think in more complex ways. From middle childhood on, our mental systems consist of both schemas and operations.

Piaget viewed intellectual growth as a process of **adaptation** (adjustment) to the world. This happens through:

- **assimilation** which is using an existing schema just as it is, e.g. an infant with an innate grasping schema will curl its fingers round any object which it finds in its hand. This rather primitive **palmar grasp** will allow it to take in all sorts of information about objects such as their weight, texture and temperature.
- **accommodation** happens when the existing schema needs to be changed in order to take in new information. The palmar grasp is useful up to a point but altering it by bringing the thumb into play opens a whole new world of little objects for the child to get to know.

- **equilibration** is the force which moves development along. An unpleasant state of **disequilibrium** happens when new information cannot be fitted into existing schemas (i.e. assimilated). Equilibration is the process by which balance is restored, for example, by bringing about accommodation. Assimilation with the new schemas can then go on.

These processes help the person to progress through the stages of intellectual development. They are also called **invariant functions** because the way they operate stays the same throughout life. An adolescent, for example, who develops a bike-riding schema, can get on any similar bike and ride it (assimilation). Faced with a moped, disequilibrium may occur. Through the action of equilibration, s/he may accommodate the schema because, although many elements of the original one are useful, it cannot be applied successfully without being changed (accommodation).

INTELLECTUAL DEVELOPMENT OCCURS IN STAGES

Piaget named four stages of intellectual development each characterised by the way the child thinks and reasons.

1   The sensorimotor stage. 0–18 months/2 years

This stage is so named because the infant knows the world only through receiving *sensations* and making *movements*, mostly reflexive ones.

Characteristics of this stage include:

- the infant exists in the present. It does not yet have a mental picture of the world, therefore it does not have a sense of **object permanence** (or **object concept**) – if it cannot sense an object, it does not exist. This is why you can hide a toy from an infant, while it watches, but it will not search for the object once it has gone out of sight. At about 8 months, the infant will understand the permanence of objects and search for them when they disappear.
- towards the end of the stage, *language* starts to appear showing that the child can now store (*mentally image* or *represent*) information that it knows about the world, recall it and label it.

2   The pre-operational stage. 2–6/7 years

This stage is called pre-operational because the child does not yet have 'operations' as part of the mental structure. It differs from the previous stage because the child is developing **symbolisation**, meaning that they can use one thing to stand for, or symbolise, another. We can see this in their make-believe play but also in their language where they use words to stand for things.

Characteristics of this stage include:

- **egocentrism**. Children seem to be 'self-centred' in that they find it difficult to take someone else's point of view. Piaget showed this in the **mountains demonstration**. A child would be shown three model mountains on a table top and asked to choose the view they could see from a series of pictures. A doll was then placed at different positions round the table and the child asked to choose a picture showing what the doll could see. Children tended to choose the view they could see themselves.
- **animism**. This is the tendency to think that non-living objects have life and feelings like a person's, e.g. when asked why it gets dark at night, an animistic child might say that it's because the sun gets tired and goes to bed.
- **failure to conserve**. If a child can conserve it means they understand that, although things may change in appearance, certain properties remain the same. There are several kinds of conservation. In **conservation of mass**, the child is shown two identical balls of plasticine and asked if they are the same. The child says yes. The shape of one ball is then changed and the child asked if they are still the same or different. The *non-conserving* child says they are different. Children at this stage also have trouble conserving number, weight, length and liquid volume (see **Fig.** 11.1).

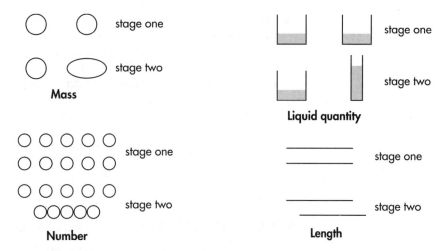

Figure 11.1 Conservation tasks

It seems that pre-operational children:

- are taken in by how things *look* and this dominates their judgement;
- find it difficult to take into account *more than one thing at a time*, e.g. in the liquid volume conservation test they cannot see that both the height and the width of the container have changed;
- cannot *reverse* an event in their minds.

3 Concrete operational period. 6/7–12 years

The child now has **operations** in their mental structure. This means they can think logically and solve problems like conservation ones, because they can mentally reverse things (e.g. picture a ball of plasticine returning to its original shape) and can take more than one aspect of a problem into account at once. The stage is called 'concrete' because children can think logically much more successfully if they can manipulate real (concrete) materials or picture them. (Maths tables in most primary school classrooms are full of equipment to help children understand concepts through using a 'hands-on' approach.) Egocentrism is lost as children learn to **decentre** and animism disappears to be replaced by more **scientific reasoning**.

4 The formal operational stage. 12 years+

66 adults should be in this stage 99

Children continue to think logically but now their reasoning is not tied to the here and now. They can deal with **abstract ideas** (e.g. no longer needing to think about slicing up cakes or sharing sweets to understand division and fractions, but using numbers instead). They can also deal with **hypothetical problems** with many possible solutions, e.g. if asked '*What would happen if* money were abolished in one hour's time?' they could speculate about many possible consequences.

EVALUATION OF PIAGET'S THEORY

Strengths:

- The influence of Piaget's ideas in developmental psychology has been enormous. He changed how people *viewed* the child's world and their *methods* of studying children. He was an *inspiration* to many who came after and took up his ideas.
- His ideas have been of practical use in *understanding* and *communicating* more effectively with children, but especially in education.
- His ideas have been *supported* over and over again by research all over the world.

Weaknesses:

- Are the stages *real*? Behaviourists would rather not talk about stages at all, preferring to see development as *continuous*. Others have queried the *age ranges* of the stages. Some studies have shown that *progress* to the formal operational stage *is not guaranteed* (e.g. Kagan's (1971) cross-cultural research suggested children in rural Kenyan and Guatemalan communities did not reach stage 4).
- Some critics think Piaget emphasised children's *intellectual* development too much and was wrong to play down the *social* and *emotional* side of development.

- Piaget's *methods* (observation and clinical interviews) are more open to *biased interpretation* than other methods.
- Many criticisms of Piaget's questioning methods have been made in a book by *Margaret Donaldson* (1978). She thought that problems were not presented to children in a way that made **human sense**. *Hughes* (1975) for example, tested egocentrism by asking children to hide a 'naughty boy' doll from a policeman doll. He found that children as young as $3\frac{1}{2}$ years old succeed at this so could **decentre**. *McGarrigle and Donaldson* (1974) demonstrated number conservation in 4–5 year olds using a **naughty teddy** to mess up the second row of counters. Younger children may make errors in Piaget's way of testing because they do not understand the testing situation as older children do. Studies like these lead us to wonder whether there really are distinctly different stages as Piaget suggested.

BRUNER'S THEORY OF COGNITIVE DEVELOPMENT

Bruner (1966) agreed with Piaget that the intellect is **organised** and that children are **active** in building up knowledge about the world. Rather than using stages, however, Bruner thought children developed increasingly sophisticated ways of mentally representing their world. He called these **modes of representation**. Children start with one and acquire two more with time. They are called:

> there are important areas of agreement between Piaget and Bruner

- **the enactive mode**. The infant stores information in the form of a kind of **muscle memory**. When they recall something, they do so through recreating the movement, e.g. an infant may recall a rattle by moving its hand and arm as it did when it last held a rattle.
- **the iconic mode**. The infant can now store **images** of things. These are often visual (we can 'picture' things) but can be from other senses too.
- **the symbolic mode**. Not everything can be 'pictured'. The symbolic mode allows us to mentally represent more abstract things **symbolically**, e.g. in numbers or words.

A key difference between Piaget and Bruner is in their view of the importance of **language**. Bruner thought its appearance was responsible for the shift to symbolic representation. Piaget proposed that the appearance of *operations* marked the shift to logical thought and that language (symbolic representation) came after.

Bruner and Kenney (1966) demonstrated the difference between the iconic and symbolic modes in children aged 3–7 years using the task illustrated in **Fig**. 11.2.

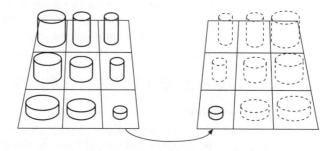

Figure 11.2 Bruner and Kenney's glasses experiment – the transposition task

Once children had studied the arrangement of glasses, the display was removed and they were asked either to **reproduce** it as before or **transpose** it (produce a mirror image of the original given one glass to start from). The ability to reproduce the display occurred earlier than the ability to transpose it. Younger children had an iconic image in their heads which was inflexible. Older children could symbolise the relationship between the glasses and this more flexible mode of representation enabled them to solve the problem.

APPLICATIONS TO EDUCATION

Piaget's theory

In Piaget's view educational activities should be fitted to the child in the pre-school years. This is reflected in the sorts of toys provided at each stage:

- The **sensorimotor** child is *practising* innate schemas and *developing* new ones. Toys are typically ones which are interesting to gaze at, which have various textures and which make sounds or simple movements. Others which allow them practice and mastery of movements are also appropriate, e.g. trolleys to push, shape-sorters, simple puzzles and 'activity centres'.

- **Pre-operational** children will be old enough to go through *nursery* and *infant* school. They will need toys which help with physical, manipulative, social and imaginative play. Physical toys like climbing frames help develop spatial awareness. Manipulative toys, like sorting games or bead threading, can help with grading and counting. Social and imaginative play such as dressing up or using a 'home corner' help children to understand others' points of view and represent things symbolically. Sharing out the juice and snacks can help with conservation concepts. The possibilities are endless.

- **Concrete operational** children's play can be much more cooperative and involve more complicated rules. Board games and team games are now possible and creative, imaginative activities continue to aid language development.

- The **formal operational** child (and adult!) can play games involving complex, abstract reasoning and will often enjoy those requiring strategy to outwit an opponent.

66 assimilation and accommodation are important throughout 99

66 children lose egocentrism and can use rules 99

Piaget's theory has had a great influence in more formal education, particularly in introducing more child-centred approaches in nursery and infant school, in teaching maths at junior level and science at secondary level. The approach is based on the following:

- **The nature of development.** *Maturation* is important in intellectual development although the right kind of *experience* can help things along.
- **The nature of the child.** The child is naturally *curious* and motivated to learn.
- **Discovery learning.** Children will *find things out* for themselves if we give them the right kind of materials and set problems in ways which fit their stage of development.
- **The teacher's role.** This is to know each child's state of *readiness* to learn and arrange activities or ask questions which fit the child and *challenge* their thinking. This should allow for *assimilation* and be just enough to bring about *accommodation*. The right balance ensures that the child is not discouraged or bored.
- **The child's role.** This is be *actively involved* in the learning process.
- **Interaction with others.** Piaget emphasised this less than others, such as Bruner, but still thought that *social interaction* with others was useful, if it included argument, discussion and exposure to more mature ways of thinking.

Bruner's theory

Bruner's approach to education is similar to but differs from Piaget's in some important ways:

- **Language** plays an important role in pushing the child forward.
- We should **actively intervene** in learning rather than wait for the child to be ready. However, we should still work within what the child could realistically achieve. (Vygotsky (1967) called this working within the child's 'zone of proximal development' or **ZPD**.)
- Knowledge develops **spirally** so a child can understand anything at some level providing it is presented in an appropriate way.
- There is far more emphasis on the **social side of learning**.

66 Piaget saw the social side of development as less central than did Bruner 99

Applying the theory involves the use of:

- **Scaffolding.** This is where the teacher (working within the child's ZPD) helps them to solve a problem through *supporting* them to a solution rather than giving the solution. The teacher **scaffolds** by doing things such as providing the child with the *elements* of a problem, *encouraging* and taking an *interest*, drawing the child's *attention* to important information, or even *demonstrating*. The teacher constantly adjusts the level of guidance given to the needs and abilities of the child until the child's knowledge is ready to stand alone and the scaffolding can be taken away.
- **Tutors other than teachers.** Bruner thought that any **expert** could work with a child to help them learn. **Parents** are one kind of expert. In **peer tutoring** the

tutor is another pupil who is not that far ahead of the learner so can work naturally in the learner's ZPD. **Cooperative group work** in classrooms should have the same good effect. Carefully designed computer assisted learning (**CAL**) packages called **Intelligent Tutoring Systems**, based on the idea of branching programmes, are a different kind of expert.

2 > LANGUAGE
DEVELOPMENT

A DESCRIPTION OF LANGUAGE DEVELOPMENT

For centuries it has been maintained that it is language which sets humans apart from animals. This is not to say that animals do not communicate, but human language is unique. Language develops at an *amazing speed*. Children have to learn to form words and sounds (the **phonology**) of the language, arrange them in the right order (understand **syntax** or grammar) and make meaningful sentences (understand **semantics**). While language is developing, children seem to understand more than they can say, i.e. they have a better **passive** than **active vocabulary**. Here is the usual sequence of events with very approximate age ranges:

- 0–4 months. At first the infant only seems to make **discomfort** sounds but **pleasure** sounds are soon added.
- 4–9 months. **The babbling stage**. Infants start to produce strings of speech sounds known as 'phonemes', e.g. bababa, mumumum, dadada. Babies everywhere in the world babble in the same way as if it is a *universal* tendency. Even *deaf babies* babble.
- 9–18 months. **The holophrastic stage**. Infants produce single word utterances, building up the phoneme system for their own language. These words may be **over-extended** meaning that they are too widely applied (e.g. calling all women 'Mummy'). The words are often combined with a gesture which helps to give the meaning, e.g. 'Daddy' + pointing at a slipper means 'That's Daddy's slipper'. The word plus the gesture make a holophrase.
- 18 months–2½ years. **The telegraphic stage**. Simple, two-word sentences are produced consisting of a **pivot word** and an **open word**. Many different open words can be attached to one pivot. With a vocabulary of between 50 and 270 words there are many possible combinations. Telegraphic speech omits **functor words** which make a sentence complete. Functor words are the kind you would leave out of a telegram, hence the name of the stage, which was coined by *Roger Brown* (1965).
- 2½–4 years. This stage does not have a specific name. Children complete their phoneme system, add about 50 new words a month to their vocabulary and perfect their grammar. At this time they may make many **virtuous errors** where they apply a grammatical rule to an irregular verb or plural, e.g. saying 'goed' instead of 'went' or 'mouses' instead of 'mice'.
- 4–6 years. The child will probably have a vocabulary of around 2,000 words and will add to it for the rest of its life. Language is now as competent as an adult's.

THEORIES OF LANGUAGE ACQUISITION

Learning theory

Behaviourists argued that verbal behaviour is just another kind of learned behaviour so it can be explained using the principles of **operant conditioning** and **observational learning**. Learning and experience (**nurture**) is seen as more important than inbuilt, genetic influences (**nature**). *Skinner* (1957) thought the baby's babbling behaviour could be shaped by the use of **selective reinforcement**. **Successive approximations** to the desired words are reinforced until use of language becomes skilled. Non-reinforced responses should fade away. In this way, the babbling which all babies do can be **shaped** into whatever language their parents use. There are three kinds of verbal behaviour which are shaped:

remember shaping from chapter four

- **Mands** – these are sounds which are appropriate to whatever the child wants to communicate about, e.g. 'b' for biscuit is rewarded with a biscuit.
- **Tacts** – these are sounds that are appropriate by chance. The parent assumes they have meaning and responds with praise, attention etc. The child might just happen to say 'da' when Daddy walks in and get a very positive response from Daddy.

- **Echoic responses** – these are direct imitations of adult speech.

In addition, children's grammar should be perfected by having grammatically correct speech reinforced. Much of our language, including correct grammar, may also be acquired through **observing** and **imitating** models around us.

Evaluation of the learning theory approach

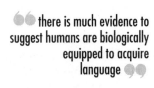
learning theory does not go far enough

It seems obvious that children will not acquire language unless they are exposed to others using it and learning theory can account for speech performance (**production**) very well. It has problems for the following reasons:

- Conditioning and observational learning are relatively *slow* processes, and cannot account for the amazing speed with which children acquire language.
- If children only use language which they have observed others use or have been rewarded for they should *not* produce telegraphic speech or make virtuous errors, but they do! It is as if they have an underlying understanding of grammar and sometimes misapply it.
- Some children imitate language a great deal, others do not, but this has no effect on their overall rate of language acquisition.
- Some critics doubt that grammar (syntax) is learned by imitation. From observations of parents and children talking, parents seem more concerned about the *truth* and *accuracy* of what children say than its *grammatical correctness*. If this is the case, the children should end up speaking the truth ungrammatically!
- Children seem able to extract the principles of language to make up new sentences which make sense but which they have never been rewarded for or heard another person say.

Nativist theory

Nativist explanations stress the importance of innate (inborn), biological determinants of language. *Noam Chomsky* (1975) suggested that humans alone have a 'language acquisition device' (**LAD**) which helps them to pick up language once they are exposed to it. Languages all have things in common. Chomsky called these **linguistic universals**, e.g. vowels and consonants, syllables, sentences, nouns and verbs. These make up the **deep structure** of the language and innate understanding of these allows the child to extract the meaning of a sentence no matter how it is phrased. The **surface structure** may be different (e.g. 'The dog bit the man' or 'The man was bitten by the dog') but the deep structure is the same.

Evaluation

there is much evidence to suggest humans are biologically equipped to acquire language

Evidence for Chomsky's theory includes the following:

- Children usually acquire language with speed and apparent ease.
- Cross-cultural evidence shows children everywhere go through the same stages of language acquisition suggesting an innate influence. (Remember, deaf babies babble too.) It's as if language is **maturational**, rather like learning to walk.
- We have highly specialised breathing and vocal apparatus which prepare us to produce language. There are also **language areas** in the human brain specialised for receiving, understanding and producing language.
- Almost all children acquire some language regardless of intellectual ability.
- People produce language even under the most difficult circumstances, e.g. when severely physically disabled.
- There is some evidence to suggest that language development goes through a **sensitive period** when children's brains are developing and they are maximally sensitive to language input. If they are not exposed to language in this period it may never fully develop. *Curtiss* (1977) describes the case of Genie, who was neglected and severely deprived of normal social contact until she was discovered aged 13 years and 7 months. She had been punished for making any sound and her only social contact had been with her brutal father and almost blind mother. Although Genie could understand a few words, and picked up some rudimentary two-word utterances and longer sentences, speech training did not improve her language past essentially telegraphic speech.

Possible weaknesses include:

- Chomsky's theory is better for explaining language **competence** (as opposed to **performance**) which learning theory does better.
- There is no direct evidence for the existence of an LAD.
- There may be more *coaching* by parents than this theory allows, e.g. some psychologists talk of the tendency of parents to alter their language when talking with their children, i.e. they use a baby talk register (**BTR**). Parents thus work within the child's range of understanding (**ZPD**), subtly correcting and expanding on children's speech.
- Others think theories such as this play down the importance of **social interaction** in language development, preferring to see development as a combination of maturation and experience.

THE DEBATE ABOUT ANIMALS AND LANGUAGE

One way to attempt to resolve the nature–nurture debate in language development is to see if it is possible for animals to acquire language. If they can be trained, it would suggest language is learned. If not, the idea of an LAD, unique to humans, would seem more plausible. At the same time, such studies help satisfy academic interest about whether animals think. This difficult debate could be helped if animals could use language to communicate their thoughts to us. We might then need to rethink our ideas about how we differ from animals and the way we treat them for our own ends.

> two reasons for engaging in this debate

What is human language?

We must be clear about what language is. Clearly, a parrot can be taught to imitate language, but it does not seem to communicate like humans do. *Hockett* (1960) suggested that human language has certain characteristics which he called **design features**. If we can show evidence of these in animals, we may be able to argue that they use language like humans do. Some of the features are:

- **Displacement**. The language can be used to refer to things not actually present in time or space, i.e. we can talk about things in the past or future and about things which are out of sight.
- **Productivity**. The language can be used to produce an infinite number of novel utterances and even to create new words.
- **Prevarication**. The language can be used to talk about the ridiculous or impossible and to lie or tell jokes.
- **Cultural transmission**. The language can be passed down the generations.

Attempts to teach language to animals

In the early days, researchers attempted to teach chimpanzees to talk. *Kellogg and Kellogg* (1933) raised a chimp called *Gua* with their own child. Eventually it seemed Gua could understand about 70 words but she said nothing herself. *Hayes and Hayes* (1951) tried to train their chimp, *Vicky*, to vocalise using operant conditioning, but at age 3 she could only produce four words. The breakthrough came when researchers decided chimps' vocal apparatus would never allow them to speak and that sign language was more appropriate.

Gardner and Gardner (1969) began with a 1-year-old chimp called *Washoe*. They taught her sign language using a combination of *moulding* her hands and *rewarding* her. After four years, Washoe knew 132 American Sign Language (**ASL**) signs. Washoe showed some similarities to human children's language acquisition, e.g. she over-extended meanings of signs and began to use two-word combinations. She also showed evidence of:

- **displacement**, e.g. by signing about things hidden in boxes;
- **productivity**, e.g. by making up new words such as 'water bird' for swan;
- **prevarication**, e.g. pointing to a green frog and signing 'that red' then rocking in apparent amusement;
- **cultural transmission** – it is claimed that Washoe was seen trying to teach signs to her own baby.

Other well-known studies were carried out by:

- *Premack* (1971) who trained *Lana* to communicate using plastic shapes which symbolised objects like 'apple' and actions like 'insert';
- *Patterson* (1978) who trained a gorilla called *Koko* to use ASL;
- *Terrace* (1979) who trained a chimp called *Nim Chimpsky* to use ASL;
- *Rumbaugh* (1977) who trained chimps to use a keyboard to communicate in strings of symbols which she called **Yerkish**.

Evaluation of animal language studies

Terrace (1974) made many criticisms of studies which attempted to teach sign language to chimps:

- He claimed that chimps used language very differently from children. They produced few spontaneous signs. Instead, they seemed simply to imitate what the trainer had been signing. It was as if the trainer was **cueing** the chimp.
- He said that the chimps' sign order was often *incorrect* and *repetitive* as if they had no real understanding of what they were communicating.
- Chimps often interrupted their trainers and showed little evidence of being able to *take turns* in communication like children do.

Researchers and their critics still hotly debate the issue of whether chimps really can acquire language. Certainly chimps do not acquire the sophistication of human language but they do, with a great deal of painstaking encouragement, show some of its characteristics. A new and constructive approach has been developed by *Sue Savage-Rumbaugh* (1990) who teaches Bonobo chimps to communicate using a large, portable sign board called a **lexigram**. Their coaching is much more like a child's would be. Instead of learning symbol by symbol, chimps pick up how to use the signs through:

- constant exposure to the trainer's example;
- by using the lexigram themselves alongside all their daily activities;
- hearing spoken language alongside all their activities.

The chimps can respond to verbal instructions alone. Their *understanding* of language still outstrips their *ability* to produce it, rather like a young child's does. Nevertheless, most researchers would agree that, although chimps can be trained in the rudiments of language production, they do not do it with the ease and speed that humans do, suggesting a *qualitatively different* way of using language.

EXAMINATION QUESTIONS

MEG specimen paper 4 (Higher), Option 1

Spend 35 minutes on this question

Source

Psychologists are interested in how children acquire language. Children have been shown to use *rules* – for example, adding 'ed' to a word to make it refer to the past:

I walk

I walk<u>ed</u>

Sometimes they make mistakes because they do not realise that a word is an exception to this rule.

A psychologist recorded the following conversation:

Child: My teacher holded the baby rabbits and we patted them
Mother: Did you say your teacher held the baby rabbits?
Child: Yes
Mother: What did you say she did?
Child: She holded the baby rabbits and we patted them
Mother: Did you say she held them tightly?
Child: No, she holded them loosely

[Gleason, 1967]

This conversation can be used as evidence that gaining language involves more than just imitation.

(a) How can you tell that the child above is not learning by imitation?   [1]

(b) Suggest **one** reason why continually correcting children's language mistakes does not always improve the child's use of language.   [1]

(c) Parents talk to children in special ways. What have psychologists found out about this?   [4]

(d) For your Psychology coursework you are going to carry out a study of language development in children.
   (i) Outline how you would do the study.   [2]
   (ii) Identify **two** practical problems that you might face when carrying out the study.   [2]

(e) Evaluate **one** theory of how children acquire language, using psychological evidence.   [8]

[Total 18 marks]
(MEG)

TUTOR ANSWER

MEG specimen paper 4 (Higher), Option 1 Source B

(a) The child makes a virtuous error ('holded') and does not correct it when the parent correctly says 'held'.

(b) The child may feel discouraged if it looks on constant correction as punishment.

(c) Parents may coach a child's language in subtle ways. One suggestion is that parents alter their language to suit the child's level of understanding. This used to be called talking in 'motherese' but the term baby talk register is now preferred. Parents work within the child's range of understanding (the ZPD) conversing with the child and correcting and expanding its speech.

(d) (i) Language development could be studied using a longitudinal research design where a sample of children was selected at birth and visited at regular intervals. Records of the children's speech could be in the form of written accounts and audio- or video-tapes. These records could be analysed to see how language changes with age.

   (ii) A problem with a longitudinal research design is that participants may drop out of the study so much time and money is wasted on collecting data that ends up incomplete. Another problem is that if there is a flaw in the research design at the start it carries on throughout the study.

(e) Learning theorists believe we learn language through operant conditioning and observational learning. Skinner suggested that, through operant conditioning, adults shape babies' babblings into language until it becomes very skilled. Speech sounds parents may reward are called mands (sounds close to an appropriate word), tacts (sounds that are correct by chance), and echoic responses (imitations of speech). Much of our language may also be acquired through observing and imitating important models around us.

Clearly, children would not learn language unless they were exposed to it and this theory explains language production well, but there are some problems with it. Learning cannot be the whole story. It is too slow to account for the speed with which children acquire language. It also cannot explain why children's speech contains word orders, novel sentences and virtuous errors that they would never have heard from an adult or been rewarded for. Parents also seem more inclined to correct the truth of what children say rather than their grammar so children should end up speaking the truth ungrammatically. Finally, children who imitate language a great deal are no faster at acquiring language in the end than children who imitate very little. Chomsky concluded that the role of innate, biological factors in acquiring language was far more important than learning.

STUDENT'S ANSWER

SEG sample paper (Higher Tier), Section E
Spend 35 minutes on this question

(a) According to Piaget, how do we learn? [9]

> Piaget thought that children are naturally curious and will learn willingly if the right materials are provided for them. This is known as discovery learning. For Piaget, learning is the result of growing up (maturing) and experiences. Experiences can slow down or speed up our learning but we will all reach maturity in the end. Learning involves adaptation to the world and this happens through assimilation and accommodation. When the child is born it has reflexes known as schemas. These grow and change. Assimilation is when we learn about something new using the old schema. Accommodation is when the old schema isn't enough and we have to change it to take in something new. Later, the child will develop operations. These allow him to deal with more complicated information.

❝❝ a good answer 9/9 ❞❞

(b) What is meant by egocentrism? [3]

❝❝ give an example 2/3 ❞❞

> Very young babies and children up to about 7 are egocentric. This means that they can only see things from their own point of view and cannot take another person's point of view.

(c) Describe an example of egocentric thought or behaviour. [6]

> Piaget tested egocentrism in children in the pre-operational stage (2–7 years). He showed a child three model mountains on a table. He then showed them some
>
> pictures of three mountains and asked the child to pick the one they could see. All the children could do this. He then asked them to say how the mountains would look from other sides of the table. The children could not do this showing that they were egocentric.

❝❝ explain a little more fully 5/6 ❞❞

(d) Explain how Piaget's ideas have influenced the toys and activities of children. [12]

[*Total 30 marks*]
(SEG)

> We now have toys to match every stage of children's development according to Piaget. In the sensorimotor stage (0–2 years) babies like toys that are interesting to look at and feel and that make interesting noises. Parents buy them activity centres to practise simple movements with. In the pre-operational stage (2–7 years), children will play more with other children and will need toys to help them play make-believe, such as dressing-up clothes. They also need plenty of exercise and story-books to look at and listen to. Concrete operational children (7–12 years) like team games and other games with rules. (They can now understand rules.) Formal operational children (12 and upwards) can understand abstract ideas so they enjoy more complicated games, clever jokes and solving mysteries.
>
> At school, they may have discovery learning. The teacher sets up activities for them to do which match their stage of development. She allows them to practise what they can already do and challenges them when she thinks they are ready. She is trying to encourage assimilation and accommodation. Primary school children learn maths using special equipment as well as books. Older children might learn science by discovering things for themselves. Children of all ages can get involved in discussions with brighter children to encourage them to think at a higher level.

❝❝ 9/12 ❞❞

❝❝ 25/30 Plenty of sound psychological content. The answer to part (d) does not specifically address the question, i.e. how Piaget's ideas have **influenced** toys and activities, although it does show how they fit in with Piagetian stages **❞❞**

A Review Sheet for this chapter can be found on pp. 245–6.

CHAPTER 12

PERCEPTION

GETTING STARTED

This chapter begins with a consideration of what perception is and discusses some important influences on perception. It then goes on to consider the nature–nurture debate and perception, that is the argument over whether we are born being able to perceive or whether we have to learn to perceive.

So what do we mean by perception? Broadly, we are talking about how the brain makes sense of or processes information detected by the sense organs. There are six sensory systems each specialised to pick up a particular kind of information from the world:

- the visual system for sight;
- the auditory system for hearing;
- the tactile system for touch;
- the olfactory system for smell;
- the gustatory system for taste;
- the kinaesthetic or body sense system for telling us about our body's position and movement.

Here, we will be concentrating on the visual system because, for humans, it is one of the most important and dominant senses.

Perception appears on the NEAB, MEG and SEG syllabuses. MEG students need all of this chapter. NEAB students can leave out the second section on the nature–nurture debate. SEG students need only this second section, but will find it useful to read through the opening sections of the chapter to familiarise themselves with the jargon.

1. PERCEPTUAL PROCESSES

2. THE NATURE–NURTURE DEBATE AND PERCEPTION

ESSENTIAL PRINCIPLES

SENSATION AND PERCEPTION

Sense organs pick up information from the world. The eyes are specialised to pick up **light energy** from a range known as the **visible spectrum**. Light energy, once detected, is converted into **electrical impulses**. This is a process known as **transduction**. These messages travel to the **visual cortex** in the brain for further processing. These reactions to a visual stimulus are what we mean by **sensation**. **Perception** refers to how these sensations are *translated, organised* and *reconstructed* (**processed**) in order to make sense of them. All forms of perception, not just visual perception, happen in the brain. The sensory system's function is simply to make sure the brain gets the information it needs to do its job.

💬💬 be able to define sensation, perception and transduction 💬💬

THE VISUAL SYSTEM

When light hits the front of the eye, light rays are focused by the curved **cornea** and the flexible **lens** on to the light-sensitive **retina** which lines the back of the eye. Light-sensitive cells called **rods** and **cones** are stimulated and they send messages along the **optic nerve** to the **visual cortex** for processing. Rods and cones are especially dense around the **fovea**, and it is here that our vision is most acute. See **Fig**. 12.1.

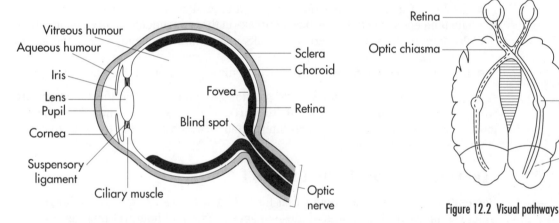

Figure 12.1 Human eye (vertical section) showing the main components

Figure 12.2 Visual pathways

When we look ahead, information from the *right* of our **visual field** hits the inside *left* of each eyeball and information from the *left* hits the inside *right*. The arrangement of the **visual pathways** ensures that information from the right of the visual field goes to the left visual cortex and information from the left of the visual field goes to the right visual cortex. This is possible because of the crossing over of the pathways at the **optic chiasma** (see **Fig**. 12.2).

PERCEPTION – MAKING SENSE OF SENSATIONS

The image which hits the retina is *upside-down*. It is also very *small* and *two dimensional* (flat). In spite of this, we perceive an image of the world which is the right way up, full size and three dimensional (it has depth). We have a very powerful impression of looking out on the world through our eyes when, really, we are seeing with our brain. How this is achieved is what interests psychologists.

We *organise* and *interpret* visual information into a world of objects against backgrounds. The objects are perceived as occupying different positions in the *space* around us. They are also seen as having certain characteristics which remain stable or *constant*. How are these three aspects of perception achieved?

OBJECT PERCEPTION AND THE GESTALT APPROACH

Gestalt psychologists think we have *innate tendencies* to organise visual input into **figures against backgrounds**. We do this by picking up certain features of the visual input and applying **laws of organisation** to them. The most basic of these laws is the **Law of Pragnanz**. This states that, when we are interpreting visual information, the perception we arrive at will be the simplest and most uniform one. In other words it will have **Gestalt** or **good figure**. We arrive at this Gestalt by applying the following laws (see **Fig**. 12.3):

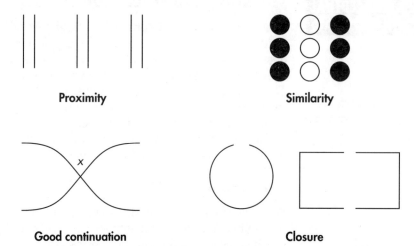

Figure 12.3 Gestalt laws of organisation (Common fate not illustrated)

- **the law of proximity** – things which are close together tend to be seen as a unit;
- **the law of similarity** – things which are alike tend to be seen as a unit;
- **the law of good continuation** – we tend to assume smooth continuity in stimuli and tend not to see things as having breaks in them or sudden changes of direction;
- **the law of closure** – if there are breaks in a stimulus we tend to close the gap to 'tidy it up';
- **the law of common fate** – things which move together are seen as a unit.

A good way of summing up the Gestalt position on perception is in the statement **the whole is greater than the sum of its parts**. This means that when we apply the laws of organisation we arrive at an interpretation which amounts to more than the stimuli which meet the eye.

PERCEPTION OF DEPTH OR DISTANCE

Remember that the visual images that hit the back of eye are *two dimensional*. The brain will take certain features of these images (cues) and interpret them in order to tell us where objects are in the space around us. People who have the use of only one eye (**monocular vision**) see depth very well because they have use of monocular cues to depth. People with vision in both eyes (**binocular vision**) have two more cues to help them.

Monocular cues to depth

Most of these cues are similar to the tricks an artist might use when drawing a land-scape (see **Fig**. 12.4).

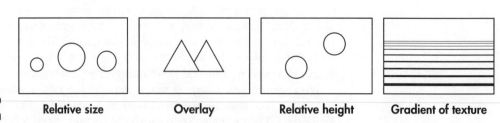

Figure 12.4 Monocular cues to depth

Relative size   Overlay   Relative height   Gradient of texture

- **Relative size**. Objects look smaller in relation to each other the further away they are.
- **Overlay**. Nearer objects often obscure part of our view of further objects.
- **Relative height**. On a horizontal surface, more distant objects are higher in the visual field than closer ones.

- **Gradient of texture**. The texture and detail of closer objects is more distinct than in more distant objects.
- **Motion parallax**. When we are moving around, nearby objects appear to move past us faster than more distant objects.
- **Accommodation**. When we look at something, the lens of the eye changes shape (accommodates) to bring the image into sharp focus. For closer objects it becomes more rounded and for distant objects it is flatter. It is thought that the brain can pick up messages from the muscles which change the shape of the lens and this tells it about the distance of the object from the viewer.

Binocular cues to depth

- **Retinal disparity**. Because the eyes are a few cm apart they pick up slightly different (*disparate*) images. We are not aware of this because the brain fuses the two images into one. Disparity is a very powerful cue to depth. A nearby object gives us two very disparate images. More distant objects give us less disparate images. The degree of disparity will tell the brain something about how distant an object is.
- **Convergence**. The closer an object is, the more the eyes turn in towards each other to focus its image on to the retina. The brain can pick up messages from the muscles controlling convergence and this will tell it something about how far away the object is.

PERCEPTUAL CONSTANCIES

Visual images change constantly yet we see a world which is familiar and stable. We achieve this through an understanding of perceptual constancies. In other words we understand that, even though the visual image of an object might change, certain properties of it stay the same. Examples include:

- **Shape constancy**. An object, e.g. an opening door, casts a continually changing visual image on the eye. We do not perceive the door as changing shape. Instead we see the door as staying the same shape but changing its position in relation to ourselves.
- **Size constancy**. Objects look smaller the further away they are. We do not see them as shrinking or expanding. Instead we see them as staying the same size while changing in their distance from us.
- **Colour constancy**. The illumination on objects changes all the time but we do not see them as changing colour. Instead, we see them as keeping the same colour and the colour or amount of light falling on them as changing.

GREGORY'S 'HYPOTHESIS TESTING' THEORY OF PERCEPTION

Gregory (1977) suggests that, while the image which reaches the eye is rich in information, the messages about it which reach the brain have lost much of this information. This means that the brain has to make a *best guess* about how to interpret these messages and this may involve some inference. There could be more than one interpretation. Therefore, Gregory thinks that the brain forms a number of **hypotheses** about what it is seeing, tests them and chooses the most likely one.

66 perception involves
guesswork 99

Sometimes, there is more than one equally likely interpretation of a visual input. Gregory was particularly interested in studying what happens in these circumstances. He thought it demonstrated very clearly hypothesis testing at work. Four lines of evidence included:

1. **Ambiguous stimuli** (see **Fig**. 12.5). These include *Jastrow*'s duck–rabbit figure (1900), *Leeper*'s (1942) old/young woman figure and the *Necker cube* (1832). In all cases, we can make two hypotheses about what the drawing is. Usually we cannot decide on one or the other so our perception wavers between them.
2. **Depth perception demonstrations**. The **hollow face illusion** consists of a model of a face which is hollow (inside out) yet when we look at the face we interpret it as a normal face. In this case, our experience of faces is that they are overwhelmingly never hollow so this is the hypothesis chosen by the brain as the most likely one. Only when the hollow face is rotated does the hypothesis break down and we see it for what it really is. The **Ames room** (1952) is another example of

  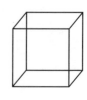

The duck-rabbit	**The old/young woman**	**The Necker cube**

Figure 12.5 Ambiguous figures

this misinterpretation. It is a distorted room which people look into through a peep-hole. They see it as an ordinary room until objects are placed inside. The brain can choose between a 'distorted room with normal size objects in it' hypothesis and a 'normal room with distorted objects in it' hypothesis. People nearly always choose the second hypothesis because their experience is that rooms are not odd shapes.

3. **Geometric illusions and size constancy**. Visual illusions which are created by lines and angles are known as geometric illusions (see Fig. 12.6). Gregory uses the idea of **misapplied constancy scaling** to explain why these work. He suggests that the brain interprets the figures as being *three dimensional*. In the case of the Muller-Lyer illusion the lines and fins could be seen as representing the inside corner of a room or the outside corner of a building. For the lines to cast retinal images of the same size, we would have to be close to a corner in a room but far away from a corner of a building. The brain 'scales' the perceived size of the figures to fit this hypothesis and so we see one line as longer than the other. Gregory thought Westerners were very susceptible to geometric illusions because they lived in a **carpentered world**, that is, a world full of straight lines in rooms and buildings.

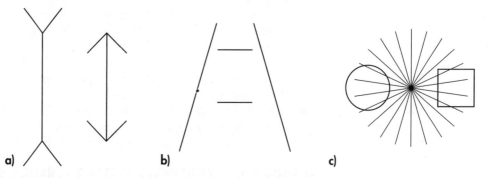

Figure 12.6 Geometric illusions
a) The Muller-Lyer illusion
b) The Ponzo illusion c) The Orbison illusion

a)   b)   c)

4. **Natural illusions**. The moon illusion refers to the fact that the moon (and sun) appear to be larger when they are nearer the horizon yet the size of the retinal image of the moon does not change according to where it is in the sky. Gregory can explain this using the misapplied constancy scaling argument. A moon close to the horizon is judged in relation to familiar objects at ground level. Next to them it is perceived as being larger. The size of a moon in the middle of a dark and featureless sky is judged more accurately.

Evaluation

- Some theorists, e.g. *Gibson* (1979), argue that the brain does not usually have to deal with visual input which is so unusual and lacking in information. Gibson thinks it is hardly surprising that perception breaks down in these circumstances. He argues that visual input from the real world is normally so rich in information that perception is *immediate* and does not involve guesswork.
- *Allport and Pettigrew* (1957) provided some support for Gregory's carpentered world hypothesis when they showed that Zulus living in traditional cultures were not as susceptible to geometric illusions as Westerners. Traditional Zulu buildings are curved and the surrounding world is full of natural objects. (However, this finding may have more to do with Westerners being more familiar than Zulus with interpreting pictures. *Hudson* (1960), showed pictures of hunting

scenes to members of a remote African tribe and found they did not use depth cues such as relative size to interpret them as Westerners did.)

- *Day* (1980) showed that the Muller-Lyer illusion is just as powerful if the fins are replaced with other shapes that do not suggest a three-dimensional figure (see **Fig**. 12.7). It is difficult to see how the misapplied constancy argument could explain this.

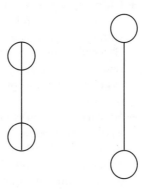

Figure 12.7 The Muller-Lyer illusion works without depth cues

SET AND PERCEPTION

> perception is seen as an active process

Many psychologists agree that perception is an *active* process. By this we mean that it involves *selecting, interpreting* and *organising* incoming information. This makes sense if we consider that people receive much more information than they can actually process. Some way has to be found of filtering out what we need. Some psychologists talk of people having schemas, others prefer to use the term **set**. *Allport* (1955) defined set as: 'a perceptual bias or predisposition or readiness to perceive particular features of a stimulus'.

Another way to think of 'set' is as a temporary *lowering* or *raising* of our threshold for perceiving something. Set can determine both *what* we choose to perceive and *how we make sense* of it. In other words, set acts as:

- a selector
- an interpreter.

Some of our tendency to select some things to attend to rather than others can be put down to *hard-wiring* in our attention systems. For example, visual stimuli which are *bright*, *intense*, *moving* and *repetitive* are often attention grabbing and so more likely to be perceived. Psychologists have also experimented with the effects of other kinds of set:

- **Instructions**. *Chapman* (1932) asked participants to look at briefly displayed cards on which there were arrangements of capital letters. Cards varied according to the number of letters, the letters themselves and the layout on the card. Participants were asked to report on either the number of letters, the letters' identity or the arrangement of the letters. They could do this very well if instructions were given before they saw a card. Giving the instructions afterwards was no help.
- **Context**. *Minturn and Bruner* (1951) used an ambiguous figure which could be read as either a B or a 13. If the figure appeared in a row of capital letters, it was more often seen as a B. In a row of numbers it was more often seen as a 13. We may also fail to see some things because of their context. The second 'the' in **Fig**. 12.8 is often missed for this reason.

Figure 12.8 A demonstration of the effect of context on 'set'

- **Past experience.** *Bruner and Postman* (1949) used ambiguous playing cards (e.g. red hearts and black spades) and presented them briefly to participants. At very short exposures participants did not seem to notice the problem and decided on either red hearts or black spades. At longer exposures, they sometimes reported seeing purple or brown hearts. It seems they mixed together what they knew from past experience of playing cards with what they were actually seeing.
- **Culture.** Some research suggests that members of certain remote tribes do not seem as susceptible to **geometric illusions** as are Westerners. This may have something to do with a set produced by the kind of visual worlds they are used to. However, the evidence is *mixed.* Some studies show no difference at all. Some researchers think so-called differences are due to the different amounts of experience of interpreting two-dimensional pictures of three-dimensional objects or scenes.
- **Reward.** *Lambert et al.* (1949) trained 54 3–5-year-old children to turn a handle for a poker chip. Some children could exchange these chips for sweets. Children were then asked to estimate the size of the poker chip by adjusting a spot of light to match it. Rewarded children over-estimated the size of the chip by 13% compared to 5% in non-rewarded children.
- **Motivation.** Short-term physiological states such as hunger can induce a set. *Sandford* (1936) showed participants ambiguous pictures at intervals during four hours of food deprivation. Participants reported seeing more food-related objects in the pictures as time went on. In a follow-up study, Sandford found the effect of deprivation was more pronounced at participants' usual mealtimes than at other times.
- **Emotion.** There are several examples here. *Solley and Haigh* (1958) showed that children's drawings of Christmas pictures were much more elaborate in the two weeks before Christmas than afterwards when the excitement had worn off! *Lazarus and McLeary* (1951) gave some participants electric shocks at the same time as showing them certain words. Participants were later shown these words, along with other neutral ones, for times too brief to perceive consciously. Words associated with shock provoked greater emotional reactions (measured by **GSR** or a Galvanic Skin Response) than did neutral words.
- **Perceptual defence and perceptual sensitisation.** These are special examples of the emotional meaning of a stimulus affecting how readily a person perceives it. *Bruner and Postman* (1947) showed how participants took longer to recognise **taboo words** than neutral words when they saw them very briefly. It was as if the perceptual system put up a guard or defence against something potentially threatening. *Carpenter et al.* (1956) went on to show how some people recognised taboo words faster than neutral words as if they were more open, or sensitised, to them. These rather odd findings suggest that we have a pre-conscious mechanism which screens incoming information before we become consciously aware of it. This is referred to as **subliminal perception**.

SET IN REAL LIFE

Banyard and Hayes (1994) offer a number of examples to show how set affects real-life perception:

- In **advertising**, the mood created by a TV advertisement (happy or sombre) could affect how the viewer felt about it and how much they remembered.
- When we leave a motorway after **driving** very fast, traffic on minor roads may seem to be moving very slowly. It may take some time for us to readjust our speed.
- When we are **reading** we may sometimes make mistakes with individual words. This may be because we expect to see a particular word because of the context or it may be because a word reminds us of a similar one that we are more familiar with.
- There is a similarity between the idea of a **schema** and set. We may use these when we *select* and *interpret* information about others in our social world. In this sense a *stereotype* or **implicit personality theory** acts as a kind of set so it is not something confined only to visual perception.

66 Can you add to these examples? 99

Psychologists question whether abilities are *innate* (nature) or *learned* through experience (nurture) or more usually to what extent they interact. This is sometimes referred to as a debate between **nativists** (for the nature side) and **empiricists** (for the nurture side). The debate is important for a number of reasons, e.g.:

- it is an academically interesting question;
- we need to know how development happens so that we can make sure it is going along normally. If development is largely due to nature there may be little we can do to help if it is not progressing well. If it is due to nurture we should be able to intervene to put things right.

STUDIES OF HUMAN NEW-BORNS AND INFANTS

The obvious place to start is with human infants. We need to study what they can see when they are born but there are some difficulties with this:

- They have *short concentration spans*.
- Their *ability to focus* is limited to about 30cm.
- They may be *sleepy or preoccupied* with other physical needs so they are not easy to test.
- They have *postural difficulties* and need to be supported.
- They *cannot tell us* what they see so we have to devise ways of testing them so that we can **infer** (guess) what they see from watching their *behaviour*. We may not always guess correctly.
- For *ethical reasons* we cannot interfere with their visual experience for the sake of answering scientific questions so the amount of control we have in this respect is limited.
- There may be a *bias in the sample* of infants studied, e.g. children of university lecturers or children of parents prepared to give up the time it takes for testing.
- If we wait until they are mature enough to concentrate, hold up their heads etc. *experience* will have had time to influence the child.

Form perception

Fantz (1961) devised **the visual preference technique**. He reasoned that infants would look longer at things which interested them so he presented them with two visual stimuli at a time and measured the length of time they gazed at one or the other. He discovered that babies aged 1–15 weeks liked contrast in patterns but also preferred some patterns over others. **Fig**. 12.9 shows their order of preference for five stimuli.

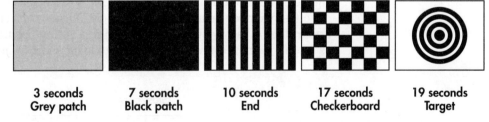

Figure 12.9 Examples of stimuli used by Fantz in his studies of pattern perception in infants (showing seconds per minute infants gazed at them)

| 3 seconds | 7 seconds | 10 seconds | 17 seconds | 19 seconds |
| Grey patch | Black patch | End | Checkerboard | Target |

Visual acuity

Visual acuity refers to how much *detail* a person can see. Using the visual preference technique, Fantz showed infants a black and white grid paired with a grey patch at a distance of 15 inches. Infants gazed longer at the more interesting grid. Fantz then used grids with finer and finer lines. Eventually the grid would appear grey to the infant who would show no preference for the grid or the grey patch. Fantz showed that, at less than 1 month, infants could tell the difference between grey and a grid with lines 1/8 inch wide. By 6 months they could tell lines 1/64 inch wide from grey showing that their ability to perceive detail *matures* with time.

Face perception

Fantz prepared three black and pink face-like patterns as shown in **Fig**. 12.10. He presented these to infants aged between 4 days and 6 months in all possible pair combinations and measured their visual preference. Infants showed a slight preference for

Organized face   **Scrambled face**   **Face shape with hairline**

Figure 12.10 Stimuli used by Fantz in his studies of infants' perceptions of faces

the organised face pattern compared to the scrambled face which had the same amount of detail. They showed little interest in the hair-line stimulus.

Later researchers have argued that Fantz's studies do not show convincingly that infants innately recognise faces. The stimuli used in the laboratory are not as interesting as a real face. They are not as colourful and do not move. Later research using pictures of faces as well as *real faces* has shown that, as early as 12 hours after birth, a baby will show more interest in its *mother's face* than in that of a female stranger. Other studies have shown infants will *imitate facial expressions* only minutes after birth. But perhaps babies do not recognise faces as faces. Instead it is likely that a face combines many features (e.g. movement, sound, colour, symmetry) which attract the infant's interest and make it more likely that it will learn quickly about faces themselves.

❝❝ this could have survival value ❞❞

Depth perception

Gibson and Walk (1963) used the **visual cliff** to test the depth perception of infants old enough to crawl (aged 6–14 months) (see **Fig**. 12.11). The infant would be placed on the centre board and the mother would try to entice it to cross to her over the 'solid' side or the apparent drop. These were the results:

- 67% crossed on to the solid side only
- 8% moved on to both sides
- 0% moved to the 'drop' side only
- 25% did not move.

Gibson and Walk concluded depth perception was present at least as soon as the baby could crawl. However, this does *not* show that it is innate. To extend their study, Gibson and Walk used the young of animals who were mobile at birth, such as chicks, goats and kittens, and found that they avoided the drop as much as did human infants. Other researchers showed that 2-month-old human infants placed directly on to the glass over the 'drop' became quiet and still as if they sensed something unusual. It was only at 9 months that this caused distress. Later research suggested that the depth cues which tell the infant about the drop are **relative size** (of the black and white squares) and **motion parallax** (of the table surface and the floor).

To test younger infants aged 6–20 days, *Bower et al.* (1970) devised the **looming apparatus**. A baby would be supported in a sitting position and a solid shape (such as a sphere) moved towards its face (stopping short of hitting it!). Infants showed a

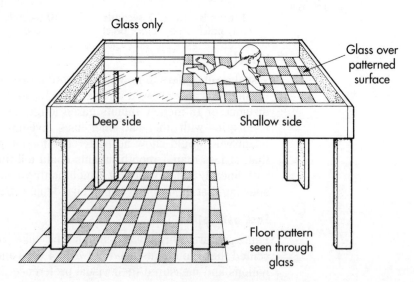

Figure 12.11 Gibson and Walk's visual cliff

marked **avoidance reaction** by leaning back, opening their eyes wide and, some
times, moving their hands up in front of their faces. This seems to suggest innate perception of depth but babies may have just been startled by the rapidly expanding
image or by the air movement caused by the object. To check this, Bower showed
babies a *rapidly expanding image* on a screen or gave them *air current* alone and
found little reaction.

Size constancy

To test size constancy, *Bower* (1966) devised the **peekaboo technique**. First the
infant must be trained to show it recognises a stimulus, then it can be tested for size
constancy:

Stage 1 – conditioning a head turn

- An infant is securely supported in a sitting position and shown a 30cm cube at 1m
  away.
- The infant soon tires of the cube and turns its head away.
- The experimenter appears, says 'Peekaboo!' and rewards the baby's head turn
  with tickles and attention. (This is, of course, a form of **operant conditioning**.)
- After doing this several times, the infant quickly learns to turn its head for reward
  whenever it sees the cube.

Stage 2 – testing for size constancy

The infant is tested using a 30cm cube at 3m, a 90cm cube at 1m and a 90cm cube at
3m. If size constancy is innate, the most head turns should occur to a 30cm cube
regardless of its distance, followed by the 90cm cube at 1m which differs in size but not
distance and the 90cm cube at 3m which differs in both size and distance.

Bower concluded that infants could understand size constancy. He counted:

- 98 head turns for the original cube
- 58 head turns for the 30cm cube at 3m
- 54 head turns for the 90cm cube at 1m
- 22 head turns for the 90cm cube at 3m

Bower also used the peekaboo technique using *rectangles* as stimuli. He concluded
that infants also have an innate understanding of **shape constancy** because they
seemed to recognise a rectangle even when it was at an angle and appeared to be a
trapezoid shape.

ANIMAL STUDIES

Studies of the development of visual perception in animals are carried out to help us
with the nature–nurture question for a number of reasons:

- A problem with studying infants is that it would be *unethical* to manipulate and
  control their visual experience to see what happens to their visual abilities. With
  animals more intervention is allowed.
- More highly controlled studies are possible with animals so we can be more
  confident about cause and effect than we can with correlational studies on humans.
- We can assume that animals and humans have a great deal in *common both
  genetically and behaviourally* so what applies to one species (e.g. chimpanzees) will
  also apply to a closely related one (e.g. humans).
- Some animal species *reproduce* and *develop faster* than humans so we can see the
  effects of early experience more quickly.
- It is easier to be *scientifically objective* with animals than it is with humans.

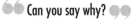 Can you say why?

However it is important to remember that:

- Not everyone would agree that research findings about animals can be transferred
  to humans.
- The kinds of deprivation used in animal studies are usually far more extreme than
  anything a human might experience.
- There have been many objections to animal studies on ethical grounds.

Deprivation studies

These studies are based on the reasoning that, if visual abilities are innate, they will not be affected if the animal is deprived of normal vision. They will simply start up as soon as normal vision is allowed. On the other hand, if they need experience to develop, deprivation of normal visual input should mean that they do not develop.

Riesen's studies

Riesen (1965) reared three chimps from birth to 7 months of age:

- Debi experienced nothing but total darkness;
- Kova had 1½ hrs a day seeing light through diffusing goggles but spent the rest of the time in darkness;
- Lad was raised in normal conditions.

Debi's vision was destroyed through damage to her retinae. Clearly the visual system needed light to keep it healthy. Kova's visual system was healthy but her vision seemed to be retarded. Her perception of patterns was poor and she did not use her vision to avoid objects. She found it difficult to follow moving objects with her eyes. Lad's vision was perfectly normal. Riesen concluded patterned light is essential for normal perception to develop. It is not enough just to experience disorganised or diffused light.

Hubel and Wiesel (1962) suggested that experience is necessary to develop specialised **feature detecting cells** in the visual cortex. These cells allow us to see lines of different orientations or to detect dots or movement.

Blakemore and Cooper's stripy tube experiments

Blakemore and Cooper (1970) reared kittens in the dark except for five hours a day when they were placed on a glass shelf suspended half-way down a large tube. On the sides of the tube were painted black and white *vertical* stripes and these were the kittens' only visual experience. Other kittens were only allowed experience of tubes with *horizontal* stripes painted on them. Blakemore and Cooper claimed the 'vertical world' kittens behaved as though they were blind to horizontal lines and the 'horizontal world' kittens seemed unable to perceive vertical lines. Normal visual experience is clearly essential for normal development to occur. Unfortunately, we are not yet sure why. It could be that:

- kittens could see normally when they first opened their eyes but the stripy tube experience had caused specialised cells in the visual cortex to die away (**atrophy**);
- the specialised cells were not present at the start and experience was necessary to cause them to develop;
- the cells for seeing normally are present but immature and need experience to finish the process of development.

Held and Hein's kitten carousel

Held and Hein (1965) reasoned that our vision was mainly to help us move around in the world and that we needed to combine movement and vision if vision were to be really useful to us. They devised the apparatus shown in **Fig**. 12.12. Two kittens spent three hours a day for several weeks in the kitten carousel until they had completed 30 hours. The carousel allowed one kitten to move and see normally. The other could see normally but was carried in a 'basket'. When they were tested, the active kitten had normal use of sight and used vision well to move around. The passive (carried) kitten had a healthy visual system but did not seem able to use its vision to move about so well. It seems that sight is only really useful to a kitten if it is active in using it.

❝❞ our vision has important functions ❝❞

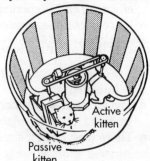

Figure 12.12 The kitten carousel (From Held, 1965)

CROSS-CULTURAL STUDIES

If perception is learned we would expect people from different environments to perceive differently. This is one reason why psychologists are interested in studying perception in different cultures. See chapter two for problems with such studies. Examples include:

- *Turnbull* (1961) claimed that *pygmies* living in dense forest had trouble with **size constancy** because they were not used to judging size over long distances. When he took a member of the tribe for a jeep ride over open plains, the pygmy mistook a distant herd of buffalo for insects and a distant boat on a lake for a piece of floating wood.
- *Segall and Campbell* (1963) claimed that *Zulus* are less susceptible than *Europeans* to the Muller-Lyer illusion. This may be due to Europeans' greater experience with a **carpentered world** of straight lines and angles. On the other hand, it could be due to Zulus being less familiar with interpreting drawings.
- *Annis and Frost* (1973) compared *Canadian Cree Indians* living in traditional tepees with *urban Canadians* whose buildings are more often rectangular. The problem was to judge whether two straight lines, presented at different angles, were parallel. Cree Indians were much better at this suggesting that they were affected by their environment in a different way to urban Canadians.

RECOVERY FROM BLINDNESS STUDIES

Adults who recover their sight after a period of blindness are interesting to psychologists because, unlike infants, they can talk about what they see. And again, unlike infants, they have a lifetime of experiences other than visual ones and their visual systems may have changed in important ways. Studies include:

- *Von Senden*'s reports of 66 case studies between 1920 and 1931. He found great differences between cases. Some were successful in using vision, others needed a great deal of training to make use of it, suffered emotional problems or gave up in spite of great determination to succeed.
- *Gregory and Wallace* (1963) described the case of **SB** who had lost his sight at 10 months of age and regained it after a corneal transplant at the age of 52 years. SB had led a very successful life as a blind person and was keen to use his new sight. When he was tested he showed good **figure–ground** perception but his **depth perception** was not very good. He could use sight to move around but relied heavily on touch to help identify objects. He never learned to read more than simple words although his drawing improved with time. In the end, SB reverted to the life of a blind person, he suffered from depression and died three years later.

READJUSTMENT STUDIES

These studies are based on the idea that, if we have to learn how to see, we should be able to readjust to see the world correctly if the input is changed in some way. *Stratton* (1897) wore a special lens which turned his visual world upside-down and left to right. At night he slept blindfolded. At first Stratton found any kind of activity very difficult. His senses of vision, hearing and movement no longer fitted in with each other. Only after several days did Stratton learn to move around more successfully but he reported that he never saw the world the right way up or the right way round. Instead he learned to adapt his movements which suggests that the movement sense is more flexible than the visual sense.

CONCLUSION

To sum up:

- **Studies of infants** show how well developed perceptual abilities are but, clearly, they need time to reach the same level as adults'. There may be sensitive periods in the first two or three years when normal experience is necessary for full development to take place.
- **Animal studies** all seem to show how important experience is but they do not

enable us to resolve the nature–nurture debate. Deprivation may actually destroy innate abilities rather than simply causing them to lie dormant.

- **Cross-cultural studies** suggest that experience matters but many of the 'differences' found may be more due to difficulties in testing people fairly than to real differences in perception.
- **Recovery from blindness studies** are fascinating but, as each case is unique it is difficult to draw firm conclusions.
- **Readjustment studies** tend to show that some perceptual abilities are more flexible than others. Also, people can learn to adapt to distorted input but they never really see the world normally.

These days we do not tend to ask whether an ability is innate or learned. Instead it is more usual to ask how nature and nurture *interact*. This is a very difficult question to answer and the debate tends to be inconclusive because:

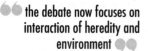 the debate now focuses on interaction of heredity and environment

- We cannot fully separate nature and nurture in order to test their influence separately. An *animal* has to have an *environment* to exist in. You cannot have one without the other.
- Some abilities may be partly innate and only develop fully with the right kind of experience. This experience might need to happen during a limited **sensitive period** in early life if development is to be normal. If an individual misses this sensitive period they may never develop the ability. We may misinterpret this, taking lack of ability to show that only experience matters when, in fact, both genetics and experience are important.

EXAMINATION QUESTIONS

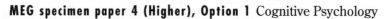

MEG specimen paper 4 (Higher), Option 1 Cognitive Psychology

Spend 25 minutes on this question

Source

Culture and experience affect the way that we interpret our perceptual world. A psychologist showed the following picture to members of a rural African community.

They believed that the man was trying to kill the elephant.

They could not interpret the information in the picture that gave cues about which animal was further away because they were not used to looking at and interpreting pictures.

People from Western cultures, where pictures are a common part of life, interpreted the scene differently. They believed that the deer was the intended victim.

(a) Identify **two** depth cues that are present in the picture. [2]
(b) The source gives an example of cross-cultural study.
 (i) Give **one** reason why psychologists carry out cross-cultural research. [2]
 (ii) Give **two** difficulties with this type of research. [2]

(c) Studying newly born children (neonates) is another way that psychologists have studied perceptual abilities. Why is this type of study used? [2]

(d) Culture affects how we see things. What have psychologists discovered about how emotion or motivation affects perception? [4]

[Total 12 marks]
(MEG)

TUTOR ANSWER

(a) Overlay (superposition). Height in the horizontal plain.

(b) (i) Cross-cultural studies can help in nature–nurture debates to show whether different environmental experiences are related to differences in behaviour. This can give us an idea of whether heredity or environment matter more in determining behaviour.

(ii) There are sometimes difficulties in translating test materials from one language to another in a way that retains the original meaning. There can also be difficulties in remaining objective about different cultures. Researchers have to try to ensure their own cultural biases do not affect how they view another culture.

(c) If psychologists want to know whether perceptual abilities are innate, it is important to study neonates to see what they can and cannot perceive before they have had any visual experience.

(d) Solley and Haigh showed that excitement in children as Christmas approached led them to draw much more elaborate Christmas pictures before the event than after. Lazarus and McLeary gave participants electric shocks at the same time as showing them certain words. When these words and others were later shown to the participants, their emotional reactions to the 'shocked' words, as shown by their GSR readings, were greater than to the other words.

STUDENTS' ANSWERS

1.   NEAB specimen paper (Tier Q) Question B1

Spend about 14 minutes answering this question

Look at the diagram below and answer the questions which follow.

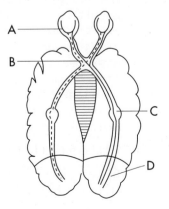

(a) Identify the parts labelled A–D in the diagram and complete the box below. [4]

C = lateral geniculate
nucleus

3/4

A	retina
B	optic chiasma
C	
D	visual cortex

(b) Identify and describe **one** binocular depth cue used in everyday life [2]

the brain puts them
together 2/2

Retinal disparity. The two eyes pick up slightly different pictures of the world and put these together to see depth.

(c) How do psychologists explain that we perceive in **three** dimensions yet our retinal images are in **two** dimensions [5]

mention perception as an
active process **or**
the role of experience 4/5

The eyes pick up a flat image that the brain converts to a 3D image. To do this, it looks for cues like retinal disparity, convergence, overlay, relative height and gradient of texture. The brain works out the distance of things from putting this information together.

[*Total 11 marks*]
(NEAB)

9/11 Some of these answers are just enough for the marks awarded

2. **SEG paper 2, 1994. Section B**

Spend 40 minutes on this question

(a) What is perception? [3]

3/3

Psychologists distinguish between sensation and perception. Sensation is the reaction of the eye and the visual system to light energy. Perception is making sense of the sensation when it reaches the brain. There may be some guesswork involved.

(b) Describe **one** study of animal perception. [6]

more details about method
needed

Blakemore and Cooper carried out a study of kittens. The kittens spent time each day in large drums with black and white vertical stripes painted on the inside. At the age of 5 months, their vision was tested. They didn't recognise anything with horizontal edges. They only reacted to vertical edges like the lines they had been reared with. It might be that the kittens had an innate ability to see all kinds of lines but the cells in the visual cortex that let them do this died away through lack of use. Or it could be that there is a sensitive period (3–15 weeks) for development of line-detecting cells and the kittens missed it through being in the tube. The study suggests kittens need normal visual input to develop useful vision and supports the nurture side of the nature–nurture debate.

just 5/6

(c) Describe **one** study of human perception [6]

aim of the study should be
here

Gibson and Walk constructed an apparatus known as the visual cliff. This is a large table covered with a check pattern and strong glass. On one half of the table the check pattern is directly under the glass. On the other half it covers the floor so it looks as if there is a drop. They took 36 infants between 6 and 14 months and placed them in the centre of the table. The mother tried to get them to cross to her, sometimes over the 'cliff' and sometimes over the other side. Nine refused to move, three crawled over the cliff side only but 24 would only cross what seemed to be the safe side. The babies seemed to be able to see depth and became distressed if they thought there was danger. Those who did cross seemed to use their sense of touch to test the safety of the glass. These findings do not tell us for sure that depth perception is innate because the babies were old enough to crawl and would have had experience of seeing depth.

5/6

(d) What is meant by the nature–nurture debate? [6]

explain why it is a
debate

This is the debate over whether we are born being able to perceive (nature) or whether we have to learn to make sense of the visual world (nurture). These days,

5/6

psychologists do not think of it being one or the other. They think nature and nurture interact but they still do not understand how.

(e) How have psychological studies added to the nature–nurture debate on perception? [9]

good

Robert Fantz used the visual preference technique to show that babies' perception of detail improves with experience. He also showed them face patterns, one regular face, one scrambled and one with just a hair-line. Babies looked longer at the regular face showing they were innately attracted to it. Gibson and Walk showed babies could perceive depth by the time they were old enough to crawl. Using the looming technique, Bower showed depth perception in even younger babies. He also showed that babies have size constancy through using the 'peekaboo' technique.

explain how these studies relate to the nature–nurture debate

Riesen reared a chimp in total darkness and another with diffusing goggles. Compared to a normal chimp the dark-reared chimp was virtually blind. The chimp reared with goggles had a healthy visual system but did not seem able to use it. Blakemore and Cooper's stripy tube experiment showed kittens become blind to certain kinds of edges if they do not have experience of them at a young age. The kitten carousel experiment showed that kittens need to practise using their vision by moving around otherwise they can't use it properly.

Many psychologists think the nature–nurture debate on perception still has to be worked out and that it is a mixture of the two. The kind of experiments they would need to do to find out on humans are mostly unethical so would not be allowed. Animal studies overcome this but may not tell us much about human perception.

6/9

[*Total 30 marks*]
(SEG)

24/30 Some very good material. It is important to spell out why studies are relevant to the nature–nurture debate in (e) rather than leaving the examiner to work it out from the answer

A Review Sheet for this chapter can be found on pp. 247–8

13
MEMORY

GETTING STARTED

Memory is a topic which appears on the NEAB and MEG syllabuses only. NEAB students need to study the whole chapter. All MEG students need this chapter because it is a compulsory, core topic, but MEG students need not study the final section on brain injury and amnesia.

For both syllabuses you need to know some of the ways in which psychologists explain how memory works and why we forget. You also need to know how these ideas are applied to help improve memory and prevent forgetting. Another important area of memory research is in the field of eyewitness testimony, that is the recall of people who have witnessed events such as crimes. Understanding how they recall such events and how their recall may be inaccurate can be vital when witnesses attend identity parades or give evidence in court.

1. DEFINITIONS

2. WAYS OF TESTING MEMORY

3. MODELS OF MEMORY

4. ORGANISATION IN LTM

5. APPLICATIONS OF THEORIES AND RESEARCH INTO MEMORY AND FORGETTING

6. EYEWITNESS TESTIMONY

7. BRAIN INJURY AND AMNESIA

ESSENTIAL PRINCIPLES

1 **DEFINITIONS**

💬💬 an example of the
information processing
approach 💬💬

Memory is a system which is vital to our survival. If we could not store information about past experiences, we would be lucky to exist for more than a few minutes! For psychologists, the term *memory* covers three important aspects of information processing:

1 **Encoding**. When information comes into our memory system, it needs to be changed into a form that the system can cope with. (Think of this as similar to changing your money into a different currency when you travel from one country to another.) For example, a word which is seen, heard or read may only be stored if it is changed (encoded) into an image, a sound or a meaning.
2 **Storage**. This concerns the nature of memory stores, that is, how long they last, how much they can hold and what kind of information they hold.
3 **Retrieval**. This refers to getting information out of a memory store. There are a number of different kinds of retrieval:

- **Recall**. This happens when you bring information out of a memory store and reproduce it, e.g. in an exam or when you recite a nursery rhyme.
- **Recognition**. This is when you realise you have encountered something before because, when you see, hear or read it again, you know it is familiar.
- **Redintegration**. This happens when you rebuild a memory as you go along. The police may get helpers to act out a crime or event in the hope that it will 'jog' the memories of witnesses who saw the actual crime and help them to reconstruct their memory of the event.

For memory to work well, you need to efficiently encode, store and retrieve information. Failure to remember (**forgetting**) may result from not doing any one of these properly.

2 **WAYS OF
TESTING MEMORY**

Psychologists have devised a number of ways of testing people's memory:

- **Free recall**. Participants may be given something to be remembered (e.g. a list of words) and then asked to reproduce it in any order they like. Witnesses also use free recall when they try to describe an event or someone's face for an *identikit picture* or *artist's impression*.
- **Cued recall**. People are given clues or 'memory joggers' to help them retrieve information, e.g. the first letter of a key word. Many of the memory aids to be described later use cues to recall.
- **Memory span procedure**. A small number of items are presented for recall and the participant asked to recall them in the same order. If this is done correctly, a longer list is presented. The memory span is the largest number of items that can be correctly recalled.
- **Serial learning**. Participants are presented with a list of items to learn and recall in order.
- **Paired associate learning**. Participants learn pairs of items and are then given the first item of the pair and asked to recall the second item.
- **Recognition testing**. Participants are exposed to something to be remembered and then, after a time interval, are asked to pick it out from a number of similar others. This is what happens when witnesses to crimes look at *identity parades*.

3 **MODELS OF
MEMORY**

ATKINSON AND SHIFFRIN'S MULTISTORE MODEL OF MEMORY

Atkinson and Shiffrin (1968) suggest that memory is made up of a series of stores (see **Fig**. 13.1). These are the sensory information store (SIS), the short-term memory (STM) and the long-term memory (LTM). The stores differ in their encoding, storage and retrieval characteristics. (This model is sometimes called the two-process model of memory because of the two major stores, STM and LTM.)

The SIS

Incoming information is registered by the senses and held in the system until the image fades. To demonstrate this, *Sperling* (1960) showed participants three rows of

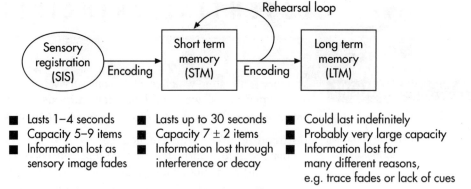

Figure 13.1 Atkinson and Shiffrin's multistore model of memory

four mixed numbers and consonants for a very brief time. He then played them a tone (high, medium and low) to prompt them to recall the top, middle or bottom line. Participants could do this easily if they recalled immediately. Sperling thought:

- information is held as a *sensation* in a sensory system (e.g. the visual system);
- the *capacity* of the SIS is between five and nine items;
- the SIS *lasts* about one-quarter of a second (later researchers have shown that the SIS can last up to four seconds and some unusual individuals (called **eidetic imagers**) can hold the image for even longer);
- forgetting is due to the sensation in the sensory system *rapidly fading away.*

The STM

Information selected for further processing passes from the SIS into the STM. It is thought that:

- the STM holds information in the form of images, sounds or meanings, e.g. information about a word might be stored in terms of its appearance, how it sounds or what it means;
- we can store seven items (+ or − two) in the STM. The items can be **chunks** of information, e.g. a telephone number with twelve digits could be reduced to three or four chunks;
- items in STM last up to 30 seconds;
- two suggestions have been made about how information in STM is forgotten. **Trace decay theory** says we lose items because they fade away. **Interference theory** says items are lost because when we exceed STM's capacity, something has to go to make room. Information in STM is kept 'alive' by rehearsing (repeating) it.

Two key pieces of evidence about lifespan and capacity of STM are:

66 the 'retention interval' is the length of time the trigram was stored before recall 99

- *Peterson and Peterson* (1959) gave participants a three-consonant **trigram** to remember (e.g. KDL) and then a large number (e.g. 485) immediately afterwards. To prevent participants from rehearsing the trigram, they had to count backwards in threes from the number for a time and then recall the trigram. The longer participants counted, the less likely they were to recall it. The point at which they could not recall it gives us an idea of how long STM lasts, i.e. a maximum of 30 seconds (see **Fig**. 13.2).
- *Miller* (1956) used the memory span procedure to test how many items participants could hold in the STM. Using strings of numbers or consonants, he found the average number of items was seven (Miller's **magical number seven**), give or take two. This means, our STM is capable of holding between five and nine items.

The LTM

Information which is rehearsed enough will transfer into LTM. (Frequently used telephone numbers tend to do this.)

- information in LTM is encoded in many forms – we know LTM contains knowledge, facts, beliefs, pictures, skills, language and musical knowledge among many other things;
- LTM seems to have an unlimited capacity;
- LTM seems to have an indefinite lifespan;
- there are many reasons why LTM information is forgotten. Possibilities include decay of the memory trace, interference (where new material pushes out old or

old material prevents new material from entering LTM) and cue dependent forgetting (where the material we need cannot be retrieved because we have no cue or 'key' to unlock the store).

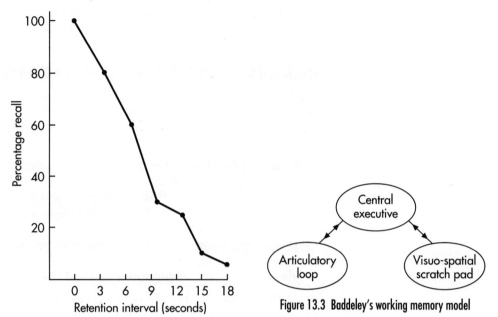

Figure 13.2 Typical results from Peterson and Peterson's (1959) studies of the lifespan of STM

Figure 13.3 Baddeley's working memory model

Further evidence for the multistore model

The primacy and recency effect
Murdock (1962) asked participants to learn a list of words and free recall them. He found that words presented either early in the list or at the end were more often recalled, but the ones in the middle were more often forgotten. Murdock suggested that words early in the list were put into LTM (**primacy effect**) and words from the end went into STM (**recency effect**). Words in the middle of the list had been there too long to be held in STM and not long enough to be put into LTM.

section 13.7 gives more detail

Physiological evidence
Milner (1967) quoted evidence from studies of brain-damaged, amnesic or alcoholic people who have a good LTM but very poor STM. *Stroke* victims and some *elderly* people may also have problems with STM. People who suffer from the alcohol related **Korsakoff's syndrome** may have problems with LTM but not STM but the pattern is not always that clear. (See the section on amnesia at the end of this chapter for more detailed information.)

Evaluation of Atkinson and Shiffrin's model of memory

1 The model suggests *rehearsal* helps to transfer information into LTM but some studies show it is *not essential*. We may, for example, remember parts of a lecture or a book simply because they are funny, interesting or relevant in some way.

2 *Baddeley* (1986) has suggested that the STM was not just for brief storage of information. He thought it also actively processed the information and decided what to do with it. The **articulatory loop** deals with verbal information and **the visuo-spatial scratchpad** deals with visual information. The **central executive** decides how to share out the limited resources of STM (see **Fig**. 13.3).

3 Atkinson and Shiffrin thought everything was held in the same LTM but this doesn't seem very likely. Other psychologists have argued we have more than one kind of LTM. Here are some examples:

- **Mental imagery.** *Paivio* (1971) carried out a great deal of research into this kind of LTM. It seems some of our LTM consists of 'images' from all our senses, e.g. visual images of someone's face, auditory images of the sound of their voice, olfactory images of the way they smell.

- **Declarative and procedural memory.** *Cohen and Squire* (1980) suggest we have two LTM stores. Declarative memory stores things that we know. It is like a personal diary, dictionary and encyclopaedia all in one. We would use this memory to answer questions in a quiz or to tell a friend about things that have happened to us. Procedural memory is where we store knowledge of how to do things such as how to ride a bike, do a jigsaw puzzle or hit a tennis ball.

Atkinson and Shiffrin's model has been important in encouraging new research and theory about memory. Points 2 and 3 above elaborate on the model rather than contradicting it. The levels of processing approach, however, offers an alternative view.

CRAIK AND LOCKHART'S LEVELS OF PROCESSING THEORY

Craik and Lockhart (1972) disagreed with Atkinson and Shiffrin's idea that memory consisted of separate stores. Instead, they suggested that memory depends on what we do with information when it comes in, in other words, how we process it. We can process it on a shallow level or a deep level:

- **Shallow processing**. This takes two forms. **Structural processing** is when we encode only the physical qualities of something, e.g. the typeface of a word or how the letters look. **Phonemic processing** is when we encode its sound. Shallow processing only involves **maintenance rehearsal** and leads to fairly short-term retention of information.
- **Deep processing**. This involves **semantic processing** which happens when we encode the meaning of a word and relate it to similar words with similar meaning. This means we are using **elaborative rehearsal** which leads to longer-term retention.

To test this, *Craik and Tulving* (1975) presented participants with a series of words, one at a time, for very brief exposures. Before each word appeared participants were asked a question (which served to tell them how to process the word). For example:

- **structural processing** – 'Is the word in upper case letters?'
- **phonemic processing** – 'Does the word rhyme with …?'
- **semantic processing** – 'Does the word go in this sentence …?'

Participants were then given a long list of words into which the original words had been mixed. They were asked to pick out the original words. The results were:

- structural processing – 18% correct
- phonemic processing – 50% correct
- semantic processing – 80% correct.

Deep processing leads to much better retention than shallow processing. It follows from this that we forget things because they have not been processed deeply enough.

Evaluation of the levels of processing approach

66 problems with testing processing depth 99

1 Deep processing takes more *effort* than shallow processing and it could be this, rather than the depth of processing, that makes it more likely people will remember something.
2 Deep processing takes *longer* than shallow processing so it could be this, rather than the depth of processing, that makes it more likely they will remember something.
3 We do not know *why* deeper processing should aid memory. The levels model does not explain this.
4 The levels model has been criticised for *over-simplifying things* so various changes and additions have been suggested:

- **Elaboration**. *Craik and Tulving* (1975) found that it was not just depth of processing that affected retention but also the degree of elaboration a person carried out, e.g. just to think of the definition of the word 'table' is deep processing but not very elaborate. We can elaborate 'table' more by thinking of different sizes of tables, made of different materials for different uses thus making it more likely that we will remember 'table'.
- **Distinctiveness**. *Eysenck* (1979) suggested that if we can make something we want to remember stand out in some unique way we are more likely to remember it. This is because the memory trace is distinct from other similar ones and will not get confused with them. We remember some events, such as personal successes or disasters, because they stand out as being unusual or distinctive.
- **Context**. *Tulving* (1979) suggested that the setting (context) in which something is learned is encoded along with the material to be remembered. Stated simply, if we learn something in a particular setting we are more likely to recall it in that setting than in a different one regardless of how deeply we processed it.

- **Personal relevance.** *Rogers et al.* (1977) found that participants who processed words in terms of whether they applied to them in some way (e.g. Do you own one of these? PARROT) remembered them even more than semantically processed words.

THE CONSTRUCTIVIST APPROACH TO MEMORY

Bartlett (1932) took a very different approach to the study of memory than the two process or levels models described earlier. Bartlett suggested:

66 this emphasises the active nature of memory 99

- We do not simply store a copy of something that we want to remember. Instead memory is seen as an *active* process. We *construct* our memories by combining existing knowledge with the new, incoming material. Retrieval involves *reconstructing* the resulting memories. It follows that people may remember quite different things about the same event because they have each constructed their memories in their own way.
- We will learn more about real-life memory if we give people *meaningful* things to memorise rather than lists of words. Bartlett used stories, faces and pictures in his tests of memory.

In one study, Bartlett used a story called **'The War of the Ghosts'** which is about 300 words long. Participants were asked to read it and, fifteen minutes later, to recall everything they could about it. Bartlett followed up some of the participants later on to test their recall. (One person was tested ten years later!) He found that people's accounts of the story changed in predictable ways. These changes seemed to serve to make the story neater or more logical so that it fitted in with the participant's personal interpretation of events. Changes were:

- **omissions** – certain details were left out;
- **rationalisations** – details were sometimes added if the participant had made additions and needed to justify them;
- **alterations in importance** – aspects of the story might be played up or down;
- **changed order** – this might make the participant's version of the story 'flow' better;
- **added affect** – if participants had reacted emotionally to the story (e.g. disgusted or amused) this often affected the way they recalled it.

In other studies, Bartlett used line drawings (see **Fig**. 13.4). Participants studied them and then drew them from memory talking about it as they went. He found people tended to interpret and recall the drawing in a way that fitted with their own knowledge and the words they used to describe it.

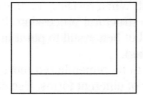  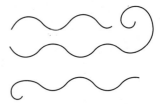

Figure 13.4 Examples of line drawings used by Bartlett

66 'effort after meaning' summarises how people deal with information to be remembered 99

Bartlett used the term **effort after meaning** to explain his results. People do not passively receive information to be remembered. They work on it and change it until they understand it in their own way; forgetting results from the distortions, omissions and additions that occur and make the remembered version different from the original.

Evaluation of the constructivist approach

1 Bartlett has given us an important alternative to other memory models by focusing more on memory as it is used in *everyday life*.
2 The approach can be *difficult to test* because people's responses to the materials used are not easy to score.
3 The approach causes us to consider *how people differ* in their recall of the same event. This is important in eyewitness testimony (see later).
4 Bartlett's ideas have been developed into a **cognitive approach to memory**. This approach asks what memory is *for* and how it fits in with other cognitive systems such as language and perception. (Other approaches have focused more on the *structure* of memory.)

4 ▷ ORGANISATION IN LTM

Information in LTM is not stored any old how. It tends to be **organised**. *Bower et al.* (1969) showed how presenting words organised into categories helped people to recall 65% of the words compared to 19% if the same words were disorganised. They also found evidence that people *spontaneously* categorise disorganised lists.

Collins and Quillian (1972) thought that information in LTM was organised into **hierarchies**. When we want to retrieve something we start at the top of the hierarchy and work down until we find it, e.g. for information on 'sticklebacks' we might start at 'animals', move to 'fish', then to 'freshwater fish', and on to 'small fish' until we find what we want.

Another reason for thinking LTM is organised is that we seem to know immediately if something is not stored. If it is stored we may experience a feeling of knowing (**FOK**) or a tip of the tongue (**TOT**) feeling. We usually know if it is worth searching and the search is not random.

Finally, the way memories trigger each other off suggests they are all connected in some way. We use this idea when we organise information to be remembered before trying to memorise it.

5 ▷ APPLICATIONS OF THEORIES AND RESEARCH INTO MEMORY AND FORGETTING

IMPROVING MEMORY

All the models of memory give us ideas about how to improve memory and prevent forgetting. We can apply the ideas to simple tasks like remembering a shopping list and to complex tasks such as revising for an exam.

66 know how theories can be applied 99

Recommendations and developments from the multistore model

- **Rehearsal** (repetition) keeps sensations alive in the SIS making transfer to STM more likely. Rehearsal in STM makes transfer to LTM more likely.
- **Chunking**. If STM holds seven (+/− two) items we should not overload it. Chunking reduces the number of items to be stored so loss is less likely.
- **Cues**. We need cues to 'hook' information out of LTM so we should build them into our attempts to memorise things. We should then never experience a FOK or TOT that we cannot get past.
- **Imagery**. Many studies have shown the power of imagery as an aid to recall. We should use this whenever we can to mentally picture things to be remembered.
- **Declarative and procedural memory**. Much of what we learn for exams involves declarative memory but, if we have to learn a skill, we should learn by *doing*, not by watching.

Recommendations and developments from the levels of processing model

- Deep processing is important. When revising for an exam it is not enough to scan a piece of text. This is only structural processing. It would be better to read it aloud (*phonemic processing*) but better still to put it in your own words or teach it to a friend (*semantic processing*).
- Find ways to make material to be remembered more *elaborate* or *distinctive*. Put revision notes into a number of different forms. Use colour.
- Try to learn and recall in a similar setting (context). You cannot take your study into the exam room but you can take *reminders* to trigger memory such as the same pens and pencils, desk layout and sweets you had when revising.
- Try to make material *personally relevant* whenever you can.

Recommendations from the constructivist approach

Effort after meaning can cause you to distort, add to or lose the original information. Accurate retrieval depends on avoiding these things.

The role of organisation in memory

We can make things much easier to memorise if we organise them first so that retrieving one thing leads to retrieval of another.

EXAMPLES OF MEMORY AIDS

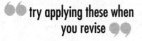
66 try applying these when you revise 99

Memory aids (mnemonics) often combine recommendations from different models of memory. When you have read through this section, spend some time thinking which models fit with each technique. (This will help you to process deeply too!)

- **Hook or peg systems**. This involves learning a rhyme to hook or peg new material on to, e.g: 'One is bun, two is shoe, three is tree, four is door, five is hive, six is sticks, seven is heaven, eight is gate, nine is line, ten is hen.'

  The trick is to form a mental image of the first item to be remembered that links with bun. The second item is linked with shoe and so on. To recall we bring back the rhyme to help conjure up each image. A house number, say 126, could be remembered by combining a bun, a shoe and some sticks.
- **Method of loci**. This is a special kind of peg system where we use a well-known journey or place for the hooks. We take a mental walk round, placing things to be remembered at particular points. To recall, we simply take the mental walk again.
- **Rhymes, phrases and stories**. Examples include the rhyme 'Thirty days hath September...' for days in each month and 'Richard of York gave battle in vain' for the colours of the rainbow. Spelling rules include 'Take off the E before I N G' and 'I before E except after C'. Many people remember the order of the planets from the sun by linking them together in a story.
- **Brain maps**. *Tony Buzan* (1980) recommends these for remembering large amounts of material, say for an exam. **Fig**. 13.5 shows the beginnings of a brain map on memory that you might like to complete. Brain maps cause us to chunk information, process it deeply, organise it and connect it all up. It is easy to visualise, especially if you use colours for different branches.

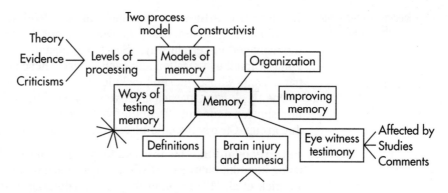

Figure 13.5 The beginnings of a brain map on memory

- **PQRS**. This study technique forces you to use deep processing. The letters stand for:

  Preview. Scan the material to get the general idea of what it is about.
  Question. List questions you hope to answer from the material.
  Read. Do this actively, seeking answers to the questions.
  Summarise. Recall the information by writing it down in your own words.

- **Apply constructivism**. Avoid the distorting effect of effort after meaning. Keep checking your recall for accuracy by going back to the original source, checking with the teacher, having discussions with friends, practising examination answers and having them marked.

All the techniques so far described are for remembering *past information*. To remember things for the *future* diaries, calendars, timers and lists are all worthwhile.

6 EYEWITNESS TESTIMONY

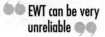
EWT can be very unreliable

The real world's emphasis of the constructivist approach makes it especially useful in the field of eyewitness testimony (**EWT** – the account someone gives of an event, such as a crime, after it has happened). Bartlett's warnings about the effects of *effort after meaning* are important here. Psychological research has shown how even the most honest and well-intentioned witness to a crime can be inaccurate yet we still rely heavily on EWT in the law courts.

BIASES IN EWT

EWT can be affected in a number of ways:

- **Violence**. EWT seems to be more accurate for non-violent crimes than for violent ones. This is especially true of women's EWT.
- **Time**. EWT often contains over-estimations of how long a crime lasted.
- **Confidence**. EWT given by very confident witnesses tends to be believed more but there is no evidence that it is more accurate.

- **Age**. Older witnesses tend to be less efficient at face recognition perhaps because their stereotypes and expectations are stronger (*O'Rourke*, 1989).
- **Ethnic group**. EWT is less accurate if the witness is from a different ethnic group to the person seen, say committing a crime.
- **Knowing the suspect**. *Stephenson* (1992) showed how experimenters could unknowingly communicate correct answers to participants in experiments. It is therefore possible that police officers, who strongly suspect someone, could communicate that to a witness looking at an identity parade or photos of suspects.

STUDIES OF EWT

Staged crimes. Buckhout (1979) staged a 'shooting' of a professor in front of 141 eye-witnesses (students and others). The eyewitnesses:

- over-estimated the time the crime lasted for;
- over-estimated the weight of the gunman;
- under-estimated the age of the gunman.

Seven weeks later, only 40% of the witnesses could identify the gunman from photographs. Even the 'shot' professor could not identify him so victims are not necessarily better witnesses than bystanders. In similar research, Buckhout (1980) used a line-up of suspects and found only 14% of witnesses could pick out the right 'criminal'.

 leading questions can affect recall

Leading the witness. Loftus and Palmer (1974) showed participants a film of a car crash. Later they were asked questions about the film. The wording of the questions was changed in certain ways. Some participants were asked 'How fast were the cars going when they smashed into each other?' These people estimated faster speeds than participants whose question included the word 'hit' instead of 'smashed into'.

One week later, participants were asked if there had been any broken glass. The film showed none but 32% of the 'smashed into' group said yes compared to 14% of the 'hit' group. Clearly it would be safer to ask for unaided recall whenever possible.

Face recognition. This is called for when witnesses try to recall the face of a suspect using identikit pictures, artist's impressions, albums of 'mugshots' or identity parades. Bahrick et al. (1975) found that face recognition was accurate 90% of the time if the test picture of a face was the same as the one the participant saw originally. Face recognition is not good if:

- the face is seen from a different angle;
- the context the face is seen in is new;
- changes are made, e.g. moustache added.

It is thought that the right person is picked in 45% of identity parades but witnesses are easily confused by changes in appearance. Even a change of clothes can cause confusion. Also, an innocent person who happens to be dressed like the criminal was at the time of the crime might be wrongly chosen. Accuracy of identification in a line-up can be improved if suspects appear in different line-ups from each other rather than all together in the same line-up.

COMMENTS ON EWT

People are very ready to believe EWT but it can be very inaccurate. What lessons can we learn from this?

- We should be aware of all the biases that affect EWT.
- We should ask witnesses to free recall whenever possible and avoid leading questions.
- Police officers, who may witness more crime than most, need training in EWT.
- People often remember more details of the crime than the criminal. Reconstructing the crime can often jog their memories of the criminal.
- Evidence from eyewitnesses is not enough on its own. It needs to be backed up with other kinds of evidence such as forensic evidence or medical information.

7 > BRAIN INJURY AND AMNESIA

Psychologists are interested in the effects of brain injury on memory because it can help them to test their existing models of memory or to create new models to fit the findings.

BRAIN INJURY

Brain injury can result from:

- **drugs**, such as alcohol;
- **disease**;
- **deterioration** through old age;
- **trauma** resulting from a blow to the head or something penetrating the brain;
- **stroke** – a haemorrhage in the brain leading to a blood clot and death of an area of the brain;
- **brain operations**.

AMNESIA

Amnesia is a term used to describe failure in the memory processes. There are two main types of amnesia but pure forms of them are rare.

- **Retrograde amnesia** is loss of memory for events *before* a brain injury occurred.
- **Anterograde amnesia** is the inability to learn and store new memories *after* a brain injury occurred.

STUDIES OF AMNESIA

The case of HM

HM has been studied by many psychologists (e.g. *Milner* 1966). In 1953 HM had brain surgery to help reduce the severity of long-term epilepsy. The operation helped with the epilepsy but left him with serious *anterograde* amnesia. His case is special because we know exactly what his brain injury was. Some findings about HM include:

- His personality and intellectual abilities (e.g. mental arithmetic) seem untouched.
- He can hold conversations.
- He appears to have no memory at all for the people he met or things that happened to him after the operation. He has not learned to recognise nursing staff, cannot remember having recently done things and cannot learn new words.
- He can remember people and events from before the operation but cannot remember their recent visits to him or anything new about them. This means he can retrieve from LTM laid down before the operation.
- His STM works normally if he rehearses items. If he stops rehearsing he loses them completely.
- He seems to have problems transferring information from STM to LTM. We assume this is because he shows a recency effect but no primacy effect on a serial position test.

this is a key piece of evidence for the two process model

Korsakoff's syndrome

Korsakoff's syndrome is associated with **alcoholism**. Excessive alcohol damages the **liver**, which then becomes unable to metabolise the vitamin **thiamine**. Thiamine is essential for normal brain function and one of the symptoms of deficiency is amnesia. The type of amnesia is not as clear cut as HM's. There is usually severe *anterograde* amnesia and some *retrograde* amnesia. This means Korsakoff's sufferers are generally unable to form new memories but can usually retrieve old ones. We are not yet sure which parts of the brain are involved in the amnesia part of the syndrome.

Unlike HM, Korsakoff's sufferers can store new information in LTM if they really work on it but storage is *disorganised* and *inefficient*. One reason for this seems to be that there are problems with **time tagging** material to be remembered so if a Korsakoff's person is asked to recall the first list from a number of lists they usually cannot do it. They seem to have problems with both *storage* and *retrieval*.

Alzheimer's disease

Alzheimer's disease is a kind of **dementia** (loss of intellectual functioning associated with old age). It is different from age-related dementia, such as senile dementia, because it begins earlier in life, usually in the 50s. Alzheimer's leads to widespread degeneration in the **cortex** and **sub-cortical regions** of the brain and the effects on memory are very varied. Sometimes there is anterograde amnesia, sometimes retrograde amnesia, sometimes a mixture of both. There is some speculation that the effect is due to there being too little of a certain **neurotransmitter** but research into this is still going on.

EXAMINATION QUESTIONS

MEG specimen paper 3 (Higher), Option C, Source: Memory

Spend 27 minutes on this question

MICHAEL: 'Where did you go for your holidays this year?'
PATRICK: 'I went to Greece again. I was really impressed.'
MICHAEL: 'What, by the beaches?'
PATRICK: 'No, by the Greek waiters' memories. Whenever we ordered our food, they never wrote anything down. And there was only one occasion when they made a mistake. The waiter was taking our drinks order and there were 9 of us. Halfway through the order, another waiter interrupted him by asking him something about the menu. When he brought the order, there were some items missing. He apologised and said he would have remembered if the other waiter hadn't interrupted his train of thought.'

    (a) The drinks order consisted of 9 items. Why would the waiter have done
        well to remember all of them?   [2]
    (b) Briefly describe a model of memory that you have studied.   [4]
    (c) Give one practical application of memory research.   [2]
    (d) Using psychological evidence, explain why people forget.   [10]

[Total 18 marks]
(MEG)

TUTOR ANSWER

(a) Miller showed that the capacity of STM is seven plus or minus two items, i.e. five to nine items. To remember nine items means that the waiter was at the top of this range.

(b) Craik and Lockhart thought that memory was a by-product of how deeply information was processed. For example, in remembering words we could process their physical features or their sound (structural or phonemic processing). Shallow processing involves only maintenance rehearsal and memory traces are not very long lasting. Deep processing means we process the meaning of something, i.e. semantic processing. This involves elaborative rehearsal and means the memory traces last longer.

(c) The levels of processing theory suggests that when we revise, we should avoid just reading or reciting notes because these are forms of shallow processing. Instead we should think about the meaning of the notes, e.g. by putting them into our own words or a different form.

(d) Atkinson and Shiffrin's two process theory of memory says we forget things in different ways at different stages of the model. Information is forgotten from the SIS if it is not maintained long enough to transfer to STM. Information is lost from STM for one of two reasons. Either we exceed STM's capacity and something has to go (interference theory) or the trace decays because it is not rehearsed. (The Petersons showed items in STM have a maximum life of 30 seconds if not rehearsed.) Information may be lost from LTM through decay of memory traces. We may also be unable to retrieve something because it is poorly organised or we do not have the cues we need to get information out of LTM. Old information can be knocked out of LTM by new and old may block the entry of new.

    The levels of processing theory suggests we forget information because we do not process it deeply enough. In recognition tests, semantic processing leads to 80% success rate, phonemic processing to 50% and structural processing to only 18%.

    Bartlett's constructivist model of memory suggests we forget information because we change it through 'effort after meaning' to fit our schemata. We may do any of the following: omit information, rationalise the addition of new information, alter the importance of some items, change their order or add effect. Bartlett used 'The War of the Ghosts' story to demonstrate these things and thought effort after meaning could explain why eyewitnesses forget or distort so much of what they saw of an event.

STUDENTS' ANSWER

NEAB specimen paper (Tier Q) Question B3

Spend about 15 minutes answering this question

Two groups, each with 10 participants, were given the following list of letters to learn.

F B I B B C G C S E I T V O B E

The 16 letters were projected onto a screen in 5 sets as shown below.

Order of presentation

	Set 1	Set 2	Set 3	Set 4	Set 5
Group 1	FBI	BBC	GCSE	ITV	OBE
Group 2	FB	IBBC	GC	SEIT	VOBE

The participants were asked to recall the sets of letters 24 hours later.
The results of the study were as follows.

Group	Total number of sets of letters recalled correctly
1	40
2	20

1/1

(a) Describe the results. [1]

Group 1 participants learned twice as many sets of letters as group 2

(b) What can be concluded from these results about how people remember things? [3]

just enough 3/3

People can remember more if they organise letters into chunks that mean something.

(c) Rubhia has just seen a bank robbery. She is asked to go to the police station to give a statement. How might the words the police use in their questions affect her memory of the robbery? Support your answer with evidence from psychological studies. [4]

good, now relate this to the study described 3/4

The police should try not to ask Rubhia leading questions. They should word questions carefully. In one study testing recall of a car crash, a question with the words 'smashed into' in it led people to say the cars were travelling faster than if the question had the word 'hit' in it.

(d) The police took Rubhia back to the bank where the robbery took place. Explain why this might improve her recall of the event. Support your answer with psychological theory and evidence. [6]

4/6

The police were trying to jog her memory by taking her back to the scene of the crime. She might be reminded of things she had forgotten. Bartlett showed that if people get emotional about something it can cause them to forget, but if Rubhia felt calmer when she went back it might help her remember.

[*Total 14 marks*]
(NEAB)

11/14 Very concise answers. In (d) mention of context cues, constructivism and Bartlett's research would give the answer more weight

A Review Sheet for this chapter can be found on pp. 249–50.

14

INTELLIGENCE, PROBLEM SOLVING AND CREATIVITY

GETTING STARTED

This chapter is for SEG and MEG students only. SEG students studying Option D need the first two sections on intelligence. You need to know how psychologists have attempted to define and measure intelligence and some of the uses and drawbacks of intelligence testing. There is also the important question of the role of nature and nurture in intelligence.

MEG students studying Option 1 need the sections on problem solving and creativity but not the section on intelligence. Problem solving is an area of animal and human thinking which psychologists have studied in detail. Creativity is thought by some to be a special kind of problem solving which is why it is included here.

1. INTELLIGENCE

2. THE NATURE–NURTURE DEBATE AND INTELLIGENCE

3. PROBLEM SOLVING

4. CREATIVITY

ESSENTIAL PRINCIPLES

●● intelligence has been defined in many ways ●●

DEFINITIONS OF INTELLIGENCE

We all seem to know what is meant by 'intelligence' but a little thought will show that it is not at all easy to define. The many different definitions that have been suggested say intelligence includes being able to:

- reason in the abstract
- think logically
- take in new information
- learn from experience
- adapt to the environment and adapt the environment in order to survive in it
- solve problems
- do IQ tests!

In general, approaches to intelligence fall into one of three categories:

- **Psychometric approaches**. These involve *measuring* intelligence using tests to arrive at an IQ score. Intelligence is seen as a quantity of knowledge or ability. Within these approaches there is a debate over whether intelligence is a general ability or a number of separate abilities.
- **Cognitive-developmental approaches** (e.g. *Piaget*). Intelligence is seen as *the ability to adapt flexibly* to the environment. In this view, differences in the quality and maturity of thought are more important than quantity of knowledge.
- **Information-processing approaches**. These more modern approaches examine *cognitive processes* such as attention, memory and problem solving. Such processes might lie at the root of intelligence and account for differences in how people do when assessed by either of the first two approaches.

MEASURING INTELLIGENCE

Infants can be assessed using a developmental test which gives them a developmental quotient or **DQ**. An example of such tests are the **Bayley Scales of Infant Development**. These measure the child's *sensory* and *motor* skills such as being able to grasp a moving object or make a small tower using building blocks. DQ is not a good *predictor* of later intelligence. Its main use is to ensure that an infant is developing at a normal pace.

Stern (1912) introduced the idea of intelligence quotient or **IQ**. This is calculated by comparing a child's actual age (chronological age or **CA**) with their Mental Age (**MA**). MA is calculated from scores on an intelligence test. A child whose CA is 6 years may answer test items as well as most other 6 year olds. The MA is thus 6. If that child answered as well as most 8 year olds, MA would be 8. IQ is arrived at by dividing MA by CA and multiplying by 100. This ensures that a child whose MA and CA match has an IQ of 100. In other words:

MA/CA x 100 = IQ.

Here is an example for a child performing below the MA for their age group:

6/8 x 100 = 75 = IQ.

●● practise working through this formula ●●

IQ tests are designed so that most children (about 68%) score somewhere between 85 and 115 points. This is the normal range for IQ. However, these days IQ is rarely worked out this way. This is mainly because CA goes on increasing after MA stops increasing. The IQ formula makes it look as if intelligence decreases rapidly with age which is nonsense. Instead, people's IQ scores are now compared against the **norms** for whatever age group they are in.

Modern intelligence tests often have parts to them which measure:

- general knowledge
- verbal ability, e.g. word meanings, spellings
- numerical ability, e.g. calculations
- spatial ability, e.g. dealing with shapes and patterns.

Examples of modern tests include:

- The **Stanford Binet Intelligence Scales** cover a wide age range and give a 'profile' of scores from different tests, for example verbal, numerical and spatial reasoning and tests of short-term memory.
- **The Wechsler scales** come in three forms for different age groups. There is the Wechsler Adult Intelligence Scale – revised (WAIS-R), the Wechsler Intelligence Scale for Children – revised (WISC-R) and the Wechsler Pre-school and Primary Scale of Intelligence (WPPSI). Each test gives a full-scale IQ and two sub-scores for verbal and performance IQ. Verbal items include vocabulary test, arithmetic and comprehension. Performance items require people to complete pictures, arrange pictures into a story sequence and assemble objects or puzzles.
- **The British Ability Scales** (BAS) consist of 23 tests measuring visual, verbal and general IQ and can be used with children and adolescents up to 18 years of age. Its most unusual part is a test of speed of **information processing** (which could be an ability that underlies all other types of test score).
- **Raven's Progressive Matrices** is an unusual test because all the items are *non-verbal*. They consist of problems concerning patterns and shapes and are thought to test *abstract reasoning*. They are useful because they are suitable for people of any age, race, sex or educational level.
- **The Mill Hill Vocabulary Scale** is a *verbal* scale to go with Raven's Progressive Matrices. It consists of two sets of 44 words. Each set increases in difficulty and participants have to define the words or find one from a short list that means the same as a given word. Children with an MA of 5 years can usually define the first few words on the list and ability increases with age. Only a very few adults can define the most unusual of the words.
- The tests so far described are individual tests given one to one. There are some group tests of which the **AH series** is an example. These assess people from school-leaving age upwards and tend to be used for selection to *apprenticeship*, various *occupations* or *higher education*.

USES OF INTELLIGENCE TEST SCORES

Bee (1992) lists a number of uses of intelligence test scores:

- **Selection**. Is a child ready for school or to move up a year?
- **Predicting school performance**. The correlation between IQ scores and other kinds of school test is about +0.6 suggesting a tendency for children with higher IQs to do better and for children with lower IQ scores to do less well. However, the correlation is *imperfect* so the predictions we can make from knowing a child's IQ are not 100% reliable.

> 66 remember correlation is not the same as causation 99

- **Diagnosis**. Some tests can be used to detect weaknesses in particular areas (e.g. numerical ability).
- **Sorting**. IQ test scores could be used to **stream** children. They may also be used to detect children at the very high and low end of the ability range who may, therefore, have **special needs**.
- **Accountability**. Test scores can be used to assess the effectiveness of teaching or to compare the success of different schools.

LIMITATIONS OF INTELLIGENCE TESTS

- IQ tests do not tell us about a person's *potential* or *general competence*. They only tell us about how the person tackles the narrow range of items on the test.
- We should not take a person's IQ score as fixed for life. Children in particular may show changes in IQ scores from one testing occasion to another. This could be because they may behave differently if they are tired, upset, keen or interested. There is also evidence that children can become **test wise** – they improve their scores through being coached.

> 66 IQ really indicates a point within a range of possible scores 99

- There are many important abilities that are not measured by traditional IQ tests, for example:

  - **social intelligence** – being able to get along with others;
  - **musical intelligence**;

- **physical intelligence** – such as having good coordination or being a good sportsperson;
- **creativity** – being able to come up with new and useful ideas;
- **adaptability** – being 'streetwise', being able to fit into different environments.

- Some critics think IQ tests are biased in favour of certain types of people. One reason for this could be because they contain items which are familiar to people from particular backgrounds especially the culture of the white, middle-class male. Certain groups of black people may not do so well on these tests leading us unfairly to conclude that they are less intelligent. Raven's Progressive Matrices are one attempt to overcome such culture bias but not all psychologists agree that culture-free tests 'work'. They think it is more a matter of knowing how to approach a test rather than the test items themselves that leads to differences in scores between people from different cultural backgrounds.

 *culture-free tests are very difficult to devise*

- Some psychologists argue that people will find out what their IQ is, misunderstand it and label themselves as failing in some way. The danger is that the *label* becomes *self-fulfilling* – people with low scores start to fail at things and 'grow into' the label.
- If we cannot agree on what intelligence is, should we really be measuring it and using the scores in ways which affect people's lives? This is an important ethical point but it can be argued that tests do have *some* good uses.

2 ▷ THE NATURE–NURTURE DEBATE AND INTELLIGENCE

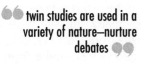 *interaction is the current focus of the debate*

Early debates asked how much of intelligence was inherited and how much learned. These have now been discarded in favour of questions asking how heredity and environment *interact* with each other to affect intelligence. This is still an important debate because it raises questions about the inherited inferiority of certain groups of people on the grounds of class, race or gender. Beliefs in such inferiority have been used to excuse all kinds of **discrimination**.

this is an important concept to grasp

An important, though rather difficult, idea to grasp is **heritability of intelligence**. Instead of asking how much of intelligence is inherited, psychologists make a **heritability estimate** which is a different thing altogether. Heritability is the amount of the difference in intelligence between people that can be accounted for by heredity. For example, if people grew up in exactly the same environment and had exactly the same experiences, differences between them would be entirely due to genetics. In this case the heritability estimate is 100%. On the other hand, if a group of genetically identical people grew up in different environments, differences between them would be entirely due to experience. In this case, the heritability estimate would be 0%. Of course, there are not many genetically identical individuals and we all have different experiences so heritability estimates end up somewhere between 0% and 100%.

STUDIES CONCERNING NATURE–NURTURE AND INTELLIGENCE

Twin studies

twin studies are used in a variety of nature–nurture debates

These studies compare genetically identical (monozygotic, **MZ**) twins who have been reared *together* with MZ twins reared *apart*. The reasoning is that, if intelligence is largely inherited, the twins' IQs should be very similar regardless of their experiences.

In the 1950s and 1960s *Sir Cyril Burt* studied 53 pairs of separated MZ twins. He claimed the correlation between their IQs was +0.86. The IQs of MZ twins reared together correlated only a little higher at +0.91. Burt concluded that heredity was much more important than environment in determining intelligence. In 1962, *Shields* reported a correlation for MZ twins reared apart of +0.77 and *Newman et al.* (1937) gave a figure of +0.67 in their study.

These correlations tend to be higher than those for non-identical (dizygotic or **DZ**) twins or siblings but how convincing are they? *Kamin* (1974) claims that Burt invented some of his data. He has also pointed out that separated MZ twins often experienced very *similar* environments, perhaps being brought up in different branches of the *same family,* going to the *same school* and spending *social time together*. This makes it difficult to separate the effects of nature and nurture.

Family studies

Another way to look at the nature-nurture issue is to compare correlations between people who vary in how similar they are genetically. *Erlenmeyer-Kimling and Jarvik* (1963) did this and gave the following correlations:

- MZ twins reared together   +0.87
- MZ twins reared apart   +0.75
- Siblings reared together   +0.55
- Siblings reared apart   +0.47
- Parent–child pairs   +0.50
- Second cousins   +0.16
- Unrelated pairs   –0.01.

It looks as though heredity plays a vital part in determining intelligence but many of these results include data from Burt's studies. There are also a number of ways in which the data were distorted that makes them very unreliable. They were discredited long ago but are still often quoted in books! More careful studies make heritability estimates of between 30% and 60% but even these findings have problems.

Adoption studies

If intelligence has more to do with heredity than environment, children's IQs should correlate more highly with their *natural* parents' IQs than with their *adoptive* parents' IQs. *Burks* (1928) found correlations between adopted children and their adoptive parents of only +0.13. *Skodak and Skeels* (1949) found a much higher correlation of +0.44 between the IQs of adopted children and their natural parents. Again this looks like support for the nature side of the debate. However, *Kamin* (1974) argued that, in the 1920s children were nearly always placed with better-off families. In the 1940s, children were placed in adoptive homes that were carefully chosen to be similar to the natural parents' home so it is impossible to say whether heredity or environment matters most.

> 💬💬 this meant little variation in parents' IQs so correlation is depressed 💬💬

> 💬💬 it is hard to compare two such different studies 💬💬

Studies of social class differences

Statistics repeatedly show that children from lower social classes score lower on IQ tests than children from higher social classes. In 1975, *Broman et al.* published a study of 50,000 4 year olds in which they measured children's IQs and plotted them against social class. IQ rose with social class and with the mother's level of education. DQ tests show no differences. The differences appear as the child grows and widen as the years go by. However, it is virtually impossible to separate out the effects of environment and heredity in such studies. Children from poorer or lower-class homes may miss out on all sorts of stimulation, dietary needs and health care which could affect their IQ.

> 💬💬 the effects here are very complex 💬💬

Enrichment studies

If intelligence is largely inherited, attempts to improve it should not work. Programmes to enrich the experience of children from deprived homes are designed to show this idea is wrong and to give children a boost before they start school.

Project Headstart began in the USA in 1965. There were many different types of enrichment on this programme. Some children had home visits from teachers. Others attended different kinds of pre-school. Some of these pre-schools were quite formal, others freer and more **discovery-learning** based.

Most programmes resulted in IQ gains of up to ten points in the *short term* but it seems these gains do not last very long. Follow-up studies, however, have shown lasting gains in things *other than IQ* for example, in *behaviour* in school, in various tests of *academic achievement* and in later *employment*. Researchers call this the **sleeper effect** and they are unsure about why it happens. One suggestion is that these programmes improve children's *self-esteem* and *confidence* in their ability. Another is that there is a change in the whole *family's attitude* to schooling which helps to support and encourage the child. This is a good reason for involving the family in the programme if possible.

> 💬💬 Project Headstart worked for unexpected reasons 💬💬

Race and intelligence

Jensen (1969) and *Eysenck* (1971) have argued that differences in IQ scores between black and white Americans and British whites and West Indians are due to genetic differences between races. This unpopular conclusion has been widely criticised. For example, there is very little genetic difference between members of different races. Also the role of environment is largely ignored. Studies of children who are black, white or of mixed race and raised in similar environments show that the children's IQs are very similar.

CONCLUSIONS ON THE NATURE–NURTURE DEBATE AND INTELLIGENCE

None of the studies outlined in this section tell us just how nature and nurture interact to determine intelligence as measured by IQ scores. The nature–nurture debate on intelligence is likely to remain inconclusive because:

this is a very complex debate

- It is impossible to separate the effects of environment and heredity. We cannot have one without the other.
- For ethical reasons, we cannot do **controlled breeding** experiments with humans or bring them up in **controlled environments**. All the research studies outlined earlier have to wait for genetic or environmental differences to arrange themselves. This means psychologists can never be absolutely sure about the reasons for differences in intelligence.
- Some aspects of intelligence may emerge through **maturation** or in a **sensitive period**. It then looks as though environment was responsible when, in fact, it was not at all responsible or only partly so. This complicates the picture for psychologists.
- Genetically determined characteristics may be more open to influence by the environment than we allow for. Some genetically determined characteristics may be more open to such influence than others.
- We will probably never be able to measure so-called '**genetic potential**' so we will never know whether it has been reached.
- There is much debate about the worth of IQ tests as a measure of intelligence. People's performance on them is known to be open to many influences other than differences in intelligence, e.g. *motivation, unfamiliarity, practice*. Also there are many important intellectual qualities that IQ tests do not tap.

One way round the nature–nurture debate is to see nature and nurture as interacting in complicated ways that we still do not understand. A useful way to think of this is to use the **rubber band hypothesis**. This means we can picture genetic potential as a rubber band which is stretched by experience but can only be stretched so far. Differences between individuals can be explained by both differences between stretchability of rubber bands and different amounts of stretching. Two individuals could also achieve the same IQ test score but we will never know the exact combination of influences that brought it about.

3 ▸ PROBLEM SOLVING

DEFINING PROBLEM SOLVING

Problem solving is a form of thinking that we use when we need to reach a goal which is not readily available. Cognitive psychologists are especially interested in studying the thought processes by which people reach such goals. *Lefrancois* (1983) says that problem solving in everyday life covers such varied things as finding the answer to a quiz question, applying mathematical rules, finding the way round a maze, solving a crossword clue or inventing something.

there are many kinds of problem solving

In the1960s *Guilford* made an important distinction between:

- **convergent thinking** where there is one correct or best solution to a problem; and
- **divergent thinking** where there are several possible solutions to a problem. Some psychologists call this kind of problem solving **creativity**.

WAYS OF STUDYING PROBLEM SOLVING

Comparing animals and humans

Both animals and humans need to solve problems and comparing how they do it can help us to understand what is involved. *Thorndike*'s (1898) cats, for example, solved the problem of escaping the puzzle box by trial and error. However, not all animal (and very little human) problem solving happens in this way. *Gestalt psychologists* such as *Kohler* (1925) think that both animals and humans are capable of **insight**. Kohler presented apes with the problem of how to reach a banana which was outside their cage or dangling from the ceiling. Sticks and boxes were provided. After unsuccessful attempts to reach the banana, an ape would sit and seem to ignore the problem. It would then solve it in one go by using the boxes to stand on or the sticks to help reach the banana. There was no period of trial and error. Apes appeared to experience what humans call the **Aha!** or **Eureka! effect**. Since both animals and humans experience this kind of insight it seems that it is not necessary to have language to solve some sorts of problem. Indeed, humans often solve a problem without being able to explain how.

Laboratory studies

Unlike apes, humans can let us know their thought processes when they solve problems by talking aloud as they work. This is known as **verbal protocol**. Studies of protocol, and the moves people make when they solve problems, tell us that human problem solving is rarely random or haphazard. Instead, humans use **strategies** to solve problems, as we will see. In laboratory studies of problem solving psychologists require participants to move from an **original state** to a **goal state** and give them **rules** by which they can do this. One example of this is a series of tests devised by *Wason and Johnson-Laird* (1972). The participant is presented with four cards on which are written R, G, 2 or 7. The problem is to see if the following rule is true: 'If there is an R on one side of the card there is a 2 on the other.' The participant has to check the rule by turning over as few of the cards as possible. (Incidentally, most people check R and 2, rather than G and 7. Can you see why this will not help them verify the rule?)

Another frequently used problem concerns three **cannibals** and three **missionaries** who are on the left bank of a river and need to cross to the right. There is one boat which will hold up to two people. You should never leave more cannibals than missionaries on either river bank and the boat cannot cross the river if it is empty. What is the fewest number of trips the boat will need to make to transport all six people across?

Computer simulation

If you want to test an idea (**model**) about how humans solve problems one way to do it is to programme a computer with information about the original state and goal state of a problem and the rules for solving it. You can then run the programme and see if it performs like a human would (i.e. *simulates* human problem solving). If it does then your model is probably an accurate one. If not, then you can modify the programme until it mimics a human more closely.

WAYS OF SOLVING PROBLEMS

Algorithms

In algorithmic problem solving there is a correct answer which you are guaranteed to find in the end. It operates rather like trial and error where you try a solution, discard it and try another. A diagram of a simple algorithm is given in **Fig**. 14.1.

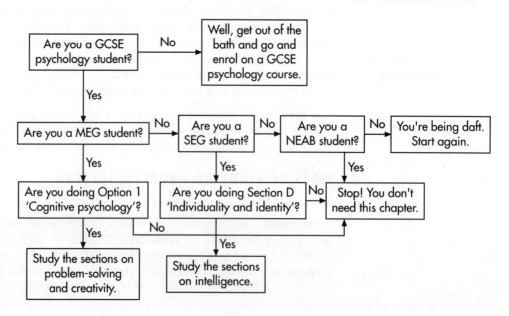

Figure 14.1 An algorithm to help you solve the problem of how to use this chapter

We do not always carry such well-organised algorithms in our heads. Our algorithmic problem solving can be very *haphazard* or *well organised*. For example, in using the algorithm approach to solve an anagram, you may randomly reorganise letters in the hope of hitting on the answer or you may try out every possible combination of letters in careful sequence.

Some algorithms can be extremely complicated and difficult for psychologists to identify. Computer programmes that play **chess** are one such example. We need the computer to consider every possible legal move in response to what its opponent does, the goal being to win the game. Such a programme is possible in theory but only now are we devising programmes that can give human chess masters a good game!

Algorithmic problem solving has some uses for humans. However, it is often very slow and only really useful for problems with *one definite answer* rather than several equally good answers. You may have already realised, for example, that you do not usually solve anagrams in quite the way described. Instead, you probably use strategies – in other words, **heuristics**.

Heuristics

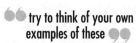
rules of thumb help us to solve problems

Heuristics are **rules of thumb** or **strategies** for solving problems which we hope will pay off. Whenever you are looking for a solution to a problem you are working in what psychologists call the **problem space** (the set of all possible answers). The main advantage of heuristics is that they cut down on problem space so we can search for a solution in a more manageable area and may reach an answer more quickly. The drawback is that, if we choose the wrong problem space to work in, we may not arrive at the answer at all.

Here is an example. The problem space for the anagram YHTUO is quite large if you choose to solve it algorithmically and try out all the possible ways these letters can be arranged. People who solve anagrams rapidly do not depend entirely on algorithms which take up lots of problem space. Instead they often cut it down by, for example, not considering combinations beginning with HT or UY. The rule of thumb is that these letter orders do not occur at the start of English words so they can be disregarded straight away.

try to think of your own examples of these

In real-life problem solving we may combine different kinds of heuristics. Here are three heuristics that psychologists have identified in their research:

1. Means-ends analysis

When people problem solve in this way they:

- are clear about where they are now (the original state);
- figure out where they want to be (the goal state);
- figure out the means to get there;
- break the problems into steps or sub-goals and tackle them one by one.

You might use this when you need to hand in an essay by a certain date. You could break it down into sub-goals such as select topic, read around, write rough copy, have it marked, rewrite essay, get copy to teacher. At each stage you reduce the distance between the original state and the goal state. Successful students often do this. They realise that handing in an assignment is really a set of sub-problems to be solved and that they are more likely to succeed if they break it into manageable chunks and limit the problem space at each stage. Psychologists find that people solving the missionaries and cannibals problem often *spontaneously* break it down into sub-problems.

Research has shown that, sometimes, means–ends analysis involves seeming to move further away from the solution in order to make progress. For example, you may have to move one or two people back over the river in order to achieve the goal of moving all six. You may have missed a lesson on material needed for an essay and need to spend time copying up before you can begin solving your essay-writing problem.

To test out this model of human problem solving, *Newell and Simon* (1972) created a computer simulation called the General Problem Solver (**GPS**) which is programmed to use **means–ends analysis**. When the GPS does the cannibals and missionaries problem, it seems to perform rather like a human. This lends weight to the idea that humans are in some way 'programmed' to solve problems using means–ends analysis.

2. Analogies

This involves using prior experience to help solve a problem. It is as if we think to our-selves 'this problem is similar (analogous) to one I solved earlier so I will use the method of solving the old problem to help me solve the new one'. We do this when-ever we solve a new maths problem analogous to others we have practised in class. This is also a method children may use when they learn to read. If they can read 'though', when faced with 'although' they mentally ignore 'al' read 'though' then add 'al'. The simpler analogy helps us to solve the more complicated problem. Like all heuristics, analogies do not always work, e.g. when you need to read 'thought'.

3. Backward search

Most of our problem solving involves working forward in time but a heuristic which sometimes helps in problem solving is to work backwards from the goal state to see how to get to it. An example would be to start in the centre of a maze and work back through it to find the start point. We can sometimes solve mathematical problems using backward search, and understand jokes too. To understand the punchline 'Rude Olf the Red Nose reigned here' requires you to work back through the story that led to it.

FACTORS AFFECTING PROBLEM SOLVING

Gestalt psychologists, such as Köhler, used the term **Einstellung** to describe the way in which people sometimes get stuck in thinking about problems a particular way and so may not reach a solution. Here are some examples:

Set

A set is a fixed way of responding to a problem usually as a result of prior experience. Set can interfere with insight in many ways. *Wason and Johnson-Laird* (1972) gave par-ticipants the sequence 2, 4, 6, 8, 10 and asked them to produce new lists to show that they had worked out the rule behind the list. The rule was simply that numbers increased in size (1, 6, 7, 9 would have obeyed the rule) but participants' new lists nearly always had equally spaced numbers in them and they found it hard to discover the rule. *Duncker* (1945) showed participants the array of dots shown in **Fig**. 14.2 and asked them to draw four straight lines which would cross through all the dots. They were not allowed to go over the same line twice and could not take the pen off the paper. Set seemed to cause problems because people thought they had to stay within the array of dots.

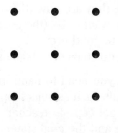 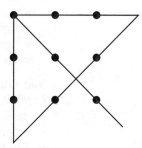

Figure 14.2 The problem and solution to one of Duncker's demonstrations of 'set'

Luchins (1942) induced a short-term set in his water jars problem. Participants were told they had three jars of different volume and they were to use them to measure a specified amount of liquid, for example:

| | Use jars of these volumes | | To measure this volume |
A	B	C	
9	20	3	5
4	12	1	6
20	59	4	31

The rule to apply is B – A – 2C. Once people discovered this, they developed a set so when they were faced with a new problem which did not follow the rule they were slower to solve it than people who had not been 'set'. Clearly, set can be useful but there are also times when we need to be flexible.

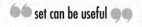 set can be useful

Functional fixedness

Duncker (1945) showed how problem solving can be held up by our tendency to think of objects only in terms of their usual uses or *functions*. In one problem, he asked participants to fix a candle to a wall so that it would burn properly. They were given a candle, thumbtacks in a box, matches and some irrelevant materials. The solution was to fix the thumbtack box to the wall and stand the candle on it. People tended to think in terms of using the matches to melt the candle to stick it to the wall, or to try to tack the candle to the wall! They did not always think of altering the function of the thumbtack box and using it as a shelf to hold the candle.

`4 > CREATIVITY`

DEFINING CREATIVITY

There are many different ideas about what creativity is. *Guilford* thought of it as **divergent thinking**. Such psychologists argue that scores on conventional IQ tests, which measure **convergent thinking**, do not correlate well with creativity scores so they must be *different abilities*. Other psychologists see creativity as including *originality* or *novelty, usefulness, fluency* and *flexibility.*

Hudson (1966) found that **convergent** thinking schoolboys tended to opt for sciences, maths or classics and had hobbies to do with mechanical things. **Divergent** thinkers tended to go for the arts and biological subjects. They were less conventional and preferred more sociable hobbies. We do not know why such differences exist (although it could have something to do with Social Learning, i.e. what boys have been reinforced for doing in the past and the kinds of models they were exposed to).

Gestalt psychologists (e.g. *Wallas* 1926) think of creativity as a kind of **insight** which results from going through these stages:

- **Preparation**. This involves becoming familiar with a problem through research or getting to know the 'tools of the trade'.
- **Incubation**. Time passes while we 'sit on' the problem. At this stage we seem unconsciously to 'mull it over'.
- **Illumination**. This is where we experience insight. An idea seems to, quite suddenly, just come to us.
- **Verification**. There is a period of checking to see if the insight is a good one.

MEASURING CREATIVITY

Probably the best-known tests of creativity are the **Minnesota Tests of Creative Thinking**. Items from the tests include:

- How many uses can you think of for:

  - a brick?
  - a silk stocking?
  - a paperclip?

- How many ways can you think of to improve a bicycle?
- A picture would be provided and the person asked to provide as many titles as possible.
- Name as many words ending in -tion as you can (in a given time limit).
- Name as many round, edible objects as you can.
- Discuss the consequences for people of no longer needing or wanting sleep.

Items on such tests are scored for:

- **fluency** – the number of different responses;
- **flexibility** – the number of times the participant shifts from one class of responses to another;
- **originality** – the number of unusual responses.

this is a serious problem in creativity testing

A problem with such tests is that there is little evidence that high scores on them are related to a person's *actual* creativity so some people question whether the tests are valid. (For example, famous artists do not always score highly on divergent thinking tests.) In fact *Hudson* (1968) found he could get schoolchildren to *act creatively* by asking them to answer questions as if they were 'bohemian artists' (as opposed to 'inhibited scientists'). This finding suggests that we can all be creative if we want! More recent evidence suggests that creativity is just another kind of intellectual ability but some people combine it with a *personality type* or *motivation* which makes them seem unusual. They may be more inclined to take risks or have more *self-confidence, curiosity* and *perseverance* than others. There are many examples of 'creative geniuses' whose school reports were average but this is hardly surprising if school exams mostly rate convergent thinking.

schools are not to blame for not spotting creativity

ENCOURAGING CREATIVITY

We seem to value creativity so it makes sense to find ways of encouraging it. There are currently two main ways to do this:

1. Brainstorming (*Osborn* 1957) brings together people from different backgrounds in groups of five to twelve. They are set a problem to discuss in as free and wide-ranging ways as possible. Rules are set such as:

- no one is allowed to judge the value of anyone else's ideas during the discussion (this includes non-verbal signs of approval or disapproval such as laughter or frowns);
- say all your ideas out loud even if they are only half formed;
- encourage each other to change or combine ideas;
- encourage quantity of ideas;
- encourage wild and unusual ideas.

Once all the ideas have been sifted through, useful ones often remain. There is also evidence that it helps people to improve their creativity scores.

2. Lateral thinking (*DeBono* 1970) is a general approach to all problem solving and is not focused on one problem as brainstorming is. People are given exercises to do which it is hoped will encourage them to think of unusual, creative solutions. In one such exercise people are presented with geometric patterns (see **Fig**. 14.3) and asked to think of as many things that it could be as possible.

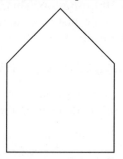

Figure 14.3 An example of a geometric pattern used to encourage lateral thinking

Lateral thinkers are also encouraged to:

- challenge the judgements and assumptions which lead to *Einstellung*;
- brainstorm;
- learn to find out the important parts of a problem;
- challenge the old and create the new.

DeBono introduced the word **po** to be used in lateral thinking. When we think logically, we say 'no' to ideas which are not useful. Lateral thinkers do not use 'no'. Instead they say 'po' to remind themselves to think laterally.

EXAMINATION QUESTIONS

SEG paper 2 1995 Section B, Question 4

Spend 40 minutes on this question

(a) What is IQ?   [3]

(b) Describe **one** advantage of the use of IQ tests.   [6]

(c) Explain **two** reasons why IQ tests might not accurately measure a child's intelligence. [*12*]

(d) Explain why psychologists study the development of twins. [*9*]

[*Total 30 marks*]
(SEG)

TUTOR ANSWER

SEG paper 2 1995 Section B, Question 4

(a) IQ stands for Intelligence Quotient. It can be calculated by comparing a person's actual age with their mental age as measured by an intelligence test. These days IQ is usually calculated by comparing a person's score with the norm for their age group.

(b) IQ tests can be used to predict performance at school. The correlation between IQ scores and other school tests is about +0.6. This means IQ tests are a fairly good predictor of how children can do in school so it is a useful but not a foolproof one. All we can say is that school IQ test scores are fairly well matched to school test scores. This can give us some idea of how children are likely to do and allows us to help them in ways that are most useful to the child.

(c) IQ tests seem to suggest IQ is fixed for life but we should not make this assumption. Children's IQ scores change from one testing time to another. This can happen because they may vary in how tired, interested or upset they are so they may do better or worse on different occasions. It is also possible to raise a child's IQ up to fifteen points through coaching. It is more sensible to think of an IQ score as a point about which the IQ can vary. It simply gives us a general idea of what a child can do.

IQ tests have also been criticised for being biased in favour of certain groups of people, especially white, middle-class males. If a person is not a member of this group they may not do so well on a test because the items do not draw on the kind of knowledge shared by white, middle-class males. It is important to develop tests that are as culture fair as possible. Raven's Progressive Matrices are an attempt to do this. The test consists of problems using patterns and shapes and is thought to test abstract reasoning. It may be fairer than other tests because it does not have a large verbal element which could favour certain groups of people over others.

(d) Psychologists are interested in studying twins mainly because it can help to throw light on the nature–nurture debate, i.e. the argument over the extent to which environment and heredity determine our behaviour. Identical (MZ) twins reared together or apart are especially interesting. They are genetically identical so, if characteristics are determined mainly by heredity, environment should make little difference. Any differences that do arise between them can probably be put down to environmental influences.

In the 1950s and 1960s, Sir Cyril Burt studied IQs of MZ and DZ (non-identical) twins reared together or apart. MZ twins reared together share environment and heredity so they should be the most alike. When reared apart, they only share heredity but should still be alike if environment has little influence. DZ twins are no more alike genetically than siblings, but do share very similar environments if reared together. Reared apart, they share neither environment nor heredity so should not be at all alike.

In general, Burt found the predicted trend was followed. In particular, the correlation between the IQs of MZ twins was much higher than for DZ twins, even when the MZ twins had been reared apart, suggesting that heredity was more important than environment in determining intelligence. Burt's findings have been seriously questioned like other studies showing a similar trend.

For ethical reasons psychologists cannot decide how twins are brought up just to answer a nature–nurture question. They have to wait for separations of twins to occur. There are some cases where twins were reared apart and then discovered each other as adults. When reunited, they may find remarkable similarities possibly because they are looking for them! Even in psychological studies, separated twins may be brought up in very similar homes making it virtually impossible to decide the role of nature and nurture. However, twin studies are probably the nearest psychologists can get to controlling the effects of heredity and environment in humans.

STUDENT'S ANSWER

MEG specimen paper 2 (Foundation), Option 1

Spend 34 minutes on this question

Source B

A large group of schoolboys were asked this question:

'How many uses can you think of for a paperclip?'

One group of boys could only think of a few ideas. They were trying to find the 'right' answer and approached the question in a very logical way. This is known as *convergent thinking*. These boys were generally the ones who were good at sciences like physics and chemistry.

     The second group showed *divergent thinking*. They could think of many uses, including some unusual ideas. These boys were generally the ones who were better at arts subjects like literature and history.

(a) According to the study, what were two differences between the divergent and convergent thinkers?   *[2]*

2/2

Divergent thinkers could think of many uses for a paperclip whereas convergent thinkers could only think of a few. Divergent thinkers tended to be good at arts subjects, convergent thinkers tended to be good at sciences.

(b) The participants (subjects) in the study in Source B were schoolboys. What is a problem with this sample?   *[1]*

1/1

The sample only represented schoolboys so findings could not be generalised to others, e.g. schoolgirls.

(c) What could be a practical application of the findings about convergent/divergent thinking?   *[3]*

good answer 3/3

One practical application might be in selecting people for jobs. Divergent thinkers might do well in occupations requiring creative, original thought (e.g. advertising). Convergent thinkers might do well in jobs requiring more focused thought (e.g. some branches of science).

(d) Choose **one** of the following and outline how it interferes with our ability to solve problems.   *[3]*

[Tick your choice]
functional fixedness ✔   learning set ☐   principle of closure ☐

be explicit about why this is functional fixedness 2/3

Functional fixedness. Duncker showed how people's tendency to think of objects only in terms of their usual functions can stop them solving problems. He gave participants a candle, matches, thumbtacks in a box and some irrelevant materials. They had to find a way of fixing the candle to a wall so that it would burn properly. People did not always think about emptying the thumbtack box, standing the candle in it then attaching the box to the wall.

(e) How could psychologists help people to improve their problem-solving ability? [8]

" good section **"**

Brainstorming and lateral thinking are two ways to improve problem-solving ability. In brainstorming, people in groups of five to twelve are set a problem to discuss. The idea is to come up with a wide range of solutions so rules are set to guide the discussion. No one is allowed to judge their own or anyone else's ideas. People should say all their ideas out loud. Group members should encourage each other. They should produce as many ideas as possible and put forward wild and unusual ideas. All the ideas that result can then be sifted through and the useful ones considered. There is some evidence that brainstorming improves people's creativity scores.

" add other ways of encouraging lateral thinking **"**

" 7/8 **"**

Lateral thinking is a general way of approaching all kinds of problems. People are given exercises to do to encourage them to think in unusual and creative ways. They are encouraged to avoid Einstellung by challenging their existing judgements and assumptions, brainstorm, sift out the important parts of a problem, challenge old ways of doing things and create new ways. Where logical thinkers might use the word 'no' when they reject solutions, lateral thinkers use the word 'po' to remind themselves to use lateral thinking techniques such as those described above.

[*Total 17 marks*]
(MEG)

" 15/17 High marks here for clear, relevant answers **"**

A Review Sheet for this chapter can be found on pp. 251–2.

CHAPTER 15

PERSONALITY AND TEMPERAMENT

GETTING STARTED

Personality appears on both MEG and SEG syllabuses but their requirements are different. However, all students should begin by looking at the definitions of personality offered at the beginning of the chapter.

For MEG students personality is a compulsory, core topic so you should then go on to study the sections on the Humanistic approaches of Rogers and Kelly and the alternative approaches of Eysenck and Cattell.

For SEG students, personality is only relevant if you are studying Option D. You can skip sections on Humanistic and alternative approaches and go straight on to look at Psychodynamic, Behaviourist and Social Learning approaches to personality. You should finish the rest of the chapter ending with the section on temperament.

1. THEORIES OF PERSONALITY

2. TEMPERAMENT

ESSENTIAL PRINCIPLES

1 ▷ THEORIES OF PERSONALITY

❝❝ personality is hard to define ❞❞

WHAT IS PERSONALITY?

Personality is a term which psychologists (or anyone else) find very difficult to define. Much depends on which theory of personality you accept. We tend to think of personality as a *fairly stable* collection of characteristics (**traits**) which make our own and others' behaviour consistent over time and place. This definition is not acceptable to everyone, as we will see. Theories differ in many ways including:

- whether people's personalities are a *unique* collection of traits or whether they share the same characteristics to different degrees;
- whether we can *measure* personality and, if so, whether it is better to think of people as general types or a more specific collection of traits;
- whether personality is *fixed* early on or whether it *changes* all the time;
- whether there is anything at all *consistent* about people which even deserves the name 'personality'.

HUMANISTIC APPROACHES TO PERSONALITY

The Humanistic approach is often called the **Third Force** in psychology because of its important influence after the first and second forces of psychoanalytic theory and Behaviourism. Humanistic approaches emphasise the following (and these ideas are reflected in the personality theories of *Rogers* and *Kelly*):

- We should study the *whole person* and not reduce them to biological levels or just their behaviour.
- The scientific approach to studying people is inappropriate. We should try other ways of understanding them. In particular, we should try to see the world from *their point of view*.
- We should concentrate on trying to understand people's experience of living, in other words, their experiences of *conscious awareness*.
- We should see people as *free* to decide how to behave rather than being constrained by biological forces or learned patterns of behaviour.
- People are basically positive and *good*.
- People are motivated to grow personally and become all they are capable of becoming. Humanistic psychologists call this **self-actualisation**.

Rogers' self theory

Carl Rogers (1951) developed a psychotherapeutic technique known as **client-centred therapy** and his personality theory grew from this. Central to Rogers' theory is the idea of **self**. Some of his key ideas are as follows:

- Our **self-concept** is our sense of personal identity built up from *evaluations* from others, *comparison* with others and our own *experience* of living. It includes our thoughts and feelings about ourselves and our attitudes and values.
- How we feel about our self (**self-esteem**) depends a great deal on how others treat us. We all need **positive regard** from others, that is their (preferably unconditional) approval, interest and acceptance.
- Rogers also thought we have an **ideal self** which is the person we would like to be. For most of us there is a gap between the self-concept and ideal self but we can live with it. For some people, however, the gap between self-concept and ideal self is so large that they become very unhappy and may need help.
- Whatever the situation, we are all motivated to **self-actualise**, i.e. to grow personally until we achieve our potential.
- No one can decide for us the best way to 'grow' personally but we can, as clients, be encouraged to find our own way by a **facilitator** (which is a term Rogers preferred to 'therapist').

❝❝ the facilitator and client are equals ❞❞

Personality assessment and change

For use in client-centred therapy Rogers developed a technique of self-assessment called the **Q-sort**. This helps people clarify their own self-concepts and to communicate them to their facilitator. The Q-sort consists of cards on each of which is a statement such as 'I am satisfied with myself' or 'I am a popular person'. The client sorts the cards into several piles ranging from 'not at all like me' to 'very like me'. Once a note has been made of this 'sort', the client can then be asked to sort the cards again to show the ideal self. The two 'sorts' can be compared to see where there are important gaps between self and ideal self.

During client-centred therapy, the facilitator would **counsel** the client using particular techniques and by showing **warmth**, **empathy** and **positive regard**. In this supportive atmosphere a troubled client would begin to understand and accept themselves and others more easily and decide what to change and how to change it. Rogers could use the Q-sort to see how therapy was going along, especially to see if the gap between self-concept and ideal self was closing.

Kelly's personal construct theory

Kelly (1955) saw people as 'scientists' who form theories about the social world and test out and revise these theories in the light of experience. Just like a scientist, a person **construes**, or understands the world in their own way. If we can discover the words, or **constructs**, a person uses to describe this world, we have, in effect, discovered their personality.

Personality assessment and change – the repertory grid technique

A personal construct is a **dimension** with two extremes (e.g. warm–cold) on which we can place someone. The repertory grid technique encourages a person to bring into the open their own set of personal constructs in the following way:

- A number of important others in a person's life (such as mother, father, brother, best friend, teacher, disliked person) are listed across the top of a grid.
- The person is asked to fill in the actual names of as many of these as they can.
- They are then asked to compare three of these at a time (for example, mother, best friend, disliked person) and say one way in which any two are alike but different from the third. The resulting constructs are written down the side of the grid (in this example, the person might choose 'accepting–rejecting').
- The process continues until the person runs out of ideas. By this time we will have a fairly complete idea of how they construe themselves and others, and thus, a good idea of their personality (but full analysis of the grid goes beyond this).

For Kelly, the personal construct system gives us a kind of *anchor* for understanding the world. It should serve us well in trying to make sense of ourselves, others and the world, but it should not be *too loose* or *too rigid* and it should be *open to change*. Kelly argued that certain mental disorders could be linked to such problems with personal construct systems resulting, perhaps, in behaviour which is *erratic* or *over-controlled*. In the right kind of therapeutic situation, a client could reconsider and challenge their existing construct system and, possibly, alter it so that the world is seen in a more balanced way.

Evaluation of the Humanistic approach

- Humanistic psychologists have given us ways of assessing self or personal constructs. These have practical uses in therapies which aim to change the self-concept or personal construct system.
- They have given us a fresh way of looking at people, i.e. as *individuals* rather than as a person like any other to be pigeon-holed or categorised in a rigid way.
- People may not be as 'self-aware' as we would like them to be when they are assessing the self or thinking up personal constructs. Also they may deliberately withhold information if they feel it would be unacceptable to express it.
- Some psychologists find the vagueness of ideas such as self-actualisation or personal constructs unacceptable and difficult to test.
- It can be argued that 'self-report' methods lack precision.

> this approach gave us a fresh new way of viewing behaviour in humans

ALTERNATIVES TO THE HUMANISTIC APPROACH – EYSENCK AND CATTELL'S THEORIES

Eysenck and *Cattell* take a **psychometric approach** to personality. This means they believe it can be *measured* with personality tests based on statistical techniques. One such technique is **factor analysis** which allows us to take a large number of personality trait names and reduce them to a more manageable number by putting together those that are similar and giving them one name. Unlike the Humanistic psychologists, psychometricians think that people can all be *categorised* using the same system. However, Eysenck and Cattell differ on what that system is.

Eysenck's personality theory

In 1944, *Eysenck* began to build his theory by studying 700 neurotic patients. From this he proposed that personality was biologically based and could be adequately described using two main dimensions:

there are physiological bases to these

1. **Introversion–extraversion** (E). Typical extraverts are **stimulus hungry**. They seek out stimulation and are outgoing, sociable, excitable and impulsive. They may take more risks and tend to be more aggressive. They are not always reliable. Typical introverts are retiring and quiet. They prefer to plan things carefully, usually manage to keep their feelings under control and rarely lose their temper. They are generally reliable.

   Eysenck proposed we all need to keep activity in the central nervous systems (CNSs) at a comfortable level. For extraverts this takes more effort which is why they seek out more stimulation. Introverts reach the right activity level more easily so tend to avoid stimulation.

2. **Neuroticism–stability** (N). Neurotic people are anxious, moody and often depressed. They may have difficulty sleeping as well as other psychosomatic problems. They may react strongly to emotionally arousing events and have difficulty recovering. Stable people are slower to react and are usually calmer, more controlled and less worried.

   Eysenck argued that neurotic people tend to have autonomic nervous systems (ANSs) that are more easily aroused and slower to recover than the ANSs of stable people.

Most of us fall somewhere between the extremes of these two dimensions and a person's position on them can be measured using the Eysenck Personality Inventory (**EPI**). Extreme scores are quite rare and could be associated with deviant behaviour or mental disorder.

Later Eysenck suggested another dimension called **psychoticism** (P). This is measured using a questionnaire called the **EPQ**. Most people score low on P. High scorers tend to be solitary individuals who show little concern for others and who may be aggressive and insensitive.

Although Eysenck thought these main **types** were most useful for describing personality, he also thought that within each type there was a larger number of **traits** and that each trait would lead people to **habitually respond** in specific ways. His model of personality is thus a **hierarchical** one with a number of levels.

Research into the personality types

- If a personality theory is *biologically based,* we can use *twin studies* to test it. *Shields* (1962) studied identical (**MZ**) twins reared apart and found that E and N *correlated quite highly* even though the twins had experienced different environments. The correlations for non-identical (**DZ**) twins was lower, as we would expect. (But there are many problems with twin studies. See, for example, twin studies in the nature–nurture debate and intelligence.)

the research findings are mixed

- Eysenck proposed that we inherit different kinds of nervous systems which make us likely to react in different ways. If the extravert's CNS is harder to arouse than the introvert's, the extravert should not be as *easy to condition* as the introvert. *Franks* (1956) claimed to have shown this with a classically conditioned eyeblink reflex. In another area of conditioning, one reason why introverts tend to be more *conformist* could be that they have also been more easy to condition socially. However, the evidence on conditionability is mixed.

- *Spielman* (1963) found differences in extraverts and introverts in their *tolerance* for a boring, repetitive task. Extraverts' tolerance was much less. Spielman thought this might be because the task was not stimulating enough to cross their high arousal threshold.

- If the CNSs of introverts and extraverts differ we should be able to show differences in EEG readings of the *electrical activity in their brains*. However, *Gale* (1983) thought that only about half of such studies showed differences which could be related to personality and that there might have been design faults with these.
- There is some evidence that the autonomic nervous systems of *neurotic patients* respond strongly to external stimuli and recover slowly (but there is little evidence of this in non-patient high N scorers).
- *Farrington et al.* (1982) found that *delinquent boys* have higher P scores than non-delinquents but Eysenck admits the P scale is inferior to the other two scales and so is possibly less convincing.
- *Eysenck and Eysenck* (1985) found some evidence that people who commit *anti-social or criminal behaviour* score high on P, N and E but the links are not very strong.

Cattell's theory of personality

Rather than describing personality using major types, Cattell thought it was more useful to measure a number of different traits. He distinguished between **source traits** that underlie behaviour and **surface traits** or the general behaviour we actually show. Cattell thought it would be more useful to identify the source traits because they are at the root of behaviour and *more stable* than surface traits. He began by identifying 18,000 trait names in the English language. These had to be reduced. To help him do this he looked at three sources of information about the personality:

- **L-data**. This is the 'life record' and consists of ratings of a person *given by others* who know that person well, e.g. through school reports or references or other ratings of their behaviour.
- **Q-data**. These are *self-ratings* given on personality questionnaires.
- **T-data**. These are the results of *objective laboratory tests* of behaviour, e.g. physiological measures and other reactions to tests.

Through factor analysis of Q- and L-data he eventually arrived at sixteen personality factors which he could measure in his questionnaire aptly named the **16PF**. The factors are:

1. reserved	outgoing
2. less intelligent	more intelligent
3. emotionally unstable	emotionally stable
4. humble	assertive
5. sober	happy-go-lucky
6. expedient	conscientious
7. shy	venturesome
8. tough minded	tender minded
9. trusting	suspicious
10. practical	imaginative
11. forthright	shrewd
12. self-assured	apprehensive
13. conservative	experimenting
14. group dependent	self-sufficient
15. undisciplined	controlled
16. relaxed	tense.

Research evidence concerning the sixteen personality factors

- *Cattell et al.* (1970) looked at the relationship between personality and **criminality** using the 16PF. They found weak evidence that criminals were more likely to be humble, sober, expedient, imaginative, apprehensive, undisciplined and affected by feelings
- Cattell used the 16PF to produce **profiles** of people in **different occupational groups**. These profiles could then be used to help select suitable new recruits (although we have to be aware that people can sometimes fake their answers if they want to give a particular impression).

Cattell and Eysenck differ in other important ways

- If we go on to factor analyse these sixteen traits we end up with a smaller number of surface traits, two of which Cattell called **exvia–invia** and **anxiety**. These are rather like Eysenck's E and N but Cattell thought they were too general to be useful. (This area of disagreement has much to do with the different types of factor analysis preferred by Eysenck and Cattell.)

- Cattell also disagreed with Eysenck that abnormal groups were *extremes* of the personality types. Instead, he thought the abnormal personality was different in *quality* from the normal type rather than in quantity.
- Cattell thought a complete assessment of personality must take into account a person's *mood* and *motivation* at the time of completing a questionnaire as this could change their answers. For this reason, he devised the **Eight State Questionnaire** to use alongside the 16PF.
- Cattell's 16PF tends to be used more in educational settings and for selecting people for different occupations. The EPI is more likely to be used to research into the personalities of criminals and people with mental disorders.

Evaluation of Eysenck and Cattell's theories

- The methods of assessing personality are reliable and based on thorough statistical information.
- Both theories have produced much interest and research.
- Both theories are clear and easy to understand.
- Both theories have been criticised for over-simplifying something as complex as human personality and for pigeon-holing people in a way which might play down important differences between them.
- As we shall see, some theorists think it is wrong to see personality as something which is fairly fixed and measurable. If this were the case, people's personalities would be *stable* across *time* and *situations* but there is evidence that they are not.

THE PSYCHODYNAMIC APPROACH

Psychodynamic theorists such as Freud agree on the following:

there are different levels of consciousness

- The most important influence on behaviour is the **unconscious mind** (although we also have a pre-conscious and a conscious mind). Freud proposed the unconscious consists of **instinctive drives** that are mainly life preserving, sexual (**Eros**) or aggressive and destructive (**Thanatos**).
- The personality develops over time as a result of the instinctive drives *interacting* with experience.
- The personality develops in **stages** roughly defined by age. The stages are like **sensitive periods**. What happens to us during a stage has long-lasting effects on our personality. The different experiences people have in these stages account for differences in personality.

Freud's theory of psychosexual development

there are other psychodynamic approaches

Here we will concentrate on Freud's **psychoanalytic theory** as one example of the psychodynamic approach. The theory was developed as a result of studying many wealthy Viennese patients who came to him for help with **neurotic problems**. Freud used a variety of methods to tap into people's unconscious minds (e.g. **free association, analysis of slips of the tongue**). He produced **clinical case studies** of his clients and eventually based his theory of personality development on about twelve key cases. (This theory has already been mentioned in connection with sex and gender and moral development.)

The structure of the personality

Freud saw the adult personality as having three parts called the id, ego and superego. The id is present at birth, the ego appears by about 3 years of age and the superego by 5 or 6. One way in which people's personalities differ is in how powerful these three parts of the personality are in relation to each other.

- **The id** is an *animalistic*, asocial part of the personality. It consists entirely of biological, instinctive, life-preserving, sexual and aggressive energies. If a need arises, e.g. through hunger or a threat to safety, the id demands *immediate action* to restore calm. It cannot tolerate delays so we say it operates on the **pleasure principle**. It is like a demanding infant.

- **The ego** is a more *social* part of the personality that functions to satisfy the id's demands in more socially acceptable and realistic ways. Because of this, it is said to operate on the **reality principle**. The ego's role is to balance the demands of the id and superego. It is like a reasonable adult.
- **The superego** is the *moral* part of the personality and it is said to operate on the **morality principle**. It has two parts called the **ego-ideal** and the **conscience**. The superego watches over the ego's attempts to meet the id's demands and seems to pass judgement on how successful the id is being. The ego-ideal part makes us feel *worthy* and good if the ego does a good job. The conscience will make us feel *guilty* if the ego does not do well.

Ego defence mechanisms

The ego has a number of defence mechanisms, or *emergency measures*, which it can use to protect itself from unpleasant feelings of anxiety or guilt. These feelings can arise because the person feels threatened by a real danger or because the id or super-ego become too demanding. Here are a few examples:

- **repression** – the ego pushes the id's demand into the unconscious and holds it there;
- **displacement** – the ego finds a safe target for the id's needs (for example, you may feel aggressive towards your boss but to show it would lose you your job so you go and throw things instead);
- **denial** – the ego argues that there is no problem to worry about;
- **projection** – pretending that your unacceptable impulses belong to someone else, not yourself;
- **sublimation** – the ego finds an outlet for the id's need which is almost as good as the real thing (for example a person with a strong, but thwarted, reproductive need might find satisfaction in caring for children or other needy people).

Psychosexual stages of personality development

Freud thought we go through four main stages of personality development. At each stage, the id seeks a zone of the body (an **erogenous zone**) from which it can gain feelings of pleasure. Our personalities are affected by how successful the id is at gaining enough pleasure at each stage. If there is *too little* or *too much*, **fixation** may result. This means that energy becomes tied up in the stage and unbalances the personality. The stages are:

66 fixation is a key concept 99

- **The oral stage**. 0–1 year. The id focuses its pleasure seeking on the *mouth* and everything to do with feeding and sucking. **Orally fixated** adults may enjoy oral pleasures such as eating, drinking, smoking, talking, pencil-chewing and thumb-sucking. They may choose careers involving these or other oral activities. Depending on how good or bad their experiences were they may become optimistic, cheerful and generous or the opposite.
- **The anal stage**. 1–3 years. The id now focuses its pleasure seeking on sensations to do with *bladder* and *bowel* function. The **ego** develops during this stage as the infant finds that it can no longer be completely dependent on others to meet its needs. **Anally fixated** adults often **sublimate** their feelings through working with or enjoying things which *symbolise* faeces, such as money, pottery clay or garden soil. A person who was frustrated in this stage may be orderly, stubborn and thrifty. An over-indulged person may be the opposite of these as well as confident, self-reliant and independent.
- **The phallic stage**. 3–5 or 6 years. The id now focuses its pleasure seeking on the *genitals*. A **phallic fixated** person may enjoy work or leisure activities involving exhibitionism and heroism such as acting or dangerous voluntary work. Phallic personalities are often courageous, reckless, curious, vain and proud or the opposite of these.

During the phallic stage children go through very important conflicts which result in the formation of the **super-ego**. For boys this is called the **Oedipal conflict** and for girls the **Electra conflict**. (You should now look back to the psychodynamic explanation of sex and gender for a detailed account and evaluation of these ideas, chapter 9.)

- **Latency**. 5 or 6 years to puberty. This is not a stage but a period of relative calm when the child increases its intellectual and social skills through school and friendships. This is also a period of further ego development.
- **The genital stage**. Puberty onwards. The adult personality and sexuality are now expressed and we can see the results of experiences in the earlier stages.

Evaluation of Freud's theory of personality development

66 Freud's theory has had enormous influence 99

- The theory has been very *influential* in our thinking and in inspiring other psychodynamic theorists.
- Many Freudian ideas, such as *defence mechanisms,* have *wide appeal* and their names occur often in everyday conversation even if there is little reliable research evidence that they exist!
- The idea of *oral fixation* is supported in a study by *Yarrow* (1973) which linked short time periods spent feeding in infancy with later thumb-sucking. (But we don't know whether these children had a stronger urge to suck all along which led them to feed quickly and thumb-suck later.)
- There is some evidence for the existence of the *personality types* predicted by Freud. For example, *Kline* (1972) gives support for the anal personality type (but there is little evidence that this is connected to the type of toilet-training experienced in childhood).
- The theory acknowledges the importance of *biological* and *environmental forces* in shaping personality.
- It is also *practically useful* because it provides an effective therapeutic technique.
- The idea that personality is decided so early on in life is a rather *pessimistic* one. Strictly speaking, the only way to change an unbalanced personality would be to undergo lengthy psychoanalysis.
- Freud's *methods* (clinical case studies of small numbers of neurotic, Viennese adults) have led some critics to question whether the ideas can really be applied to ordinary children and to people everywhere.
- Many of the key elements of Freud's theory (e.g. unconscious mind, instincts, defences) *cannot be observed directly* or shown to exist. They are, therefore, difficult to test.

THE LEARNING THEORY (LT) APPROACH

As you will recall from chapter four, Behaviourists think most of our behaviour is **conditioned**. *Skinner* suggested behaviour is *shaped and maintained by its consequences.* The consequences of our actions include **reinforcement** and **punishment** and some actions seem to bring about no consequences at all.

For radical (extreme) Behaviourists:

- personality is just another expression of learned behaviour. It is brought about in the same way as any other learned behaviour and is nothing unusual or special. We may learn to be outgoing because friendly behaviour is *positively reinforced* or we may become aggressive because of the reinforcing attention it gets us;
- occasional (*partial*) reinforcement of behaviour tends to make the behaviour more persistent and resistant to extinction. (In everyday life we are not reinforced every time we are friendly or aggressive. Instead, it tends to be now and again.)

Examples of supporting research

- *Walters and Brown* (1963) found that children could be encouraged by reward to hit a large, inflatable clown doll harder and in more imaginative ways. What is more, they transferred (**generalised**) their aggression to play situations with other children.
- *Sears et al.* (1957) carried out a study of **child-rearing styles** and their effects on children's behaviour. They found that **permissive parents** rarely stopped their children from being aggressive but occasionally stepped in with quite severe punishment. Their children were more aggressive than children of more consistent parents. The permissively parented children had found aggression generally paid off. It also got them occasional attention from an otherwise indifferent parent.

- *Patterson* (1989) has suggested a number of influences which might lead a child to become uncooperative or out of control. One factor might be **negative reinforcement**. For example, a parent might ask a child who is playing with friends to come indoors for a meal. The child doesn't want to and makes a fuss. The parent backs down to escape the fuss and the child gets its way. Both have been negatively reinforced by behaving in a way which ended an unpleasant situation so they are both more likely to behave this way in the future.

SOCIAL LEARNING THEORY (SLT)

As we saw in chapter four Social Learning theorists accept that much of our behaviour results from conditioning but they also think we learn from **observing** and **imitating** certain important **models** around us. These models can be friends or family members or people we see in films or on TV. The 'company we keep' is therefore very important.

SLT predicts we pick up both **pro- and anti-social behaviour** from observing others. We can learn to be friendly and helpful in just the same way that we can learn to be aggressive or dishonest. If you look back to chapter four you will find a list of the kinds of models most likely to be imitated and the kinds of behaviour learned. For example, SLT predicts that we learn both specific behaviour patterns from others and their general attitudes and standards of behaviour.

Examples of supporting research

- SLT predicts that what a model does is more important to the observer than what it says. *Grusec et al.* (1978) found that asking or telling children to be generous was less likely to encourage children to be generous than actually showing them how to be generous. It is a matter of 'practising what you preach'.
- SLT takes into account a learner's *thought processes* when they are deciding how to behave. It is not merely a matter of reinforcing the desired behaviour. *Bandura* (1982) found that he could help people overcome anxiety and nervousness by getting them to think of themselves as more capable.

Evaluation of Learning Theory and SLT

- LT and SLT give us a straightforward explanation of how personality develops and changes. It seems to make good *common sense*.
- LT and SLT can explain why our personalities may not be consistent. There is a much quoted piece of research by *Hartshorne and May* (1928) who showed that boys' honesty varied in different situations. LT and SLT would say that the boys had learned different responses in different situations (e.g. home and school) and were simply showing the behaviour that had been reinforced or modelled in each place.

  Mischel (1968) developed this idea into an approach to personality known as **situationism**. He argued against approaches which see personality as fixed. He said there is *very little consistency* in personality. Instead, we get an *illusion* of consistency because we tend to see people, and ourselves, in similar circumstances all the time. (It can come as a shock to us to see them, or ourselves, behaving differently in a new or different situation but this is exactly what learning theories and situationism warn us to expect.)
- LT and SLT think it is possible to change people's personalities which could be a good thing if we could change aggressiveness or unfriendliness or encourage people to be more honest or generous.
- Some people criticise LT for seeing people as puppets or machines with little freedom to choose how to behave. SLT helps to answer this criticism because it brings the social side of life and people's thought processes into the picture.
- For other evaluative points about LT and SLT see chapter four.

2 > TEMPERAMENT

66 know this definition 99

DEFINING TEMPERAMENT

Some psychologists think that we each have *a fundamental, inbuilt way of responding to the world and other people*. They call this **temperament**. Parents are often heard to say that their children were different from the very start. It is almost as if at least some parts of the personality are innate and other people notice these differences early on.

Bee (1992) says temperament theorists agree on the following:

- individuals are *born with* a particular kind of temperament;
- people with different temperaments *differ physiologically*, e.g. in how quickly and how much their nervous systems react to stimuli;
- temperamental differences are present from the start and *last into adulthood;*
- temperament *affects how we respond* to the world and others, therefore it affects the way others respond to us.

TYPES OF TEMPERAMENT

Thomas and Chess (1977) suggested children may be classified as one of three types (the first one being the most usual).

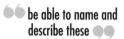
be able to name and describe these

- **The easy child** – This child is happy and adaptable, regular in sleeping and eating habits and welcomes a certain amount of stimulation.
- **The difficult child** – This child is often irritable and slow to adapt, has difficulty establishing regular sleeping and eating and often reacts negatively to change.
- **The slow to warm up child** – This child is not as negative as the difficult child or as positive as the easy child. Regular patterns are established moderately easily and the child will adapt to change in time. There is a kind of passive resistance to new things.

Buss and Plomin (1989) suggested three temperament dimensions, which means that most children can be placed somewhere between each of the following extremes:

- **active–lethargic**
- **emotional–impassive**
- **sociable–detached**.

Kagan et al. (1990) suggested one basic dimension:

- **inhibition** – the extent to which we approach or withdraw from new situations, objects or people.

SUPPORT FOR TEMPERAMENT THEORIES

Twin studies

If we are born with our temperaments and they are biologically based, genetically similar individuals should have similar temperaments. Of particular interest in this respect are identical (monozygotic or **MZ**) twins reared *apart*. If we find their temperaments are similar, in spite of different experiences, the idea that temperament is innate gains strength.

Many popular accounts of MZ twins, reunited after years apart, show the twins to be remarkably similar in all kinds of ways. This is true even of twins who did not previously know of each other's existence. The similarities are hard to explain unless we accept the idea of innate characteristics. However, it is important to remember that very similar reunited twins make good news stories and people may be enthusiastic about looking for similarities but ignore important differences.

Goldsmith and Gottesman (1981) studied 500 pairs of twins at 8 months, 4 years and 7 years and rated them on a number of dimensions of temperament. Twins were rated separately by different people to guard against bias. Even with this precaution, MZ twins were still rated as much more similar than were DZ (dizygotic or non-identical) twins.

Bee (1992) warns against reading too much into these findings. She says that recent research shows little similarity in MZ or DZ twins' temperaments in the first year. In fact, they seem to grow more alike with time as if temperament takes time to unfold.

Physiological studies

Kagan et al. (1990) found that measures of heart-rate, muscle tension and dilation of the pupils correlated at about +0.6 with their measure of **inhibition**. Such measures are quite good *predictors* of this type of temperament. This lends support to the idea that it has a biological basis.

Consistency of temperament over time

A number of studies show that temperament is quite stable over time. *Rothbart* (1986) found consistency of difficult and easy behaviour in a longitudinal study of infants at 2, 9 and 12 months. *Korn* (1984) found consistency of temperament in adolescents followed up as adults. Unfortunately, although such studies suggest consistency there is little evidence that temperament in *infancy* correlates with temperament in *later life*. This could be for any one of the following reasons:

- measures of temperament for infants are rather different from those used with older individuals so it is hardly surprising that they *do not compare well*;
- temperament is *not consistent* over time;
- temperament is innate but it *takes time to unfold* or mature.

Temperament and our response to the world

Temperament theorists think that our temperaments influence how we interact with the world and with others and that others' behaviour towards us is affected by this. Such an idea is very difficult to test and the evidence is patchy. *Thomas and Chess* (1977) quote one success story of a person who was a **difficult** baby who reacted intensely and negatively to anything new. His parents started to think they were incompetent but, with help, they learned to cope. For example, they became able to predict what kinds of situations would cause negative reactions and introduced the infant to them *gradually* and *repeatedly* instead of *suddenly*. Childhood and adolescence were fairly smooth because there were few changes but, in young adulthood, a move away from home to college began to cause problems. By this time, Dr Thomas was able to help the young man to deal with his temperament and adapt more successfully to his new life.

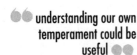
understanding our own temperament could be useful

Children with difficult temperaments may be more *vulnerable* in situations involving stress or change. The reactions of family members to these situations and to the difficult child could determine how successfully the child copes. Unravelling all these influences in order to test them out is very difficult in practice. There are also obvious ethical reasons why psychologists cannot take control of a child's experiences in life simply to test out an interesting theory.

Evaluation of the temperament approach

- There is some promising evidence for the idea of temperament (as outlined above).
- Temperament theory is a good balance for strongly environmental theories such as LT and SLT. The idea of innate temperament *interacting* with experience to produce personality appeals to common sense.
- There is a problem finding measures of temperament for infants which compare well with measures of temperament for other stages of life. This makes it hard to support the idea that temperament is innate.
- The different theories of temperament give rise to different measures and this makes it harder to compare research findings in meaningful ways.
- There are practical and ethical barriers to testing how temperament and environment interact.

EXAMINATION QUESTIONS

MEG specimen paper 3 (Higher), Section C

Spend 18 minutes on this question

Source: Personality

According to Eysenck, introverts are supposed to be better at vigilance tasks than extraverts. Vigilance involves being able to concentrate for a long period of time at a task. In one study, the researcher measured the personality type of 15 participants using the Eysenck Personality Inventory. These participants were then given a vigilance task and the number of errors were recorded. The researcher plotted the scores of the personality inventory and the number of errors made on the vigilance test. The results are shown in the scattergram below.

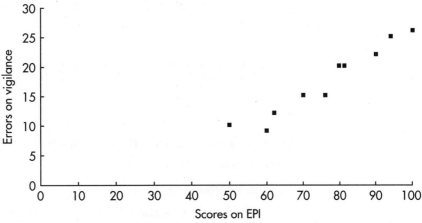

Correlation between personality type and vigilance

(a) What could the researcher conclude from the results of this study? [2]
(b) Give one disadvantage of using correlational research. [2]
(c) According to Eysenck, why are introverts better at vigilance tasks? [3]
(d) Briefly describe one other theory of personality that you have studied. [5]

[*Total 12 marks*]
(MEG)

TUTOR ANSWER

MEG specimen paper 3 (Higher), Section C

(a) The researcher would conclude that there is a positive correlation between scores on the EPI and number of errors on a vigilance task. (The higher the EPI score, the greater the number of errors.)

(b) Correlation only tells us about the relationship between two variables. It does not allow us to talk about cause and effect, i.e. we cannot say that one causes changes in the other.

(c) Spielman found that introverts and extraverts differ in their tolerance for repetitive and boring tasks. He thought this was because low levels of stimulation were not enough to cross the extravert's high arousal threshold. The vigilance task would, therefore, not be enough to keep their attention which is why they make more mistakes.

(d) Kelly's personal construct theory is an example of a Humanistic approach to personality. Kelly thinks that people construe the world in their own way and the key to understanding their personality lies in discovering which constructs they use. Kelly used the repertory grid technique to do this. Participants compare others who are known to them in groups of three and think of a way in which two of them are alike but different from the third. This generates a list of bipolar constructs (e.g. warm–cold) and this list will tell us how that person construes themselves, others and the world.

A personal construct system helps us to select from and organise the vast amount of information that we have to deal with about the world. Kelly thought that a system should be fairly open to change through everyday experience but that too flexible or too loose a system could, in extreme cases, lead to mental disorders. In this case, therapy might help to achieve a better balance in the system.

In common with other Humanistic approaches, a strength of Kelly's theory is that it invites us to see the person as a whole, unique individual. Problems with it include difficulties with testing some of its underlying assumptions about humans (such as basic goodness) and the use of rather subjective self-report techniques such as the repertory grid.

STUDENT'S ANSWER

SEG sample paper (Higher Tier), Section D

Spend 35 minutes on this question

(a) What is temperament? [4]

66 4/4 99

Temperament is a fundamental, inbuilt style of responding to others and the world. Each child is born with a different character.

(b) Describe **one** way in which temperament has been studied [6]

66 rather brief 99

66 explain type of behaviour 99

66 4/6 99

Twin studies are one way of finding out if temperament is inherited. If identical twins are studied, their temperaments should be the same even if they are reared apart and have different environments. There is some evidence for this but the studies are not very well controlled. Goldsmith et al. studied 500 pairs of twins and had their behaviour rated separately by observers. The identical twins were rated as being much more similar in temperament than non-identical twins.

(c) Describe the findings of **one** study of temperament and explain the conclusions which can be drawn from those findings [6]

66 explain why 99

66 explain conclusions 99

66 3/6 99

One study was done to see if temperament stayed the same throughout life. Korn found that temperament in adolescents was similar when they grew into adults. This study supports the idea that temperament is innate. One problem with it is that it did not follow up these adolescents from when they were babies so we don't know whether they had always had temperaments like that or whether they had been learned.

(d) Compare and contrast **two** different explanations of personality development [14]

[*Total 30 marks*]
(SEG)

Learning theorists think that we learn our personalities through the process of conditioning. Operant conditioning says we learn through the consequences of our behaviour so if we are rewarded for being extravert and punished for being introvert, we will become more extravert. Parents shape children's personalities by the way they react to their behaviour. Child-rearing style can affect the child in this way. If the parent is permissive, lets the child do what it wants and only steps in if the child is too noisy or naughty, the child is likely to grow up thinking it can do what it likes. If the parent always gives in to the child this is likely to have the same effect. Social Learning Theory grew out of Learning Theory. It says that we also learn by observation of role-models and imitation of them. If we see others behaving in particular ways and being rewarded for it, we may be encouraged to copy them so that our personality is really just a way of behaving. Learning theories are useful because they can explain why we seem to have different personalities for different situations. Different situations bring out different things in us.

Freud thought that our personalities formed in childhood depending on the experiences we have. Children go through four stages of personality development: the oral, anal, phallic and genital stages.

There is a period of latency before the final stage. At each stage, the biological id part of the personality demands pleasure from a different part of the body. Too little or too much pleasure can leave the child fixated in that stage. An anally fixated person could be mean, stubborn and orderly. The ego develops in the anal stage and the superego develops in the phallic stage. The ego helps the id to deal with reality and the superego gives us our sex-role and morality. Some people have very weak egos and experience a lot of anxiety about how to cope with the id. Some people have very strong superegos and have a lot of anxiety from guilt. The best kind of personality is one where there has been a good balance of pleasure in each stage and the id, ego and superego work well together. Freud's theory has been criticised for being unscientific and difficult to test but there is some evidence for the personality types he suggested.

66 8/14 99

66 19/30 Good answers on the whole but more explanation would have helped in places. Part (d) is let down by failure to compare and contrast explicitly 99

A Review Sheet for this chapter can be found on pp. 253–4.

CHAPTER 16

BIO-PSYCHOLOGY

GETTING STARTED

This chapter is for MEG and NEAB students only. It opens with a general account of some of the biological bases of behaviour. It then goes on to examine stress and emotion.

If you are an MEG student, read through the opening section on Biological Bases of Behaviour to help you understand later sections. (If you are doing Option 4 you will need to know this section in detail.) All MEG students should go on to study Stress which is a core, compulsory topic for you. It is not necessary for you to study the final section on Emotion.

NEAB students would benefit from studying the whole chapter. Stress and emotion are important, compulsory topics on the NEAB syllabus.

1. BIOLOGICAL BASES OF BEHAVIOUR

2. STRESS

3. EMOTION

ESSENTIAL PRINCIPLES

1 **BIOLOGICAL BASES OF BEHAVIOUR**

THE NERVOUS SYSTEM

The nervous system can be divided into sections as shown in **Fig**. 16.1.

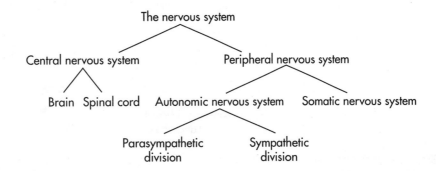

Figure 16.1 Divisions of the human nervous system

The central nervous system (CNS) divides into the **brain** and **spinal cord**. We will look at the divisions and functions of the brain soon. The spinal cord's main functions are to carry information to and from the rest of the body to the brain and to bring about **reflex actions** (automatic responses to stimuli).

The peripheral nervous system (PNS) consists of all the other parts of the nervous system apart from the brain and spinal cord. The **somatic division** carries messages to and from the voluntary muscles and sense organs. The **autonomic nervous system** (ANS) is a *self-regulating* system controlling internal organs and glands. It looks after all the activities in the body of which we are normally unaware, e.g. regulating heart-beat and breathing and digestion. The ANS has two divisions. The **sympathetic division** is, generally speaking, an excitatory system. It prepares us for *fight, flight* or *frolic* through *physiological arousal*. Functions which are not immediately essential, such as digestion, may be halted for a time while the person deals with a situation. We are all familiar with the results of sympathetic action. Consider, for example, how you feel before an exam or when looking forward to something you expect to enjoy. The **parasympathetic division** dampens down this arousal when it is no longer necessary to 'fight, flee or frolic' and restores calm to the system. Table 16.1 shows some of the activities of the ANS.

❝ it is very important to know about ANS function ❞

Organ or gland	Sympathetic action	Parasympathetic action
Digestive organs	Digestion inhibited	Digestion maintained
Liver	Sugar released into blood	Sugar stored
Pupils	Dilate	Constrict
Heart	Heart-rate increased	Heart-rate decreased
Salivary glands	Secretion of saliva inhibited	Secretion of saliva maintained

Table 16.1 Some effects of the ANS

The endocrine system has close links with the ANS. It is a system of *ductless glands* which release **hormones** (chemical messengers) *directly* into the blood stream. The hormones travel round the body and affect various *organs* and *muscles*. Their effect is to support the activity of the ANS. The main endocrine glands are illustrated in **Fig**. 16.2.

Psychologists are particularly interested in the action of the CNS, ANS and the endocrine system because of their role in such things as *stress, emotion* and *mental disorders*.

NEURONS, SYNAPSES AND NEUROTRANSMITTERS

Neurons are **nerve cells** and there are billions of them making up the human nervous system. Messages are carried along the neuron in the form of *electrical impulses*. Neurons do not touch each other. They are separated by minute gaps called **synapses**. The only way one neuron can communicate with another is by sending chemical

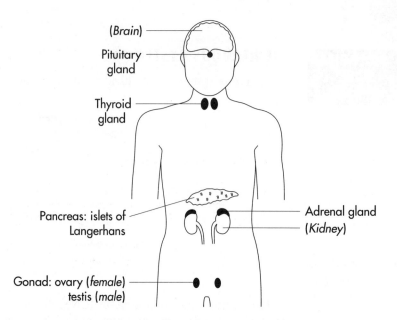

Figure 16.2 Position of the main endocrine glands in humans (the relative position of other organs is shown in italics)

messengers called **neurotransmitters** across the gap. The neurotransmitters stimulate the next neuron to send another electrical impulse and so the message goes on. If this happens, the synapse is **excitatory** but, sometimes, the synapse will be **inhibitory** and damp down activity. This is because there must be a way of controlling the amount of activity in the nervous system. The rate at which nervous transmission happens is very fast indeed (see **Fig**. 16.3).

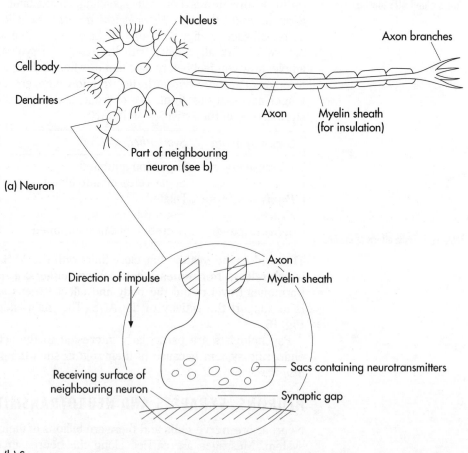

Figure 16.3 A typical neuron and a synapse

THE STRUCTURE OF THE BRAIN

The cerebral cortex and the cerebrum

From the outside we can see that the human brain is divided into two **cerebral hemispheres**. These are connected by a broad band of nerve fibres called the **corpus callosum**. The cerebrum is the largest part of the brain but the surface of the brain, or **cortex**, is by far the most important. It is about 3mm thick and is thrown into many folds which increases its surface area and gives it its distinctive appearance. It also looks grey under the microscope hence the term **grey matter**.

Cerebral localisation refers to where in the cortex areas for controlling certain abilities lie. Research has told us that certain cortical areas are centres for particular abilities so we now have quite an accurate 'map' of the cortex (see **Fig**. 16.4).

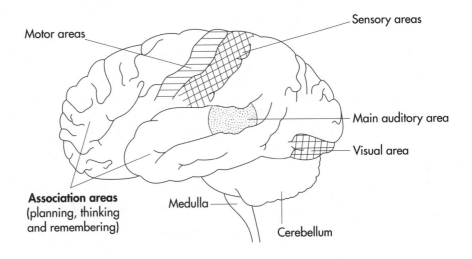

Figure 16.4 A view of the human brain showing key areas of the cortex

- **Sensory areas** receive information about touch, heat, cold, pain and body movements.
- **Motor areas** control all the voluntary movements of the body.
- **Visual and auditory areas** deal with information from the eyes and ears.
- **Language areas** control everything to do with receiving, understanding and producing language. There are several areas. (Not shown in Fig. 16.4.)
- **Association areas** deal with all the things we call higher mental processes. These include thinking, problem solving, planning, remembering.

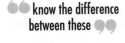 be able to sketch a diagram showing these

The remainder of the cerebrum is devoted to connecting up all parts of the brain. It consists of many, densely packed nerve fibres and makes up the **white matter**.

Cerebral lateralisation and cerebral dominance

know the difference between these

Cerebral lateralisation refers to the fact that the two cerebral hemispheres of the brain are not identical in their function. For some abilities, one side actually *dominates* the other. Language is one such example because language centres are mainly in the left hemisphere. In right-handed people, the left hemisphere is usually dominant for language but in left-handed people the pattern is not so reliable. We might expect them to be right-hemisphere dominant, but this is not the case. They are either left dominant or the dominance is less extreme than in right-handed people. Another finding is that right-handed males generally show much stronger lateralisation of language abilities than do right-handed women. Damage to the man's left hemisphere affects language more than the same damage would in a woman. Some of our abilities are not at all strongly lateralised so there is no dominance. Examples include vision and hearing which are dealt with about equally by both hemispheres (see **Fig**. 16.5).

Some other areas of the brain

The cerebellum has much to do with controlling and coordinating movement. When we learn the movements necessary to walk, speak, ride a bicycle or swim the

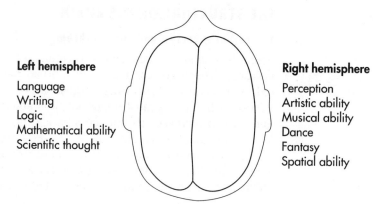

Left hemisphere

Language
Writing
Logic
Mathematical ability
Scientific thought

Right hemisphere

Perception
Artistic ability
Musical ability
Dance
Fantasy
Spatial ability

Figure 16.5 Dominant abilities in the right and left hemispheres of the brain

knowledge is stored in the cerebellum so they become automatic and we never forget how to do them.

The **thalamus** could be thought of as a kind of *relay station* or sorting office. It organises incoming information and distributes it to the appropriate area of the brain for further processing.

The **hypothalamus** acts rather like a *thermostat*, detecting needs in the system and taking the action necessary to meet them, e.g. in the control of temperature, blood sugar or fluid level. To do this it works closely with the endocrine system by communicating with the main gland of that system (the **pituitary gland**) (see **Fig**. 16.6).

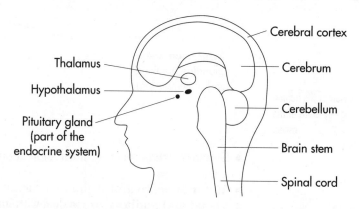

Cerebral cortex
Thalamus
Hypothalamus
Cerebrum
Cerebellum
Pituitary gland (part of the endocrine system)
Brain stem
Spinal cord

Figure 16.6 A cross-section through the human brain

METHODS OF STUDYING THE BRAIN

Studies of accidental brain injury

For *ethical* reasons, it is not usually possible deliberately to damage a person's brain in order to observe the effect. We have to wait for people to have accidents, be injured in fighting or have strokes. We can then try to link up the kind of brain damage they have with its effects on their behaviour and abilities. Much of what we know about localisation of function comes from such studies. Unfortunately, because there is no control over the position of the damage, a great deal of *guesswork* is involved in interpreting findings. We may be able to see the extent of the damage by conducting a *post mortem* on the brain but then we do not have the living person to help us check out our findings.

Deliberate damage to the brain

This is an area which raises important ethical problems with both humans and animals (see chapter two).

- **Electrode implantation.** *Lashley* (1950) studied brain areas to do with sleep by implanting electrodes in the brains of cats. *Hubel and Wiesel* (1962) studied the visual cortex of cats looking for evidence of feature-detecting cells.
- **Split brain studies**. Splitting the corpus callosum to separate the two cerebral hemispheres has been used in an attempt to reduce the severity and frequency of severe epileptic fits. We now know that this affects some aspects of perception. This, in turn, tells us something about the role of the corpus callosum, what the two hemispheres do and how they communicate.

- **Ablation**. Ablation (cutting out) certain parts of the brain has been tried as a control for problem eating or aggressive behaviour. Destruction of a small part of the brain is called a **lesion** and this can be done using an electric current or a chemical. Some lesions can be caused with *anaesthetic drugs* whose effects soon wear off.
- **Pre-frontal lobotomies**. These were first carried out by *Moniz* (1936) and involved destroying the frontal lobes of the brain or separating them from the rest of the brain. It was thought to help people suffering from anxiety, obsessionality and phobias. Some lobotomies may be carried out to control chronic and severe pain. **Leucotomy** involves cutting only the neural pathways and is less severe.

Techniques which do not involve brain damage

- **Electrical stimulation of the living brain** without damaging it is possible. *Penfield* (1955) claimed he could get patients to recall past events when he stimulated points on the surface of the brain using electrodes.
- **Electrical recording techniques**. These involve attaching sensors in specific positions on a person's scalp and measuring electrical activity in the brain. These can then be related to different states of awareness such as alertness, arousal, relaxation or sleep.
- **Drugs and chemicals**. The effect of these on the brain can tell us something about brain function. Some kinds of mental disorder respond well to certain **drugs** (e.g. schizophrenia and anti-psychotic drugs). Because we know what the drug's action is, this can give us clues as to which neurotransmitters may be malfunctioning in the ill person's brain. **Radioactive chemicals** can sometimes be injected into the brain so that we can detect tumours or see which parts of the brain are active at different times.
- **Brain scans**. Techniques such as **CAT** and **PET** scans can give us a three-dimensional picture of the brain which is useful in diagnosis and in discovering *differences* between brains of normal and mentally ill people.
- **Comparative studies**. These involve studying how the brain has *evolved* by comparing different animal species. We can sometimes link up differences in their behaviour to differences in their brain structure.

2 > STRESS

WHAT IS STRESS?

There are a number of ways of defining stress. Some definitions focus on things *external* to a person such as noise or pace of work. Other explanations focus on the individual's *internal* responses to stressors both physically and psychologically. Others combine these two views seeing stress as an interaction between external demands and internal reactions.

❝❝ this third view is the most usual ❞❞

It is important to remember that some stress is an important part of normal life and its effects are often *positive*. Most research, however, focuses on the negative effects of stress because of its apparent connection with health problems. A simple definition of psychological stress which has negative effects goes like this: 'Stress results when we perceive a discrepancy (*mismatch*) between the demands of a situation and our ability to cope with them.'

SOURCES OF STRESS (STRESSORS)

Stressors can arise outside the individual, within the individual or be a combination of both. Examples are:

Noise

Burns and Dobson (1984) say that noise is most stressful if it is *unpredictable* and *uncontrollable*. If noise is constant we usually become used to it and can block it out. If we can control it we can get rid of it. Either way we can reduce its ability to annoy us. Noise from neighbours can be particularly stressful because it is both unpredictable and uncontrollable.

Temperature

Surprisingly, *moderately* hot, rather than very hot or very cold temperatures seem to be connected with more frequent riots or other civil disturbance (*Baron and*

Ransberger 1978). However, we do not really know if this is due to individuals feeling more stressed or because people are more active in more pleasant temperatures and tend to have more contact with each other.

Pollution

This covers many situations ranging from having to put up with cigarette smoke to worries about a wide range of hazardous substances in the air, water or food. *Threat* of pollution is another problem. More than a year after the Three Mile Island nuclear plant accident, researchers showed how people living close to the plant felt more stressed than people living near a similar plant where there had been no accident.

Architecture

Cochrane (1995) suggested that stress linked to living in high-rise blocks as opposed to low-rise buildings had more to do with the *quality of relationships* with neighbours than with the actual *quality of the housing* or how *densely populated* an area was. Other research has shown the importance of how space is used within buildings, e.g. open-plan offices are generally less popular than other kinds of office because workers perceive them as noisy and lacking in privacy.

Work patterns

There are many potential stressors connected with work (apart from the fact that some occupations are dirty, noisy or dangerous). Workloads which are *too light* or *too heavy* can be equally stressful. Research has also shown that people find work more stressful if their role is unclear, relationships with colleagues are difficult, their job is insecure, they feel dispensable or there are no chances to advance their career.

Controllability at work

In a famous study of **executive monkeys** *Brady* (1958) restrained two monkeys in a harness and gave them electric shocks to the feet every now and then. The monkeys did not know when the shocks would occur, but one of them (the executive) could postpone a shock for 20 seconds by pressing a lever. Of course, it had no way of knowing if it had been successful. After 23 days, during which monkeys alternated six hours on and six hours off the apparatus, the executive monkey died from a perforated ulcer.

Disruption of bodily rhythms

Many of our waking, sleeping and other bodily rhythms revolve around and within the 24-hour clock. Upsetting the rhythms through *shift work*, changing *time zones* or through *illness* can have negative effects. *Hawkins et al.* (1978) studied nurses during the first seven nights of night shifts and found that some bodily rhythms shifted to the new schedule more easily than others, e.g. sleep–waking shifted more quickly than hormonal or temperature cycles. The first night for these nurses was the worst!

Critical life events

Holmes and Rahe (1967) suggested that major life events, good or bad, were potentially stressful so they devised the **Holmes-Rahe Social Readjustment Ratings Scale** (SRRS) to measure the impact of different events. There are over 40 'events' on the scale and people mark those which have affected them in the previous twelve months, e.g. death of a spouse, Christmas, change in financial state. High scores have been found to relate to an *increased chance* of physical or mental illness but the link is rather *weak*. Some critics argue that the scale does not allow for *individual differences* in reactions to events. Others criticise it for putting positive and negative events together.

Daily hassles and uplifts

Lazarus (1981) agreed that critical life events are important but he thought it would also be useful to measure the 'hassles and uplifts of everyday life'. The hassles scale has 117 items such as 'losing things' and 'rises in the price of common goods'. The uplifts scale has 135 items including things like 'feeling healthy' and 'relating well to spouse/lover'. Lazarus studied 100 45–64-year-old men for twelve months using these scales and found that hassles scores were positively related to physical and psychological ill health and uplift scores were negatively related to such things.

THE EFFECTS OF STRESS

Physiological responses

Hans Selye (1950) used the **General Adaptation Syndrome** (GAS) to describe how we react to stress on a physiological level. It has three stages:

1 **The alarm stage.** This involves arousal of the **sympathetic nervous system** (SNS) to prepare us for fight, flight or frolic (as explained in the opening section of this chapter). SNS arousal mobilises the body's resources to react appropriately. How does it do this?

- First, the **hypothalamus** signals a need to the **pituitary gland**. This is the 'command centre' for the endocrine system and it sends out hormonal messages to other glands, stimulating them to release their own hormones.
- The **adrenal glands** are thus stimulated by the pituitary hormone **ACTH** to release hormones such as **adrenaline** and **noradrenaline**. These cause heart and respiration rate to speed up and increase blood pressure. At the same time, digestive processes may be suspended and blood sugar released to energise the muscles.
- When the need for SNS arousal has passed, the **parasympathetic nervous system** restores calm.

SNS arousal is clearly very useful to us. As humans were evolving, they would have needed it to help them survive. Unfortunately, modern life may be such that the need for SNS arousal *does not pass*. In this case we move into stage 2.

2 **The resistance stage.** If the stressor remains, the body has to adapt to its presence. SNS arousal decreases but remains quite high. The ability to cope with new stressors is reduced and immunity might be affected.

3 **The exhaustion stage.** Eventually the body runs out of coping resources. Blood sugar levels drop and, in extreme cases, severe **hypoglycaemia** (low blood sugar) can lead to death. A variety of physical illnesses may be more likely at this stage, e.g. high blood-pressure, ulcers, asthma and heart disease.

Physical effects of stress

These can be assessed by:

- measuring hormone levels in the urine or blood;
- measuring heart-rate, respiration rate or blood pressure;
- taking GSR measures, i.e. measuring the electrical conductivity of the skin which changes with the level of arousal;
- testing for enlargement of the adrenal glands (a longer-term side-effect of over-activity).

Psychological responses

People under stress report a variety of psychological symptoms, e.g.:

- negative emotions such as anger, depression, anxiety, aggressiveness;
- feelings of helplessness as if they can do nothing to escape the situation or improve it;
- low self-esteem;
- inability to concentrate;
- feelings of listlessness and apathy;
- feeling a need to smoke or drink more or take mood-changing drugs.

COPING WITH STRESS

Broadly speaking, there are two ways to deal with stress. One is to tackle it at a *physical level*, the other is to focus on the *psychological level*.

Physical approaches

- **Cry!** A good cry can relieve some of the tension caused by stress. Some researchers claim that there is evidence of *stress-related chemicals* in the tears we cry when distressed. One way of interpreting this is that it helps to clear them out of the system. However, the quantities in which they are released may not make much difference. Crying may be effective simply because it encourages others to offer *comfort* and *support* or because it enables us to acknowledge that we are running out of coping resources.

- **Drugs.** As stress tends to raise blood-pressure, **Beta-blockers** (which act on the PNS) can help to reduce it and feelings of stress should also reduce. A variety of other drugs to reduce anxiety, such as **Valium** or **Librium** could be used, bearing in mind that long-term use could lead to **dependency**.

- **Biofeedback.** This involves monitoring a measure of arousal, such as heart-rate or blood-pressure and finding a way of amplifying it and feeding it back to the person in the form of a sound or picture on a screen. People find that they can take control of their physical reactions to stress and reduce them. With practice, they should be able to recognise the signs and do something about them before they get out of hand.

◖◗ this is based on operant conditioning ◗◗

- **Progressive muscle relaxation** (PMR). For some people, simply learning to relax can be very helpful. They are taught a technique of focusing on and relaxing groups of muscles over the whole body. This is the first stage in the treatment known as **systematic desensitisation** where a person (e.g. a social phobic) learns to remain relaxed while facing a series of evermore fearful situations (e.g. ranging from small- to large-scale social situations).

◖◗ this is based on classical conditioning ◗◗

- **Meditation.** There are a number of meditation techniques to choose from, all with the same calming effect. Typically, the meditating person finds a quiet place where they are unlikely to be disturbed and may go through *breathing exercises* and/or repeat a **mantra** – a special word – to help them relax. Meditation and PMR are both known to reduce blood-pressure and they do this as well as, or better than, biofeedback without the need for special apparatus.

- **Exercise.** This can improve the fitness of the heart and circulation and improve people's recovery rate after exertion. Fit people do seem better able to resist the physical effects of stress.

Psychological approaches

There are many different psychological approaches to dealing with stress. Some focus on dealing with the *problem* (the stressor), some focus on the *emotions* and some tackle *both*.

- **Ego defences.** *Sigmund Freud* (1856–1939) suggested that we can deal with the anxiety caused by threatening situations by psychologically 'defending' ourselves against them. Repression is a well-known example. It involves pushing anxious thoughts into the unconscious mind. We may also 'deny' a problem or 'displace' our feelings by taking them out on something other than the stressor. The problem with these defences is that they do not deal with the problem directly. It is still there to bother us.

The next three techniques are suggested by *Sarafino* (1990).

- **Increase social support systems.** People seem better able to resist stress if they have friends, family or colleagues around to support them. Sarafino suggests we work hard on making sure we have such support systems so that we can survive stress better and look after others when they need us.

- **Improve physical fitness.** We already know that a fit body resists the physical effects of stress better but being fit can improve psychological well-being too. This may be because we learn to value ourselves more and give attention to our own needs. If the form of exercise is social it makes it more likely we will spend time with others building support networks.

- **Prepare yourself beforehand** (if possible). If we know we are going to face a difficult situation, we may be able to reduce its effect by preparing for it. We know, for example, that young children cope better with separation from parents if they are carefully prepared. *Janis* (1985) showed that adults facing surgery coped better if they were *moderately anxious* rather than very anxious or not at all anxious. This suggests people would benefit from finding ways of keeping their anxiety at a moderate level.

- **Improve personal control and hardiness**. *Kobasa* (1986) suggests three ways of dealing with stress:
  1. **Focusing**. Learn to recognise signs of tension in your own body so that you can become aware of what is causing them and do something about it.
  2. **Reconstructing** stressful situations. Look back at a stressful situation and list ways in which it could have turned out worse or better. This helps to get it in perspective.
  3. **Compensate** through self-improvement. Encourage yourself by doing some things you *are* good at, then improve coping for the future, e.g. develop examination skills, learn how to manage time or take assertiveness training.

DISTRESS AND EUSTRESS

There are wide *individual differences* in people's reactions to stressors. What is stressful for one person may be challenging to another. What is manageable for us on one day may be unmanageable the next. Techniques for coping with or reducing stress need to take these things into account. Some psychologists think it is helpful to start by finding out what a potential stressor *means* to an individual. If they see it as a *threat* this will probably lead to a destructive state of **distress**. If they see it as *positive* it may lead to a constructive state known as **eustress**. Distress can even be turned into eustress using one or a number of the techniques described above.

a useful distinction to draw

3 > EMOTION

WHAT IS EMOTION?

The answer is that psychologists do not seem to be able to agree on a definition! We do, however, know what emotion involves:

- **Physical changes**. *Activity in the ANS* accompanies emotion, e.g. arousal in the *sympathetic* nervous system or calming by the *parasympathetic* nervous system. This prepares us for fight, flight or frolic or helps us recover (as described earlier in this chapter).
- **Subjective experience**. This is the *'feeling'* we describe ourselves as having, e.g. happy, sad.
- **Cognitive aspects**. This is to do with whether we see the situation as positive or negative.
- **Expressive behaviours**. This is to do with what we say and do, e.g. admitting to feeling anxious, wearing an anxious expression or adopting an anxious body posture.
- **Behavioural consequences**. What we do as a result of feeling an emotion, e.g. go to our GP for tranquillisers or go out with friends to share happiness.

MEASURING EMOTIONS

If we want to measure emotions we must remember how many different levels it operates on. Typical ways of measuring emotion are:

- **Physiological measures**. These are similar to the techniques we might use to measure stress, e.g. looking for signs of arousal in the SNS such as increased heart-rate, respiration rate or blood-pressure.
- **Subjective report**. This means that, using a questionnaire or interview, we ask people to describe to us how they are feeling.
- **Facial expression or bodily posture**. *Ekman* (1972) thinks that the way we express emotions is probably innate. This is based on **cross-cultural studies** showing how similar people's expressions are when they are feeling fear, happiness, sorrow, anger, disgust or surprise. It follows that we should be able to get a crude measure of emotion from monitoring people's expressions.

None of these measures is particularly satisfactory because, on their own, they do not give us a complete picture. Other problems are:

- some people have more control over their physical reactions than others;
- some people may not answer questions honestly or they may hide their emotions very effectively;

- cross-cultural research has shown that, in some cultures, certain emotions are more easily distinguishable than others, e.g. expression of happiness is more easily agreed on than anger or fear.

THEORIES OF EMOTION

We all know that emotions usually come with a change in the way we feel physically. This is due to arousal of the ANS. Generally speaking, the sympathetic nervous system tends to be aroused when we experience emotions such as excitement, fear or anger. *The parasympathetic nervous system* tends to dominate when we feel sadness or grief. It would be tempting to think that there is a different physical state to go with each emotion but this does not seem to be the case. The physical reactions for anger and fear, for example, are very similar but the subjective feelings are different.

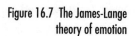 a key point

One of the great problems for emotion theorists is to explain how physical sensations and psychological factors go together to create emotion.

The James-Lange theory of emotion

James and Lange (1884–5) suggested that, when we experience emotion, bodily changes come first and emotional feelings after. For example, we perceive a threat and the SNS immediately prepares us for fight or flight. It is only then that we perceive ourselves as being 'afraid' or 'angry'. As James and Lange said 'We are afraid because we run; we do not run because we are afraid.' This would make good sense in a situation where we needed to save ourselves first and worry about it later (see **Fig**. 16.7).

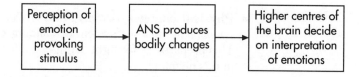

Figure 16.7 The James-Lange theory of emotion

The Cannon-Bard theory of emotion

In 1927 and 1937 respectively *Cannon and Bard* raised objections to the James-Lange theory:

- People who have spinal cord injury or disease do not get feedback from the body about physical changes but they are still capable of feeling emotion.
- Changes in the ANS are quite slow compared to how quickly we feel an emotion.
- Very similar physical states can occur for different emotional feelings. If James and Lange are right we should have different physical states for different emotions.

Cannon and Bard suggested an alternative (see **Fig**. 16.8). They thought that information from a stimulus went to the **thalamus** (the relay station). The thalamus would then alert both the ANS (via the **hypothalamus**) and the higher brain areas. Physical and psychological reactions to emotion therefore happened at the same time.

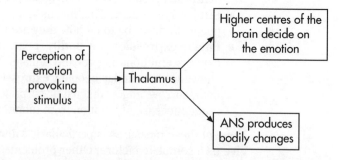

Figure 16.8 The Cannon-Bard theory of emotion

Unfortunately for Cannon and Bard:

- Damage to the hypothalamus or thalamus does not leave a person unable to feel emotional or react physically to an emotion-provoking stimulus.

- *Ekman et al.* (1983) have produced evidence that some emotions can be distinguished at a physical level. They did this by asking participants to hold facial expressions for certain emotions for ten seconds while he measured their physical reactions. This evidence weakens Cannon and Bard's case against James and Lange but it does not show that all emotions are physically distinguishable.

Schachter and Singer's cognitive labelling theory

Schachter and Singer (1962) knew that simply injecting a person with an adrenaline-like substance (**epinephrine**) was not enough to produce a full emotional experience. They thought the way we interpreted a situation added to the physical feelings and led us to experience an emotion (see **Fig**. 16.9.) To test this, they gave volunteers an injection of '**Suproxin**' which was meant to improve performance on a visual perception test. This was a cover story. Participants were, in fact, in one of four groups:

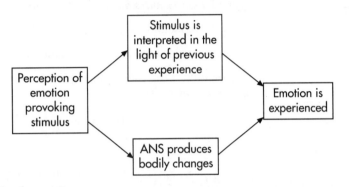

Figure 16.9 Schachter and Singer's cognitive labelling theory of emotion

1 **Control group**. These participants had received an injection of saline solution.
2 **Experimental group A** (epinephrine *informed*). These participants had been injected with epinephrine and told of the likely effects.
3 **Experimental group B** (epinephrine *misinformed*). These participants had received epinephrine but were given false information about its likely effects, e.g. told they would experience numbness or itching.
4 **Experimental group C** (epinephrine *uninformed*). These participants had received epinephrine but were not told what to expect.

Half the subjects in each of these groups then waited alone in a room for a while to complete a questionnaire. The remaining participants were individually shown to a room in which there was another person. This person was introduced as someone who had undergone the same treatment as the participant (but was actually a stooge acting for the experimenters). Half the participants witnessed this person behaving *angrily*, the rest saw the person behave *happily*. The reactions of participants were assessed by the questionnaires they were filling in and by observers.

Schachter and Singer found that control and epinephrine informed participants were *not affected* by the behaviour of the stooge. Epinephrine misinformed and uninformed participants were much *more affected* by the stooge. Schachter and Singer thought that this was because they could not account for the way they were feeling physically and so used the stooge's behaviour to help them decide on a label for their emotion.

❝❝ be clear about the design of this experiment ❞❞

Evaluation

- The study has been criticised for artificiality. Emotions are probably much more complex than the adding up of artificially caused physical feelings and a single incident of someone else's behaviour.
- People differ in their reaction to epinephrine and this was not controlled.
- There are some doubts about whether the observers were 'neutral'. Some of them may have known which group the participants were in and this could have affected the observer's judgement.
- Some emotional reactions seem to be *automatic*, i.e. they do not involve cognitive appraisal (see, for example, the case of **Little Albert** in chapter four).
- We can also learn to *suppress* our reactions to emotion-provoking stimuli. *Seligman et al.* (1967) showed how dogs subjected to inescapable electric shocks do not take an escape route when it is offered. Seligman called this **learned**

helplessness and suggested it could explain some forms of depression. People may experience a series of unpleasant events which they cannot control. The end result is that they are passive and unemotional in situations which would normally provoke a reaction.

EXAMINATION QUESTIONS

NEAB paper 2 1994 Question 2

Spend 20–25 minutes answering these questions

A psychologist had an hypothesis about children.

'Three year olds can hide their emotions.'

He conducted the following experiment with a group of 20 children. Children were tested **one at a time**.

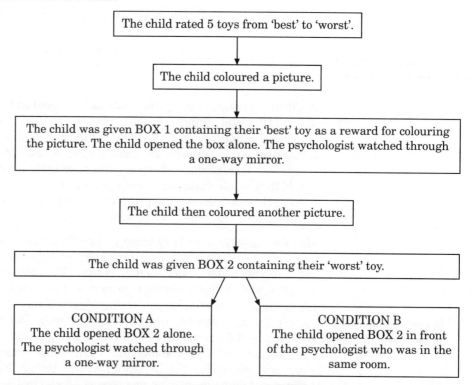

The psychologist recorded the number of children who smiled after opening each box. The results of the study can be seen in the table below.

Number of children who smiled after opening each box.

	CONDITION A	CONDITION B
After opening BOX 1	10	10
After opening BOX 2	1	10

(a) What was the **dependent variable** in this study? [1]
(b) (i) Do the results support the hypothesis? Explain your answer. [3]
　　(ii) Explain why the children's feelings should not be measured only by the expression on their faces. [2]
　　(iii) State another way that can be used to measure emotion. [1]
(c) (i) When a person knows that he or she is in danger the sympathetic nervous system is activated. State **four** bodily changes which can occur. [4]

      (ii) Changes brought about by the sympathetic nervous system play an important part in the James-Lange theory of emotion. Briefly describe the James-Lange theory of emotion. [3]

     (iii) Explain **one** criticism of the James-Lange theory of emotion. Support your answer by referring to experimental studies. [6]

[Total 20 marks]
(NEAB)

TUTOR ANSWER

NEAB paper 2 1994 Question 2

(a) Whether the children smiled after opening the box.

(b) (i) Yes, the hypothesis is supported. Children who were alone did not smile when they opened the box containing their worst toy. When the psychologist was present, they smiled in both conditions suggesting that they were able to cover up their disappointment.

    (ii) Facial expressions can hide our true feelings so they are not always a reflection of the emotion being experienced. It would be better to take other measures into account as well.

    (iii) Emotional reactions can be monitored by measuring the GSR. This is the change in electrical activity that occurs when we are emotionally aroused.

(c) (i) 1 heart rate
      2 pupils dilate
      3 sugar released into blood
      4 digestion inhibited.

    (ii) James and Lange say that when we perceive an emotion-provoking stimulus, we experience bodily changes first and emotional feelings afterwards, i.e. the SNS reacts immediately and we then interpret the situation as positive or negative. They said 'We are afraid because we run, we do not run because we are afraid.'

    (iii) Schachter and Singer thought that physical changes alone were not enough to produce the full range of emotional experience. They suggested that the emotions we feel result from combining physical changes with an interpretation of a situation. They arranged an experiment with four conditions. Control participants were given an injection of saline solution. Other participants were given an injection of epinephrine which has a similar effect to adrenaline. Of these participants, some were accurately informed about the drug's likely effects, some were misinformed and some were uninformed. All the participants were told a cover story – that they had been given 'Suproxin' to test its effect in a vision test.

        Participants were then exposed to either a happy or an angry stooge. Measures taken by self-report on a questionnaire and by observations of participants suggested the uninformed and misinformed group needed to explain their feelings and took on the stooge's mood. The other participants were not affected because they could explain their feelings. Schachter and Singer took this as support for their theory.

STUDENTS' ANSWERS

MEG June 1993 Module 4

Spend 23 minutes on this question

Source: Stress and Performance

Some athletes are now using psychological research to help improve their performance. The early research on performance and arousal was based on the Yerkes-Dodson Law. According to this law, we perform a task best when we are moderately aroused. (See diagram below). However, more recent research appears to suggest that arousal on its own does not determine performance.

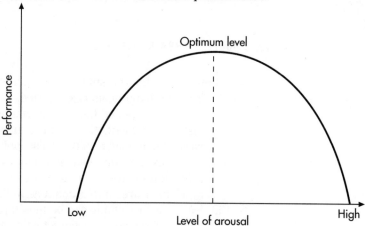

The Yerkes-Dodson law of arousal

Cognitive anxiety (which is a measure of a person's attitudes and feelings towards his/her performance) is also important in determining performance. In one study, 200 athletes completed questionnaires which measured both their psychological arousal (Does your heart race before the event?) and their cognitive anxiety (Were you worried about your performance?). The results seem to suggest that it is the **relationship** between cognitive anxiety and arousal which determines performance. If cognitive anxiety is low and the person is feeling confident, then a high level of physiological arousal does not harm performance. However, if cognitive anxiety is high and there is also a high level of arousal, then performance may be lowered because the person feels stressed.

[Adapted from *New Scientist*, 25/7/92]

(a) According to the text, what is meant by the term *cognitive anxiety*? [1]

Yes, Well read! 1/1

Cognitive anxiety is a measure of a person's attitudes and feelings towards his/her performance.

(b) According to the Yerkes-Dodson Law, what happens to performance when the person is over-aroused? [2]

2/2

The Yerkes-Dodson law states that over-arousal will lead to a decrease in performance. This would be more likely to happen if high arousal was seen as stressful.

(c) The psychologists used a questionnaire in this study. Give **one** advantage and **one** disadvantage of using this method to measure arousal [4]

nice and clear 4/4

advantage. Questionnaires are good for collecting large amounts of data relatively quickly and inexpensively.
disadvantage. People might be concerned about making a good impression in their answers so what they say they do and what they actually do are not the same.

(d) Devise **one** other question which could be used in a questionnaire to measure cognitive anxiety. [2]

2/2

'Do you feel confident just before an event is due to start?'

(e) The Yerkes-Dodson Law was based on laboratory experiments in which subjects were asked to repeat simple tasks. Why might this make it difficult to apply the research to **athletic** performance? [3]

Findings from lab. research may not tell us much about behaviour in real-life settings. This is because tasks in labs are done in highly controlled conditions and the feelings participants have about them may be different from the feelings they experience when taking part in a real athletic event.

❝ Yes, and the tasks are not the same either 2/3 ❞

(f) Describe **one** way in which a psychologist might help reduce the athlete's cognitive anxiety. [3]

One way would be to use systematic desensitisation. The athlete would draw up a list of anxiety producing situations and arrange them from least worrying to most worrying. They would also be trained in relaxation techniques. The athlete would then relax and imagine each situation on the list in turn starting with the least worrying and working up to the next when they were ready. Eventually they would be able to cope with the most worrying situation at the top of the list.

❝ 3/3 ❞

[*Total 15 marks*]
(MEG)

❝ 14/15 Good concise answers showing a good grasp of psychological ideas ❞

A Review Sheet for this chapter can be found on pp. 255–6.

CHAPTER 17

AGGRESSION

GETTING STARTED

This chapter is for MEG and SEG students. For both syllabuses you need to study aggression but the emphasis is quite different for the two boards. All students should begin by looking at the definitions of aggression and then select the relevant sections.

MEG students studying Option 4 need to look at differences in aggression between animals and humans. You should then go on to the section on cultural differences in aggression. The theories you need are the biological and ethological ones, although a quick look over the remainder of section 17.3 would give you a wider view.

If you are an SEG student studying section C you should pick up the chapter at the beginning of ethological theory and go on to the psychodynamic and learning approaches. You should finish the rest of the chapter with the sections on child-rearing styles and reduction of aggression.

To get the most from this chapter you should make sure you thoroughly understand the contents of chapter four. Many of the ideas raised there appear again here.

1. ANIMAL AND HUMAN AGGRESSION

2. CULTURE AND AGGRESSION

3. APPROACHES TO AGGRESSION

4. CHILD-REARING STYLES AND AGGRESSION

5. REDUCTION OF AGGRESSION

ESSENTIAL PRINCIPLES

DEFINITIONS OF AGGRESSION

Many psychologists make an important distinction between two types of aggression.

be able to define aggression

- **Hostile aggression**. The intention behind this type of aggression is to harm someone or something. It is an end in itself. In humans it is often referred to as **violence**.
- **Instrumental aggression**. This kind of aggression happens when a person wants to achieve a goal but something or someone else is in the way. The aggression is not purposely directed at the obstacle. It is simply a means to an end.

1 > ANIMAL AND HUMAN AGGRESSION

There are many reasons why humans and animals show aggression and these are often seen as important to their survival. They may, for example, use it to defend territory, establish dominance, retain a mate, protect and discipline their young, defend themselves or find food.

Lorenz (1966) and *Eibl-Eibesfeldt* (1979) claimed that animal and human aggression were not alike. They thought animals had ways of stopping aggression before it became too serious but humans were uniquely aggressive. Not everyone agrees with this idea.

When an animal is threatened by another there are many ways of responding:

- **escape**, e.g. run off, use distractions like 'playing dead' or making an unpleasant smell;
- **threaten in return** in the hope that the aggressor will back down, e.g. chimps might glare, stamp, swagger, throw rocks and wave branches;
- **ritualised fighting**, i.e. 'go through the motions' in a stereotyped way which is designed to avoid real harm or danger;
- **make appeasement gestures**, e.g. a dog might roll on to its back, a baboon might adopt a posture of sexual presentation. These actions seem to defuse the situation. Appeasement gestures are important because they avoid conflict and therefore reduce risk for the aggressor and the victim. Whether this is for the good of the individual animal or for the species is not clear.

It would seem that animals are very good at avoiding direct conflict but there are still examples of animal behaviour which do not fit this idea:

- *Goodall* (1978) reported on chimps killing chimps from other groups;
- males taking over a group of chimps may kill the infant chimps of other males.

Does human aggression show evidence of threat, ritual and appeasement gestures? It has been argued that very aggressive species (including humans) have very few appeasement gestures because, normally, they deal with aggression by *getting away*. This may no longer be an option because humans are very *crowded*. They find this *unpleasantly arousing* but *cannot escape*. There are, therefore, more opportunities to irritate each other but few chances of defusing aggression.

This view has been criticised on the grounds that:

- humans have many appeasement gestures, e.g. cringeing, begging, smiling, crying;
- humans also have rituals, e.g. football supporters may sing, chant, wave banners and hurl abuse without actually fighting with each other.

Lorenz has suggested that the reason why humans are so aggressive is not that there are no appeasement gestures. They have many effective ones and only a few people do not respond to them. The problem for humans is their *advanced technology* (e.g. bombs, weapons) which overcomes their instinctive ways of avoiding aggression (see the ethological approach later in this chapter).

2 > CULTURE AND AGGRESSION

Cross-cultural studies can help to tell us something about 'human nature'. If we find patterns in behaviour (such as aggression) which are similar regardless of environment we may be able to argue that it is a general human characteristic. However,

❝❝ see chapter two ❞❞

cross-cultural studies of aggression come down more on the side of Social Learning Theory (SLT) than anything else.

- You should look back to *Mead*'s (1935) studies of New Guinea tribes (the **Arapesh**, **Tchambuli** and **Mundugumor**) in the section on cross-cultural aspects of sex and gender in chapter nine, p. 107. The way in which children are reared in these cultures had an effect on their gender-role and, consequently, on how ready they were to show aggression.
- *Bronfenbrenner* (1970) compared **child-rearing patterns** in Russia and the USA. In the USA children were encouraged to show **individualism**, i.e. to look after themselves. But the message to these children was mixed. Aggression and self-ishness might be disapproved of in the family but children may see these things modelled on TV by people they admire. Also, as adolescents they may be encouraged to reject family values and 'challenge the system' or 'drop out'. Russian children received a clearer message that **cooperation** is valued as well as community spirit and being a good citizen. This was true for children, adolescents and adults. Selfishness and aggression were not encouraged.
- *Lambert* (1971) compared six cultures, i.e. the USA, Kenya, India, Okinawa, Mexico and the Philippines. He looked at parenting style, use of punishment, control of aggression and contact with extended family. He also observed children with their peers. The great variation he found between cultures suggests that learning experiences are far more important than human nature.

THE BIOLOGICAL APPROACH TO AGGRESSION

Biological explanations of aggression call on the role of the nervous system, hormones and genetics. These systems are related but we will separate them here.

The role of the nervous system

Various, more primitive, parts of the central nervous system (e.g. **the limbic system**) have been linked to aggression. Electrical stimulation of a region of the **hypothalamus** (part of the limbic system) can cause a cat to stalk and kill. A different part will cause the cat to hiss and act defensively. *Delgado* (1967) implanted electrodes in various regions of the hypothalamus of a monkey and a bull. He could cause the monkey to become more dominant and the bull to stop charging by stimulating these hypothalamic regions via the electrodes using a remote control device.

❝❝ primitive aggression centres? ❞❞

Hormones

Castration in many mammal species has been reported to reduce aggression, probably because production of the male hormone, **testosterone**, is stopped. Giving chickens extra testosterone raises their rank in the pecking order. The link between testosterone and aggression in human males is less clear.

Female reproductive hormones also play a role. In some bird species, egg-producing hormones increase aggression. In humans, pregnant women injected with extra progesterone had children who were rated more aggressive as adolescents (*Reinisch* 1981).

Genetics

Ebert and Hyde (1976) found they could create strains of aggressive or non-aggressive female house mice through **selective breeding** which suggests a genetic basis to aggression.

In humans **XYY** males turn up slightly more often in prison populations than in non-prison populations. This has sometimes been taken to indicate that these people are 'supermales' and more aggressive than XY males. However, there is no evidence that XYY males are more aggressive than XY males or that they have more testosterone. XYY males generally have slightly lower IQs and it has been suggested that they crop up more often in prisons because they are not very good at avoiding arrest and conviction!

It is generally thought that human males are more aggressive than human females. The reason for this is not clear. It could be due to genetic differences or to different learning experiences.

THE ETHOLOGICAL APPROACH TO AGGRESSION

Konrad Lorenz (1966) suggested that aggression in animals and humans is instinctive. His approach is often called a **psychohydraulic model**. This model pictures aggressive energy as constantly renewing itself and being stored in a kind of *reservoir*. Excess energy must be released from time to time and this normally happens when aggression is called for in the course of everyday life. If there is no opportunity to release excess energy, it may spill over and show itself either as an *unprovoked outburst* or as a **vacuum activity** in which the animal goes through the motions of being aggressive for no obvious reason.

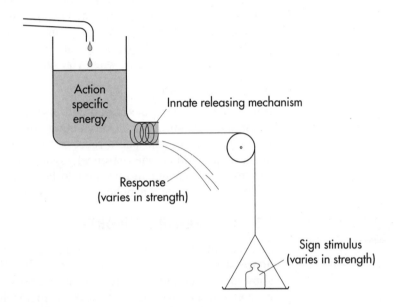

Figure 17.1 Lorenz's psychohydraulic model of instinctive behaviour

Given that aggressive energy must be expressed, animals have evolved ways of protecting members of their own species from harm. This is especially important in species that could easily kill each other. They have developed **appeasement gestures**, **rituals** and other **stereotyped behaviour patterns** to protect themselves. Lorenz argued that *human language* and *tool use* evolved very rapidly. This meant that they could be very clever in devising ways of harming each other. Sadly, they did *not* evolve ways of defusing aggression at the same rate and so human aggression is potentially deadly and a threat to the survival of the whole species. Criticisms of this view include:

- humans do seem to have *some* appeasement gestures and rituals;
- findings from animals cannot always be transferred to humans;
- there is no physiological evidence for a psychohydraulic system;
- there is *increasing evidence* of killing between members of certain animal species;
- human aggression is more complex and varied than much animal aggression;
- our ability to use language may save us from destruction – wars can be successfully settled through negotiation, truces and treaties.

THE PSYCHODYNAMIC APPROACH TO AGGRESSION

❝❝ Freud can explain many aspects of behaviour ❞❞

Freud's (1856–1939) psychoanalytic theory is an example of the **psychodynamic approach**. Freud, like Lorenz, saw aggression as **instinctive** and operating according to the **psychohydraulic model**. Freud thought we have life-preserving, reproductive instincts (**Eros**) and aggressive, destructive instincts (**Thanatos** – the 'death instinct'). Like Lorenz, Freud believed we must express our aggressive instinct from time to time. If we do not (repression), we run the risk of being destructive. (Some people may turn this excess aggression on themselves and become depressed or suicidal.) Criticisms of this approach include:

- the idea of a death instinct is not widely accepted;
- unaggressive people do not always become depressed or suicidal;
- there are many ideas in Freud's theory which are difficult to test because they are not directly observable;

- Freud's theory was based on clinical case studies of neurotic adults and may not be applicable to other kinds of people.

THE LEARNING THEORY (LT) APPROACH TO AGGRESSION

(You should make sure you have understood chapter four to get the most from this section.)

LT sees aggression as being learned by the same processes as any other learned behaviour:

Classical conditioning

Aggression may be seen as an automatic response (UCR) to a threatening stimulus (UCS). Certain neutral stimuli may become **cues** for aggression (CSs) through being associated with UCSs. For example, someone might threaten you (UCS) which makes you feel aggressive (UCR). If they are waving a gun about at the same time, the gun could become a CS so that, when you see a gun in the future, you feel aggressive.

Operant conditioning

Aggressive behaviour is **shaped** and **maintained** by its consequences, i.e. **reinforcement** and **punishment**. All very young children seem to show some aggression and how their parents and peers react to this will affect how likely they are to show it again. This could be one reason why males seem to be more aggressive than females. Aggressive behaviour in males could be seen as more fitting so it is more often reinforced. In females it may be disapproved of or ignored.

SOCIAL LEARNING THEORY

SLT accepts the importance of **conditioning** but **observation** and **imitation** of aggressive models is also important. In his **Bobo doll studies**, *Bandura* (1965) showed that children readily absorb aggressive behaviour from certain kinds of models but are more likely to show it themselves if they saw the model praised or experiencing no unpleasant consequence.

An important extension to SLT is the role of models on TV and in other media in influencing aggression. We do not yet know for sure what the effects of violence in the media are. There is much evidence to show that more aggressive children watch more violent TV but this is only a correlation. It does not tell us the reason for the link.

Criticisms of the LT and SLT approach include:

- the biological side to aggression may be played down too much;
- there are objections to applying a learning theory based on animal research to humans;
- LT in particular does not pay enough attention to people's thought processes. SLT is better in this respect.

FRUSTRATION AND AGGRESSION

Dollard et al. (1939) hypothesised that aggression was a very likely response to frustration. This idea neatly links Freudian and LT approaches. If we are blocked in our *instinctive need* to express aggression, *frustration* results. This is uncomfortable. We need to find an *outlet* for the aggression so it may be *displaced* on to a *scapegoat*. Which scapegoat we choose may be the result of *learning*.

4 **CHILD-REARING STYLES AND AGGRESSION**

A number of studies (e.g. *Sears et al.* in the 1950s) have identified types of child-rearing style which we can call **democratic**, **authoritarian** and **permissive**. How do these link with aggression?

In 1967, *Coopersmith* studied 1,700 10–12-year-old middle-class boys. His main interest was in the origins of **self-esteem** but he also looked at **child-rearing styles** and tried to link them to other aspects of the boys' *behaviour* (e.g. aggression). As other psychologists have done before and since, Coopersmith categorised parents as follows:

- **Democratic parents** tended to have sons with *high* self-esteem. Such parents were warm, accepting and interested in the child. They made clear rules and enforced them fairly, consistently and with discussion. Aggression was *low* in this group.

- **Authoritarian parents** tended to have sons with *low* self-esteem. These parents were cold and rejecting and used harsh discipline (sometimes inconsistently). They expected obedience and no arguments. Their sons tended to be aggressive but not in front of the parents!
- **Permissive parents** also had sons with *low* self-esteem. These parents were not necessarily cold but did not take a great deal of interest in the child. They occasionally stepped in with inconsistent and rather harsh discipline. Aggression was *high* in their sons.

Although Coopersmith's research focused on self-esteem his findings about aggression are useful here. He noted that all children can be very aggressive in the early years but become less so as they grow older. Boys with authoritarian or permissive parents, however, continued to be aggressive (often towards objects rather than people). There are a number of possible reasons for this:

- as SLT would predict, authoritarian and permissive parents act as *aggressive models* and the child learns to be aggressive by observing and imitating them;
- the child comes to regard aggressive behaviour as the *norm* for adults (SLT again);
- the child of permissive parents never learns to lose its early high levels of aggression – it finds aggression continues to *pay off* (LT);
- the child of permissive parents finds aggression is a good way of getting at least some attention – the fact that the reinforcing attention is on a **variable ratio schedule** only makes matters worse (LT);
- the parents' behaviour and the child's own low esteem are *frustrating* – the child needs to *displace* its resulting anger on to something else, i.e. a *scapegoat* (psychodynamic theory).

Look also at the earlier section on culture and aggression.

5 > REDUCTION OF AGGRESSION

Recommendations about reducing aggression depend on which theory we accept.

THE BIOLOGICAL APPROACH

To control behaviour on this level, we would need to carry out surgery on the brain, inject people with hormones or breed them selectively. Clearly there are serious practical and ethical problems with all of these!

THE ETHOLOGICAL APPROACH

66 ethological ideas can work for humans 99

If we accept that humans do respond to **appeasement gestures** one useful application of this approach would be to train people in how to use them to help defuse a situation. People working in potentially violent situations, e.g. the police, prison service or psychiatric units, can learn how to use *speech* and *body language* to reduce the risk of a threat against them turning into violence. Another recommendation would be to encourage discussion as much as possible so that we can use our *advanced intellectual powers* to overcome our weak control of our biological aggression.

THE PSYCHODYNAMIC APPROACH

Early childhood would be the place to begin controlling aggression. The child would need to be reared in a way which ensured the development of a *well-balanced* id, ego and superego. Also, when aggressive urges do threaten to escape, children should be encouraged to find ways of **sublimating** them, e.g. through sport or of **displacing** them on to other targets. People can also off-load aggression by watching others be aggressive, e.g. on TV or in sport. They can express aggressive fantasies in stories or dreams. Far from being a bad thing, Freud thought that watching such things as sport and violence served to protect people from destroying each other.

LEARNING THEORY

An LT approach based on classical conditioning would recommend *the removal of cues* (CSs), such as guns, that would be likely to trigger aggression. Operant conditioning theorists would recommend the use of *reward* and *punishment* to control aggressive behaviour but these need to be used with care:

- **Punishment** should reduce aggression but often has the opposite effect. It may work in the short term but it can make the punished person angry, frustrated and resentful. It models aggression as a way to control others and, on its own, does not teach a person what they should have done instead. There is some evidence that occasional, well-deserved punishment given to a child by a parent can work well if their relationship is a loving and secure one.
- **Rewarding non-aggressive behaviour** is a better alternative to punishment. The idea is to give lots of attention to children when they are being good and to ignore aggressive behaviour as much as possible (unless harm is being done). Eventually, the child will be spending so much time being good that they have little opportunity to be aggressive. *Brown and Elliot* (1965) successfully applied these ideas in a class of nursery schoolchildren. With older children a token economy can have the same effect.

SOCIAL LEARNING THEORY

In Bandura's experiments we saw that aggressive models who are praised or experience no unpleasant consequence are more likely to be imitated than punished models. It is important to understand that children who saw a model punished were *no less aggressive* than children *who saw no model at all*. It therefore seems more important to avoid showing children models who are rewarded for aggression rather than to show them models who are punished.

SLT would also recommend that we provide **non-aggressive models**, especially those who show us how to deal with aggression in less destructive ways. **Assertiveness training** tries to achieve this by teaching people how to deal with their own and others' aggression in a way which leaves everyone feeling OK.

FRUSTRATION AND AGGRESSION

There will always be frustrations in life. In fact, a life without frustration could be very frustrating! The recommendation from this approach would be to *learn acceptable ways* of expressing the aggression which sometimes arises from frustration.

BUILDING EMPATHY

This has not been mentioned before. It is based on the idea that people are aggressive towards others because of **deindividuation**. This means that either the aggressor or the victim might lose their identity in some way, for example through being in a big crowd or wearing a uniform and this allows aggression to occur. *Feshbach* (1971) thought that people find it hard to be aggressive to another unless that person has been 'dehumanised', thus policemen may be lumped together as 'pigs' and young men as 'thugs'. *Feshbach and Feshbach* (1969) developed a way of teaching primary schoolchildren to empathise with others more (i.e. see things from the other's point of view). They did role play and had practice in 'reading' others' emotions. This led to decreases in aggressive behaviour. In the real world, bringing people together to discuss their differences might increase empathy because it involves personal contact and better understanding.

CONCLUSION

Aggression in humans and animals is very complex. All the theories described have something to offer. Together they will probably give us a fairly complete picture of this difficult area.

EXAMINATION QUESTIONS

SEG sample paper (Foundation Tier) Section C

Spend 35 minutes on this question

(a) What is aggression? [4]

(b) Outline **two** different psychological explanations of aggression. [16]

(c) From what you have learned in psychology, describe **one** way in which aggression might be reduced. [10]

[Total 30 marks]
(SEG)

TUTOR ANSWER

SEG sample paper (Foundation Tier) Section C

(a) Psychologists often distinguish between two types of aggression. Hostile aggression (violence) is intended to hurt someone or something. Instrumental aggression is when we incidentally harm someone or something because it gets in our way when we are trying to achieve something.

(b) Konrad Lorenz suggested that aggression in animals and humans is instinctive and operates according to the psychohydraulic model. This means aggressive energy builds up constantly and needs to be expressed from time to time. Usually, this will happen in the course of everyday life through work or physical activity, but if it does not, there is a danger that it may explode in an outburst of aggression. In animals, excess aggressive energy may be expressed as a vacuum activity in which it is acted out for no apparent reason.

To protect themselves from harming each other, members of the same species have evolved ways of dealing with aggression between themselves. They may use appeasement gestures, rituals and other stereotyped patterns of behaviour to put an end to a conflict. A dog, for example, may roll over to show its opponent that it does not intend to fight any more. Lorenz argued that humans' ability to plan, use tools and make weapons has evolved faster than their ability to defuse aggression. Consequently, the human race is a danger to itself and must find ways of coping with aggression if it is to avoid wiping itself out.

Sigmund Freud agreed with Lorenz that aggression is instinctive. He also agreed with the idea of the psychohydraulic model. Freud thought that we have life-preserving, reproductive instincts (Eros) but we also have destructive, aggressive instincts (Thanatos). We have no choice but to express our aggressive instincts from time to time. Mostly, we do this successfully in everyday life as explained for Lorenz's theory. Other ways of expressing aggression are through defence mechanisms. The most successful of these is sublimation whereby we are overtly aggressive in an acceptable way, e.g. through watching or taking part in contact sports or watching aggressive TV. We could also repress aggression (push it into the unconscious), but it may break free if we repress too much and result in an aggressive outburst. Alternatively, it could turn inwards and be self-destructive making us depressed or suicidal. Aggression could also be expressed by displacing it on to an innocent scapegoat. This means that we find an innocent and powerless target on which to vent our aggression.

(c) One way to reduce aggression would be to apply the Learning Theory approach. This leads to a number of ways of reducing aggression depending on how it has been learned. When aggression is learned through classical conditioning, previously neutral stimuli have become associated with stimuli (UCSs) that naturally provoke aggression (UCR). The neutral stimuli become CSs capable of setting off a conditioned response without the presence of the UCS. Such aggression can be controlled by ensuring that CSs likely to trigger aggression (e.g. guns) are removed from view.

If aggression were learned through operant conditioning, it could be reduced by controlling the consequences of behaviour. Reward of non-aggressive behaviour should help it to increase, leaving the person less time or incentive to be aggressive. Punishment, if used in a warm and secure relationship, can lead to a decrease in aggression but it needs to be used with care. It provides aggressive models to the punished person, showing them that it is a way to get what you want from others. It also leads to negative emotions in the punished person that could make matters worse. On its own it does not teach the person how they should have behaved.

Social Learning Theory extends traditional Learning Theory to add that observational learning from role-models could also be used to reduce aggression. People tend to observe and imitate models who are important to them in some way. If they see these models behaving non-aggressively they should imitate them. The model should practise what it preaches as SLT has shown that consistency between expressed views and behaviour is important. We tend to observe and imitate what models do more than what they say.

STUDENT'S ANSWER

MEG specimen paper 4 (Higher), Option 4

Spend 35 minutes on this question

Source

Robert: Did you see that television programme last night about this boy called Ken who got really aggressive every time he ate crisps? He was just sitting in a chair quietly, and someone gave him a crisp and he went crazy!

Jackie: What? Just one crisp? I don't believe it. I reckon he must have been watching lots of those violent videos.

Robert: Honestly! Apparently it's something to do with potatoes. A chemical in them makes him get aggressive. He can't help it.

(a) What is the problem with basing a whole theory of aggression on the case of Ken? [2]

❝2/2❞

Ken is just one example of a boy who watches TV. He could be unusual so his case could not be applied to anyone else.

(b) Outline psychological evidence that suggests that specific parts of the brain are involved in aggression. [4]

❝good point needing expansion 3/4❞

Most research into brain areas and aggression has been done on animals for ethical reasons so this may not tell us much about human aggression. The hypothalamus is part of the older limbic system in the brain. If electrodes are put into the hypothalamus of a cat and stimulated it can be caused to kill a mouse. Bulls can be made to stop charging in the same way.

(c) Psychosurgery is the attempt to change a person's behaviour or personality through operations on the brain.
 (i) Outline one type of psychosurgery and say what it tries to achieve. [2]

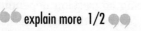 **❝explain more 1/2❞**

Limbic leucotomy has been used to help people with emotional problems.

(ii) Outline two ethical problems with psychosurgery. [2]

take care with clarity
2/2

People don't understand much about how the brain works and psychosurgery is irreversible. There is the ethical problem of getting people to consent to something they don't understand.

(d) What have studies of animal aggression told us about human aggression? [8]

[*Total 18 marks*]
(MEG)

6/8

Lorenz thought that aggression in animals and humans was instinctive and that, if it wasn't expressed, it could boil over. Animals have evolved appeasement gestures and rituals to protect themselves from harming or killing each other, e.g. a lion might roll on its back when it is losing a fight. Some people think humans had appeasement gestures and rituals but lost them. However they are very clever and can plan imaginative ways to kill each other. Other people think humans do have appeasement gestures and should learn to use them to stop aggression before it gets serious. Criticisms of this approach are that findings from animals cannot be transferred to humans and that animals do sometimes kill each other in spite of having appeasement gestures and rituals.

14/18 Good answers. Go for accuracy and detail in (d)

A Review Sheet for this chapter can be found on p. 257.

THE ETHOLOGICAL APPROACH

GETTING STARTED

This chapter is mainly for MEG students studying option 4 but SEG students might find it useful to look over the material to be sure that they are aware of the influence of inborn characteristics.

Ethology is generally defined as the study of animal behaviour in its natural environment. The ethological ideas outlined here stem mainly from a group of European ethologists working in the first half of the twentieth century. Konrad Lorenz and Niko Tinbergen are the key figures. Their influence on psychology has been as important as that of the Behaviourists. Both approaches studied animal behaviour but they did this in quite different ways and for different reasons. Along with the Behaviourists, ethologists have contributed much to a newer branch of psychology known as comparative psychology which seeks to compare different species to shed light on behaviour.

1. THE ETHOLOGICAL APPROACH

2. INNATE AND LEARNED BEHAVIOUR

3. IMPRINTING

4. EVALUATION OF THE ETHOLOGICAL APPROACH

ESSENTIAL PRINCIPLES

1 ▷ THE ETHOLOGICAL APPROACH

This approach:

● grew from the work of the early ethologists, such as *Lorenz* and *Tinbergen*;
● emphasises the importance of *observing* animals behaving in their *natural habitat*;
● now incorporates some *experimentation* with animals;
● has given rise to *human ethology* where humans are studied in their natural habitats – this consists mostly of observations of children;
● merged with **comparative psychology** in the 1950s and began looking at the *nature* and *functions* of behaviour between species, how it *evolved* within the species and how it *develops within the individual*.

Lea (1984) lists four applications of ethology:

● **practical** – e.g. in helping endangered species to survive. Understanding the importance of particular kinds of early experience, such as imprinting, to the survival of chicks hatched in captivity for release into the wild has improved survival rates;
● **methodological** – in developing and improving observational research methods;
● **transfer of ideas** about the behaviour of one species to another (e.g. the idea of personal space);
● **transfer of research findings** from one species to another, e.g. imprinting research.

2 ▷ INNATE AND LEARNED BEHAVIOUR

There is much debate over whether there is such a thing as truly innate (inherited) or purely learned behaviour. Few psychologists would now agree with the idea of **tabula rasa**, that is, the idea that our minds are like blank slates ready to be written on by experience. As we will see, innate tendencies often affect learning and experience often affects an apparently innate behaviour pattern. In other words, they *interact*.

INHERITED BEHAVIOUR

Early ethologists talked of **instinct** as innate behaviour but this term is not often used now because it is so difficult to define. However, behaviour that could be thought of as innate:

● has *evolved gradually*;
● has been *changed* by **natural selection** to fit the environment;
● is especially useful to animals with *short life spans* and *little parental care*.

Lea (1984) lists several characteristics of inherited behaviour:

● it is **stereotyped**, that is, it always appears in the same form;
● it is **universal** – all members of the same species show it;
● it is **independent of experience** – it appears regardless of experience or contact with others of the same species;
● it is **ballistic** – once it has been set in motion, it carries on unchanged;
● it shows **singleness of purpose** – it is never shown in other contexts;
● it is **triggered by a known stimulus**.

Such behaviour became known among ethologists as fixed action patterns or **FAPs**. An example of such behaviour was given by *Eibl-Eibesfeldt* (1970). He reared squirrels on a liquid diet and then gave them some nuts. First they ate their fill and then they went through a ritual as if they were 'burying' the nuts in their cages. It looked as if they were digging, covering the nuts and then stamping earth down over them.

Sign stimuli and super releasers

Tinbergen called stimuli such as nuts **sign stimuli**. He suggested they activate an innate releasing mechanism (**IRM**) which releases action specific energy (**ASE**) and sets off an FAP. Lorenz likened this to a kind of *flush toilet*. In response to a stimulus, the handle is activated (the IRM), water (ASE) is released and the flush happens (FAP). (You may have encountered this idea in the ethological explanation of aggression, under the title of **the psychohydraulic model**, see **Fig**. 17.1.)

Tinbergen also noticed an FAP in a male stickleback who, during the mating season, would go through an aggressive display triggered by a red stimulus. Tinbergen experimented with different kinds of stimuli and found that the strongest reaction was to a fish shape with a red patch. (Male sticklebacks have red patches on their throats during the mating season which seems to enable them to tell male rivals from plain brown females.)

Tinbergen and Perdeck (1950) also tried to find out what it was about other sign stimuli that was important. They used herring gull chicks who seem to respond to some aspect of the parent gull's beak by pecking at it. This, in turn, stimulates the parent bird to regurgitate food. The natural beak pattern is yellow with a red spot. Using different combinations of spots and colours, it was found that the most important aspects of the stimulus were redness and contrast between the spot and its background.

Movement could also be an important aspect of a sign stimulus. Lorenz and Tinbergen used a bird silhouette that looked like a hawk if it moved in one direction or a goose if it moved in another. Turkey chicks would freeze and cower in response to the hawk but not to the goose.

Other researchers have *exaggerated* the properties of sign stimuli to observe the effect. Oystercatcher eggs are similar in marking to herring gull eggs but gulls' eggs are twice the size. Oystercatchers respond much more vigorously to the larger egg and brood it rather than their own. Exaggerated sign stimuli like these have been called **super releasers**.

FAPs are not always released in the presence of a sign stimulus. A stickleback will not challenge another male unless it is on its own territory. In birds, hormonal changes to do with the seasons may encourage FAPs designed to attract a mate only when they are in the mating season.

LEARNED BEHAVIOUR

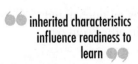
you must have done chapter four to understand this

The amount of behaviour which we could think of as inherited decreases in higher animals who live relatively longer, have more parental care and who may need to adapt in order to survive. In other parts of this guide (especially chapter four), we have already encountered the following kinds of learning:

- classical conditioning (see *Pavlov*);
- operant conditioning (see *Skinner*);
- insight learning (see *Kohler*);
- learning set (see *Harlow*);
- latent learning (see *Tolman*).

All the types of learning listed above have been shown in animals and humans. For humans we can add **SLT** to the list.

THE INTERACTION BETWEEN INHERITED AND LEARNED BEHAVIOUR

One trial learning

inherited characteristics influence readiness to learn

This is another kind of learning which both animals and humans show. It is a kind of **classical conditioning** and is best illustrated with the example of food aversion. *Seligman* (1971) described the Sauce Béarnaise phenomenon. He had eaten Sauce Béarnaise (CS) just before he became ill with stomach flu (UCS). The sickness that resulted (UCR) became linked to the innocent sauce and after one learning trial, Seligman developed an aversion to Sauce Béarnaise.

One trial learning is a good way of demonstrating the importance of both inheritance and experience in learned behaviour. Seligman suggested that some kinds of learning are very rapid because we are **biologically prepared** to make certain links. Animals and humans who eat something which makes them ill but who live to tell the tale would do well not to try the food again. In Seligman's case he knew the sauce had not made him ill but he could not convince his body of that. The connection had been made. *Garcia and Koelling* (1966) fed rats flavoured water and sounded a buzzer and followed these with either sickness or electric shock. Rats associated the water with the sickness and the tone with the shock.

Instinctive drift

Breland and Breland (1961) also showed how inherited tendencies can affect learning. They were using **operant conditioning** to train animals to do tricks that could be filmed and used in advertisements. One such trick required a pig or a racoon to put a large coin in a piggy bank. Pigs are normally very fast learners but in this case were untrainable. The coin encouraged them to root it along the ground as they would if they were foraging for food. Racoons were equally hard to train. They appeared to wash the coin by rubbing it between their paws which is the way they would treat their natural food. In both species, inherited behaviour patterns were impossible to overcome by conditioning. Their behaviour drifted back to what was instinctive.

Critical periods and sensitive periods

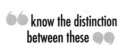
know the distinction
between these

These are a special example of how inherited tendencies and experience come together to affect behaviour. A critical period is a time in an animal's life when it seems particularly open to a certain kind of learning or experience. This openness seems to be brought on by *maturation*, i.e. when the individual has reached a certain point in their development. After a period of time, it switches off and the individual is no longer able to benefit from the relevant kind of experience. The effects of experience during the critical period were thought to be *irreversible*. A critical period has been likened to a *window* which opens briefly, and once only, to let something in before it closes forever.

Nowadays, few people would accept the idea of truly critical periods. They see such an idea as too rigid. Much research has shown that critical periods can be extended so the term **sensitive period**, which is more flexible, is preferred instead.

Examples of behaviour which might develop fully through the right kind of experience in a sensitive period are:

- **Bird song**. *Marler and Tamura* (1964) thought there was a period between 30 and 100 days of age when white-crowned sparrows would learn from hearing the adult bird's song. (Birds even learn *regional dialects* in this period.)
- **Language**. *Curtiss* (1977) reported the case of **Genie**, a girl who had been neglected and virtually isolated until she was discovered at the age of 13. Genie never learned more than a few words which seems to suggest the importance of a period of exposure to language at least before adolescence.
- **Binocular vision**. There is some evidence to suggest that we learn to process binocular input at a particular time in our early lives. It is important that young children with squints have them corrected in time to benefit from this period.
- **Attachment**. The idea that there might be a sensitive period for forming attachment bonds to others has been discussed in chapter seven. Also see **imprinting** next.

3 ▷ IMPRINTING

this was important in
Bowlby's work on
attachment

Imprinting was first defined as a special type of learning which led to a young animal forming a lasting attachment to its parent. It is an especially good example of the importance of the critical (or sensitive) period. The term has been expanded to cover more types showing its importance in developing social behaviour:

- **filial imprinting** – the early attachment of the very young animal to its parent;
- **sexual imprinting** – exposure to others of the same species resulting in sexual behaviour towards them when mature;
- **habitat imprinting** – learning to recognise 'home ground' in order to return to it, perhaps to spawn or mate.

Lorenz (1935) found that young birds, such as goslings, had a strong tendency to follow a moving object in the first hours after hatching. After a while, they would become attached to it and prefer it to any other. Most often the object would be the parent bird but, if the parent bird were not there, it could be any moving object. Lorenz easily succeeded in getting goslings to imprint on him. He thought imprinting had the following characteristics:

- it occurs during a **critical period**. Readiness to imprint in goslings increased steeply from hatching, peaking between 12 and 17 hours of age. It then dropped until it disappeared by 32 hours when it was replaced by a fear of any moving object other than the imprinted one;
- it is **irreversible**;
- it is **long lasting**.

This apparent readiness to learn so rapidly has obvious survival importance for the individual. Filial imprinting ensures it will stay near its parent so that it can be protected by it and learn from it. Habitat and sexual imprinting ensure it will find a place where there are others of its own species with whom it can mate.

Evaluation of Lorenz's assumptions about imprinting

- **The critical period**. As suggested earlier, the term **sensitive period** may be preferable to critical period. *Sluckin* (1965) kept chicks in isolation or very unstimulating environments and found they could imprint long after the critical period should have been over. He said the sensitive period is when the young animal is most likely to learn but there is not a rigid genetic time-switch as suggested by the critical period idea.
- **Irreversibility**. *Boakes and Panter* (1985) showed filial imprinting could be reversed if the imprinted young bird was prevented from escaping an object it feared. It has proved harder to reverse sexual imprinting where birds have imprinted on other species.
- **Long lasting**. Filial imprinting does seem to last until the bird reaches adulthood. Sexual imprinting seems to last even longer.

In chapter four you can see how the idea of imprinting was borrowed by people such as *Bowlby* (1965) who argued for a sensitive period for attachment between human infants and their mothers. Many psychologists suggest that the early years are vitally important for all kinds of later development. While early experiences probably are important, it would be pessimistic to think that bad ones were irreversible.

4 ▷ **EVALUATION OF THE ETHOLOGICAL APPROACH**

Some good points about the approach include:

- the ethological approach has a number of *useful applications* (see Lea earlier in this chapter);
- it has emphasised the importance of *observational methods*;
- it has emphasised the importance of observing behaviour in the *animal's natural environment* rather than in highly controlled, and possibly artificial, settings;
- it has helped to add to our *understanding* of both human and animal behaviour.

Criticisms tend to centre on the underlying ideas and the way in which some of the research findings have been interpreted:

- Some critics think Lorenz and Tinbergen *over-emphasised* the role of *innate factors* in behaviour. As we saw earlier, many behaviour patterns seem to be acquired as a result of both inherited influences and experience. A further example is the finding that gull chicks improve with practice in the accuracy of pecking at their parents' beaks which, again, shows the role of experience.
- There is *no physiological evidence* for a psychohydraulic system or for ASE and IRMs. At the moment, these are just useful ways of picturing how the system works.
- *Schneirla* (1965) doubted whether the hawk–goose experiment showed an innate freezing reaction to the hawk shape. He thought the *sudden onset* of the stimulus in the hawk condition could be responsible instead and argued a long triangular shape presented base first would have the same effect.
- The psychohydraulic model would predict that ASE must be discharged for an instinctive urge to be satisfied. A stickleback, for example would need to get rid of the ASE stored to drive the behaviour which lures a female to his nesting site. However, seeing new-laid eggs alone is sufficient to satisfy the instinct and *no energy needs to be discharged* which is contrary to the model's prediction.

EXAMINATION QUESTIONS

MEG June 1994 Module 6

Spend 18 minutes on this question

Fixed action patterns and sign stimuli

One well-known example of a fixed action pattern (FAP), discovered by Tinbergen, was the begging response of the herring gull chick. The chicks obtain food by pecking at the tip of the parent's bill. The parent then regurgitates (brings up) the food it has collected and the chick is able to feed. The adult herring gull has a white head and a yellow bill with a red spot on it.

Tinbergen wanted to discover which features of the parent's head acted as a sign stimulus for the begging response. He used a series of cardboard models of the adult's head. First, he tried varying the colour of the spot, so that all the models had a yellow bill but the colour of the spot changed.

He then varied the colour of the bill itself (without a spot). The number of times the chicks pecked at each model was counted. The results are shown in the graphs below.

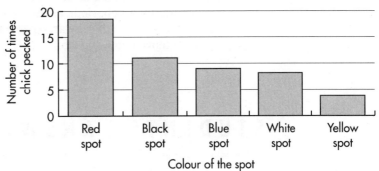

How colour of the spot affected pecking

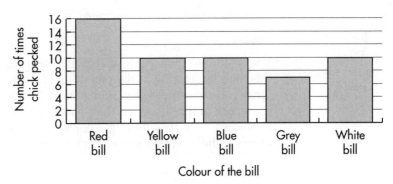

How colour of the bill affected pecking

(a) What was the aim of Tinbergen's study? [1]
(b) Use the graphs to answer the following questions.
  (i) How many times did the chicks respond to the blue bill? [1]
  (ii) Which spot colour was least effective in getting the chicks to respond? [1]
(c) What could Tinbergen conclude from this study? [2]
(d) (i) give **one** characteristic of a fixed action pattern. [1]
  (ii) Describe the fixed action pattern (or sign stimulus) of **one other animal** that you have studied. [2]
(d) (i) Why was it helpful for Tinbergen to study animals in a laboratory environment? [2]
  (ii) Why do other psychologists prefer to study animals in their natural environment? [2]

[Total 12 marks]
(MEG)

TUTOR ANSWER

MEG June 1994 Module 6

(a) The aim was to find out exactly which characteristics of the adult's head acted as a sign stimulus for the begging response.
(b) (i) 10 times
  (ii) Yellow.

(c) In the spot tests the red spot was the most effective colour for inducing pecking. In the bill colour tests, the red bill encouraged most pecking which is unexpected as the parent's beak is yellow.

(d) Once the FAP has been set in motion, it carries on unchanged to the end, i.e. it is ballistic.

(e) (i) In laboratory conditions, precise control of all variables can be taken so that the experimenter can be more confident about what exactly is influencing the bird's behaviour.

(ii) Behaviour studied in the animal's natural habitat is more true to life and natural than behaviour in the lab. (Some psychologists would also argue that it is more ethically acceptable to leave the animal in its natural habitat than move it into the lab.)

STUDENT'S ANSWER

MEG specimen paper 4 (Higher), Option 4 Biological and Comparative Approach

Spend 25 minutes on this question

Source

Young herring gulls eat food that has been regurgitated by the parent gull. They get this food by pecking at the parent gull's beak. A study by Hailman investigated this further. He used newly-hatched gulls and cardboard models. He found that the young gulls peck at a red spot on their parents' beak. They would only peck the spot if the cardboard beak was moving from side to side in the same way as the parent gull moves its head when it comes back to the nest.

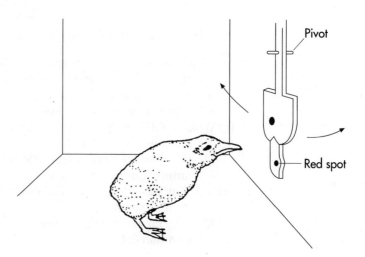

From: Nicky Hayes, *A First Course in Psychology*

The moving red spot seemed to be the trigger for the pecking behaviour.

The young herring gulls are born able to do this, but get more accurate with practice.

(a) *A fixed action pattern* is a stereotyped behaviour that is usually a response to a simple stimulus (a sign stimulus). What is the example of a sign stimulus in the Source? [1]

 1/1

Moving red spot.

(b) What evidence is there in the Source that learning is involved in the herring gulls' feeding behaviour? [1]

1/1

They got better with practice.

(c) Why would it have been important to have a cardboard model of a beak that was moving from side to side but did not have a red spot on it? [2]

66 explain more 1/2 99

To act as a control.

(d) Outline one other example that you have studied of a fixed action pattern triggered off by a sign stimulus. [4]

66 add detail and jargon 2/4 99

When a bird called an oystercatcher sees an egg outside the nest it reaches out, hooks the egg with its beak and rolls it back into the nest.

(e) Hailman's study took place in laboratory conditions.
  (i) Give **one** disadvantage of this. [1]

66 1/1 99

The bird may not behave naturally in a strange place.

  (ii) Give **one** advantage of studying animals in laboratory conditions. [1]

66 1/1 99

The experimenter has more control over what happens to the bird.

(f) Instinctive behaviour is inborn (innate). Give **one** advantage to an animal of having a behaviour that is innate. [2]

66 good point and example 2/2 99

Innate behaviour can help an animal to survive, e.g. turkey chicks crouch and freeze when they see a hawk shape overhead.

[*Total 12 marks*]
(MEG)

66 9/12 Good concise answers here with a little more detail needed in places 99

A Review Sheet for this chapter can be found on p. 258.

REVIEW SHEET (CHAPTER 2)

1 What is the main aim of observation?

2 What is the difference between inter- and intra-observer reliability?

3 Distinguish between naturalistic and controlled observation.

4 For each of the following methods give one research example and one strength and one weakness of the method:

	Example	Strength	Weakness
Non-participant observation			
Participant observation			
Case study			
Psychometric method			

5 In what two main ways are survey data collected?

6 Between what two values does a correlation coefficient vary?

7 Which is stronger, a correlation coefficient of +0.5 or -0.6?

8 Give a general definition of an experiment.

9 Identify two differences between a natural experiment and a laboratory experiment.

10 If we were investigating the effect of teaching technique on students' exam results, what would be the IV and the DV?

11 Distinguish between the cross-sectional method and the longitudinal method.

12 Identify two strengths and two weaknesses of cross-cultural research.

13 What three qualities does a good psychometric test have?

_____
_____
_____

14 Give three reasons why psychologists carry out animal research.

_____
_____
_____

15 Give two objections to animal research in psychology.

_____
_____

16 Ten ethical guidelines for research with humans are given in the text. Here are the initial letters. Fill in the appropriate word and give a brief comment on each one.

Initial letter	Comment
R	
C	
D	
D	
W	
C	
P	
O	
A	
C	

17 Identify three ethical concerns relating to research with non-human animals.

_____
_____
_____

REVIEW SHEET (CHAPTER 3)

1 What do psychologists mean by the term population?

_____

_____

2 Imagine you wanted to study moral reasoning in students. How would you define your population?

_____

_____

3 Name and define two sampling techniques.

_____

_____

4 From a population of 500, would a sample of 50 be sufficient? Explain your answer.

_____

_____

5 Provide a research hypothesis for the following:
  ● a study to see whether fast readers learn more than slow readers;

_____

  ● a study to see if income and happiness are related;

_____

  ● a study to see if a milky drink before bed helps children sleep better.

_____

6 Provide null hypotheses for each of the three examples in question 5.

_____

_____

_____

7 Suggest ways of operationalising the following variables:
  ● reading speed _____
  ● amount of learning _____
  ● income _____
  ● happiness_____
  ● milky drink _____
  ● quality of sleep._____

8 What is a 'control group' and what is its purpose?

_____

_____

9 Name the three experimental designs and give one strength and one weakness in each case.

Name of design	Strength	Weakness
a		
b		
c		

10 What are order effects?

_____

_____

11 What is counterbalancing?

_____

_____

12 Which of the three experimental designs named in question 9 would you choose to study the effect of single-sex vs mixed-sex schools on girls' exam results? Justify your choice.

_____

_____

13 On a separate sheet of graph paper plot a fully labelled scattergram using the data in Table 3.6 and estimate the correlation coefficient.

Participant	Number of cigarettes smoked per week	Number of sweets eaten per week
1	60	5
2	15	40
3	20	50
4	30	25
5	35	40
6	40	20
7	45	30
8	50	10
9	55	10
10	5	60

Table 3.6. Weekly consumption of cigarettes and sweets

14 On a separate sheet of paper plot a fully labelled bar-chart using the data in Table 3.7:

Repetition	15
Imagery	25
Repetition and imagery	30

Table 3.7 Number of words out of 50 recalled after using one of three aids to memory

15 On a separate sheet of graph paper plot a fully labelled graph using the data in Table 3.8. What does the pattern indicate?

Minutes spent typing	Number of typing errors in the last 100 words
10	2
20	3
30	5
40	7
50	12
60	17

Table 3.8 Typing time and typing errors

_____

_____

16 Calculate the mean, median, mode and range for each of the following two samples of data. What do these statistics tell you about the two samples compared to each other?

	Mean	Median	Mode
Sample A – 3, 6, 7, 5, 8, 4, 3, 9, 3, 2.			
Sample B – 8, 5, 2, 1, 8, 4, 3, 8, 9, 2.			

_____

_____

REVIEW SHEET (CHAPTER 4)

1 What sorts of behaviour does classical conditioning explain best?

_____

2 Define the term 'reflex'.

_____

3 Draw diagrams to show how classical conditioning could account for:
   a) a child's fear of men in white coats;
   b) an adult's aversion to lemon meringue pie.

4 To what might a classically conditioned fear of budgerigars generalise?

_____

5 How might you train a dog to discriminate between rectangles and squares?

_____
_____

6 What kinds of learned behaviour does operant conditioning explain?

_____
_____

7 State two ways in which classical and operant conditioning might be seen as different.

_____
_____

8 List two new examples for each of the four boxes in Table 4.1.

_____
_____
_____
_____

9 How would you use shaping to teach a rat to pick up a marble and drop it into a cup?

_____
_____
_____

10 Distinguish between negative reinforcement and punishment.

_____
_____

11 Define the term 'extinction'.

_____

12 Give a new example for each of the five reinforcement schedules described in the text.

_____

_____

_____

_____

_____

_____

13 State three ways in which SLT differs from traditional conditioning theories.

_____

_____

_____

14 What were the three conditions children encountered in Bandura's experiment?

_____

_____

_____

15 Distinguish between acquisition and performance.

_____

_____

16 State four characteristics of models which make it more likely that they will be imitated.

_____

_____

_____

_____

17 Give one example each of latent learning, insight and learning set.

_____

_____

_____

18 Give one example each of classical conditioning, operant conditioning and SLT applied in an educational setting.

_____

_____

_____

19 Give one example each of classical conditioning, operant conditioning and SLT applied in a clinical setting.

_____

_____

_____

20 State one strength and one weakness of the behavioural approach to explaining behaviour.

_____

_____

21 State two ways in which the ethics of behavioural applications have been questioned.

_____

_____

R E V I E W   S H E E T   (C H A P T E R   5)

IMPRESSION FORMATION

1 What is the difference between a central and a peripheral trait according to Asch?

_____

_____

2 Distinguish between primacy and recency effects.

_____

_____

3 Give three reasons why first impressions matter most.

_____

_____

_____

4 Give two real-life implications of research findings about primacy and recency effects.

_____

_____

5 What is meant by implicit personality theory?

_____

_____

6 What two dimensions did Rosenberg use to explain how central traits work?

_____

_____

STEREOTYPING

7 What is a stereotype?

_____

_____

8 Describe the stereotypes for a) Negroes and b) Jews discovered by Katz and Braly.

_____

_____

9 What would be a typical stereotype for a) men and b) women.

_____

_____

10 What general effects might a social filter have on information?

_____

_____

11 What is a gatekeeper?

_____

12 In what two ways might gatekeepers use the mass media to control information?

_____

_____

13 Name the three main personal filters and give an example of each.

_____

_____

_____

PREJUDICE AND PREJUDICE REDUCTION

14 What three components make up a prejudice?

_____

_____

_____

15 What are the three main sources of prejudice?

_____

_____

_____

16 Give three characteristics of the authoritarian personality.

_____

_____

17 What two things characterised the child-rearing style of authoritarian people's parents?

_____

18 Give one criticism of the authoritarianism explanation of prejudice.

_____

19 What is the frustration–aggression hypothesis?

_____

20 Give one evaluative point about the frustration–aggression approach to prejudice.

_____

21 Give two examples of how the way in which our cognitive systems work may encourage prejudice.

_____

_____

22 How did Minard show conformity to group norms could affect prejudice?

_____

23 What three learning processes might be responsible for prejudice?

_____

_____

_____

24 What is a minimal group?

_____

25 How did Tajfel think being a member of a group encouraged prejudice?

_____

_____

_____

_____

_____

26 Give one real-life and one research example of prejudice produced by group conflict.

_____

_____

27 Give an example each of tokenism and reverse discrimination.

_____

_____

28 Give one example each of racism **or** sexism in educational, judicial and employment institutions.

_____

_____

_____

29 Give one example each of how prejudice might be reduced on a) an individual b) an interpersonal and c) an inter-group level.

_____

_____

_____

30 Give three reasons why attempts to reduce prejudice are not always successful.

_____

_____

_____

REVIEW SHEET (CHAPTER 6)

SEG and NEAB students

1 Distinguish between audience and co-action effects.

_____

_____

2 Name and define the three hypotheses that have been suggested to explain audience effects.

_____

_____

_____

3 What are the two main kinds of social inhibition?

_____

_____

4 Identify two ways in which social loafing can be reduced.

_____

_____

SEG, MEG and NEAB students

5 Briefly describe one study of conformity.

_____

_____

_____

6 Name the six variations on Asch's procedure which were found to affect conformity.

_____

_____

_____

_____

7 Identify four ways in which Asch's studies can be evaluated.

_____

_____

_____

_____

8 What is meant by deindividuation?

_____

9 Identify four variations on Milgram's obedience study which affected the amount of obedience shown by participants.

_____

_____

10 What three ethical objections did Baumrind make to Milgram's study and how did he defend himself?

_____

_____

_____

_____

_____

_____

11 Name the four stages of empathy development given by Hoffman.

_____

_____

_____

_____

12 Define 'altruism'.

_____

_____

13 How does a real-life setting affect the rate of bystander intervention when compared with a laboratory setting?

_____

_____

14 List the five stages people go through when deciding how to help according to Tedeschi *et al.*

_____

_____

_____

_____

_____

15 Name Piliavin's model of helping.

_____

16 Name and define the three main social norms which affect people's tendency to help each other.

_____

_____

_____

_____

_____

MEG students only

17 Name and give measurements for the four zones of personal space suggested by Hall.

_____

_____

_____

_____

18 Briefly describe one study on the effect of space invasion.

_____

_____

_____

19 Distinguish between a territory and territoriality.

_____

_____

20 How might people mark territories?

_____

21 Give two reasons why privacy is important.

_____

_____

22 What are the three main points of Altman's theory of privacy regulation?

_____

_____

_____

23 What do we mean by the phrase 'crowding is subjective and psychological'?

_____

_____

24 Identify two effects of crowding on the rats in Calhoun's study.

_____

_____

25 What does Evans (1989) say is the main effect of crowding?

_____

_____

26 List the seven main effects of crowding on people.

_____

_____

_____

_____

REVIEW SHEET (CHAPTER 7)

1 Define the term 'attachment'.

_____

_____

2 State two ways in which the infant could be described as 'sociable'.

_____

_____

3 Name and briefly describe the three types of attachment identified by Ainsworth.

_____

_____

_____

4 What four features make for good quality day-care?

_____

_____

_____

_____

5 List three main findings from UK studies of childminding.

_____

_____

_____

6 Briefly describe one cross-cultural study of attachment.

_____

_____

_____

7 Distinguish between maternal separation, deprivation and privation.

_____

_____

_____

8 Outline two pieces of evidence which led Bowlby to state his 'maternal deprivation' hypothesis.

_____

_____

_____

_____

9 On what grounds did Rutter challenge Bowlby's idea that separation from the mother was strongly linked to later delinquency?

_____

_____

_____

10 Give two positive effects of research findings into attachment.

_____

_____

11 What are the three phases of the divorce process according to Wallerstein?

_____

_____

_____

12 List any three factors which Bee found lessened the effects of divorce on children.

_____

_____

13 List any two features of parenting that can help secure attachment to form.

_____

_____

_____

_____

REVIEW SHEET (CHAPTER 8)

1 Define affiliation.

_____

_____

2 List Schachter's four reasons for affiliation.

_____

_____

_____

3 What might younger children need friends for and how is this different from an adolescent's need for friends?

_____

_____

_____

4 What five changes are there in the sex of friends chosen at different ages?

_____

_____

_____

_____

_____

5 How did Selman test children's understanding of friendship?

_____

_____

6 What were the two main things which changed as children moved through the stages of friendship development?

_____

_____

7 List the five stages of friendship development suggested by Selman. Try to give a name and age range for each stage.

_____

_____

_____

_____

_____

_____

8 List three characteristics of rejected children according to Cole and Dodge.

_____

_____

_____

9 List two other things that we know about more popular children.

_____

_____

_____

_____

10 List three influences on attraction. For each, outline a piece of supportive research evidence.

_____

_____

_____

11 Name four theories of attraction.

_____

_____

_____

_____

REVIEW SHEET (CHAPTER 9)

1 Distinguish between sex and gender.

_____

_____

2 What is meant by 'sex-role stereotype'?

_____

_____

3 On Bem's Sex Role Inventory, what kind of scores do androgynous people get?

_____

_____

4 Regarding Maccoby and Jacklin's (1974) research into sex differences, give two examples for each of the following:

(a) myths about differences between boys and girls

_____

_____

(b) established differences between boys and girls

_____

_____

(c) areas of uncertainty about differences between boys and girls.

_____

_____

5 Give two ways in which biological sex can be defined.

_____

_____

6 What do we call someone who has biological characteristics of both sexes?

_____

7 Explain two ways in which sex hormones may affect the foetus (and therefore, later behaviour of the individual).

_____

_____

_____

_____

8 Briefly describe the Oedipal conflict and say how boys resolve it.

_____

_____

_____

_____

9 Give two ways in which other people may shape sex-role behaviour in children.

_____

_____

10 List three characteristics each of male and female role-models as portrayed on TV.

Male	Female
1	1
2	2
3	3

11 Name the three tribes studied by Mead and give a brief description of the way gender-roles were expressed in each one.

(a) _____

_____

(b) _____

_____

(c) _____

_____

12 Briefly explain the effect of food-getting vs food accumulation on the role of females according to Schlegel and Barry (1986).

_____

_____

_____

13 List the three stages of sex and gender understanding in Kohlberg's theory.

_____

_____

_____

14 What is meant by 'gender schema'?

_____

_____

_____

15 Why should we not worry if young children express very rigid sex-role stereotypes?

_____

_____

_____

R E V I E W   S H E E T   (C H A P T E R   1 0)

Moral development (SEG students 1–13 and MEG students 1–11)

1 For the following three approaches to moral development, list all the ways you can think of in which parents and peers have an influence:

Psychodynamic   Cognitive developmental   Social Learning Theory

_____   _____   _____
_____   _____   _____
_____   _____   _____

2 What are the two parts of the superego called and how do they make us feel?

_____

3 What is the main difference between heteronomous and autonomous morality?

_____

4 What would Piaget have called these types of punishment applied to a child caught stealing money from a parent's wallet:

(a) The parent should steal the same amount from the child's piggy bank.

_____

(b) The parent should take the child to the police.

_____

(c) The parent should stop the child from seeing friends that day.

_____

5 Arrange the following examples of moral reasoning into order according to Kohlberg's three levels and six stages. Put one letter in each box.)

(a) Heinz should steal the drug or his wife will die and won't be able to look after him.   ☐ *Lowest*

(b) Heinz shouldn't steal. If he's caught he'll go to prison.   ☐

(c) Heinz should steal the drug. His wife's life is more important than anything else.   ☐

(d) Heinz should steal the drug or he'll never forgive himself.   ☐

(e) Heinz should steal. It's against the law but this is a special case.   ☐

(f) Heinz should steal the drug. Everyone will think he's very brave.   ☐ *Highest*

6 According to Gilligan, how do men and women differ in what they base their moral judgements on?

_____
_____

7 Give one strength and one weakness of Gilligan's approach.

_____
_____

8 Draw a diagram to show how a child may acquire a classically conditioned aversion to hitting others.

9 Give three reasons why punishment may not be effective in teaching moral behaviour.

_____
_____
_____

10 Why do Social Learning theorists say parents should practise what they preach?

_____
_____

11 Why did Bee think it is so difficult to predict a person's moral behaviour in a given situation?

_____
_____
_____
_____

12 Using Eisenberg's model of pro-social reasoning, sort these statements into order.
A child decided to help with the washing-up because:
(a) I'll help because the job needs to be done.   ☐ *least advanced*
(b) I'll help because I can see my parents would like it.   ☐
(c) I'll help because they might play a game with me afterwards.   ☐
(d) I'll help because children should help their parents.   ☐
(e) I'll help because everyone should do their bit.   ☐
(f) I'll help because it will please my parents.   ☐ *most advanced*

13 Give two ways in which pro-social development in children could be encouraged.

_____
_____
_____
_____
_____
_____

Self (SEG and NEAB)

1 Distinguish between self-concept and self-esteem.

_____
_____

2 What are the three major sources of self-concept?

_____
_____
_____

3 List the four types of roles Mulford and Salisbury found people most often use to
describe themselves in the Twenty Statement Test.

_____   _____
_____   _____

4 Briefly describe Rosenthal and Jacobson's 'Pygmalion in the Classroom' study.

_____
_____
_____
_____

5 Give two criticisms of this study.

_____
_____

6 What did Golombok and Fivush say boys and girls are praised and criticised for in
the classroom?

	Boys	*Girls*
Praise		
Criticism		

7 List four reasons why girls may underachieve in sciences.

_____
_____
_____
_____

8 List four things parents and/or teachers can do to improve self-esteem in children.

_____
_____
_____
_____

9 What might be the effect on a low ability child of:
(a) streaming?

_____

(b) not streaming?

_____

10 Give two ways in which a teacher might improve his/her self-esteem.

_____

REVIEW SHEET (CHAPTER 11)

For MEG and SEG students:

1 What two research methods did Piaget mainly use?

_____
_____

2 Define 'schema' and 'operation'.

_____
_____

3 By what three processes does adaptation come about? Give an example in each case.

_____
_____
_____
_____
_____
_____

4 For each of the four stages proposed by Piaget:
   – name the stage;
   – give an approximate age range;
   – give two characteristics of children's thinking.

_____
_____
_____
_____
_____
_____
_____
_____
_____
_____
_____
_____

5 Outline two 'human sense' studies which have been used to question Piaget's ideas.

_____
_____
_____
_____

6 Name the three modes of representation proposed by Bruner.

_____
_____

7 Give examples of the kinds of toys appropriate to each stage of intellectual development proposed by Piaget.

_____
_____
_____

8 List five features of Piaget's theory as it is applied to education.

_____
_____
_____
_____

9 State three ways in which Bruner's approach to education differs from Piaget's.

_____

_____

_____

10 Explain what Bruner means by 'scaffolding' and 'peer tutoring'.

_____

_____

_____

_____

11 What is meant by ZPD?

_____

_____

_____

For MEG students:

12 What is meant by babbling, holophrastic speech and telegraphic speech?

_____

_____

_____

13 What three features of a baby's language are shaped according to Skinner?

_____

_____

_____

14 What is the role of imitation in the learning approach to language acquisition?

_____

_____

15 Give two criticisms of the learning approach to language acquisition.

_____

_____

16 Identify two things the LAD enables a child to do.

_____

_____

17 Give three pieces of evidence for Chomsky's theory.

_____

_____

_____

18 Name and define three of the 'design features' of language suggested by Hockett.

_____

_____

_____

19 Identify two of the criticisms of animal language studies made by Terrace.

_____

_____

20 Identify two ways in which Sue Savage-Rumbaugh's technique for training chimps to use language differs from earlier studies.

_____

_____

21 Draw a general conclusion about the success of attempts to teach language to chimps.

_____

_____

_____

_____

REVIEW SHEET (CHAPTER 12)

For MEG and NEAB students (optional for SEG)

1 Distinguish between sensation and perception.

_____

2 Give a real-life example of each of the five Gestalt laws. Make sure you name each law.

_____
_____
_____
_____
_____

3 On a separate sheet draw a small sketch of a landscape showing four monocular cues to depth.

4 Define the binocular depth cues known as retinal disparity and convergence.

_____
_____
_____
_____

5 Name three perceptual constancies.

_____
_____

6 Give one example of each of Gregory's four main lines of evidence for his theory of hypothesis testing.

_____
_____
_____

7 Make three evaluative points about Gregory's theory.

_____
_____
_____

8 What is meant by 'perceptual set'?

_____

9 Give three research examples showing the effect of different kinds of set on perception.

_____
_____
_____
_____
_____

10 Give two real-life examples of set in action.

_____
_____
_____
_____
_____
_____

For MEG and SEG students only

1 What is meant by the term 'nature–nurture debate'?

_____

_____

2 Give two reasons why it is difficult to study infant perception.

_____

_____

3 Name two studies of infant perception and say whether they support the nature or nurture side of the argument.

_____

_____

_____

_____

_____

_____

4 Give one reason for and one reason against using animals in studies of visual perception.

_____

_____

5 Name one study of animal visual perception and say whether it supports the nature or nurture side of the argument.

_____

_____

_____

_____

6 Briefly describe one cross-cultural study of perception.

_____

_____

_____

7 State two problems with drawing conclusions from cross-cultural studies.

_____

_____

8 State two reasons why recovery from blindness studies are limited in what they can tell us about the nature–nurture debate.

_____

_____

9 Outline what readjustment studies have told us about the nature and nurture of perception.

_____

_____

_____

10 Give two reasons why the nature–nurture debate is likely to remain inconclusive.

_____

_____

_____

_____

REVIEW SHEET (CHAPTER 13)

1 What three processes make up memory?

_____

_____

_____

2 Draw a diagram to illustrate Atkinson and Shiffrin's multistore model of memory.

3 What are the primacy and recency effect in memory and why do they support the multistore model?

_____

_____

_____

4 What have Baddeley, Paivio and Cohen and Squire added to the multistore model?

_____

_____

_____

5 In Craik and Tulving's levels of processing model, what types of processing are involved at the shallow and deep levels?

_____

_____

_____

6 Give two criticisms of the levels model.

_____

_____

7 Bartlett's constructivist model of memory suggests we change information in any of five ways. These begin with the letters ORACA. What does each of these stand for?

O _____

R _____

A _____

C _____

A _____

8 Make two evaluative points about Bartlett's model.

_____

_____

9 Give one piece of evidence to suggest that information in LTM is organised.

_____

_____

10 For each of the three models of memory, make one recommendation about improving memory.

_____

_____

_____

11 Describe three aids to memory and say why they work.

_____

_____

_____

12 List three biases that affect the accuracy of EWT.

_____

_____

_____

13 Briefly describe a piece of research that shows the effect of leading questions on EWT.

_____

_____

_____

14 Give three ways in which brain injury may occur.

_____

_____

_____

15 Name and define the two main kinds of amnesia.

_____

_____

16 What is thought to be the main reason for HM's amnesia?

_____

17 Name two medical conditions which could lead to amnesia.

_____

_____

REVIEW SHEET (CHAPTER 14)

INTELLIGENCE (SEG students only)

1 Name and briefly explain the three major approaches to intelligence.

_____

_____

_____

2 What does DQ stand for?

_____

3 What is the formula for IQ?

_____

_____

4 Calculate the IQ of a child with an MA of 8 years and a CA of 6 years.

_____

5 Name any two tests of intelligence.

_____

_____

6 List the four uses of intelligence test scores given by Bee.

_____

_____

_____

_____

7 Outline three criticisms of IQ tests.

_____

_____

_____

8 What is meant by a heritability estimate of 70%?

_____

_____

9 Outline two problems with the conclusions drawn by Burt after his studies of MZ twins' IQs.

_____

_____

10 Why is it so difficult to draw conclusions about intelligence from adoption studies?

_____

_____

_____

11 Identify one problem with studies of intelligence and social class.

_____

_____

12 If enrichment studies have little long-term effect on IQ what two main things do they achieve?

_____

_____

13 Give one reason why racial differences in IQ are unlikely.

_____

_____

14 Give two reasons why the nature–nurture debate on intelligence is likely to remain inconclusive.

_____

_____

15 Briefly explain rubber band hypothesis.

_____

_____

PROBLEM SOLVING AND CREATIVITY (MEG students only)

1 Define 'problem-solving'.

_____

_____

2 List the three main ways of studying how humans solve problems.

_____

_____

_____

3 What is algorithmic problem solving?

_____

_____

4 Name three heuristics giving a brief explanation of each.

_____

_____

_____

5 What is the advantage of using a heuristic?

_____

_____

6 Take six matches and arrange them so that they make four equilateral triangles. If you cannot do this what kind of Einstellung got in the way? The solution is at the end of the review sheet.

7 What is creativity?

_____

_____

8 List the four stages of creative thinking suggested by the Gestaltists.

_____

_____

_____

_____

9 List five items from creativity tests.

_____

_____

_____

_____

_____

10 What three things are scored in creativity tests?

_____

_____

_____

11 Identify one major problem with creativity tests.

_____

_____

12 Why is creativity sometimes not spotted at school?

_____

_____

13 List four things people are encouraged to do or not do when they are brainstorming.

_____

_____

_____

_____

14 What is 'po' and why is it important in lateral thinking?

_____

_____

Answer to q.6. You should use the matches to make a triangular pyramid. You may have failed through being 'set' to think of solving the problem in two dimensions only.

REVIEW SHEET (CHAPTER 15)

For MEG students only

1 List three assumptions of the Humanistic approach to personality.

_____
_____

2 What did Rogers mean by 'self' and 'ideal self'?

_____
_____

3 What is the Q-sort used for?

_____
_____

4 In Kelly's theory, what is a 'personal construct'?

_____
_____

5 List the four stages in completing a repertory grid.

_____
_____
_____
_____

6 Give one strength and one weakness of Humanistic personality theories.

_____
_____

7 What is the purpose of factor analysis?

_____
_____

8 What two personality dimensions are measured by the EPI?

_____
_____

9 Outline two areas of research into Eysenck's theory and say what the conclusions were.

_____
_____
_____
_____

10 Why does Cattell prefer sixteen personality factors to two main dimensions?

_____
_____

11 What else does Cattell measure alongside personality?

_____
_____

12 Give two criticisms of the psychometric approach to personality.

_____
_____
_____
_____

For SEG students only

1 Name the three parts of the personality according to Freud. Say which principle each one operates on.

_____
_____
_____

2 Name and briefly define two ego defence mechanisms.

_____

_____

3 Name the four stages of psychosexual development.

_____

_____

_____

_____

4 How does 'fixation' happen?

_____

_____

5 Give one result of fixation at each of the first three psychosexual stages.

_____

_____

_____

_____

_____

_____

6 Give two evaluative points about Freud's theory.

_____

_____

_____

_____

_____

7 What are the two basic assumptions of the LT approach to personality?

_____

_____

_____

_____

8 Outline one piece of research which supports the LT approach.

_____

_____

9 Outline one piece of research to support the SLT approach.

_____

_____

10 What can the LT/SLT approaches to personality explain that other theories have difficulty with?

_____

11 What is temperament?

_____

12 Name the three types of temperament identified by Thomas and Chess (1977).

_____

_____

_____

13 Outline the findings of one area of research into temperament.

_____

_____

_____

_____

14 Make one point for and one against temperament theories.

_____

_____

_____

_____

REVIEW SHEET (CHAPTER 16)

For MEG and NEAB students

1 What is the general effect of SNS arousal?

_____

2 Briefly, what is the endocrine system?

_____

_____

3 What is the function of a neurotransmitter?

_____

4 Sketch a diagram of the brain showing the location of the main cortical areas.

5 Give one example of a lateralised function.

_____

6 What is the role of a) the thalamus and b) the hypothalamus?

_____

_____

7 List two ways of studying the brain through damaging it and two ways which do not involve damage.

_____

_____

_____

_____

8 Give a brief definition of 'stress'.

_____

_____

9 List two stressors and briefly say what their effect is likely to be.

_____

_____

10 List two ways of measuring stress (you can include physical and psychological measures in your list).

_____

_____

11 What are the three stages of Selye's GAS?

_____

_____

_____

12 List three psychological responses to stress.

_____

_____

_____

13 Name two physical approaches to dealing with stress. In each case, identify a strength or weakness of the approach.

_____

_____

_____

_____

_____

14 In what three ways does Kobasa think we can improve our 'hardiness'?

_____
_____
_____

15 What is the difference between distress and eustress?

_____
_____

For NEAB students only

16 What five things are involved in experience of emotion?

_____
_____
_____
_____
_____

17 In what three ways might we measure emotion? State a problem with each.

_____
_____
_____

18 Draw a diagram to sum up each of the following:
   (a) the James-Lange theory of emotion.

   (b) the Cannon-Bard theory of emotion.

   (c) Schachter and Singer's cognitive labelling theory of emotion.

19 Give one criticism of each of the theories named in question 18.

_____
_____
_____
_____
_____

REVIEW SHEET (CHAPTER 17)

For MEG and SEG students

1 Distinguish between hostile and instrumental aggression.

For MEG students only

2 Give three reasons why animals behave aggressively.

3 Give two ways in which an animal might respond to a threat.

4 Give one way in which animal and human aggression may differ.

5 Identify the cultures compared in any one cross-cultural study of aggression.

6 Name the three main lines of evidence in the biological approach to aggression.

For MEG and SEG students

7 Briefly explain the psychohydraulic model of aggression.

8 Explain why Lorenz thought humans were a danger to themselves.

9 Give two criticisms of Lorenz's approach to aggression.

For SEG students only

10 Name the two main instincts in Freud's theory of aggression.

11 In Freud's view what two things might result from turning aggression inwards?

12 Name the three main explanations of learning given in the chapter.

13 Name and briefly define the three main child-rearing styles identified by Sears.

14 Which child-rearing style is more likely to reduce aggression?

15 Outline any two ways in which aggression may be reduced and try to identify the psychological theory the idea comes from.

REVIEW SHEET (CHAPTER 18)

1 Give a definition of ethology.

_____

_____

2 Name two famous ethologists.

_____

3 List two of Lea's applications of ethology.

_____

_____

4 List three of the six characteristics of innate behaviour suggested by Lea.

_____

_____

_____

5 Write a brief paragraph in which you correctly use the terms FAP, IRM, ASE, sign stimulus and flush toilet.

_____

_____

_____

_____

_____

6 Name three different kinds of learning.

_____

7 What three lines of evidence show the interaction between learning and experience?

_____

_____

_____

8 Give two examples of human behaviour which might develop in a sensitive period.

_____

_____

9 Why is the term 'sensitive period' preferred to 'critical period'?

_____

_____

10 Name and briefly define three kinds of imprinting.

_____

_____

_____

_____

11 What three characteristics of imprinting did Lorenz identify?

_____

_____

_____

12 Give a brief evaluation of any one of the characteristics you named in your answer to question 11.

_____

_____

13 List two strengths of the ethological approach.

_____

_____

14 Outline two weaknesses of the ethological approach.

_____

_____

_____

_____

INDEX